URBAN (IN)SECURITY
Policing the Neoliberal Crisis

Edited by:
Volker Eick and Kendra Briken

© Red Quill Books Ltd. 2014
Ottawa

www.redquillbooks.com
ISBN 978-1-926958-29-3

Printed on acid-free paper. The paper used in this book incorporates post-consumer waste and has not been sourced from endangered old growth forests, forests of exceptional conservation value or the Amazon Basin. Red Quill Books subscribes to a one-book-at-a-time manufacturing process that substantially lessens supply chain waste, reduces greenhouse emissions, and conserves valuable natural resources.

Library and Archives Canada Cataloguing in Publication

Urban (in)security : policing in neoliberal times / edited
by Volker Eick and Kendra Briken.

Includes bibliographical references.
ISBN 978-1-926958-29-3 (bound)

1. Police—Political aspects. 2. Police—Economic aspects.
3. Neoliberalism. I. Eick, Volker, 1963-, editor of compilation
II. Briken, Kendra, 1972-, editor of compilation

HV7921.U73 2013 363.2 C2013-905050-7

The production of this book has been financially supported by:
Republikanischer Anwältinnen- und Anwälteverein e.V. (RAV), Berlin
Holtfort Stiftung e.V., Hanover

Front cover: © Andreas Lohner, taken from the series "Corcoran, world leader."

RQB is a radical publishing house.
Part of the proceeds from the sale of this book will support student scholarships.

TABLE OF CONTENTS

ACKNOWLEDGEMENTS

U rban (In)Security. Policing the Neoliberal Crisis is the result of many collaborators. Most of the essays selected for this edited volume were initially presented at the conference *Policing the Crisis – Policing in Crisis* held in Berlin and organized in cooperation with the Goethe Universität Frankfurt and the Freie Universität Berlin in August 2010 (cf. http://www.policing-crowds.org). While the economic crisis unfolded we invited additional authors to participate with supplementary papers, thus extending the scope of the current edition of *Urban (In) Security* to Northern Europe and to the Global South.

Without our partners from Germany and from abroad neither the conference nor this edited volume would have been possible. We therefore would like to thank several institutions for providing us with their generous support that allowed for inviting scholars and friends for our international meeting even in times of crisis. The German political foundations Rosa Luxemburg Stiftung, Heinrich Böll Stiftung and Helle Panke (AK Linke Metropolenpolitik) provided us with financial and infrastructural support. With the financial assistance of the Canadian Embassy (through the "Understanding Canada" program) and of the US Embassy we were able to invite colleagues from North America. Two alumni organizations based in Berlin (John F. Kennedy Institute) and Frankfurt/M. (Friends of the Goethe University) financially supported the social events during the evenings (and nights).

Ellen Bareis, Johanna Hoerning, and Tilla Siegel chaired some of the panels and supported the idea of editing a book right from the start. Our friend and colleague Jenny Künkel helped us in organizing the conference. Together with Elitza Stanoeva she supported us in proof-reading this volume (clearly, the usual disclaimers apply and the responsibility for remaining mistakes is ours). Both also encouraged us to publish not just the conference papers but to invite additional colleagues to participate. Following a first collection of conference and invited papers published with *Social Justice* (38/1-2) in 2011, the subsequent papers of *Urban (In) Security* conclude our scholarly journey visiting a variety of places to investigate *Policing the Neoliberal Crisis.*

Last but not least we want to thank all our authors for their patience. Editing a book based on precarious and constantly changing (non)employment statuses and shifting workplaces, we admit, was a challenge. Accordingly, we are thankful to George S. Rigakos and the Red Quill Books collective for their respective sympathy and constant support.

URBAN (IN)SECURITY
An Introduction

Volker Eick and Kendra Briken

Throughout the last three decades, neoliberal approaches to urban governance have persistently, albeit unevenly, circulated around the world. The ascendancy of neoliberalism has been associated with a profound reordering of both the practice and discourse concerning the appropriate boundaries between states, markets, and individuals. It culminates in an insistent emphasis on the ethics and logics of the market as the fundamental basis of social organization.

As an ideology, neoliberalism can be defined as a set of political discourses that reconfigure the liberal conceptions of freedom, the individual, the market and the non-interventionist state. Yet, neoliberalism is also an evolving process, often understood as neoliberalization or "actually existing neoliberalism" (Brenner and Theodore, 2002). By now, a broad agreement among scholars exists that in its contemporary form, neoliberalization is not only a global but a glocal project (Swyngedouw, 1997) – gaining more and more momentum due to the current crisis – conducted by elites and mainstream political parties in various forms around the world (Harvey, 2005; Leitner et al., 2007; Mirowski and Plehwe, 2009; Künkel and Mayer, 2012). In parallel, a distinct transnational geography came into being marked by strategies of financialization and commodification ranging in scale from the municipal ('gentrification') to the supranational (G20, G8). Neoliberal governance in general – and its urban manifestation in particular – advocates deregulation, privatization and competitive commodification through 'neo-Schumpeterian' economic policies (Jessop, 2002). Or, as Neil Brenner already highlighted in 2001, the characteristics of neoliberal times can be understood as

> a massive assault upon established scales of sociopolitical regulation such as the nationally based Keynesian welfare state and aggressive attempts to build global, national, regional and local scalar hierarchies in which unrestricted capital mobility, unfettered market relations, intensified commodification, and a logic of 'beggar-thy-neighbor' competition are to be permanently institutionalized (Brenner, 2001: 594).

Neoliberal policies take hold of the glocal level and permeate every pore of the social. As noted elsewhere (Brenner and Theodore, 2002), 'actual existing neoliberalism' relates to regimes of coexistence and of conflict. In the public sector, this involves privatization, liberalization and the imposition of commercial criteria in the residual public sector as well as in the nonprofit sector. Neoliberalism also supports and is supported by free trade and capital mobility, facilitated by state policies focussing on financial deregulations flexibilizing labor. Peck and Tickell (2002) depicted the neoliberal 'evolution' in a linear way arguing that neoliberalization consists of three phases: a proto-phase, a roll-back phase and, finally, a roll-out phase. Whereas proto-neoliberalism refers to the theoretical stage of initiating neoliberalization (starting in the late 1940s), the two subsequent phases encompassed the development of neoliberalism as a practice. During the roll-back phase (starting in the late 1970s to early the 1980s), which was focussing closely on market logics, Keynesian policies and formations were dissolved. The second phase of the neoliberalization process is the roll-out phase (beginning in the late 1990s) that involved proactive neoliberal practices and ideas, constructing new policies and institutions such as workfare programs, public-private partnerships or community-based urban governance. The following chapters will emphasize that neoliberalization is an ongoing global project. With regard to countries as diverse as India, the UK and Germany, Lithuania and the US, the impacts of this process on the local level and on what is here referred to as provision of safety, order and security, or 'SOS policing' are highlighted.

Roll-back and roll-out neoliberalization do not unfold in a linear way, but tend to shift arrangements and institutions back and forth, absorbing parts of the Keynesian-Fordist compromise while also rolling back already rolled-out 'solutions.' In other words, this is a conflict-ridden process; hence, the neoliberal project is never stable. Furthermore, once translated into real programs, such a neoliberal project is constantly contested by workers, activists, dissenting citizens and competing capital factions in various forms of lobbying, protest and resistance (della Porta and Tarrow, 2005; Künkel and Mayer, 2012). From this point of view, it is not at all surprising that the provision of what is perceived as safety, order and security also underwent major adjustments. State, commercial and 'civil society' policing changed significantly and continue to do so with the ongoing financial and economic crisis as argued in the next chapters. Stuart Hall et al. (1978) – from where we borrowed our subhead – described in all detail, though in different terms the UK crisis of the 1970s. Due to the termination of the Fordist class compromise, triggered by the neoliberal project, the latter found itself in need of adjusted policing strategies (Henry and Smith, 2007; Brodeur, 2010; *Social Justice, 2*011; Bowling and Sheptycki, 2012; Newburn and Peay, 2012). It is against this background that two distinct analytical approaches challenge what can be understood as the neoliberal fetish of 'security.' While Neocleous and Rigakos (2011) outspokenly argue for an 'anti-security' agenda and suggest to replace the term 'security' with 'pacification,' colleagues in the field of (critical) security studies such as Krause and Williams (1997) and Buzan et al. (1998) attempt to understand the discursive effect of reframing every political issue or social problem in the realm of international relations in the context of security. An attempt shared by several authors in this volume, on the grounds of their own empirical and theoretical insights. Likewise, the category of pacification might help us to understand 'security' as a mode of governing or "a *police* mechanism" for the fabrication of a social order, while keeping in mind the capitalist structure of this order (Neocleous, 2011: 26). Contrary to the Paris School, this approach allows taking into account the 'ruling class(es) of (in)security.' Pacification focuses not only on the "management of unease" organized by transnational "professionals" allegedly knowing the "rules of the game," as Didier Bigo (2008: 6-7) puts it, but also on the state.

Inasmuch as neoliberalization does not involve the absence of state intervention, policing is not, and has never been, solely a task of the state – notwithstanding political and economic elites' clear understanding of the importance of state-police for fabricating and safeguarding a working class obedient to the needs of capital. New, however, are the coordinated attempts to respond to the consequences of the roll-back phase of neoliberalism by policing means. The resulting urban areas of devastation stigmatized as 'failed neighborhoods' in the UK (Wallace, *this volume)*, 'Banlieues' in France (Germes, *this volume*), and 'dangerous places' in Germany (Eick, *this volume*), or even whole regions as is the case in India (Ferus-Comelo, *this volume*), are one particular target for state and non-state police forces. In turn, the residents of such areas – the urban poor, the 'dangerous classes,' the alien (migrant) 'Other' – are policed not only by the state but also by private security guards of for-profit as well as nonprofit types. Furthermore, protest policing is now an endeavor that engages far more policing entities than just the state, as Juska and Woolfson show with regard to Lithuania and Fernandez and Scholl with regard to North America (all four authors, *this volume*).

Since the early 1990s, an emphasis is also placed on harmonized preemptive policing strategies on the neighborhood level, which are more in line with the roll-out phase of neoliberalism, as is the case in Germany and Sweden where participation of residents is being encouraged (Wallace, Eick, and Rodenstedt, *this volume*; cf. Herbert, 2006).

Phenomena such as nonprofit organizations deploying long-term unemployed as security forces (Eick et al., 2007), 'Community Wardens' or 'Ambassadors' supervised by municipalities (Helms, 2008), or unpaid volunteers policing sports events such as the FIFA World Cup 2006 in Germany (Görke and Maroldt, 2006) thus extend "the policing web" (Brodeur, 2010) into the realm of the 'civil society.' Referring to this, day-time and night-life consumption areas, shopping malls, bars and nightclubs are also placed under a particular mix of policing entities that would guarantee for a smoothly running neoliberal urban environment (Wakefield and Gahan et al., *all this volume*, cf. Rigakos, 2008).

This edited volume is concerned with practices and strategies developed under 'actually existing neoliberalism,' and it treats 'the urban' as a particular focal point of research on the continuous lament of (in)security (Neocleous, 2000). In times of glocal neoliberalization, the urban constitutes an important laboratory for the study of neoliberalization processes. With the deregulation and the dismantling of the welfare state in the 1980s, distributive policies were increasingly replaced by measures of reinforcing urban competitiveness. As a consequence, sociospatial polarization intensified, whereas wealth and economic opportunities became more unevenly distributed and were in greater need of policing. Roll-out neoliberalism established some flanking mechanisms and modes of crisis displacement such as local economic development policies and community-based programs to elevate increasing social exclusion. But still, the most important goal of today's urban policy is to mobilize city space as an arena of market-oriented economic growth protected by policing mechanisms either in a state-led or a private form.

Recently, references to 'the urban' in the sense of traditional city cores, suburban peripheries and metropolitan regions became contested by some scholars criticizing that the bulk of twentieth-century urban studies rested on the assumption that all too often the urban "represented a particular type of territory that was qualitatively specific, and thus different from the putatively 'non-urban' spaces that lay beyond their boundaries" (Brenner and Schmid, 2012: 11). From such a broader perspective, 'the urban' as well as 'the city' are not simply juxtaposed to the non-urban or the rural but rather embody an increasingly global, even though unevenly woven, fabric in which the sociospatial relations of capitalism are enmeshed. Attention should be focused, as Brenner and Schmid (2012) therefore argue, on a process of "planetary urbanization," within which even infrastructural configurations and sociospatial arrangements that lie well beyond traditional understandings of the urban have become integral parts of a worldwide urban condition. Be that as it may, for us, the urban core and its suburbs reflect multiple processes of differentiation which the proponents of neoliberalization seek to regulate and further commodify by particular forms of policing. The increasing devolution of nation state's responsibilities for the economy on the urban scale, combined with cuts in funding from an increasingly hollowed-out national state, has transformed the urban – and cities in particular – into places where some of the sharpest contradictions of neoliberalization proceed. Consequently, cities have become 'incubators' not only for strategies such as commercialization and commodification, privatization and place-marketing but also for the related 'innovative' experimentations with policing practices, surveillance strategies and coercive control mechanisms. This volume provides case studies of policing 'urban (in)security' that are situated within the broad spectrum of workfare (Peck, 2001; Gustafson, 2011) and prisonfare (Wacquant, 2011) either state-led or orchestrated commercially (Grayson, 2012).

While 'actually existing neoliberalism' proceeds differently at different scales and at different times, it becomes evident that since the early 1990s, all these types of policing have been affected by "a new desire to punish" (Cremer-Schäfer and Steinert, 1998), while they in turn affect such desires as well. The recourse to both the 'good citizen' and, as Spitzer (1975: 649) reminds us, the "potential trouble-makers [who] can be recruited as policemen, social workers, and attendants" lead to patterns of 'the poor policing the poor' which is a widespread phenomenon in Europe, North America and beyond. Relatively new forms of policing such as local crime prevention schemes, social work projects led by state police, and deployment of long-term unemployed as quasi-policing entities are blurring the borders of state, commercial, and 'civil society' types of policing. This edited volume offers insights into these complex changes by suggesting three levels of analysis: namely, the urban setting, the urban industry and the urban battleground.

Policing the Urban Setting (Section I)

Policing the urban setting aims at securing the competitiveness of cities and at safeguarding their profitable management. By using the concept of scale, *Margit Mayer* analyses the challenges that such a situation evokes for global and urban social movements. Inasmuch as the slogan of 'the right to the city' reaches beyond the urban environment and is concerned not only with particular demands or rights, the 'urban frontier' is but one contestation on a global scale. At the very same time, however, local movements emerge, demanding better living conditions, healthcare and welfare provision, jobs, decent housing or merely shelter, and an end to evictions. To challenge the current neoliberal urban setting, it is thus necessary to 'make connections' not only between the global and local engines of exploitation, commodification and injustice but also to connect with those grassroots initiatives, groups, movements and individuals that are fighting against the neoliberal agenda on different scales. An additional challenge is to remain flexible within diverse spatial contestations without running the risk of being incorporated or neutralized. Further complications arise from the fact that alterglobalization movements emerge which are not necessarily based in the local environment, in which they stage their protests.

While Mayer tackles the question how to organize an urban setting against the neoliberalization of the city, *Andrew Wallace* further argues that policing the urban setting might start either in advance of any coercive form of police action or as a particular type of fine-tuning of neighborhoods after such police interventions have occurred. Policing of individual behavior within the trope of 'community' and the respective eradication of incivilities within neighborhoods have taken on an increasing importance in the orchestration of urban renewal within marginalized or peripheral housing estates. In his chapter, Wallace addresses a particular filtering of community 'securitization,' to borrow a term from the Copenhagen and Paris School, linking new techniques of civic policing to a broader agenda of social discipline which was first 'rolled out' (Peck and Tickell, 2002) under the 'third way' government in the UK. Such policies of discipline and security generate intersecting processes of activation, coercion and empowerment of policing within and between localities, which attempt to entrap all citizens in complex moralized spaces of order and control. Problematic populations are controlled, but they are also constituted and differentiated as control agents within the pursuit of a broader program of civic reconstruction.

The chapter provided by *Samantha Ponting* and *George S. Rigakos* and the photographs taken by *Andreas Lohner* (reproduced in this volume) look at civic construction. Here, policing of the urban setting is treated in its architectural dimensions – the wall – and is analyzed as a particular form of 'Othering,' of containment and exclusion with the aim of 'pacification.' While the beginnings of the capitalist security regime were rooted in the securitization of property and the wage labor system on an urban scale, common functions of security today involve safeguarding of exploitable labor by dividing the international working class socially and spatially on a global scale. The management of populations is central to this regime, and border security walls, gated 'communities,' and 'ordinary' walls in our cities remain its characteristic facets. In turn, policing of the urban setting is preoccupied with evoking the 'good citizen,' the obedient urban dweller, and the consumption-ready individual as the decisive role model promising undisturbed consumption opportunities.

Policing as Urban Industry (Section II)

To a growing extent, the commercial security industry is delivering the tools and strategies for the urban consumption areas. Commercial security companies, at least since the early 1990s, have started to conquer public spaces, to develop particular expertise in policing and surveillance, and are thus challenging the ordinary understanding of policing as state police (Rigakos, 2002; Wakefield, 2003; Eick, 2006; Button, 2007; Eick and Briken, 2011). While the 21st century is witnessing what has been called the "pluralization of policing" (Jones and Newburn, 2006; cf. Eick et al., 2007) further discussed in section II, policing in terms of wage labor has been widely neglected. Commercial security companies, at least since the early 1990s, have started to conquer public spaces, to develop particular expertise in policing and surveillance, and are thus challenging the ordinary understanding of policing as state police (Rigakos, 2002; Wakefield, 2003; Eick, 2006; Button, 2007; Eick and Briken, 2011). Such a void in research is even more surprising as current studies claim that the commercial security industry will grow further and take over more tasks formerly executed by state police either through additional manpower or new technologies (ESRAB, 2006; Berenberg Bank and HWWI, 2008; Freedonia Group, 2008; VDI and VDE, 2009). The growing scales and scopes of commercial police provision are one of the developments addressed in section II 'policing as urban industry.'

The second topic addressed in this chapter is based on a related observation. Critical research on globally emerging neoliberal workfare systems has shown that according to employers and (conservative) politicians alike, 'work' nowadays is either to be perceived by workers and unemployed as a 'gift' or as a 'duty': While 'work' should be understood as a 'gift' for those in the labor market, those without jobs should understand (waged) labor as a 'duty' to strive for. This is particularly true for the growing part of the low-wage workforce that is constantly hired and pushed back and forth between work, workfare, and unemployment. The chapters by *Volker Eick* on Germany, *Peter Gahan*, *Bill Harley*, and *Graham Sewell* on Australia, *Alison Wakefield* on the UK, and *Anibel Ferus-Comelo* on India argue that the commercial security industry in particular is one of the service sectors confronted with such working conditions under 'actually existing neoliberalism.' The struggles against such exploitation are currently very sporadic and rare, even though trade unions of the 'developed world' start to understand that confronting global players is important for successful collective action at home and abroad.[1]

Policing the Urban Battleground (Section III)

Events such as the 'Battle of Seattle,' the mass-mobilization against the G8 summit in Rostock-Heiligendamm (Germany), and the Occupy Wall Street movement demarcate thriving mobilizations of the recent years – and political and police responses have widely been understood as unsuccessful by the global elites and the police alike (Lichbach and Almeida, 2001; della Porta et al., 2006; Fernandez, 2008; Seferiades and Johnston, 2012). The staging of these protests by the alterglobalization movement therefore saw one of the first waves of 'strategic incapacitation' (Noakes and Gilham, 2007). The second wave, beginning in 2011, targeted the Occupy Wall Street movement as it was met by a heavily policed 'globopolis' (Bowling and Sheptycki, 2012) backed by the FBI-coordinated crackdown – a fact that was only revealed in December 2012 (Wolf, 2012).

As the chapters in this section demonstrate, trade unions, the alterglobalization and urban social movements

---

1   For the situation in the US, cf. www.standforsecurity.org; for Germany, cf. http://www. strikeinformer.com/germany/; for the worldwide struggles against union busting, cf. www.uniglobalunions.org (index 'Cleaning/Security').

are confronted with external challenges such as new and more sophisticated crowd policing strategies and excessive force by 'kleptocratic' neoliberalists and their police forces, as *Arunas Juska* and *Charles Woolfson* highlight in the case of protest policing in Lithuania. In addition, they have to respond to what *Lois Fernandez* and *Christian Scholl* call 'counter-insurgency' strategies even including military forces. On the other hand, social movements are confronted with internal challenges such as dangers of being coopted or neutralized (highlighted in particular by Mayer in section I).

While aforementioned chapters are based on empirical research on staged counter-summits, in her discursive analysis *Mélina Germes* describes a positional warfare between the French youths of the *Banlieues* and two police forces. The encounters include weaponry but also a post-colonial 'warfare wording.' As the French anthropologist Didier Fassin (2012) recently pointed out in his ethnographic participatory research on the Paris-based 'brigades anti-criminalité,' urban policing does not focus on sustaining a public order, but on reproducing a special social order. Thus, policing the urban battleground does not only emerge as brute force by state police but is inscribed in the daily police routine. As *Ann Rodenstedt* argues in her chapter on Sweden, policing might include, as also Wallace has shown in his chapter, 'generating community' by non-state patrols, even including night watch schemes provided by parents.

About half of the essays selected for this book were initially presented at the Berlin conference 'Urban Security Work Spaces: Policing the Crisis – Policing in Crisis' which was held in cooperation of the Goethe Universität Frankfurt and the Freie Universität Berlin in August 2010, whereas the rest of the papers have been especially produced for this volume.[2] The collection thus draws together a variety of disciplinary approaches, including criminology, economy, geography, labor studies, management, political science, social work,

---

2   We are grateful to Jenny Künkel who helped us with the conference organization and with discussing parts of this volume.

sociology, urban planning, and visual arts. In geographical terms, this volume tackles – from different angles – developments within the realm of policing in Australia, France, Germany, India, Lithuania, Mexico, Northern Africa, Sweden, the UK and the US. It therefore offers an intriguingly heterogeneous as well as – paradoxically – homogeneous view on urban policing. Last but not at least with the aim to explore the potentials for citizen and workers' resistance against the ongoing neoliberal exploitation. In short, the aim of the book is to contribute to the current empirical, theoretical and political debates on crime control in a glocal perspective.

References

Berenberg Bank & HWWI. Hamburger WeltWirtschaftsInstitut (eds.) 2008. *Strategie 2030 – Sicherheitsindustrie*. Hamburg: HWWI.

Bigo, Didier 2008. "Globalized (In)Security: the Field and the Ban-opticon." In: Didier Bigo and Anastassia Tsoukala (eds.), *Terror, Insecurity and Liberty*. New York: Routledge: 5–49.

Bowling, Ben and James Sheptycki 2012. *Global Policing*. London: Sage.

Brenner, Neil 2001. "The limits to scale? Methodological reflections on scalar structuration." *Progress in Human Geography*, 25 (4): 591–614.

Brenner, Neil and Christian Schmid 2012. "Planetary Urbanization." In: Matthew Gandy (ed.), *Urban Constellations*. Berlin: Jovis: 10–13.

Brenner, Neil and Nik Theodore 2002. "Cities and the Geographies of 'Actually Existing Neoliberalism.'" *Antipode*, 34 (3): 349–379.

Brodeur, Jean Paul 2010. *The Policing Web*. Oxford: Oxford University Press.

Buzan, Barry, Ole Wæver, and Jaap De Wilde 1998. *Security: A New Framework for Analysis*. Boulder, CO: Lynne Rienner.

Button, Mark 2007. *Security Officers and Policing*. Aldershot: Ashgate.

Crawford, Adam and Stuart Lister 2004. *The Extended Policing Family*. Leeds: University of Leeds.

Cremer-Schäfer, Helga and Heinz Steinert 1998. *Straflust und Repression*. Münster: Westfälisches Dampfboot.

della Porta, Donatella and Sidney Tarrows (eds.) 2005. *Transnational Protest and Global Activism*. Lanham: Roman.

della Porta, Donatella, Abby Peterson, and Herbert Reiter (eds.) 2006. *The Policing of Transnational Protest*. Aldershot: Ashgate.

Eick, Volker 2006. "Preventive Urban Discipline: Rent-a-cops and the Neoliberal Glocalization in Germany." *Social Justice*, 33 (3): 66–84.

Eick, Volker and Kendra Briken (eds.) 2011. "Policing the Crisis – Policing in Crisis" (Special Issue). *Social Justice*, 38 (1-2).

Eick, Volker, Jens Sambale, and Eric Töpfer (eds.) 2007. *Kontrollierte Urbanität*. Bielefeld: transcript.

ESRAB. European Security Research Advisory Board 2006. *Meeting the Challenge: the European Security Research Agenda*. Luxembourg: European Communities.

Fassin, Didier 2011. *La Force de l'ordre: Une anthropologie de la police des quartiers*. Paris: Seuil.

Fernandez, Luis A. 2008. *Policing Dissent*. London: Rutgers University Press.

Freedonia Group (eds.) 2008. *World Security Services to 2012*. Cleveland, OH: Freedonia Group.

Görke, André and Lorenz Maroldt 2006. "Tanzen verboten! Eine lateinamerikanische Fiesta in Leipzig." *Der Tagesspiegel*, June 26: 3.

Grayson, John 2012. "Britain as a private security state: first they came for the asylum seeker..." *Open Democracy*, March 9, http://tinyurl.com/7jt255f (accessed March 11, 2012).

Gustafson, Kaaryn S. 2011. *Cheating Welfare*. New York: New York University Press.

Hall, Stuart, Chas Critcher, Tony Jefferson, John Clarke, and Brian Roberts 1978. *Policing the Crisis. Mugging, the State, and Law and Order*. London: Macmillan.

Harvey, David 2005. *A Short History of Neoliberalism*. Oxford: Oxford University Press.

Helms, Gesa 2008. *Towards Safe City Centres? Remaking the spaces of an old-industrial city*. Aldershot: Ashgate.

Henry, Alistair and David J. Smith (eds.) 2007. *Transformations of Policing*. Aldershot: Ashgate.

Herbert, Steve 2006. *Citizens, Cops, and Power*. Chicago: University of Chicago Press.

Home Office 2001. *Policing a New Century: a blueprint for reform*. London: HMSO.

Jessop, Bob 2002. "Liberalism, neoliberalism, and urban governance: a state-theoretical perspective." *Antipode*, 34 (3): 452–472.

Jones, Trevor and Tim Newburn| (eds.) 2006. *Plural Policing: a comparative perspective*. New York: Routledge.

Krause, Keith and Michael C. Williams (eds.) 1997. *Critical Security Studies. Concept and Cases*. London: University College London.

Künkel, Jenny and Margit Mayer (eds.) 2012. *Neoliberal Urbanism and Its Contestations. Crossing Theoretical Boundaries*. London: Palgrave.

Leitner, Helga, Jamie Peck, and Eric Sheppard (eds.) 2007. *Contesting Neoliberalism*. New York: Guilford.

Lichbach, Mark and Paul Almeida 2001. *Global Order and Local Resistance*. Los Angeles: University of California, Riverside.

Mirowski, Philip and Dieter Plehwe (eds.) 2009. *The Road from Mont Pelerin*. Cambridge, MA: Harvard University Press.

Neocleous, Mark 2000. *The Fabrication of Social Order*. London: Pluto.

Neocleous, Mark 2011. "Security as Pacification." In: Mark Neocleous and George S. Rigakos (eds.), *Anti-Security*. Ottawa: Red Quill Books: 23–56.

Neocleous, Mark and George S. Rigakos (eds.) 2011. *Anti-Security*. Ottawa: Red Quill Books.

Newburn, Tim and Jill Peay (eds.) 2012. *Policing. Politics, Culture and Control*. Portland, OR: Hart.

Noakes, John A. and Patrick F. Gillham 2007. "'More than a March in Circle': Transgressive protests and the limits of negotiated management." *Mobilization*, 12 (4): 341–357.

Partnership for Civil Justice 2012. "FBI Documents Reveal Secret Nationwide Occupy Monitoring." *Justice online*, 22 December, at http://tinyurl.com/d5zhkwq (accessed 5 February 2013).

Peck, Jamie 2001. *Workfare States*. New York: Guilford Press.

Peck, Jamie and Adam Tickell 2002. "Neoliberalizing space." *Antipode*, 34 (3): 380–404.

Rigakos, George S. 2002. *The New Parapolice*. Toronto: University of Toronto Press.

Rigakos, George S. 2008. *Nightclub*. Montreal: McGill-Queen's University Press.

Seferiades, Seraphim and Hank Johnston (Eds.) 2012. *Violent Protest, Contentious Politics, and the Neoliberal State*. Farnham: Ashgate.

Social Justice 2011. "Policing the Crisis – Policing in Crisis" (Special Issue, edited by Volker Eick and Kendra Briken). *Social Justice*, 38 (1-2).

Spitzer, Steven 1975. "Toward a Marxian theory of deviance." *Social Problems*, 22 (5): 638–651.

VDI & VDE (eds.) 2009. *Marktpotential von Sicherheitstechnologien und Sicherheitsdienstleistungen*. Berlin: VDI/VDE.

Swyngedouw, Eric 1997. "Neither Global nor Local: 'Glocalisation' and the Politics of Scale." In: Kevin Cox (ed.), *Spaces of Globalization: Reasserting the Power of the Local*. New York: Guilford: 137–166 .

Wacquant, Loïc 2011. "The Wedding of Workfare and Prisonfare – revisited." *Social Justice*, 38 (1–2): 203–221.

Wakefield, Alison 2003. *Selling Security. The private policing of public space*. Cullompton: Willan.

Wolf, Naomi 2012. "Revealed: how the FBI coordinated the crackdown on Occupy." *The Guardian*, 29 December, at http://tinyurl.com/d7pmkyb (accessed 5 February 2013).

SECTION I
Policing the Urban Setting

Volker Eick and Kendra Briken

Contemporary urban conditions are marked by what some scholars call a 'post-political' police order of managing the spatial distribution and circulation of things and people in an urban setting (Swyngedouw, 2009). Under 'actually existing neoliberalism' (Brenner and Theordore, 2002), policing urban settings relies on a variety of technologies, infrastructures, skills, and duties deployed, more often than not, with a moralizing undertone. They are – always contested – parts of profit motivated strategies and tactics for ordering, policing and even evicting people, things or functions from one to another designated area. As Neocleous (2009: 26) argues in turn, "we need to understand security not as some kind of universal or transcendental value but rather as a mode of governing or a political technology of liberal order building." In other words, policing the urban setting is about hierarchy, ordering, and distribution.

While Swyngedouw might be right in arguing about "a consensually agreed neo-liberal arrangement,"[3] in the first chapter of this section *Margit Mayer* investigates practices and opportunities for contemporary glocal movements and nongovernmental organizations – on both the local and the global scale – to achieve "new spatial politics for a just

---

3   Cf. "Cities and Inequalities in a Transnational World." at http://cgs.illinois.edu/jacs2012 (accessed 30 April 2013).

city," and she analyzes how the shifting scalar organization of statehood is reflected in grassroots movements' similar reorganization in multi-scalar ways. She further highlights that "on each and every scale," specific fields of social and power relations "need to be realized and confronted if cooptation or neutralization are to be prevented."

Obviously, particular forms of crowd control aim at the 'neutralization' of social movements, and 'networking' is of growing importance for both the movements and the law enforcement agencies involved in policing dissent (cf. section III). Mayer, in addition, emphazises that fighting for particular rights and struggling for the 'right to the city' might bring about contestations within and among local and global movements. She emphasizes that they need to be addressed in order to achieve a just city and thus a just world on a glocal scale.

Policing the urban setting relies on state police and commercial security provision analyzed in section II of this volume but also attempts to responsilize the citizenry in neocommunitarian ways to allow for self-policing endeavours. *Andrew Wallace* in his chapter on the 'urban ordering' of British cities – by New Labour but also looking at the current conservative-liberal coalition – identifies three interlocking processes he argues to be framing the turn to self-regulating neighbourhoods: The retrenchment of the welfare state, exacerbated by recent recessionary and fiscal crises, together with the emergence of policies of 'place making' and "models of communitarianism which found expression in moralising New Labour government interventions in the lives and spaces of the poor," give rise to models of community self-policing with "strategic importance in delivering sanitized and responsible urban spaces." For Wallace, "poor-on-poor scrutiny of personal conduct has become a key signifier of a 'remade' poor community and an 'active' post-industrial, post-bureaucratic citizenship" with the "aim to construct sanitized, remoralized civic spaces with an emphasis on eradication deviant or 'antisocial' behavior."

Constructing sanitized spaces and containing anti-social 'undesirables' is also a topic for *Samantha Ponting* and *George S. Rigakos*. In a historical perspective, they investigate 'walling' as an example of architectures of exclusion and thus as part of a "broader race- and class-based pacifying mission." As they highlight, "Just as colonization exported a culture, walls today work to preserve a distinct Western cultural composition ... through pacifying, homogenizing, and criminalizing" with the aims, among others, to ensure exploitable labor and to divide the international working class socially as well as spatially. As biopolitical structures walls are part and parcel of wider attempts of the ruling classes to make labor more productive through segregation, to help reinforcing a system that privileges the global protection of private property, and to signify that there is a 'dangerous' population and an oppositional population against such threats and in need of 'protection.'

The visual artist, *Andreas Lohner*, provides us with his view, speaking directly to the chapter provided by Ponting and Rigakos, on walling. The photographs are taken from his Corcoran projects, "casa mia" and "world leader," both dating back to 2007, and "multi purpose," first published in 2008 (Lohner, 2008). 'Corcoran' refers to the male-only state prison located in the city of Corcoran, Kings County, California. The German futurologist Rüdiger Lutz describes Corcoran as 'frozen terror' and as a possible scenario for the nearer future; a vision, that inspired Lohner's project.

His photographs, reprinted here, emerged out of a workshop coordinated by Paolo Riolzi and Francesco Jodice at the Freie Universität Bozen, entitled *"Die Anderen"* (The Others), thus bringing to the fore processes of 'Othering,' a topic also captured within this volume in section III. From a vertical position, Andreas Lohner took pictures of walls and fences with his 35mm camera focusing the lens on the ground while leaving walls and fences in fuzziness. For him 'Corcoran' is not just a prison facility but refers to borders more generally and thus is a synonym for so-called security and demarcation systems even reaching beyond the urban setting.

URBAN (IN)SECURITY: POLICING THE NEOLIBERAL CRISIS

References

Brenner, Neil 2001. "The limits to scale? Methodological reflections on scalar structuration." *Progress in Human Geography*, 25 (4), 591–614.

Brenner, Neil and Nik Theodore 2002. „Cities and the Geographies of 'Actually Existing Neoliberalism.'" *Antipode*, 34 (3): 349–379.

Jessop, Bob, Neil Brenner and Martin Jones 2008. "Theorizing sociospatial relations." *Environment and Planning D*, 26 (3): 389–401.

Neocleous, Mark 2011. "Security as Pacification." In: Mark Neocleous and George S. Rigakos (eds.), *Anti-Security*. Ottawa: Red Quill Books: 23–56.

Lohner, Andreas 2008. "Corcoran", at http://andreaslohner.com/PN_3_08_S12f.pdf (accessed 5 February 2013).

Lutz, Rüdiger 2005. "Meine Zukunftswerkstatt-Revision. Ein persönlicher Rückblick auf die letzten 30 Jahre", at http://www.thur.de/philo/gast/ruediger/lutz4.htm#szenarien (accessed 5 February 2013).

Swyngedouw, Erik 2009. "The Antinomies of the Postpolitical City." *International Journal of Urban and Regional Research*, 33 (3): 601–620.

TOWARDS GLOCAL MOVEMENTS?

NEW SPATIAL POLITICS FOR A JUST CITY

Margit Mayer

Asking whether the expansion and selective use of movements' scalar strategies have implications for their chances of challenging neoliberal power relations, this chapter concentrates on one particular type of place-specific movement. It explores the ways in which movements for a just city articulate the 'global' in struggles that take place 'locally' and vice versa, how transnational movements have rediscovered 'the local.' Drawing on examples mostly from the Euro-American zone, the chapter finds that urban movements encounter, on each and every scale, specific fields of social and power relations, which need to be recognized and confronted if cooptation or neutralization are to be avoided.

It is no news that urban politics occurs not only in cities. Even before political relations between cities, nation states and supranational institutions have become fundamentally reconfigured with the onset of neoliberal globalization, urban politics have played out not only within municipalities, but have also been carried out by regional and national governments as these set up frameworks and parameters, provide renewal or infrastructure programs at one point, housing development at another, or cut back and cancel such programs in favor of revitalization programs or stimuli to enhance locational economic competitiveness. Transborder networks and partnerships which cities have been building across national boundaries are also no novelty. What is new, though, is a differentiated shifting of decision-making sites, which has found its way into the urban politics debates under the label of re-scaling (Brenner, 2004; Keil and Mahon, 2009). As Jessop et al. (2008) remind us, the concept of (re)scaling emerged at a time when inherited global, national, regional, and local relations have become recalibrated through post-Cold-War capitalist restructuring and state retrenchment, propelling particularly supra-national and subnational arenas to the forefront of sociospatial regulation. Capturing the rescaling of state activities since the crisis of Fordism, it brought into focus the mutable, contested, yet very real hierarchical structures of neoliberalism in which actors continually seek to harness the different advantages which different scales of politics offer them (Mayer, 2008: 417).

This re-scaling of decision-making processes has been applied to many contested issues and in different directions: which issues get down-scaled to local and urban authorities, which get up-scaled or externalized to supra- or extra-national bodies, and how these shifts affect power relations between ruling and challenging groups is of crucial importance for the opportunities and potentials of social movements.

As a consequence, the shifting scalar organization of statehood is reflected in grassroots movements' similar reorganization in multi-scalar ways. Responding to where contested decision-making takes place, movements mobilize not only locally, but also regionally, supra-regionally, nationally, and also globally, making use of technological innovations and social media as well as of the emergence of global publics (cf. Nicholls et al., 2013). This also goes for urban social movements, which nowadays fight for 'the right to the city' not merely on-site, but world-wide, at global summits as well as with regional, continental and larger campaigns and networks. Having identified specific institutions and actors of corporate globalization as responsible for the degradation and polarization of their – and not only their – city, they push for an urbanization that respects the urban dwellers' claims and desires – as opposed to those of corporate investors or developers. As they challenge the re-scaled architecture of both state and corporate power, (urban) social movements have been developing new scalar practices, which imply new possibilities as well as new risks and problems, which have however hardly been explored and are thus not yet very well understood.

At the same time, urban movements have also made increasing use of another sociospatial dimension: networks, which span space and frequently traverse hierarchical scales. They build links between local struggles and transnational organizations, between place-based contestation and global NGOs, thereby bringing into contact vastly different movement lexicons and political cultures. The resulting multitude of forms of connectivity between urban movements around the world has hardly been conceptualized. The literatures on transnational social movements tend to distinguish between two types of practices: On the one hand, they identify transnational (advocacy) networks that push for the democratization of international institutions and agreements, organize campaigns to that end, or draft alternative charters; to the extent these networks pursue urban agendas, they do so with the goal of strengthening the participation and access rights of city dwellers, especially of those most powerless and poor. Distinct from these transnational NGO-type organizations and networks, they see local initiatives that experiment with and implement direct-democratic projects committed to social justice principles, from participatory environmental policy to participatory budgeting that have proliferated throughout the world to form a source of counter-hegemonic politics (Santos and Rodriguez-Garavito, 2005; Smith, 2008; Tarrow, 2005b).

A definition of transnational protest includes not just the transnational advocacy networks that have launched campaigns to democratize international institutions such as the World Trade Organization, World Bank, or International Monetary Fund, but also those activists' networks that organize the events and campaigns critically accompanying the summits of representatives of the neoliberal world order such as the G8/G20. These counter summits provide a space not just for challenging and publicizing the social and ecological destructiveness of corporate globalization, but also to exchange insights and experiences with other (local) activists from around the world, and to plan and coordinate joint civil disobedience and other actions in the common struggle for the right to the city. The way this occurs is, invariably, strongly influenced by the respective local movement milieu (of e.g. Seattle, Genoa, Quebec, Prague, Rostock or Chicago).

Since the first meeting of the World Social Forum in 2001 and thanks to the countless regional and national Social Forum meetings around the world, an alternative, counter-hegemonic form of globalization has been taking shape. Its activists and organizations have, over the last decade, been taking the core issues of the alter-globalization movement, the struggles against privatization, dispossession, and eviction, from the global summits back to their cities – of the first as well as second and third worlds.

This multi-scalar jumble of interurban movement connectivity does not appear to be structured by any causal relationships between, e.g., location in the scalar hierarchy and movement strength. Neither can we observe that up-scaling of struggles brings more effective results, nor can one say: the closer to the grassroots, the more authentic or radical the movements will be (nor is the inverse invariably the case: the more inter- or transnational a campaign, the more aloof or easily co-opted its activists). Are movements more successful if they employ a bigger repertoire of spatial strategies? Do place-based movements overcome their localism only if they expand their spatial strategies? Looking at examples from these new local/global arenas and their relationships with each other, this chapter finds that such questions are not answerable by abstract accounting of the various spatial strategies employed in contentious urban politics. Revealing the new opportunities as well as the new challenges urban movements encounter in this emerging multi-scalar architecture requires that we look closely – not just at the spatial forms, but at the social actors who act, embedded in particular (multidimensional) spatial forms and making use of particular 'glocal' scales and networks. The chapter thus seeks to 'politicize' the space/scale/network concepts suggested by Jessop et al. (2008), i.e. to bring politics into their multidimensional, polymorphic framework of socio-spatial analysis. That means, the differentiation and transformation processes that have taken place amongst the various urban contestants during the phase of roll-out neoliberalism have to be accounted for. As state actors from the municipal to the U.N. level have cultivated partnerships with grassroots organizations as well as NGOs in their search for best practices, the struggles within and against neoliberal urbanization have taken on many faces (cf. Künkel and Mayer, 2012). In this situation, we need acute awareness of the political meaning of sociospatial categories as well as of traditional movement vocabularies, as their substance is transforming in front of our eyes. Categories such as 'empowerment' or the 'right to the city' have come to mean rather different things in different contexts. Depending on context, some distinctions become even more important than they have been in the past: for example the distinction between NGOs and social movements matters a great deal in terms of political implications, but is not always clearly made (e.g., Sikkink [2005] or Cumbers et al. [2008: 190] use the terms interchangeably).

In order to make these arguments, the chapter first looks at the ways in which classical urban-based movements have come to refer to and make use of the global scale, either by protesting the negative effects of globalization in the city, or by harnessing scales of discourse and politics beyond their local one, thus diversifying their strategies and activities in a multi-scalar way (*Local Protest*). Second, it looks at the ways in which transnational networks and campaigns have taken up the claims and demands of urban movements and thereby impact on the local movement milieus (*Transna-*

tional Protest). The interplay of these different clusters of 'glocal' movements creates a novel multiscalar architecture of urban protest, in which impetus from supra-national scales may boost local grassroots movements, and particular urban initiatives may turn into beacons of the global social justice movement. Drawing on these cases, the last section traces some of the tensions and conflicts that have emerged between mobile transnational activism and the locally or community-based groups, between activists from resource-rich first world countries and those representing urban struggles in the global South, and between radical calls for a fundamental transformation of cities the way they exist today versus demands for 'good urban governance' and 'rights' to the city.

Local protest: urban movements scaling upwards

In the course of the last few decades' globalization, cities and local politics have acquired new significance in two ways, and as a consequence, urban movements have taken on new roles:[4] First, the shift towards decentralization in a series of policy fields (particularly in labor market and social policy fields) has expanded municipalities' pertinent powers and functions and simultaneously entailed an opening of local governance arrangements, through which municipalities now harness the expertise and experience of local NGOs and social movement organizations. Secondly, the upgrading of cities as engines of economic growth has enhanced their autonomy vis-à-vis national governments and turned them into important nodes and actors within worldwide networks. Since this upgrading of the role of cities has not been accompanied by improvements in the living conditions or increased access to decision-making processes for the majority of urban dwellers, local struggles

---

4   More detail on these connections is provided in Hamel et al. (2000) and Mayer (2007a, 2012).

over social justice have become more pronounced. Activists as well as supportive academics realize more and more that their struggles and projects are hampered if they remain locally confined, and that they need to connect with similar struggles in other places or with movement actors on other, 'higher' scales. "[To] build effective social justice strategies … efforts must emphasize the formation and mobilization of a consciousness of justice and a multi-scalar understanding of place that can be linked with other local scale ventures and/or larger scale actors" (Pendras, 2002: 831).

GLOBALIZATION IN THE CITY

Local struggles against corporate urban development and the "entrepreneurial city," which challenge the make-over of central business districts (CBDs) and concomitant gentrification processes, increasingly confront global investors and developers. Ever since (the third wave of) gentrification is being pushed as an instrument of intra-urban competition, global finance capital has been flowing into large-scale development projects in CBDs (Smith and DeFilippis, 1999), justified by local politicians pointing to job creation, tax revenues and gains from tourism. While North American cities have been leading this development, Europeans have also advanced gentrification as a tool in the global urban competition. "Urban regeneration" programs have been designed to help cities make themselves attractive and remove "irritants" such as the homeless or other potentially 'blemishing factors'. Local governments in this situation often strive to be global capital's active partner, no longer even pretending to regulate or control development (Smith, 2002: 443). Movements challenging this form of urban development have galvanized across Europe, as for example in coordinated "Downtown Action Weeks" that took place simultaneously in 20 German and Swiss cities to protest not only the intensifying global location competition and the corresponding image marketing campaigns, but also the 'cleansing' of the downtown citadels, the marginalization of whole neighborhoods and groups of residents that do not 'fit' into this type of entrepreneurially branded city. Mobilizations against privatization and commercialization of public space and against the deregulation and deterioration of public services in European as well as North American cities are well documented (Hamel et al., 2000; Low and Smith, 2006; Leitner et al., 2007), struggles against gentrification less so (but see Slater, 2014).

Also, many North American as well as European cities are sites of protests by 'undocumented' migrants who contest the role and position forced on them within northern nations, which treat them as outsiders while crucially integrating their labor power into the expanding economies of the urban centers of the global political economy (Rosewarne, 2001). The Sans-Papiers in France, for example, have been claiming, through demonstrations and occupations, their presence in first world metropoles as decisive and thus their right to membership as valid before the granting of any citizenship rights (McNevin, 2006: 143-144). With actions such as the occupation of the headquarter of the French Construction Confederation they emphasize their prominent role in meeting labor shortages in key urban industries as well as the tight connection between formal and informal economic sectors. Such migrant organizations of 'immanent outsiders' – integrated into the urban economy yet excluded from social and political participation – have formed networks, together with advocacy groups, across Europe and beyond (e.g. NoBorder Network; No-one is illegal).[5] They also have a strong presence at meetings of the European Social Forum (see below) as well as at the Social Forum meetings in the U.S., which indicates that they are making use of the transnational organizational structures of the global justice movement, parallel to their local actions.

---

5   Cf. http://www.noborder.org/ for the former; http://www.noii.org.uk/ and http://toronto.nooneisillegal.org/ for no-one is illegal campaigns in Britain and Canada.

Supra-local scales of politics

Another strand of local protest is made up by residents of abandoned and deindustrialized districts as well as their advocates, who contest the effects of neoliberal globalization with strategies as varied as squatting vacant buildings or developing self-help structures. These neighborhoods represent the obverse of the booming CBDs; their (unemployed, welfare-dependent, or otherwise precarious) residents are targeted, in this era of roll-out neoliberalism (Brenner and Theodore, 2002), with a novel type of sociospatial program designed to 'stop the downward spiral' presumably characteristic of blighted areas. In Europe, the community organizations active in such districts have increasingly become integrated into (often EU-supported) neighborhood development programs, which address social exclusion with territorially oriented empowerment approaches, social capital building, and even microcredit programs, i.e. instruments that were originally developed to combat urban poverty in the global South (Mayer and Rankin, 2002). Involving community-based organizations in policies to combat urban decline and poverty has a longer tradition in North America. Policy diffusion in this realm is as transnational as community-based movements seeking to learn from so-called best practice in 'successful' cases of harnessing civil society energies to stop decline.

When such movements shift scale to the international level, they do not necessarily become transnational movements. As Tarrow and McAdam (2005) have found, transposition of part of the movement's activities (rather than its transformation) is the more common pattern. This pattern can be observed when urban (anti-poverty) movements forge transnational networks of support as an operational strategy to improve their constituencies' lot. An illustration of this is presented by the Kensington Welfare Rights Union (KWRU) in Philadelphia, which harnessed global human rights discourses and organizations for their concerns. The Kensington neighborhood, which lost most of its local businesses and jobs in the course of the 1970s and 80s, had the highest poverty concentration in Pennsylvania by the beginning of the 1990s. In 1991 six women on welfare took over an abandoned welfare office, set up a community center, and began to mobilize for better social services.

> Through direct action campaigns, including the takeover of empty HUD housing by homeless families, we have housed more than 500 families, fed and obtained utility services for thousands, and educated on the streets for basic skills (Babtist and Bricker-Jenkins, 2002: 204).

After passage of Clinton's welfare reform in 1996, the KWRU organized, together with other anti-poverty-groups, a 140 mile march to the state capital Harrisburg to protest the loss of benefits. But its members soon realized that even at the state level their struggle remained constrained. They therefore broadened their framework from a civil rights to a human rights focus, and linked up with anti-poverty groups internationally, especially with groups active in third world countries. With their 1998 month-long 'March of the Americas' from Washington, D.C. to the United Nations in New York they involved international activists, especially from Latin America, in order to highlight that U.S. poverty needs to be understood in global context (Smith, 2008). Because Washington "could not be counted on to protect and promote the economic human rights of its residents, ... we turned toward the court of world opinion symbolized by the U.N. Social and Economic Council" (Babtist and Bricker-Jenkins, 2002: 207). In 1999, KWRU globalized its struggle further by taking the Poor People's Economic Human Rights Campaign (PPEHR) to the Hague Appeal for Peace, where nearly 10.000 people working in peace and human rights groups from more than 100 countries gathered. Since 2001, KWRU activists regularly participated in the World Social Forum. Together with the Center for Economic and Social Rights (Ford Foundation, 2004: 26-27) they have been pressuring international human rights institutions such as the UN Human Rights Commission in Geneva and the Inter-American Human Rights Committee (Smith, 2008: 207).

The dual strategy KWRU was applying – on the one hand addressing, with community action and programs, the concrete problems of urban poverty, and on the other developing and using international contacts with NGOs and human rights institutions as well as, through the WSF process, with similar movement groups active elsewhere – helped to publicize the concerns of anti-poverty groups and also to make visible the connections between struggles against the marginalization of 'redundant' people and neighborhoods around the globe.

Yet another field of urban contestation in the struggle over neoliberal urbanism is that of community participation, often framed as 'practical utopia,' where urban residents seek to expand their input in municipal planning and decision-making processes. A variety of such projects and initiatives to expand participatory democracy and citizenship rights – whether through participatory budgeting, innovative forms of involving citizens in planning, or policy-specific round tables – have been diffused and propagated via transnational networks. UN Habitat and the World Urban Forum offer opportunities for disseminating and sharing such experiences and best-practice models, and also for persuading local policy makers of the advantages of such participatory programs and direct-democratic procedures. Networks and cooperative linkages have also emerged between cities – to further sustainable development, employment, or civic engagement.[6]

---

6   Such partnerships and networks are globally supported by the World Bank, through its various *good governance* programs, or nationally, as by the German Bertelsmann Foundation (which initiated a so-called *Civitas Network* of civil society-oriented municipalities); the latter network elaborated quality criteria for citizen-oriented municipalities (Pröhl et al., 2002), which detail desired forms of civic engagement in a variety of municipal policy fields (Roth, 2003).

In spite of the growing salience of cities in the global context, movement claims cannot be restricted to the local/ urban scale, because locational competition, financial crisis, and privatization measures have robbed municipalities of resources and room to maneuver. Even before the 2008 recession made its impact felt, urban movement groups have begun to wonder whether local authorities are an appropriate addressee for them, as their capacity for public provisions had been diminishing more and more. These shrinking resources have certainly been an additional reason for the growing supra-local orientation of urban movements.

Transnational protest: the (right to the) city in the global justice movement

The mobilizations labeled by Europeans as 'alter-' or 'anti-globalization movements' and by North Americans as 'global justice movements' are most manifest in the protests against supra-national organizations such as the WTO and IMF and against summit meetings (e.g. of the G8),[7] as they seize on the political opportunities and public attention which these meetings create. They are also manifest in the 'open space' of the World Social Forum and in the national, regional and local Social Forums, which have created novel transnational spaces of activism, within which urban protest claims and milieus have carved out a space (cf. previous section). But the global justice movement itself also addresses more than hegemonic globalization: it also addresses the city, and not only in symbolic actions at urban sites where the command and control functions of the global economy are concentrated (such as headquarters of multinational corporations, banks and investment firms, stock exchanges, etc.). Over the last few years the anti-globalization movement has explicitly identified the city as place where the negative

---

7   Mobilization against globalization can be dated back to 1986, when over 80,000 people protested against an IMF meeting in Berlin. In the early 1990s, in North America struggles emerged against GATT, in Europe movements such as Reclaim the Streets (Routledge, 2003: 347).

effects of the global neoliberal project become tangible for
many different groups, and where it therefore makes sense
to organize the resistance against the neoliberal project
(Köhler and Wissen, 2003).

SUMMIT PROTESTS
Since 1994 international mega-events have been staged where
thousands of people rally against the multilateral economic
and financial institutions and their political representations.
Whether at G8 summits or at meetings of global institutions
such as WTO, IMF, World Bank, or FTAA, each time movements organize and coordinate across national boundaries and
political differences. In order to articulate broad, plural resistance against neoliberal globalization, they aim to disturb or
disrupt the meetings, and to network and exchange with each
other at parallel 'alternative summits' (cf. Ainger, 2009).

In preparations well in advance of the events they develop
formal as well as informal coalitions and networks that
build on existing local, regional, national and global organizations, which then cooperate during the days of the protest,
in demonstrations, blockades, assemblies, workshops and
cultural events, always creating unique happenings.

While the transnational network organizations Attac,[8]
People's Global Action,[9] Reclaim the Streets,[10] and various
European and North American anarchist and autonomous

---

8   Attac (Association pour la Taxation des Transactions pour l'aide aux Citoyens),
     founded in 1998 in order to implement the Tobin tax worldwide, constitutes a network
     of professionalized NGOs that is particularly well grounded in France, Germany, and
     Switzerland, cf. http://www.attac.org.
9   People's Global Action (PGA) owes its genesis to an encounter between activists and
     intellectuals organized by the Zapatistas in Chiapas in 1996. In 1997, the idea of a network
     between different resistance formations was launched by ten social movements including
     Movimento Sem Terra (Landless peasants movement) of Brazil and the Karnataka State
     Farmers Union of India. Since its official birth in 1998 PGA consists of leftist groups from
     the global South as well as North to inspire people to resist corporate domination through
     civil disobedience and people-oriented constructive action, cf. Routledge (2003); Tarrow
     and McAdam (2005: 143); http://www.nadir.org/nadir/initiativ/agp/en/.
10   Reclaim the Streets formed in Britain in the mid-1990s, initially as a radical environ-
     mental movement that transformed urban industrial landscapes into eco-friendly oases,
     occupied city streets and concrete-covered squares to build gardens and celebrate
     parties. Later RTS activists began to disrupt business-as-usual in public spaces with
     provocative interventions and protest parties, cf. http://rts.gn.apc.org/.

groups play central roles in carrying out these events, the local movement organizations of the summit hosting city are equally crucial.[11] At the Seattle protest (WTO, 1999) it was not just the usual leftist and anarchist groups and the environmental, women's, and faith-based organizations, but also the longshoremen, Teamsters, and other union groups who had already carried out the local strikes of 1919 and 1934 (Levi and Olson, 2000); in Genoa (G8 2001) it was the *Centri Sociali Autogestiti,* the self-managed social centers of the local alternative milieu (Piazza, 2007). And it was local movement organizations from Berlin, Hamburg, and Hanover that mobilized in 2007 for the protest against the G8 in Heiligendamm and the counter-summit in Rostock, together with supra-regional groups of the 'Block G8' Campaign,[12] the Interventionist Left,[13] Dissent!,[14] and Attac.

Building on the legacy of prior summit protests, the actions around Heiligendamm/Rostock reveal the urban edge of the anti-globalization movement in all its diversity. The traditional dual strategy to be both on the street and inside where negotiations take place works however less and less well at G8 meetings than at WTO, IMF or World Bank summits. This is due to the gradual transformation of the function of G8 meetings: while they initially served to mediate between competing state and capital interests, their task has shifted to legitimating global rule as benevolent. The summits are supposed to show that global problems (debt at the Cologne summit, poverty/ Africa at Gleneagles, climate change at Heiligendamm)

---

11   With regard to the protest events in Seattle, on which most research so far has focused, Hadden and Tarrow (2007) note that the majority of the participating organizations and individuals were of local origin.

12   'Block G8' constituted a broad coalition including large organizations such as Attac and the Left Party, but the local Hanover Coordinating Committee played a key coordinating role and also initiated the Rostock action conferences.

13   The Interventionist Left (http://www.dazwischengehen.org/site/gruppen-der-il) spearheaded the block 'Make Capitalism History,' but was also part of the 'Block G8' coalition.

14   The 'anarcho-globalists' of the Dissent! network mobilized autonomous and anarchist activists from all over western Europe (dissentnetzwerk.org).

can be resolved through these meetings. At Gleneagles the British government even presented itself as extension of the claims of social movements, while the Heiligendamm summit was to convey the impression that the leaders of the industrial nations were actually going to do something about climate change (Müller and Sol, 2007).

The themes of urban social movements were explicitly present at these counter summits: workshops offered discussions on how local activism can internationalize the struggle against displacement, eviction, speculation, privatization, and for the right to housing, water, land and the city;[15] one workshop sought to create a better understanding of the relationship between global finance capital and urban restructuring: under the heading of "Global financial markets, privatization, and investments" European and North American urban activists and researchers shared information and experiences with Asian and Latin American movements,[16] mediated by INURA[17] and the Habitat International Coalition.[18] At a "Gathering of homeless, marginalized and tenants," representatives of community and homeless organizations from Brazil, Japan, France and Germany discussed the globalization of the struggles for the right to housing. In spite of the interactions and information sharing at such events, however, follow-up evaluations noted self-critically that "we succeeded only in very rudimentary fashion to build bridges to local struggles, whether to self-organized groups of unemployed, to homeless initiatives, or to the residual activists from the strikes at Gate Gourmet, Siemens or Opel" (Samsa, 2007).

---

15   Cf. the website of Habitat (http://www.habitants.de/en/campaigns/g807/) which describes urban movements at G8 Heiligendamm.

16   Cf. http://www.habitants.de/en/campaigns/g807/agenda/index.php/art_00000030.

17   INURA (International Network of Urban Research and Action), founded in 1991, is a transnational mix of movement organization, alternative professional association, and network.

18   Habitat International Coalition is an alliance with worldwide membership for the right to housing, dedicated to advocacy for the poor. It seeks to derive practical and strategic lessons from experiences around the world, cf. http://www.hic-net.org/.

THE (WORLD) SOCIAL FORUM, WORLD URBAN FORUM, AND SOCIAL URBAN FORUM

The World Social Forum was initially designed as a counter summit to the World Economic Forum in Davos and reflected a desire to shift energies from street protests toward generating alternatives to neoliberal globalization. The first meeting in Porto Alegre, Brazil, 2001, drew many more participants than the French and Brazilian organizers had anticipated. At the second WSF, participants were called on to organize similar processes in their own places and at whatever scale made sense to them. Since then, this novel form of alternative globalization has not only convened annually on the world scale, reflecting both the global historical conjuncture and the particular conjuncture and social struggles of the host country and region (Conway, 2008), but also in regional as well as national and local gatherings.[19] The WSF has evolved into a completely novel socio-spatial and political praxis, a globally diffused political form that is regularly enacted on different scales and unites a broad spectrum of distinct movements and organizations, from all over the world,[20] in the struggle against neoliberal globalization, oppression, and discrimination. The large variety of different, and not only western, currents, and the broad scope of political positions and – insurgent as well as institutionalized – action repertoires, provide hardly a basis for consensus, except with regard to nonviolence, but even this is contested.[21] With its slogan "Another world is possible!" the WSF articulates a radical critique of contemporary neoliberal realities without

---

19   Self-organized Social Fora appeared on every continent: After the violent repression of the anti-G8 protest in Genoa in 2001 local Social Fora sprang up all over Europe. In the Americas, hemispheric social forum gatherings took place in Quito, Ecuador (2004) and Guatemala City (2008). In 2006 the WSF meeting took place in polycentric form, i.e. dispersed over three sites (Caracas, Bamako, Karachi). Groups that were involved in the Seattle protest also participated in the WSF in 2001 and 2002, and later organized Social Forum Gatherings in Atlanta (2007) and Detroit (2010); cf. http://www.ussf2010.org/.

20   As with the earlier events, the meeting in Belém attracted masses of participants – 130,000 from 142 countries – but the majority come from the region, in this case "the Forum remained an overwhelmingly light-skinned, young, urban, Brazilian and Portuguese-speaking space" (Conway, 2009).

21   The WSF Charta outlines the goals and political character of the forum, cf. http://www.forumsocialmundi.org.br.

however specifying its features in much detail. The diversity and variety of participating movements are, in fact, highlighted as positive, valorized as an important source for a progressive societal transformation.

Besides the human rights, environmental, climate change, women's, unions', indigenous and other movements, urban and community-based organizations use the open space of the WSF to encounter and learn of 'others' and to share information across places and scales. While local groups that visit and participate in WSF events still remain local movements (as Tarrow and McAdam insist), they become not only more eager to embrace transnational commitments (without abandoning their domestic ones), but they also use access to this transnational space to support each other and to spread. Compared with counter summits, WSF events are more dominated by (international) NGOs and formal organizations. While local movement activists obviously participate – often in large numbers –, they partake here in an arena significantly shaped by transnational networks and organizations (many established or funded by UN programs) dedicated to urban problems, as e.g. the World Urban Forum (WUF).[22] The thousands of WUF participants who congregated 2002 in Nairobi, 2004 in Barcelona, 2006 in Vancouver, 2008 in Nanjing, and 2010 in Rio de Janeiro encompass the spectrum of urban actors: government leaders, mayors, and members of national, regional, and international associations of local governments, non-governmental and community organizations and international associations of local governments, professionals, academics, youth, women and slum dwellers groups. However, WUF meetings have been accompanied and challenged by simultaneous Social Urban Forums[23] which are much smaller but bring together more grassroots and social movement organizations. World

---

22 The WUF was established by the United Nations to examine the problems of urbanization, cf. http://www.unhabitat.org/categories.asp?catid=535.

23 The Social Urban Forum in Rio was called by social movements and organizations of Rio de Janeiro including favela-based groups, cf. Marcuse (2010).

Urban Forums are held to dialogue and network as well as to draw up reports and appeals. Activist networks such as the International Alliance of Inhabitants (IAI)[24] and the Habitat International Coalition (HIC)[25] make use of such UN-sponsored forums as well as of the WSF process to launch their campaigns against the effects of neoliberal globalization in (not only third world) cities. They use these arenas for global campaigns (e.g. *Housing and Land Rights*) and appeals for a new *Urban Social Pact*, and also for drafting charters for the 'right to the city', which, over the last few years, has become a joint focus of international human rights groups, UNESCO institutions, and the urban-oriented NGOs just mentioned.

The organizations pushing this type of a 'right to the city' agenda see some of its elements as already implemented, as for example the participatory municipal budget.[26] Furthermore, they point to digital democracy as implemented in the city of Bologna, which provides free internet access to its residents; or to youth governments that have been installed in the Latin American and Caribbean region with the help of UN-Habitat.

All of these statutes and charters seek to influence public policy and legislation in a way that combines urban development with social equity and justice. They strive to put "our most vulnerable urban residents" rather than investors and developers at the center of public policy, and in this effort enumerate specific rights which a progressive urban politics should protect. Thus, contrary to Lefebvre's definition of the right to the city,[27] which

---

24   Founded in Madrid in 2003, the IAI has brought together a large network of grassroots associations of urban residents from many parts of the world. It seeks to coordinate actions to "jointly stand against the perverse effects of exclusion, poverty, environmental degradation, exploitation, violence, and problems related to transportation, housing and urban governance produced by the neoliberal globalization," cf. http://eng.habitants.org/who_we_are/.

25   Cf. http://www.hic-net.org/.

26   Cf. http:///www.participatorybudgeting.org.

27   Born out of the context of May 68 in Paris, the right to the city for Lefebvre meant the "creative surplus of the city, which points beyond the rationality of economics and state planning, as well as the right to participate in urban centrality" (Lefebvre, 2009: 108; cf. Mayer, 2007b).

these documents frequently refer to,[28] they invoke specific struggles for particular rights (not *the* right to the city), and combine "a bundle of already-existing human rights and related state obligations, to which, by extension, local authorities are also party".[29] The right to the city in these declarations entails the human rights to housing and work, food and clean water, health, security, access to public infrastructure, participation in decision-making, and many more. These rights are supposed to hold for all "urban inhabitants," both as individuals and as collective, but some groups are mentioned as deserving particular protection (the poor, ill, handicapped, and migrants get mentioned). These charters do not set binding, globally enforceable guidelines, but rather are proposed to work as blueprints for municipalities and NGOs interested in *good urban governance*. Their goal is to establish effective legal monitoring mechanisms and instruments to ensure the enforcement of recognized human, social, and citizenship rights. Towards this end, UN-Habitat campaigns such as the 'Global Campaign on Urban Governance' proselytize the charters, using toolkits on participatory decision-making, transparency in local governance, and participatory budgeting to demonstrate how these principles can be implemented in practice.

Contrary to Lefebvre's right to the city, which builds on a class-based concept of difference, these charters and declarations as well as their repertoire build on a more general concept of diversity, in which civil society as a whole appears as worthy of protection from (destructive) global forces – as if it did not itself harbor economic and political actors, who participate in and profit from the production of poverty, discrimination, and racism. They thus obfuscate the fact that both civil society and 'the city' are themselves deeply divided by class and power.

---

28   Cf. UNESCO-UN-Habitat Discussion Paper of March 2005, http://www.hic-net.org/articles.asp?PID=229.

29   Cf. UNESCO-UN-Habitat Discussion Paper of March 2005, http://www.hic-net.org/articles.asp?PID=229, paragraph 7.

Yet, one might still argue that, once fully realized, these enumerated rights might spell a significant improvement for disadvantaged urban inhabitants. For one, the public recognition through governmental and UN institutions certainly lends added weight and legitimacy to movement demands and enhances the status of the groups articulating them. But these charters and the coalitions devising and promoting them often tend, in the process, to modify the political content and meaning of the original movement demands. The laundry-list of rights thus boils down to claims for inclusion in the current system as it exists, rather than aiming to transform the existing system – and in that process ourselves. This type of rights discourse merely targets particular aspects of neoliberal policy, e.g. in combating poverty, but not the underlying economic policies which systematically produce poverty and exclusion. Both concepts of the right to the city are actually present at WSF meetings, but some of the documents published[30] tend to reflect the institutionalized version of a "top down agenda agreed on by some NGO networks who already know what the rights are, but want to build a larger alliance … for which they need a name and branding" (Unger, 2009).

The transnational forms of cooperation with NGOs and UN institutions thus provide urban movements with rich opportunities for exchanging and networking with multiple emancipatory struggles, and to link up with grassroots mobilizations in cities of the global South and North – if often at the cost of diluting their radical demands.

ANTI-GLOBALIZATION MOVEMENTS DISCOVER THE LOCAL/THE URBAN

The experiences gained at summit protests as well as those from WSF meetings are brought home. Conference delegates report back to their home organizations, and counter summit participants often import inspirations gained and lessons learned. Lesley Wood described how activists from New York

---

30   As e.g. the 'Urban Movements Building Convergences at the World Social Forum, WSF 2009,' at http://www.hic-net.org/content/convergencies-wsf2009.pdf.

City and Toronto tried to transfer the 'Seattle model' to their home cities. After participating in the G8 protests in Seattle they experimented with some of the hallmarks of transnational summit protest such as black block street fighting tactics, blockade strategies, affinity groups, spokes councils, and radical puppet theater (Tarrow, 2005a: 63). Importing these forms turned out to be more difficult in Toronto than in New York, and implanting action repertoires seems to be harder than to transfer the themes of neoliberal globalization from the global to the local setting. Still, "report backs" have become an important tool also for the participants of the US Social Forum in Atlanta and Detroit. After these big meetings, activists share their experiences and observations at back home gatherings with members of their local community, reflecting the process orientation of the Social Forum (Smith et al., 2008: 46).

The localization and urbanization of global-scale movements occur in a variety of ways and with varying impact.[31] Especially since transnational networks such as Attac, Global Action Network, and Reclaim the Streets have become aware that free trade and market deregulation not only wreck sustainable production structures in the global South, but also threaten unions and consumers in the North, they have refocused their activities to national and local scales in these first world regions. In addition to their efforts to democratize international institutions, they now also emphasize the local impacts of global neoliberal restructuring in their home cities. Many have moved the defense of public urban services and infrastructures to the top of their agendas, while others (like Reclaim the Streets) zero in on the detrimental effects of corporate-driven urban restructuring. In Germany, the more than 200 local Attac groups have, since 2003, turned towards the local impositions of neoliberal restructuring, from the privatization of public utilities to the dismantling of social services. In similar fashion, the

---

31   Because movement activists confront different situations as they import and translate experiences and insights gained on higher scales into their distinct local environments, this leads to significant differences in the "down-scaling" of global issues and strategies (cf. Tarrow, 2005a: 60; 2005b: chapter 3).

Social Forums that have sprouted across Germany since 2003 have bundled the work of local progressive initiatives, rank and file union groups, autonomous as well as church and charitable organizations. They align themselves with the WSF Charta of Principles (stressing cooperation in non-hierarchical networks), in order to "locally benefit from the dynamics of the WSF process."[32] This local-scale instantiation of the anti-globalization movement emphasizes alliance building and networking just like the global enactment does. German Social Forum groups have, in the face of mounting attacks on social rights, sought to bring together the splintered protests of students and childcare workers, jobless and handicapped, migrants and welfare recipients, arguing that their fragmented protest does not find resonance with left parties, church representatives, or other established organizations such as unions. With their political networks they have been seeking not only to coordinate and support the activities of these diverse and often isolated groups, but also to break up the climate of resignation and instigate a public critique of neoliberal social policies.[33]

Together with Attac, the Social Forums have also carried the global campaign against the General Agreement against Trade and Services (GATS)[34] into the cities: they organized protests and referenda against the privatization of public goods such as municipal utilities, and petitioned for plebiscites against cross-border leasing of public facilities to US finance trusts.[35] In many cities the protests succeeded in stopping or preventing these deals, as for example the plan to lease out the Frankfurt subway grid.

---

32 Leitlinien der Zusammenarbeit im Berlin Social Forum (Guidelines of cooperation in the Social Forum Berlin), which were adopted May 2003, at www.wikiservice.at/esf/wiki.cgi?BSF-Leitlinien.

33 Cf. http://germany.indymedia.org/2003/03/44293.shtml.

34 The GATS extends liberalization efforts from the sphere of goods to the one of services. How and by whom services are provided has impacts on basic human rights (to health, to education) and development (e.g. access to water, public transport, financial services, etc., i.e. GATS links economic processes directly to social and human rights, cf. UN High Commissioner for Human Rights (2001).

35 This form of selling off public infrastructure was wildly popular in German municipalities before the global financial meltdown (Rügemer, 2008).

Anti-globalization movements that have newly entered the urban stage have brought fresh momentum to the local movements, helping them overcome their fragmentation, and supporting their consolidation as well as their professionalization. In 'localizing' the issues of the transnational movements, they contributed to the transfer of repertoires associated with the work of transnationally oriented organizations, such as professional PR work, sophisticated media orientation, and a flexible action repertoire utilizing pragmatic as well as militant action forms. Especially the dual tactics tested at summit meetings, where activists operate both in the negotiation arenas (as representatives or advocates for various disadvantaged groups and as partners of business and state actors) as well as in the streets (with demonstrations, blockades, creative spectacles, clowns and puppets) have found their way into the urban movement practices. In both dimensions urban movements have since enhanced their organizational and professional skills. Whether engaging in theater actions against workfare jobs in front of employment offices, or warding off evictions of squatted buildings or social centers, their action forms increasingly tend towards media savvy, professionally managed events, and slick websites report on their actions, link to related ones carried out by others, and help spread the message and build the networks. The shift of the anti-globalization movements toward the city has thus given a boost to place-based movements, and global/local connections and mutual learning processes have frequently politicized local projects and initiatives. These transscalar diffusions of the anti-globalization movement have also put the city, and the struggle to reclaim the city, on top of the agenda of transnational struggles (cf. Portaliou, 2007).

The diffusion of knowledge and experiences goes both ways; not only have the anti-globalization movements and WSF events impacted on local struggles, but particular local/national instantiations of the Forum Process have also impacted on the WSF (Smith and Juris, 2008). This last example of local-national-global connectivities and diffusion processes reconnects the circle which these last three sections have been describing: we are back to 'urban movements scaling upwards.' All the cases sketched in these sections illustrate that every one of the scales in which the (right to) the city is fought over is shaped by specific power relations and conflict structures. The political and discursive context, the particular features of the actors, and the opportunity structures are particular to each case. But the various instances also reveal that the struggle for a just city takes not only different scale-differentiated, but also distinct place-based, territorially-anchored, and network-specific forms. All of these socio-spatial dimensions would need to be accounted for in order to adequately understand the shifts and reconfigurations in the contemporary social and political power relations (cf. Jessop et al., 2008; Brenner, 2009). The brief survey presented in this chapter provides but an initial impulse; more systematic empirical research on the practices of movements on the various scales of urban politics and their interactions is necessary to identify the opportunities and possibilities set up by these shifts. A few preliminary clues may, however, be gathered from our initial synopsis, which the final section will present.

Implications for the opportunities of multi-scalar struggles for the city

The battle for another, better city is fought in a variety of differently scaled, partially overlapping arenas simultaneously, constituting a complex set of relations of global and local engagement: alliances and networks forged at WSF meetings or alternative counter summits may reverberate as productively on local struggles as do the global activities of human rights and anti-poverty groups. Simultaneous actions at different sites around the world signal the global connectedness of local movements, thus politicizing them as constitutive elements of counter-hegemonic globalization. Also, local struggles defending social rights or pushing for direct-democratic practices transcend their local limitation

(and potential regressive bent) through transnational inter-
connectedness. But to realize these potentials requires
specific preconditions: there is no automatic mechanism
enhancing the movements' strength and mobilizing power
through these connections. For 'glocal protest' to be strong
– this much has become clear – the movement milieus of
the host locality play a crucial role.[36] But the connection
between local movement milieus and transnational urban
politics is complicated. When an online discussion forum on
social movements raised the question how best to describe
the process "whereby social movement leaders ... gravitate
away from small and local actions to more diffuse national
or international ones,"[37] replies ranged from neutrally
descriptive terms such as "institutionalization" and "action
diversification" to pejorative classifications such as "cooptation" and "bureaucratization." The cases of local/global
activism presented in this chapter reveal, however, that the
transnationalization or up-scaling of urban movement activities does not always and without fail imply simultaneous
processes of depoliticization or NGOization. Rather, we
find the whole spectrum of political positions at every scale,
from radical anti-neoliberal (frequently in tandem with
direct action and blockade type of repertoires) to narrower,
more pragmatic demands (targeting select aspects of neoliberal politics, as, for example, combating poverty, without
challenging the underlying economic system) usually put
forth by NGOs and movement entrepreneurs, often in
collaboration with multilateral organizations (cf. Wallace,
2003). While the splits and divisions emerging within the
urban movement landscapes and the dilemmas they create
for emancipatory struggles are addressed in some initial
research (cf. Twickel, 2010; Mayer, 2013), the activities,
collaborations and alliances that have formed in the global

---

36   The relocation, after Genoa and Seattle, of summits to remote luxury resorts has
      robbed protests of the fertile organizational base rooted in local everyday struggles.
37   Cf. social-movement@listserve.heanet.ie, in September 2007: "... to put it in more
      practical terms: avoid leafleting on a Saturday morning outside windswept shopping
      centres, in order to attend 'important' international meetings with fellow leading activ-
      ists?"

arenas appear so complex, variegated, and ambiguous that accompanying fragmentations or shifts in political orientation and direction of the contestations have yet to be systematically investigated.

'Glocal' collaboration around summit events, WSF and other regional and transnational gatherings has in many ways invigorated urban movement activism, but also created new and problematic dilemmas. On the positive side, the interchange taking place between activists from different countries and between particular local and transnational movements can occur only via horizontal, democratic communication structures, within which multiple acts of translation have to take place, which aids and supports the emergence of pragmatic and tolerant positions (cf. Doerr, 2009). The effects of practicing respect for national, cultural as well as ideological differences are visible in the establishment of democratic local-transnational structures. And since networking and coalition-building (including with partners from outside the movement scene) is crucial to organizing the transnational events, these strategies have broadly publicized the movements' agendas and expanded the front of resistance against neoliberal strategies of privatization and social dismantling.

But success or effectiveness of social movements is not easy to define or measure – and social movement theorists disagree on the criteria: some highlight their contribution to boosting emancipatory efforts, others measure success in terms of political leverage gained. There have always been movements that, while failing in terms of emancipatory and transformative criteria, continue with some success in terms of power politics. The networks of NGOs and advocacy organizations that have been working on drafting a World Charter on the Right to the City and are designing policies that seek to guarantee sustainable, just, and democratic cities might be viewed as exemplary cases of urban movements that have gained political leverage. On the other hand, the novel spaces created by the anti-globalization movement in the social forum process (on global as well as sub-global scales) provide modalities of transformational politics, the effectiveness of which – while hardly measurable with criteria developed from traditional definitions of political power – may be significant in different ways. Osterweil (2008) for example points to the ways in which conflicts between different movement groups were resolved at the U.S. Social Forum in Atlanta as positive and transformative in that they made previously unarticulated conflicts between different political cultures visible and helped produce less dogmatic and less formulaic knowledge as well as political actors more capable of reflexive practice. Such learning processes and experiences, with potentially long-term transformative impact, have been allowed to occur at the scale and in the (open) space created by the social forum process, which brings the needs and cultures of different local struggles into face-to-face contact. Their clashes are either worked out in a context of mutual recognition and respect and in jointly struggling against neoliberalization, which harms them all – or they do not get worked out.

The successes in terms of gaining political leverage, however, often come at a price. One price is the emerging cleavage between an elite of transnationally mobile activists who dominate the flow of information and monopolize decision-making, and the home-based rank and file of the movements (cf. Cumbers et al., 2008). While urban movements in poor and developing countries do send their representatives and spokespeople to global gatherings and networks, their numbers are comparatively small due to fewer resources. Their issues and viewpoints tend to be represented instead by advocacy networks such as Habitat International Coalition, who may or may not authentically speak for the positions of shack dwellers' movements of South Africa's cities or the self-organized struggles of Latin American favelas or of South Asian informals (cf. Bayat, 2004; Pithouse, 2009).

Another price for the gain in visibility and influence thanks to participation in the transnational arena, as was shown for the networks engaged in the charter movement, is a watering down of the movement agenda. Responsible for such dilution effects is not the 'up-scaling' from local to higher dimensions of activism, but rather the specific composition of civic alliances 'from below.' As illustrated with the movements towards Right to the City charters, such statutes and the associated discourses assume and advance civil society alliances between urban inhabitants, municipal governments, and NGOs. These alliances and their participating organizations provide arenas where the content of 'good urban governance' or direct-democratic procedures may be open to the input and radical demands of activist mobilization and political pressure – if activists choose to mobilize such pressure. But there is a world of difference between the agenda of the (UN-sponsored) World Urban Forum and that of the Social Urban Forum, both of which met at Rio de Janeiro in March 2010 on the theme of the Right to the City:

> [T]he desirability/inevitability of capitalism was a foundational belief at the WUF; not so at the SUF, where it was frequently called into question ... At the WUF, the poor were dealt with as the objects, the beneficiaries of the policies there debated ... At the SUF, the poor and their movements were the subjects of concern ... Bridging the Gap, in the call for the WUF, was there seen as moving the poor a little closer to those above them; in the SUF, it was rather eradicating the distinction between above and below (Marcuse, 2010: 31-32).

In spite of such contrasts, cooperation on some immediate actions appears as possible, even if with different long-term perspectives. As Sikkink (2005) pointed out, some international institutions provide opportunity structures, even arenas for social movements, not just threats. But where the goals are too divergent, confrontation may be more appropriate. Confrontation and critique may be the only viable option with regard to the programs and initiatives sponsored by the World Bank or WTO, for which strengthening civil society networks has become a means to increase efficiency; urban poverty, which is here seen as resulting from inefficient local government, is combated by prescribing more businesslike public management. The NGOs partnering in such World Bank or WTO programs tend to comply with, rather than challenge, the standards and definitions prevalent there (Fox and Brown, 1998), and frequently grassroots groups fall prey to such views as well. Underlying these views is the assumption that, when urban inhabitants get together with municipalities to develop endogenous potential and local growth, structural contradictions between local autonomy and international competition, or between sustainability and economic growth, can be harmonized (cf. Jessop, 2000).

The problem with such thinking is that it strips the various scales of contestation of their social content and of the tensions and conflicts residing within them, making them appear either as homogenous and worth protecting (as with the local or urban scale), or as threatening but inevitable (as with the global scale). In this perspective, the various scales become reified, and the political and organizing processes, the clashes and changing relations that take place within all of them, disappear from view. In reality, of course, the scales themselves remain contested; power is unevenly distributed within each of them. If, as is suggested here, the success of collective action is measured by the movements' capacity to transform, in the course of struggle, the terrain and the constraints of conflict (cf. de Sousa Santos, 2008), then the goal is always the fundamental transformation of existing structures, and the struggle for a better city is always also a struggle about power, which can neither be left to international NGOs (even well-meaning ones) nor to local governments (even social-democratic ones).

References

Ainger, Katharine 2009. "Once beaten for stating the obvious, our time has come." *The Guardian*, March 26, at http://www.guardian.co.uk/.

Babtist, Willie, Mary Bricker-Jenkins 2002. "A View from the Bottom." In: Randy Albelda and Ann Withorn (eds.), *Lost Ground*. Cambridge, MA: South End Press: 195–210.

Bayat, Asef 2004. "Globalization and the Politics of the Informals in the Global South." In: Ananya Roy and Nezar AlSayyad (eds.), *Urban Informality*. Lanham: Lexington: 79–102.

Brenner, Neil 2004. *New State Spaces*. New York: Oxford UP.

Brenner, Neil 2009. "A thousand leaves. Notes on the geographies of uneven spatial development." In: Roger Keil and Rianne Mahon (eds.), *Leviathan Undone?* Vancouver: University of British Columbia: 27–49.

Brenner, Neil and Nik Theodore (2002): "Cities and the Geographies of 'Actually Existing Neoliberalism.'" *Antipode*, 34 (3): 349–379.

Conway, Janet 2008. "The Empire, the Movement, and the Politics of Scale" Considering the World Social Forum." In: Roger Keil and Rianne Mahon (eds.), *Leviathan Undone?* Vancouver: University of British Columbia: 281–299.

Conway, Janet 2009. "Belém 2009: Indigenizing the Global at the World Social Forum," at http://unialter.wordpress.com/2009/03/02/belem-2009-indigenizing-the-global-at-the-world-social-forum/.

Cumbers, Andy, Paul Routledge, and Corinne Nativel 2008. "The entangled geographies of global justice networks." *Progress in Human Geography*, 32 (2): 183–201.

Doerr, Nicole (2009): "Language and Democracy in Movement." *Social Movement Studies* 8 (2): 149–165.

Ford Foundation (ed.) 2004. *Close to Home. Case Studies of Human Rights Work in the U.S.* New York: Ford Foundation.

Fox, Jonathan and David Brown (eds.) (1998): *The Struggle for Accountability*. Cambridge, MA: MIT Press.

Hadden, Jennifer and Sidney Tarrow 2007. "The Global Justice Movement in the US since Seattle." In: Donatella della Porta (ed.), *The Global Justice Movement*. Boulder, CO: Paradigm: 210–231.

Hamel, Pierre, Henri Lustiger-Thaler, and Margit Mayer (eds.) 2000. *Urban Movements in a Globalizing World*. London: Routledge.

Jessop, Bob 2000. "Good Governance und die städtische Frage." In: Volker Eick and Renate Berg (eds.), *Und die Welt wird zur Scheibe... Reader zum Weltbericht URBAN 21*. Berlin: Berliner Mietergemeinschaft: 29–33.

Jessop, Bob, Neil Brenner, and Martin Jones 2008. "Theorizing Sociospatial Relations." *Environment and Planning D*, 26 (3): 389–401.

Keil, Roger, and Rianne Mahon (eds.) 2009. *Leviathan Undone? Towards a Political Economy of Scale.* Vancouver: UBC Press.

Köhler, Bettina and Markus Wissen 2003. "Glocalizing Protest." *International Journal of Urban and Regional Research*, 24 (4): 942–951.

Künkel, Jenny and Margit Mayer (eds.) 2012. *Neoliberal Urbanism and Its Contestations.* London: Palgrave.

Lefebvre, Henri 2009 (1968). *La Droit à la Ville.* Paris: Economica.

Leitner, Helga, Jamie Peck, and Eric Sheppard (eds.) 2007. *Contesting Neoliberalism.* New York: Guilford.

Levi, Margaret and David Olson 2000. "Strikes: Past and Present – and the Battles of Seattle." *Politics and Society*, 28 (3): 309–329.

Low, Setha and Neil Smith 2006. *The Politics of Public Space.* New York: Routledge.

Marcuse, Peter 2010. "Two World Urban Forums, Two Worlds Apart." *Progressive Planning*, 183: 30–32, at http://tinyurl.com/bdw896s [accessed 29 January 2013].

Mayer, Margit 2007a "Contesting the Neoliberalization of Urban Governance." In: Helga Leitner et al. (eds.), *Contesting Neoliberalism.* New York: Guilford: 90–115.

Mayer, Margit 2007b "Recht auf Stadt." In: Uli Brand, Bettina Lösch, and Stefan Thimmel (eds.), *ABC der Globalisierung.* Hamburg: VSA-Verlag: 190–191.

Mayer, Margit 2008. "To what end do we theorize sociospatial relations?" *Environment and Planning* D, 26 (3): 414–419.

Mayer, Margit 2012. "The 'right to the city' in urban social movements." In: Neil Brenner et al. (eds.), *Cities for People, not for Profit.* London: Routledge: 63–85.

Mayer, Margit 2013. "First World Urban Activism: Beyond austerity urbanism and creative city politics," *City*, 17 (1).

Mayer, Margit and Katharine N. Rankin 2002. "Social Capital and (Community) Development: a North/South Perspective." *Antipode*, 34 (4): 804–808.

McNevin, Anne 2006. "Political Belonging in a Neoliberal Era." *Citizenship Studies*, 10 (2): 135–151.

Müller, Tadzio, and Kriss Sol 2007. "Zwei Siege auf einmal? Das geht nun wirklich nicht!" at http://transform.eipcp.net/correspondence/1183042751 [accessed 29 January 2013].

Nicholls, Walter, Byron Miller, Justin Beaumont (eds.) 2013. *Spaces of Contention.* Aldershot: Ashgate.

Osterweil, Michal 2008. "A Different (Kind of) Politics is Possible." In: Judith Blau and Marina Karides (eds.), *The World and US Social Forums.* Boston: Brill: 71–89.

Pendras, Mark 2002. "From Local Consciousness to Global Change." *International Journal of Urban and Regional Research*, 26 (4): 823–833.

Piazza, Gianni 2007. "Inside the radical left of the global justice movement", at http://www.ecpr.visionmd.co.uk/.

Pithouse, Richard 2009. "Abahlali Basemjondolo and the Struggle for the City in Durban, South Africa." *CIDADES*, 6 (9): 256–257.

Portaliou, Eleni 2007. "Anti-global Movements Reclaim the City." *City*, 11 (2): 165–175.

Pröhl, Marga, Heidi Sinning, and Stefan Nährlich (eds.) 2002. *Bürgerorientierte Kommunen in Deutschland (Vol. 3)*. Gütersloh: Bertelsmann.

Rosewarne, Stuart 2010. "Globalization, Migration, and Labor Market Formation." *Capitalism Nature Socialism*, 12 (3): 71–84.

Roth, Roland 2003. "Bürgerkommune – ein Reformprojekt mit Hindernissen." In: Heinz-Jürgen Dahme et al. (eds.), *Soziale Arbeit für den aktivierenden Staat*. Opladen: Leske + Budrich: 103–125.

Routledge, Paul 2003. "Convergence Space." *Transactions of the Institute of British Geographers*, 28 (3): 333–349.

Rügemer, Werner (2008): *Privatisierung in Deutschland: Eine Bilanz.* Münster: Westfälisches Dampfboot.

Samsa, Gregor 2007. "Mythos Heiligendamm", at http://gipfelsoli.org/ Texte/Gipfelprotest/4074.html [accessed 29 January 2013].

Santos, Boaventura de Sousa 2008. "Pluralidades despolarizadas: una izquierda con futuro." In: Daniel Chavez et al. (eds.), *La nueva izquierda en América Latina*. Madrid: Los Libros de la Catarata: 359–376.

Santos, Boaventura de Sousa and Cesar A. Rodriguez-Garavito 2005. "Law, Politics, and the Subaltern in Counter-Hegemonic Globalization." In: Boaventura de Sousa Santos (ed.), *Law and Globalization from Below*. New York: Cambridge University Press: 1–26.

Sikkink, Kathryn 2005. "Patterns of Dynamic Multilevel Governance and the Insider-Outsider Coalition." In: Donatella della Porta and Sidney Tarrow (eds.), *Transnational Protest and Global Activism*. Lanham: Roman: 151–173.

Slater, Tom 2014 (forthcoming). *Fighting Gentrification*. Oxford: Blackwell.

Smith, Jackie 2008. *Global Visions/Rival Networks*. Baltimore: Johns Hopkins University.

Smith, Jackie, Jeffrey S. Juris and the Social Forum Research Collective 2008. "'We are the ones we have been waiting for.'" *Mobilization*, 13 (4): 373–394.

Smith, Jackie, Rachel V. Kutz-Flamenbaum, and Christopher Hausmann 2008. "New Politics Emerging at the US Social Forum." In: Judith Blau and Marina Karides (eds.), *The World and US Social Forums*. Boston: Brill: 41–56.

Smith, Neil 2002. "New globalism, new urbanism." *Antipode*, 34 (3): 427–450.

Smith, Neil and James DeFillipis 1999. "The reassertion of economics: 1990s gentrification in the Lower East Side." *International Journal of Urban and Regional Research*, 23 (4): 638–653.

Tarrow, Sidney 2005a. "The Dualities of Transnational Contention." *Mobilization*, 10 (1): 53–72.

Tarrow, Sidney 2005b. *The New Transnational Activism*. Cambridge: Cambridge UP.

Tarrow, Sidney and Doug McAdam 2005. "Scale Shift in Transnational Contention." In: Donatella della Porta and Sidney Tarrow (eds.), *Transnational Protest and Global Activism*. Lanham: Rowman & Littlefield: 121–147.

Twickel, Christoph 2010. *Gentrifizierungsdingsbums oder Eine Stadt für alle*. Hamburg: Nautilus.

Unger, Knut 2009. "'Right to the City' as a Response to the Crisis", at http://www.reclaiming-spaces.org/crisis/archives/266 [accessed 29 January 2013].

United Nations High Commissioner for Human Rights 2001. *Liberalisation of Trade in Services and Human Rights* (Sub-Commission on Human Rights Resolution 2001/4). New York: UN.

Wallace, Tina 2003. "NGO Dilemmas: Trojan Horses for Global Neoliberalism?" *Socialist Register 2004*. London: Merlin Press: 202–219.

URBAN (IN)SECURITY: POLICING THE NEOLIBERAL CRISIS

MY BROTHER'S KEEPER?
Generating Community, Ordering the Urban

Andrew Wallace

Introduction

The focus of this chapter is on a key strategy of urban security in neoliberal cities: the policing of individual behaviour within and through the trope of 'community'. This is not a development that has gone unnoticed by urban scholars of course (e.g. Johnstone and MacLeod, 2012) as the eradication of incivilities within neighbourhoods has taken on increasing importance in the orchestration of urban renewal within excluded or peripheral housing estates. However, in this chapter a particular filtering of community securitisation is addressed which relates new techniques of civic policing to a broader agenda of social discipline first 'rolled out' (Peck and Tickell, 2002) under the New Labour 'third way' government in the UK. A key premise of the chapter is that the various communitarianisms underpinning civic discipline within neoliberal cities consists of numerous formulations, logics and strains which have come to shape government-driven behaviour management strategies. Policy constellations concerned with authoring civility and order within the city promote regimes of community and civic space-making as well as techniques of enforcement to choreograph the renaissance of some urban districts and the stabilisation of others. This is enacted through both the activation of various community sensibilities and the now-familiar criminal-ising and civilising of the dispossessed across a range of urban topologies. As a consequence of this multiplicity, the chapter contends that uneven geographies of responsibility (Massey, 2004) emerge performing control and security in a number of ways but which consistently implicate citizens and voluntary groups in the generation of an array of spatialised cohesions, alliances and orderings. Through these processes, places and populations are becoming subject to intensified criteria of (dys)functionality which is assessing and sifting variants of individual agency and neighbourhood 'sustainability' and 'liveability' and thereby solidifying and reproducing vectors of urban difference at both individual and spatial scales. In this regard, the regulation and segmentation of the urban is assembled through moral as well as accumulationist categories and trajectories which underpin a range of securitising subjectivities and neighbourhoods within the city. This chapter seeks to excavate and analyse these contours of urban security through a focus on the interplay of 'benign' and punitive orientations of neo-communitarianism (Eick, 2011) and in so doing to destabilise and question unitary analyses of the 'civilising' of estates, downtowns or slums (see Ward, 2003). Instead, it is proposed that policies of discipline and security generate intersecting processes of activation, coercion and empowerment within and between localities which ensnare all citizens in complex spaces of order and control. Problem populations are controlled, but they are also constituted, landscaped and differentiated within the pursuit of a broader programme of civic reconstruction. Underlining these processes is a moralised account of citizenship and social relations which is articulated through socio-spaces. In setting out this framework of analysis, the chapter is able situate its reporting of a recent urban security programme within a nuanced reading of community building.

In order to support and elaborate these arguments, this chapter has three sections. Firstly, it explores the training of the public policy gaze on the integrity and possibility of subaltern spaces and cultures to argue that it is possible to situate an account of localised interventions in the life-worlds of marginal citizens within a theory of reassembled of state/civic relations that is repositioning the city and reimagining the urban. What have been described else-where as attempts to 'remake community' (Wallace, 2010a) consist of governing strategies emerging across some liberal democratic societies as cities and states manage and mobilise neoliberalism through nuanced modalities of urban containment, 'empowerment' and the generation of communitarian publics. The governmental context referred to here is the UK and the 1997-2010 New Labour govern-ment's focus on social ordering and urban sanitising, but the themes raised transcend the fixity of nation or political system, reflecting as they do upon the creation of rescaled governance spaces 'beyond the state' (Swyngedouw, 2005), the rise of 'contractual governance' (Crawford, 2003) and the emergence of neoliberal 'place making.' Within all of these frameworks, a key backdrop is attenuations of public policy which territorialise the surveillance and management of urban populations through 'opportunities' for engage-ment, continuing revanchism strategies (Smith, 1996) *and* apparently more compassionate 'post-revanchist' manage-ments and infrastructures of care (Murphy, 2009). From this perspective, an ambivalent repertoire of urban gover-nance emerges that is wholly communitarian, but which embodies a range of impulses and ensnares a multitude of subjectivities in the practicing of social order. The chapter sets out how this ambivalence materialised during the Third Way/New Labour period of office and traces its origins in a concern with the moral capacities of poor neighbour-hoods. It suggests that under New Labour, a range of urban policies were mobilised around assumptions of communi-tarian publicness tied to an interlinking range of logics and meanings encompassing class, ethnicity, history, place and trajectories of change. These acted as normative vectors for organising and practising the regenerated inner city and justified the introduction of intrusive, activating modes of civic self-policing.

Secondly therefore, the chapter offers an account of 'regeneration' policies which locate urban populations within normatively bounded 'renewal' frames of 'live-ability,' 'sustainability' and 'responsibility.' Taking the UK as a case study, it examines some of the projects of state and city-driven social renewal which are enveloping individuals and communities in uneven and unstable geographies of security. It evidences how urban policies have sutured 'communities' with interlinking processes of both civic empowerment and self-policing, yet rendering them as unstable publics of both civility and deviance. Notwithstanding Neil Smith's injunction to view such social strategies as 'highly varied and unevenly distributed' across different economic and geographical urban contexts (2002: 439), the chapter proposes that this is an emergent facet of urban governance across those cities with 'problem' populations inhabiting deindustrialised regions. We can situate this communitarian landscaping alongside strategies of gentrification, hyperghettoisation (Wacquant, 2010) and social expulsion as potential processes in a complex urbanism which is engineering, sorting and supervising both 'problem' and 'responsible' populations. In this sense, the chapter argues for a non-linear account of urban security which emphasises the reconfiguration of poverty publics through engagement and empowerment of certain populations alongside more explicitly vengeful strategies that continue to displace, deprive and control.

Thirdly, having made the argument for the ambivalence of New Labour's revanchism and rolled out discipline, the chapter focuses particularly on the 'antisocial behaviour' agenda of the New Labour government to demonstrate how individuals were implicated in projects of urban security rooted in rebuilding 'healthy' modes of urban culture, behaviour and subjectivity. The specific focus here is on the importance of 'community' as a discourse or circuit of meaning for developing a contractualist approach to behaviour management within subaltern spaces. In the UK, both the New Labour (and the 2010 Coalition) government have relied upon imaginaries of 'community' for instilling social control and pursuing moral rejuvenation. These imaginaries underpin interventions which seek to map, restructure and challenge behavioural norms by stimulating 'responsible' citizenship, achieved through the identification and repudiation of incivilities. The crucial point here is that this is achieved through a mode of self-policing in which practices and technologies of the penal state are now mediated through the scrutiny of citizen conduct *by their fellow citizens*. Citizens are constituted as either bearers or subjects of regulation with 'citizenship' and the social politicised as crucibles of behavioural scrutiny and reform (Flint, 2003). This project relies upon a repository of collectively defined norms which 'good' citizens are entitled to enact and defend as a means of building and sustaining 'community' (Burney, 2005). The chapter connects this method of control to wider projects 'activating' subjugated populations whilst locking in security and excluding disorder from the urban as part of a 'designing out' of cultural risks and harms towards a 'future-focused' trajectory for marginal spaces (Crawford, 2003). In so doing, the chapter posits an analysis of marginalisation mediated through new constellations of social and political exchange at the micro-level through which all citizens are subject to new regimes of moral regulation. These are related to wider processes of capital accumulation and privatisation, but also connect with normative moral agendas for strengthening the social capital of communities. Drawing on qualitative data generated in 2005 in a 'regenerating' neighbourhood in the northern English city of Salford, the chapter concludes with a discussion of how urban security and ordering has played out within the reconstruction of community and civic relations. For details of the methodology of this study please refer to Wallace (2007, 2010a). All names of interviewees have been anonymised in the data cited.

Transforming dysfunctional districts

The modern city has always been a locus of interplay and exchange built upon a range of needs, fears and fissures typical of human settlement and mass society. The industrialising and urbanising of the liberal democratic city underpinned an array of technologies of control designed to facilitate spaces of exchange where public order is demanded and required (city centres, commercial zones) whilst policing spaces of deviance where disorder is written into scripts of urban life (red light districts, the 'night time' economy). Logics of control were central to reproducing the structures and rhythms of modern life as cities came to embody contingent flows of economic and cultural practice and strategies of management and planning absorbed such notions of urban complexity and plurality in the course of organising and structuring pathways of labour, commerce and leisure. Simultaneously however, the perceived disorder of the urban has also long been a concern for politicians and policymakers. That is, the city has always existed as a difficult and unsettling proposition, at once seething with possibility for human endeavours, but capable of manifesting fears of chaos and volatility as well as challenging our capacity to organise, order and plan for those endeavours. Stenson (2007: 38) argues that this angst derives from uneven attempts at taming the 'vivacity' of the city through the creation of sanitised consumption spaces free from the deleterious effects of poverty and social disarray. In other words, the human debris of the capitalist urban centres, despite being either contained within the 'dark' ghetto (Wacquant, 2010), or clustered within housing projects, slums, favelas, *Banlieues* or 'sink' estates, could never be completely spatially or psychologically dispelled and represented threats and ills that could seep into the civilised city. Nevertheless, the slums were often resolutely not to be integrated within the possibilities of the urban: rather they were considered a proximal human resource for capital and commerce as well as an enemy within that could infiltrate the healthy social body through the spread of fecklessness, disease or pauperism (Furbey, 1999). For Wacquant (1997: 343), the apogee of this mentality was apparent in the classic North American ghettoes where the black poor were not just agglomerated in dilapidated inner city neighbourhoods, but actively contained within a tailor-made ethnoracial 'institutional form.' Notwithstanding Wacquant's differentiated account of urban poverty and the purported specificity of the black American experience, there are overlaps here with a general structural and institutional production of subaltern spaces through strategies of surveillance and regulation whereby 'forced settlements' (Wacquant, 2007: 20) emerge as key territories in the performance of control, exercised by agencies – the police, urban planners – operating on behalf of the state. The gaze of planners and penal managers isolate, frame and enclose a disordered terroir imbuing poverty with pathology and otherness. These by-products and constituents of neoliberal urbanism are excluded from notions of the civilised city, inscribed with discourses of danger, disorder and dysfunction and physically and discursively set apart to be policed and enclosed in tenements and public housing estates. Marginalised spaces are defined as inimical to the controlled cosmopolitanism of the modern city which is predicated on order, urbanity, sophistication and security as opposed to chaos and post-industrial blight. Of course, the 'ghetto' and other excluded enclosures were always going to be unstable, contested formations. Concentrating and accumulating populations in bounded spaces and restrictive meanings of marginality combined with limited government support conspired to generate unstable 'locals' built around material tensions and fissures linked to experiences of resistance, division and social closure – experiences that would also be used to condemn and police ever more closely (cf. Wacquant, 2010). This is in contrast to the wealthy neighbourhood which was not subject to the same behavioural and cultural parameters. The *lack* of a bounded socio-spatial neighbourhood discourse for the better off meant they were protected from the symbolic violence (Bourdieu, 1991) meted out in creating and perpetuating poor estates, given that the boundaries of their everyday were more porous and expansive and the potential for exit was always at hand.

However, latterly the governance of the poor neighbourhood has undergone a reconfiguration. No longer is 'the slum' only defined and policed according to what it is not (that is, un-productive, un-civilised, un-safe) but instead it has become subject to normative frames of identity, possibility and agency articulated through wider circuits of social and economic change. This does not negate the possibility of continued suppression of the urban poor within geographical encasements, but increasingly we need to acknowledge increased *flexibilities* in urban management which are opening up new constellations of poor neighbourhoods either as potential bulwarks against further socioeconomic decline, or as territories through which responsible citizenship can be generated, as well as sites at which entrepreneurial cities can profit from inward urban migration and globalised flows of capital investment. In other words, the 'slum' is, in some cases, no longer defined solely by its discursive and material exclusion, but is performative of new urban governance practices and bound into a re-assembling of relations between nation states, political economies and populations (Stenson, 2008). 'Slums' are no longer enactments of straightforward state control, but have been redefined as responsible actors within reconstructed civic, social and economic spheres. Once, they could be considered simply as socioeconomic 'trenches' created and exposed by neo-liberal 'roll back' (Wacquant, 2008), not to mention being grist to the mill of a colonising statehood excluding, controlling and suppressing local agency and identity but now these 'trenches' are more likely to be operationalised as sites of participation and renewal, drawn into 'new governance spaces', implicated in the regeneration of the urban and bound to neoliberal logics of security.

They continue to be subjects of a policy gaze, but one that repositions them as actors and participants in facilitating neighbourhood renaissance, 'sustainability' and 'wellbeing' thereby *supporting* neoliberal 'place marketing' (Harvey, 1989) and (uneven) forms of state retrenchment.

Each of these agendas of renewal relies to some degree on controlling behaviour deemed threatening to morally and economically vital trajectories of change and is achieved through a variety of technologies and mobilisations imprinted on 'communities' and other 'aesthetic elements' of the social (Rose, 1999). This wide-ranging 'remaking' of communities (Wallace, 2010a) came to prominence in the 1990s under 'Third Way' governments and signalled a transformation in conceptions of community and marginal space as the needs of the city and nation state were restructured and relations between citizen, state and territory were politically rearticulated. Of course, during this period traditions of excluding and containing the urban poor continued to involve visible and tangible policies of displacement and expulsion and even in places with apparently supportive infrastructures and programmes, individuals and groups continued to be subjected to asymmetrical power structures, circumscribed empowerments (Taylor, 2007) and feel that they were being incorporated within state retrenchment and urban restructuring (e.g. Wallace, 2010a).

Nonetheless, there was clearly a reorientation in how poor communities were constructed and positioned during this period and a large body of evidence emerged to show how government policy in the UK and beyond was activating or 'summoning' communities in various ways (e.g. Raco, 2005; Uitermark and Duyvendank, 2008; MacLeod and Johnstone, 2012). The portion of this literature focused on a key strategy of 'rolled out' neoliberalism (Peck and Tickell, 2002): the policing of deviant cultures and populations and the 'civilising' of previously downbeat areas often allied to the commerce-led renaissance of urban centres and peripheries (Ward, 2003). This securitising agenda relied on new spaces and subjectivities of control through which uncivil or deviant behaviours could be managed and eradicated. In the UK, we saw this most clearly articulated politically through the 'Respect' campaign as well as an array of interventions and powers for quasi-legal entities and individuals such as housing estate managers, neighbourhood wardens and citizens themselves to identify and police misconduct. It seems clear that this agenda was tied to policies of restructuring and accumulation which relied on sanitising neighbourhoods. However, the policing of the urban during this period was a complex phenomenon which 'rolled out' vernaculars of civic discipline through a number of drivers and arrangements. Before focusing on the specific implementation of the antisocial behaviour agenda, the chapter explores how the New Labour administration authorised and textured the management of individual behaviour through spatial framings. Whilst also addressing the broad agendas of welfare tightening and the deepening of the supervision of the poor *within poor spaces*, the chapter focuses on how specific regimes of micro-social relations at the local level for behavioural reconstruction were articulated through apparently benign 'opportunities' for greater empowerment, engagement and community and derived from philosophies of moral support as well as commercial exploitation.

Securing an urban renaissance under new labour

The redefinition and reorientation of marginal urban spaces can be explained with reference to a range of interlinking shifts and developments. The key premise here is that each of these are linked in their effects: governance forms which seek to secure and (re)order urban neighbourhoods through the activation of (re)moralised community sensibilities and the 'naming' and control of deviant populations. These forms operate through rationalities of community and contractual citizenship which accentuate the moral and cultural, rather than explicitly structural elements of regeneration and neighbourhood change. An important aspect is the rendering of residents and citizens as governance actors participating in the ordering of the neighbourhood. The aim is to choreograph sanitised, re-moralised civic spaces with an emphasis on the eradication of deviant or 'antisocial' behaviour in order to achieve secure, self-policed urban environments. Therefore, the need or desire to control 'the slum' did not disappear, but was being increasingly pursued in the UK through processes of ordering and closure under-written by a model of civic contract and a communitarian politics of membership. In the UK, the New Labour govern-ments grappled with the Thatcherite neoliberal settlement and encouraged both further encroachment of the private sector into welfare provision, alongside investment in projects that sought to reconfigure spaces of exclusion and poverty. The infiltration of the public realm by the logics and rationalities of commerce and management continued unabated as the public sector was increasingly governed by matrices and indices of performance management, surveil-lance and regulation, whilst patients, students and users of welfare services were reconstituted as consumers and clients whose interactions with the state and each other were governed by and through a new 'maze of contracts' (Crawford, 2003). In part, this also reflected wider gover-nance shifts based on expectations that citizens were active participants in the development and renewal of their neigh-bourhoods. These shifts functioned to re-assemble the way policies were constructed, enacted and regulated and placed greater pressure on sub-national local territories and citi-zens as sites of government and social development. In so doing, pre-existing 'local' terrain was not simply occupied by policy agencies but was made and reshaped through an array of projects and interventions designed to 'renew' and 'regenerate' (Clarke, 2008). For example, in order to 'win' funding from the flagship neighbourhood renewal programme 'New Deal for Communities' (NDC), localities had to be formed into attractive, manageable 'communities' of 'less than four thousand households' (Neighbourhood Renewal Unit, 2001: 8). In this sense, the NDC programme continued a competitive funding model introduced by the Conservative government's 'City Challenge' programme whereby localities had to form 'partnerships' comprised of local state, private sector and voluntary sector actors and compile strategy documents from which policy officials could select funding 'winners.' As has been have noted elsewhere (cf. Wallace, 2007), this was a problematic aspect of NDC in the sense that the 'communities' that resulted from this process were unstable alliances of citizens and groups attempting to maintain their 'community' identity and security against a backdrop of poverty, disillusionment and social division.

This is a theme that has gained greater currency in the UK recently since the recession and banking crises of 2008/9 and the election of the new Conservative/Liberal Democrat coalition government which has embarked on a programme of unprecedented fiscal tightening in order to reduce the UK budget deficit (HM Treasury, 2010). The new government has implemented tight public spending constraints and it has been proposed that the 'Big Society' should intervene to ameliorate cuts to welfare services such as schools, police and community facilities. This controversial Conservative-led strategy amounts to a resettling of social relations which seeks to re-energise a supposedly infantilized civic sphere and challenge sterile or ineffectual modes of state-driven social development. The 'big society' is not an entirely new governing philosophy (cf. Norman, 2010) and amounts to the intensification of neoliberalist logics within civic and social spheres as the ordering of the neighbourhoods is more deeply entangled in discourses of 'responsible' and 'sustainable' citizens and 'communities'. It remains to be seen whether further retrenchment of services will be sufficiently absorbed by voluntary and citizen action as individuals and groups grapple with their solidified role in maintaining the viability and sustainability of civil society.

In many ways, the Cameronian 'Big Society' agenda resonates closely with New Labour's adoption of communitarianism and a desire to bring forth strong, empowered communities and citizens. The urge to activate and empower populations and territories is a response to state retrenchment or fiscal tightening that specifically reflects a moralising orientation designed to change and order citizen behaviour. This is an indication of the moral dislocation thought to exist amongst both the subaltern and the respectable and reflects a particular political construction of the spatialised postindustrial malaise and need for community sustainability in times of scarcity and state withdrawal. Housing estates had to be reoriented to ensure they behave as responsible social and civic units, capable of producing and nurturing engaged, active citizens. During the period of New Labour government, this agenda was articulated by prominent politicians who borrowed the language and prescriptions of North American communitarian moralists as well as the normative critique of the third way. These strands constituted parts of New Labour's social vision and underpinned a range of policy interventions as well as discourses of government (Wallace, 2010a).

Commentators documented New Labour's particular enthusiasm for moralising notions of 'community' within some of these programmes (Imrie and Raco, 2003) and the communitarian progenitors of the 'community' leitmotif were consistently evoked (for example, Prideaux, 2005). In the 1990s, Communitarians such as Amitai Etzioni and James Q. Wilson, responding to a perceived decline in structures promoting public virtue, advocated measures to strengthen social order and communal solidarity by arguing for the (re) tethering of individual freedom to the wider community which they inhabited. Citizens were encouraged to operate *through* community, internalising collective norms and facing penalties for behaviour deviating from agreed standards of conduct. Communitarians sought to reinvigorate a moralist strand of liberal thought which linked economic security and the certainties of the industrial age with settled, strong and moralised communities. This was an analysis that sailed too closely to conservative winds for some (see Prideaux, 2005) and which, for others overplayed the disciplinary function of traditional working class neighbourhoods (Wallace, 2010a). Nonetheless, Communitarians rather successfully circulated the notion that previously secure communities were in crisis and required an injection of "moral sense" (Wilson, 1993) in order to combat political and economic dislocation. New Labour seized upon this rhetoric and embraced the "return of the agent" (Deacon and Mann, 1999: 423) to welfare analysis and organisation. Urban governance responses therefore, became more readily redefined according to questions of morality and security rather than poverty and structural change. Hence, when both New Labour and the American New Democrats strove to tackle welfare 'dependency' and get 'tough on crime' or bad behaviour, they could frame it in communitarian language about behaviour and 'responsibility' to the 'community' and define misconduct as 'anti-social' and unbecoming of a civilised social citizen. It was no longer enough for the 'welfare dependent' to get a job, for the poor were now being scrutinised for their capabilities as parents, neighbours and residents within communities. Following Wacquant (2010: 81) it is possible that what occurs during this period indentified here was analogous to processes in the USA wherein, by the 1990s, some middle and working class white citizens were keen to support the withdrawal of inner-city welfare programmes and sought the intensification of a 'law and order' agenda as their fears of the 'collapsing' ghetto percolated into vengeful policy responses. Something of a similar dynamic was at work in the UK without being as overtly racialised. New Labour politicians were convinced they had a mandate from the 'decent majority' to create these new complexes of citizenship within downtrodden neighbourhoods and impose conditional frameworks for welfare investment:

> We are not going to put taxpayers money into inner city development unless as a partnership which involves something for something...we are renovating estates but making clear that we will act when tenants behave unacceptably...we do not tolerate antisocial behaviour or lawlessness...we will put in the police and the laws to stamp it out (Blair, 2001).

In part therefore, New Labour's redrawing of territories of security was linked not only to the potential for capital exploitation, but with the regeneration of community more generally. It was also a response to the effects of deindustrialisation whereupon local crises of identity, morality and culture were said to be threatening and replacing the secure social and economic structures that configured the traditional working class community. In the UK, New Labour made a strategic and moral decision that these areas of urban Britain – largely its electoral strongholds of course – were deemed most in need of interventions that would facilitate new standards of morality and conduct. This was mainly a test of agency: were the dangerous estates of middle Britain's imagination and nightmare able to overcome their fecklessness and dysfunction and behave like the responsible communities they were once deemed to be? Would they take paid employment, discipline their children and clean up their streets and houses? This was an agenda only loosely based on a reading of the structural and institutional poverty that affected urban estates and was still bound up with a diagnosis of cultural lack and collective pathology. It was also tied to responsibilisation strategies of the late modern state wherein self-policed spaces were assembled to enable its partial exit from localised penal oversight (Crawford, 2003).

Deacon (2004) has argued this agenda reflects a 'mutualist' approach to civic responsibility which considers bonds between citizens and groups to be rooted in collectively defined notions of the common good. A vital part of this model of civic wellbeing is being able to manage and police the behaviour of those who defy or deviate from these norms in ways that harm the collective. By empowering the 'good' citizen to affect behavioural scrutiny, and possibly behavioural change in the 'bad' citizen, New Labour thought they were facilitating a renaissance in social capital and community resilience, thereby locking in circuits of responsibility in the lifeworlds of the poor neighbourhood. If structural solutions to poverty and disadvantage wreaked by the dislocations of neoliberalism were to be largely abandoned; at least social order and 'respect' could be instilled by mobilising a social division built around civility and behaviour. After all, as Labour politicians continually instructed those who raised allegedly decadent questions about this agenda, fear of crime and 'antisocial' behaviour was the number one concern of their constituents. This provided an apparently clear mandate to intensify the security of neighbourhoods and stamp out threats to economic, social and moral regeneration coming from the problem behaviour within.

Antisocial behaviour

> People have had enough of this part of the 60s consensus. ... they want rules, order and proper behaviour (Blair, 2004).

In breaking with this 'consensus,' New Labour introduced policies to ensure that the 'communities' they were assembling were stable, responsible entities. An array of measures were devised to secure 'communities' along vectors of neighbourly 'respect' and civility; enabling the responsibilisation of some citizens and newly sanctioned civic managers who could then take localised action to police behaviours perceived harmful to the 'community' and its ongoing renewal. In the Salford district studied by the author, there were an array of mechanisms, interventions and supervisions taking place which were allied to a number of regeneration agendas and trajectories encompassing moralisation and community protection, but also processes of gentrification and privatisation (although these erasures and displacements tended to be wrapped up in the community building agenda through discourses such as 'mixed' or 'balanced' neighbourhoods). The interventions utilised in securing communities such as these were nuanced and ranged from overt technologies of surveillance (for example, increased CCTV on streets, a more visible police service and new ranks of community support officers), to newly introduced civil sanctions and a widening of police powers in response to petty crime and nuisance such as Antisocial Behaviour Orders (ASBO), Acceptable Behaviour Contracts and Good Neighbour Agreements, as well as new powers of supervision for Neighbourhood Wardens and Public Housing managers through conditional Tenancy Agreements (Flint and Nixon, 2006). These new modes of supervision – all introduced or intensified under New Labour – were designed to offer graphic signals that communities, estates and families were to be watched, questioned and disciplined to a greater extent than ever before in the name of neighbourhood order, renewal and security. These were justified continually with reference to the 'priorities' of the 'good people' (Burney, 2005) who demanded a reinforcement of civility. In Salford, these new repertoires were viewed ambivalently by residents who largely welcomed, for example, the funding of a visible neighbourhood police sergeant (although many young people were unhappy about this development), but questioned the impact of this approach to monitoring and policing behaviour on some groups:

> A lot of people seem to forget that young people are part of the community, or don't want them part of the community...young people (are now seen) as a threat rather than an asset (Paul, youth worker).

The demand to control the behaviour of young people in particular was a difficult balance to strike for the neighbourhood police service:

> Yeah, because the elderly want to see high profile police for obviously the security feeling. The youths want us to get off their backs. They are, erm, always on the streets and we're always moving them on because of all the complaints (local police sergeant).

Nevertheless, the establishment of these new policing powers to control and curb behaviour was also allied to a range of strategies for designing out, cleansing and taming the spaces in which incivilities could develop and take hold. Therefore, across many sites of urban renaissance under New Labour we saw the closing of alleyways, the fencing of public space and the dispersal of groups deemed threatening to neighbourhood order (Johnstone and MacLeod, 2012). These more subtle modes of securitisation were linked in Salford to the auditing of problematic groups and 'hotspots' undertaken through resident surveys and neighbourhood mappings which identified specific behaviours and spaces to be targeted. Indeed, the first consultation of residents by the neighbourhood regeneration team contained 'young people' as a subcategory of 'community' issues to be addressed alongside transport, housing, environment and so on, immediately constructing this group as a concern for the 'community' to consider (see also Germes and Rodenstedt, *both this volume*). The resulting actions were then explicitly connected to assuaging the fears of some (usually older) residents and defending their right to use particular facilities or amenities but also to the redevelopment of 'disused' space and the exclusion from visible locations:

> Kids have hung around street corners and shops since Adam was a lad, but now that is called antisocial behaviour ('Paul', youth worker).

A further strategy at play in policing Salford was the absorbing of citizens into processes of naming antisocial behaviour. In this neighbourhood there were countless examples of residents being encouraged to inform the authorities about bad behaviour through mechanisms such as freepost envelopes left in local shops and a local antisocial behaviour telephone 'hotline' through which they could report incidents of misconduct or criminality to the police or local government agencies. The local police and welfare agencies were explicit in their request for community 'intelligence' regarding inappropriate conduct such as residents who falsely claimed welfare benefits, who didn't pay taxes or engaged in street-based incivilities and nuisance.

However, this approach did encounter some problems in practice as one might expect in an area with limited trust in the state and its officials:

> People ... won't give evidence and they won't give a statement ... I've worked in quite a few places and I've never come across it like I have in Salford, there is a massive 'no grass' culture here. ... You just don't say anything to anyone and that's sort of inbred and it's really difficult to overcome... (Local police sergeant).

Nonetheless, through these techniques of informal surveillance and reporting, we had strategies of control which still relied on traditional welfare and penal systems in part, but which were increasingly operationalised in the first instance through the scrutiny and actions of citizens and urban managers (as opposed to the police) and which related to more amorphous notions of civic harm rather than legally-determined definitions of criminality. As well as facilitating urban transformations along more profit-driven lines through various sanitisings deemed to make neighbourhoods more 'liveable,' we can argue that these self-policing measures were part of a 'contractual governance' agenda which, for Crawford (2003), was the predominant means of regulating behaviour (as well as building reciprocity and responsibility) in an era of penal crisis. When allied with New Labour's communitarianism, urban governance reforms like these were attempts to reactivate the urban poor as both agents and subjects of regeneration, management and social change. An important aspect of 'antisocial behaviour' therefore was that it was a dualistic agenda: 'respectable' inhabitants of regenerating areas were just as implicated in designing out behavioural harms as those defined as antisocial. Those who 'play by the rules' (Blair, 2004) were to be the people and groups who would lead the regeneration and who were encouraged to make claims on the behaviour of the 'antisocial' residents in their midst. ASBOs, curfews and other control mechanisms were implemented in order to enable civically 'responsible' residents to make and formalise these claims. In this regard, when Blair made the statement cited above, he was seeking to speak to the coalition almost identified by Wacquant – middle class taxpayers and 'respectable' working class constituents who were given responsibility to lead the behavioural renaissance of their localities. In Salford, it tended to be the relatively powerless who were most targeted by these technologies of control: young people, new migrants and travellers. These groups were felt to exhibit threats which played out through a number of incidents and tensions, which were either justified in the name of community building, or required further layers of intervention in order to resolve and or protect 'antisocial' groups from the excesses of this agenda. An example related to the issue of drug dealers which required an intervention from the police when it became apparent that some residents were taking self-policing to extreme lengths:

> What we do with smack dealers is we kick 'em out. We don't wait for the council or the police to do it. We go down ... throw all the furniture on the streets and they've got to go, cos they can't live there ... If they don't listen then we fucking drag 'em out ... once they start selling to young kids and once you get 1 or 2 young kids on it, you get 5 or 6 on it. Well, we're not having it, so we don't have it and it's our direct action ('Jim', resident).

In all of these discussions, a recurring theme has been the rise of community self-policing and its strategic importance in delivering sanitised and responsible urban spaces. It has been argued this has emerged as integral to managing the dislocations wrought by neoliberalism and enacting new modes of urban governance. Thus, poor-on-poor scrutiny of personal conduct has become a key signifier of a secured community and an 'active' post-industrial citizenship. However, not only have we seen how problematic this security agenda can be, there are a number of critiques of this approach to responsibilisation worth briefly mentioning here. The displacement of structural solutions to marginality and poverty by cultural solutions focused on the sociality and morality of the urban has been argued to represent a threat to some members of the 'community' who have been grist to the mill of this new governance of social change. In particular, vulnerable sub-populations such as young people and 'outsider' groups such as travellers are most likely to suffer from processes of social closure and behavioural scrutiny from fellow residents (Millie, 2007; Wallace, 2010a). Underlying this concern is a sense, in the UK context, that the concept of antisocial behaviour reflects a "victory of behaviourism over social positivism" (Squires, 2006: 157). In other words, behaviour is stripped of context to become about "motivation and intentions" (ibid.: 157) rather than possible causes that require support rather than punishment. As a result it should be noted that, in terms of New Labour, the belief that the construction of 'community' includes encouraging residents to make claims on each other risks neglecting relations of power and influence that pattern and legitimize the demonising and exclusion of certain groups whose behaviour is perceived (in the eyes of the dominant (usually adult) beholders) to be deviant. The attempt to create 'community' through behavioural and moral unity fails to recognize the complexity of social groupings and the intersection of power and social division that produce a hierarchy of definitions of 'good conduct' therein. Finally, it risks appearing like a cynical attempt to appease the supposed 'respectable' members of that grouping by 'empowering' them to effect social closure (and possibly exclusion) on others. There is certainly more work to do in understanding these dynamics of urban management and situating new constellations of socio-spatial agency as the urban poor are buffeted and re-positioned by the legacies and vagaries of neoliberal urban strategies which now seek to engage and transform and perhaps encase in circuits of civic labour, in addition to being simply discarded and displaced.

Conclusion

This chapter has presented some data relating to the securitising micropolitics of an English inner city, which occurred through a range of new powers, mappings and relations of control at the neighbourhood level. In particular, we saw how 'antisocial behaviour' became central to the reorganisation of urban security and neighbourhood viability producing conflicting ensembles of intended and unintended consequences. However, it has also argued that the rolling out of civic discipline is not analytically reducible to the more lurid processes of 'civilising' deviant populations within communities. It has suggested that this one particular formulation of remaking 'civil' social space can be tied, not just to the accumulationist 'renaissance' of neoliberal cities, but to wider reorganisations of the civic landscape which implicate all citizens, and is particularly targeted at poor neighbourhoods. This situates the control of incivilities with an array of conflicting trajectories, including historicised and classicised readings of how the character of poor communities can and should be strengthened. Further, the approach of this chapter perhaps enables us to consider how community self-policing is constitutive of 'remade' spaces wherein 'communities' are invited/coerced into generating and 'finding' antisocial behaviour and other 'threats' to their viability. In this sense, the repositioning and supervision of poor spaces *as a whole,* is conducted in part through 'their' ability to enact exacting specifications of civicness, security and order thereby controlling their troublesome elements. Apart from the well documented role of this repertoire in civilising place, this demonstrates how New Labour's integration of benign and coercive governance frames addressing the character of 'its' people and territories belied a subtle, but insidious extension and intensification of surveillance of those 'communities' as a whole and ensnared residents in complex subjectivities of empowerment, control and discipline.

References

Atkinson, Rowland and Gesa Helms 2007. "Introduction." In: Rowland Atkinson and Gesa Helms (eds.), *Securing an Urban Renaissance*, Bristol: Policy Press.

Blair, Tony 2001. "Opportunity for all, responsibility from all" Speech at the launch of the National Strategy for Neighbourhood Renewal, 15 January.

Blair, Tony 2004. "Speech to the TUC Conference." Brighton, 13 September.

Blair, Tony 2004. "Speech at the launch of the Home Office and Criminal Justice System strategic plans, London 19 July.

Bourdieu, Pierre 1991. *Language and Symbolic Power.* Cambridge: Harvard University Press.

Brenner, Neil and Theodore, Nik 2002. "Preface: From the 'New Localism' to the Spaces of Neoliberalism." *Antipode*, 34 (3): 341–347.

Burney, Elizabeth 2005. *Making People Behave.* Devon: Willan.

Cameron, David 2009. "Hugo Young Lecture." 10 November.

Clarke, John 2003. "New Labour's citizens: activated, empowered, responsibilised, abandoned?" *Critical Social Policy*, 25 (4): 447–463.

Clarke, John 2008. "Governing the Local? A Response to Kevin Stenson." *Social Work and Society*, 6 (1).

Crawford, Adam 2003. "Contractual Governance of Deviant Behaviour." *Journal of Law and Society*, 30 (4): 479–505.

Deacon, Alan 2002. "Echoes of Sir Keith? New Labour and the Cycle of Disadvantage." *Benefits*, 10 (3): 179–184.

Deacon, Alan 2004. "Justifying conditionality: the case of anti-social tenants." *Housing Studies,* 19 (6): 911–926.

Deacon, Alan and Mann, Kirk 1999. "Agency, Modernity and Social Policy." *Journal of Social Policy,* 28 (3): 413–435.

Eick, Volker 2011. "Policing 'below the state' in Germany." *Contemporary Justice Review*, 14 (1).

Flint, John 2003. "Housing and Ethnopolitics: constructing identities of active consumption and responsible community." *Economy and Society*, 32 (3): 611–629.

Flint, John and Judy Nixon 2006. "Governing Neighbours: antisocial behaviour orders and new forms of regulating conduct in the UK." *Urban Studies,* 43 (5/6): 939–955.

Furbey, Robert. 1999. "Urban 'regeneration': reflections on a metaphor." *Critical Social Policy*, 19 (4): 419–445.

Garland, David 2001. *Culture of Control.* Chicago: Chicago University Press.

Harris, Andrew 2008. "From London to Mumbai and Back Again: Gentrification and Public Policy in Comparative Perspective." *Urban Studies*, 45 (12): 2407–2408

Harvey, David 1989. "From managerialism to entrepreneurialism: the transformation in urban governance in late capitalism." *Geografiska Annaler*, 71B (1): 3–17.

HM Treasury 2010. *Spending Review 2010*. London: The Stationery Office.

Imrie, Rob and Mike Raco 2003. "Community and the changing nature of urban policy." In: Rob Imrie and Mike Raco (eds.), *Urban Renaissance?* Bristol: Policy Press.

Johnstone, Craig and Gordon MacLeod 2012. "Stretching urban renaissance." *International Journal of Urban and Regional Research*, 36 (1): 1–28.

MacLeod, Gordon 2002. "From urban entrepreneurialism to a 'revanchist city?'" *Antipode*, 34 (3): 602–624.

Massey, Doreen 2004. "Geographies of Responsibility." *Geografiska Annaler* B86 (1): 5–18.

Millie, Andrew 2007. "Tackling antisocial behaviour and regenerating neighbourhoods." In: Rowland Atkinson and Gesa Helms (eds.), *Securing an Urban Renaissance*. Bristol: Policy Press.

Murphy, Stacey 2009. "'Compassionate' strategies of managing homelessness: post-revanchist geographies in San Francisco." *Antipode,* 41 (2): 305–325.

Norman, Jesse 2010. *The Big Society*. Buckingham: Buckingham University Press.

Peck, Jamie and Adam Tickell 2002. "Neoliberalizing space." In: Neil Brenner and Nik Theodore (eds.), *Spaces of Neoliberalism.* Oxford: Blackwell.

Prideaux, Simon 2005. *Not so New Labour*. Bristol: Policy Press.

Raco, Mike 2005. "Sustainable development, rolled-out neoliberalism and sustainable communities." *Antipode*, 37 (2): 324–347.

Rhodes, R.A.W 1996. "The new governance: governing without government." *Political Studies*, XLIV: 652–667.

Rose, Nikolas 1999. *Powers of Freedom*. Cambridge: Cambridge University Press

Sassen, Saskia 2001. (2nd ed.) *The Global City*, Princeton: Princeton University Press.

Smith, Neil 1996. *The New Urban Frontier: Gentrification and the Revanchist City*, London: Routledge.

Smith, Neil 2002. "New Globalism, New Urbanism." *Antipode*, 34 (3): 429–450.

Stenson, Kevin 2007. "Framing the governance of urban space." In: Rowland Atkinson and Gesa Helms (eds.), *Securing the Urban Renaissance*. Bristol: Policy Press.

Stenson, Kevin 2008. "Governing the Local: Sovereignty, Social Governance and Community." *Social Work and Society*, 6 (1).

Squires, Peter 2006. "New Labour and the politics of antisocial behaviour." *Critical Social Policy*, 26 (1): 144–168.

Swyngedouw, Erik 2005. "Governance Innovation and the Citizen." *Urban Studies*, 42 (11): 1991–2006.

Taylor, Marilyn 2007. "Community participation in the real world: opportunities and pitfalls in new governance spaces." *Urban Studies*, 44 (2): 297–317.

Uitermark, Jan Willem and Justus Duyvendank 2008. "Civilising the city: populism and revanchist urbanism." *Urban Studies*, 45 (7): 1485-1503.

Wacquant, Loic 1997. "Three Pernicious Premises in the Study of the American Ghetto." *International Journal of Urban and Regional Research*, 21 (2): 341–353.

Wacquant, Loic 2007. "French Working Class *Banlieues* and Black American Ghetto." *Qui Parle*, 16 (2): 5–38.

Wacquant, Loic 2008. *Urban Outcasts*. Cambridge: Polity Press.

Wacquant, Loic 2009. "Designing Urban Inclusion in the Twenty First Century." *Perspecta: The Yale Architectural Journal*, 43: 165–178

Wacquant, Loic 2010. "Class, Race and Hyperincarceration in Revanchist America." *Daedalus*, 139 (3): 74–92.

Wallace, Andrew 2007. "'We've had nothing for so long that we don't know what to ask for.'" *Social Policy and Society*, 6 (1): 1–12.

Wallace, Andrew 2010a. *Remaking Community?* Farnham: Ashgate.

Wallace, Andrew 2010b "New Neighbourhoods, New Citizens?" *International Journal of Urban and Regional Research,* 34 (4).

Ward, Kevin 2003. "Entrepreneurial urbanism, state restructuring and civilising 'New' East Manchester." *Area*, 35 (2): 116–127.

Wilson, James Q 1993. *The Moral Sense*. New York: MacMillan.

Zukin, Sharon 2010. *Naked City*. New York: Oxford University Press.

'TO TAKE AN ACCOMPT OF ALL PERSONS AND THINGS GOING IN AND OUT OF THE CITTY'[38]

WALLS AS TECHNIQUES OF PACIFICATION

Samantha Ponting and George S. Rigakos

As the haze from thousands of spent tear gas canisters still lingered over Quebec City in the Spring of 2001, RCMP officials began responding to criticism that the Summit of the Americas had been a policing fiasco; the steel fences and barricades that encircled the old city and had turned residents into prisoners and demonstrators into an enemy horde was security overkill. Yes, hundreds were gassed, arrested and beaten, but despite the public outrage it elicited, the security fence was, according to the police, a stunning accomplishment. For security planners, the perimeter fence had been a success not *despite* the fact that it divided corporate and state elites from the multitude (Hardt and Negri, 2001) but precisely *because* the walls themselves had become a lightning-rod for protesters' anger (Bronskill, 2002). When the perimeter fence and the act of breaching it became the focus, the police felt they had succeeded because the fence had achieved both a tactical and ideological victory.

---

38   Sir William Petty 1927. "The London Wall" in *The Petty Papers: Some Unpublished Writings* (Vol. 1, edited by Marquis of Lansdowne). London: Constable Press., orig. circa 1690.

Indeed, walls are one of the oldest-known technologies employed to secure populations. There are walls of enclosure – city walls, gated communities, and fully-enclosed properties – and there are walls and fences that expand across borderlines. In the wake of global capitalism, an era defined by an alleged increased permeability of nation-state borders, physical barriers continue to be erected worldwide that feature state-of-the-art technologies resulting from unprecedented defense expenditures. Modern-day imperialism has caused mass displacement and increased cross-border migration, affecting segmented labor markets and the social composition of societies. New 'risks' (Beck, 1999) have arisen alongside the structuring of capitalism, and with inequalities becoming increasingly entrenched in the global economic system, walls have a significant role to play in pacifying populations.

Perhaps the most striking function of security walls is their role in processes of exclusion. As territorializing agents, walls engage with space to separate, differentiate, divide, filter, stratify and codify populations, while concurrently seeking to homogenize, civilize, and pacify in order to 'smooth' the workings of capitalism and responses to it. This entails the construction of subjectivities that alienate workers from workers in order to further the colonial project of 'divide and conquer.' As a major component of the capitalist security regime, walls and fences play a crucial role in the shaping of racialized identities, and are expressions of a hegemonic discourse that constructs the migrant other as a risk to be controlled. While this discourse mirrors colonial thought, it can further be established that the functions of walls today are reminiscent of the colonialist civilizing mission. With many walls erected along the borders of former colonial/colonized societies, the logic of colonialism is still present in the affected society's culture and system of governance, and by extension, its security infrastructure.

With inequalities becoming increasingly entrenched in the global economic fabric, old and new 'risks' accompany the structuring of capitalist relations. Thus, it is worthwhile to explore how the securitization of society constructs as well as mitigates 'threats' to the capitalist order. How has the wall been understood and used to organize social spaces as part of ensuring circuits of capital?

Towards a 'smoothing' of society

Traditionally, walls are conceived of as a form of architecture. What does this entail? According to Anke Hagemann (2007: 301), "Architecture is a system of boundaries and connections. It produces and controls different conditions in adjoining spaces – this can relate to temperature, light, acoustics, or to access for persons." At its most rudimentary level, architecture engages with space to produce and control. While architecture directly affects the physical conditions of an environment, the social implications of these changes are numerous.

The construction of boundaries is just one facet of a complex system of production. Walls produce exclusion, subjectivities, difference, privileges, and values – walls generate economic value through securing property and regulating labor and circuits of capital. As tools of pacification, walls seek to 'smooth' out conflict and produce docility.

In his theorization of the "constitution of society," Bogard (2000: 269) asks his readers to "imagine society as a production of smoothing machines." He uses the term 'smoothing machines' to refer to often contradictory processes of objectification and subjectification that 'smooth' society, sometimes facilitating social control. Citing Deleuze and Guattari, these 'smoothing machines' can be "technological, musical, maritime, mathematical, physical, and aesthetic," to which Bogard adds the category of 'social.' While walls can be conceived as aesthetic, physical (spatial-material), technological, and mathematical, framing the wall as a 'social' machine is most useful to understanding its engagement with other social processes, particularly racism and pacification. For Bogard (2000: 271), the social smoothing machine "generates blockages, exclusions, and dissipates energies. It also creates zones of inclusion, vitality, and freedom." While the wall itself may not be understood as a smoothing machine that creates zones of freedom, its antithesis – various manifestations of resistance, as in Quebec City – fulfill this role, revealing the impermanency of walls. Smoothing machines "eventually wear out and break down" (Bogard, 2000: 275) and therefore need to be reconstituted.

Walls, as smoothing machines, seek to create homogenous populations that are predictable, stable, coherent, and obedient. As capitalism requires "the constant revolutionizing of production," and the "uninterrupted disturbance of all social conditions" (Marx and Engels, 1994: 160), walls help to filter out threats to the social order, while seeking to amalgamate the governed population under one hegemonic bond: "It [the bourgeois] has agglomerated population … lumped together into one nation, with one government, one code of laws, one national class-interest, one frontier and one customs-tariff" (ibid.: 162-163). Walls can be seen as producing a "plane of consistency" whereby "the most heterogeneous matters are made to resonate together in a homogenous mixture" (Bogard, 2000: 272). Meanwhile, those that perceivably pose a threat to the national interest or national identity are differentiated from the masses and excluded. So while walls homogenize and consolidate, they paradoxically separate and produce difference.

Embedded in this process of homogenization is a process of exclusion, determined by one's adherence or rejection of the civilization's culture. 'Smoothing machines' "serve to differentiate which bodies are human from those that are not, which are deemed fully social from which fall outside the realm of civilized behavior" (Bogard, 2000: 279-280). In this light, 'smoothing machines' can perhaps be more accurately understood as 'civilizing machines' and pacifying structures.

Where some bonds are manufactured, others are severed. Where walls promote a unification of all of society, they simultaneously 'smooth over' class antagonisms. This, in effect, follows the colonial logic of 'divide and conquer.'

As the US-Mexico border wall separates Mexican workers from their American counterparts, workers north of the fence are alienated from an underpaid workforce that could conceivably take 'their' jobs. A country united on the basis of nationality weakens class identity. This stifles coordinated resistance to exploitation by valorizing territorial sovereignty and using harsh immigration tactics to feign state interest in domestic working conditions.

Contesting 'security'

Historically, walls have played a significant role in the defense of territories. Dominant narratives in the field of international relations would suggest that this is still the case. Benjamin Netanyahu and George W. Bush do not stand alone in their rhetorical salute to national security and state sovereignty. Even critical theorists have emphasized how walls are part of a reactionary effort to protect dwindling state power. Brown argues that the phenomenon of nation-state walls are a response to eroding state sovereignty, undermined by the growth of global financial and governance institutions. Accordingly, states are reacting to the effects of neoliberal rationality, which she characterizes as recognizing "no sovereign apart from entrepreneurial decision makers" (Brown, 2010: 22). And while maintaining a particular spatial order is an important component to wielding political power, and while walls may play a role in affirming a state's territorial jurisdiction, these explanations do not suffice.

The manufacturing of capitalist economic relations was a violent, coercive process that invited resistance. From the expropriation of land and the forced proletarianization of the peasantry to colonial warfare, violence infused capitalist development. Thus, its architects needed to develop structures to suppress dissent. This gave birth to the security regime under capitalism, which can more appropriately be understood as the securitization of private property and the extension and imposition of property relations and waged labor (Rigakos, 2011: 64).

The security apparatus manifests itself in the military, legal, and political institutions of capitalism, which produce a rhetoric of 'security' rooted in liberal thought. This rhetoric highlights the ideological component of securing capitalist relations, and effectively masks another central aim of security: pacification. Pacification can occur through the barrel of a gun or through ideological production. By generating what Antonio Gramsci (1971: 12) refers to as the "spontaneous consent given by the great masses," the dominant social class is able to uphold its control. Rigakos provocatively argues that "security *is* hegemony" (Rigakos, 2011: 58). This, in part, occurs through the liberal rhetoric of security: "The order of capital is an order of social *insecurity*," which "gives rise to a politics of security" (Neocleous, 2011: 24). These politics shape the development of policy, and inform such practices as racial profiling and targeted raids. Here we witness what William Rose (2002: 199) refers to as a "politicization of danger." This is necessary to legitimize actions taken to protect capitalist social relations and pacify its opponents. But the security-pacification regime also seeks to construct both self-disciplining and 'criminal' subjectivities. The capitalist wall is integral to these developments.

Self-disciplining subjects and the construction of criminalities

Michel Foucault investigates how a particular construction of the body is necessary for the functioning of capitalism. He looks at disciplinary regimes, relations of power, and mechanisms of domination. His theory of biopower, defined as "the set of mechanisms through which the basic biological features of the human species became the object of political strategy" (Foucault, 2007: 1) is relevant to understanding the extent to which walls regulate the body. Not only do walls physically control bodies through restricting movement, they also shape subjectivities. Walls facilitate discipline through shaping spaces of governance, and through constructing self-disciplining subjects. These processes are interrelated. Foucault writes, "discipline concentrates, focuses, and encloses. The first action of discipline is in fact to circumscribe a space in which its power and the mechanisms of power will function fully and without limit" (ibid.: 44-45). The fortification of territorial boundaries creates a space to govern, and by consequence, a space to discipline. Walls perform this task through spatializing difference and reaffirming social hierarchies.

During colonization, space was occupied in order to establish economic and social control over the population. Colonialism was not just about the appropriation of resources; it concerned the forceful promotion and dissemination of Western culture. Stuart Hall (1996: 616) writes, "Each [colonial] conquest subjugated conquered peoples and their cultures, customs, languages, and traditions and tried to impose a more unified cultural hegemony." The colonial civilizing mission sought to discipline colonized subjects so as to adopt them to the ways of the colonizer – as certain types of consumers and workers. Walls are likewise fundamentally a part of a colonizing mission to discipline a population into valorizing liberal values. As a vehicle for the colonial project, security has always sought to fabricate a social order.

From the walls of the everyday prison compound to the walled cities of 17th and 18th century Europe, walls can project a notion of criminality onto society's excluded. Walls are a physical imposition of disciplinary and hierarchical cleavages – a "gap" that "produces" others. In the new regime of accumulation, 'criminality' was connected to the idea of 'rebellion,' 'disobedience,' and 'disorder' (Rigakos, 2011: 41). 'Criminality' was that which threatened the social order, particularly in light of the new 'delinquent' behaviors that accompanied urbanization: gambling, drinking, adultery, and 'wandering' (ibid.: 40-41). While these actions today can directly threaten the commercial interests within a neighborhood, the construction of delinquency and the criminalization of the 'idle poor' is further necessary to mask the root causes of social instability under capitalism, develop fear and hostility among workers, and propagate a liberal logic of security that generates legitimacy for policing and military institutions whose central goal is the suppression of dissent.

Today, the state's criminalization of irregular migrants echoes 18th century attempts to divide the population. Migrants face increasingly restrictive border controls through discriminate immigration policies and increased scrutiny at the border. And while Stephen Graham (2010: 91) suggests that the 'war' on illegal immigration is being "de-territorialized," with exclusions surrounding national citizenship affecting those that "lie inside or beyond the actual geographical borders of nation-states," the spatial significance of the border should not be downplayed. Border security infrastructure propels exclusion from national spaces through defining the spatial parameters of social inclusion. Such barriers make penetrating and confronting spaces of exclusion particularly difficult for those who reject the moral codes inscribed on them. In this sense, walls express relations of power. Delinquents were excluded from society to sustain structures of power, and in the same light, migrants are criminalized and projected as 'alien' to further embed racist attitudes in the cultural fabric of society. This can stimulate a sense of nationalism that rationalizes imperialist projects overseas and pacification in the domestic sphere.

Graham importantly reminds us that under the new military urbanism, there is a "synergy between foreign and homeland security," highlighting the pervasive yet flexible application of militarized pacification technologies (Graham, 2010: XVII). In fact, by examining the earliest example of an urban security perimeter – Petty's London wall – the connections between managing outsiders and policing domestic civilians becomes even clearer.

Petty's London wall

Sir William Petty (1927: 286), while recognized for his role as the "inventor of statistics" and the "Columbus of political economy," he was also integral to the development of a new method of surveillance in England that would profoundly shape governance. Petty envisioned a system of cataloguing – a systematic statistical approach to surveillance – that would better enable sovereigns to control their populations in order to make subjects more productive. His proposed London wall was a tool to bring this system to fruition. The London wall can thus be conceived as a 'mathematical' smoothing machine, which would use data collection and codification to distribute flows and order society.

The wall is perhaps one of the first examples in recorded history whereby the city gates would be guarded "not by sword but by pen" (Mykkanen, 1994: 75). Although the wall never actually materialized, it serves as an excellent point of departure for understanding the emergence, under mercantilism, of a shift from walls constructed primarily as tools of self-defense, to walls as part of a larger political-economic project.

Rather than a defensive construction the wall was for Petty a tool to concentrate measurement for administrative purposes. It would have channeled all the different flows that were coming into and out of the city to the gates that were guarded not by sword but by pen. Gates would have been places where the relations intersected, where the proportions were established, where the invisible was rendered visible, and where empirical observations were substituted for metaphysical notions. Petty's utopia was to erect a great grid of separation, a calculating machine and organizing tool that did not leave anything outside government (Mykkanen, 1994: 75).

Petty conceived of its properties and utility. The wall was to be 100 feet in circumference, 11 feet high, and 2 bricks thick (Petty, 2009: 42). In vol. 1 no. 11 of the *Petty Papers,* he states that the wall would serve to "take an accompt of all persons and things going in and out of the Citty," to provide "a foundation of libertyes, securityes, and priviledges" and "to increase the value of enclosed lands" (ibid.). The wall would concentrate commerce through planned choke-points, where all movement of persons and goods would be made transparent (Rigakos, 2005: 284). Petty understood that walls could be used to codify and manage goods and people, not only to solidify the policing power of government, but to maximize productivity and the generation of wealth. Under mercantilism, governments were concerned with the population as a productive force (Foucault, 2007: 69).

Regulatory economic policies were to accompany the London wall. Petty proposed the establishment of a Council of Trade that would regulate plantations, manufacturers, and land and water carriage, and would enforce duty on goods (Petty, 2009: 44). As Petty's theorized wall demonstrates, the capitalist wall does not function in isolation, but as a component of a larger regulatory regime. Even during contemporary ceremonial 'crises' of security, such as summits, citizens become denizens who must not hide their faces nor approach public buildings. They can be corralled into police kettles and detained for hours, or arrested and beaten with little recourse. New "lawless" urban zones, therefore, pop up inside of which constitutional protections evaporate and the police appear as an occupation army (Fernandez, 2008). Very early too, while the wall was to physically direct human and commercial flows, it was also situated within a broader administrative structure seeking to solidify the foundations of capitalism. Of course, in the 21st century, the state continues to be concerned with the necessary components of economic productivity.

Border security today

The security fences of the US-Mexican border and the Spanish autonomous cities of Melilla and Ceuta[39] stand

---

39   Melilla and Ceuta currently reside under Spanish jurisdiction, but are disputed by Morocco. The authors do not wish to undermine the territorial claims of Morocco, but will apply the current terminologies used to describe the cities.

out as modern-day exemplars of walls as structures aimed at pacification. Indeed, their respective governments have explicitly highlighted immigration control as the primary function of the fences. Although there have been several border security fences constructed across the world in the last twenty years (Saudi Arabia, Pakistan/Iran, the West Bank, and Botswana/Zimbabwe), the US-Mexico border fence and the Morocco-Spain fences are perhaps the most evident expressions of xenophobic immigration policies. Yet, they share other stark parallels: Spain and the U.S. employ highly technological and militarized methods of border control that, although face sharp criticisms from some, are regarded as prime models of pacification by much of the international community. Spain's *Sistema Integrado de Vigilancia Exterior* (SIVE) links a range of surveillance devices to produce a detailed picture of its southern coastline, now reaching 500 km of coverage (Collyer, 2007: 672). In the US, a 'virtual fence' has been constructed, consisting of 98-foot towers crowned with cameras, radar, and other mechanisms of electronic surveillance. The physical infrastructure of the borderlands is accompanied by immigration policies that frame migrants as criminals.

Both Mexico and Morocco were former colonies of the Spanish Empire. In the case of Spain and Morocco, the fences mark a clear division between the colonizer/colonized. Although this duality is less clear between the United States and Mexico, the racial and economic stratification of these two nations can be traced to the legacy of colonialism. This has shaped conceptualizations of the migrant other that are reaffirmed by demarcating physical barriers. The economies of the US and Mexico and Spain and Morocco are very much interdependent, and while migration flows are restricted, commercial flows across borders are necessitated. Although many theorists have highlighted the tension that exists between economic globalization and the restriction of human movement, increased levels of migration can be conceived as products of global capitalist inequalities.

While internal security walls target the urban underclass, as highlighted by Petty's London wall, border security walls target the global underclass, and fortify lines that divide rich and poor societies. For migrants seeking to flee conditions of impoverishment, border security walls also restrict access to privileged spaces. And while the 'delinquents' of the modern era were largely determined by one's class, today's criminalized 'threat' is also shaped by one's racial and national identities.

The semi-porous, highly technological, and highly militarized border fences of Melilla and Ceuta and the United States, erected alongside a period of intensified economic liberalization in the U.S. and Europe, affirm a socio-political construction of the migrant other as a risk to be controlled; this reflects an effort to culturally homogenize Western society through (re)producing disciplined liberal subjects, united not by class but by other manufactured interests. Furthermore, the fences help to maintain a geographical division of labor that is favorable to the generation of profit.

THE BORDER FENCES OF CEUTA AND MELILLA
The Spanish enclaves of Ceuta and Melilla are the only territories of the European Union in mainland Africa. They remain a point of contention between Morocco and Spain, as Morocco has claimed sovereignty over the territories since its independence in 1956 (Enriquez, 2007: 219). Spain occupied Northern Morocco until this time, and territorial lines between the two regions have been in flux throughout history. Although the towns' respective populations and land masses are meek, these hubs remain geographically important. As port cities along the Mediterranean Sea, Ceuta and Melilla have historically functioned as gates to Europe for African migrants. As in the case of the US-Mexico border, many migrants have died attempting to cross the Strait of Gibraltar in efforts to access greater economic opportunities. Thus, as the only territories providing a land border between the EU

and Africa, the enclaves act as magnets for illicit migration to continental Europe (Ferrer-Gallardo, 2008: 311). Spain has faced mounting pressure internally and from the European Union, particularly following amalgamation, to seal its border to illegal migration.

The fencing of the enclaves' perimeters with Morocco began in 1995 with financial assistance from the European Union. When Spain joined the EU, the cities became increasingly understood as a part of the European frontier (Driessen, 1998: 100). The fences mark an effort to preserve European civilization by keeping the 'other' out. Henk Driessen writes that "the reinforcement and remaking of this frontier have not only affected the political and economic relationships in the wider region but also the cultural categories used to divide people into 'us' and 'them'" (ibid.). Thus, the border fences between Melilla and Ceuta and Morocco do not function merely as territorial divides. As frontiers to Europe, they represent profound social, economic and cultural divergences between the West and the East, the colonized and colonizer, Africa and Europe, Islam and Christianity, and whites and racialized people. In Melilla and Ceuta, the construction of the physical barriers functions as "a symbolic performance aiming to (re)mark and (re)mind the limits of socio-spatial identities delimited by the border" (Ferrer-Gallardo, 2008: 313-314).

Spain is by no means racially or culturally homogenous, but border reinforcements have been used to bind together the Spanish people into one collective identity (Ferrer-Gallardo, 2008: 315). Stuart Hall (1996: 616) writes, "however different its members may be in terms of class, gender, or race, a national culture seeks to unify them into one great cultural identity, to represent them all as belonging to the same great national family." Spanish nationalism itself is very much shaped by opposition to 'Moors;' it was built on policies of ethnic, religious, and cultural homogenization (Ferrer-Gallardo, 2008: 315). This effort to homogenize Spanish society relies not only on a racialized construction of Moroccans, but also on the physical control of their bodies. The security fences permit the Spanish government to more effectively engage in this form of direct physical control.

As in the case of Petty's wall, the Spanish fences control the movement of people through a system of calculation and codification. The fences perform the role of filtering. "The functional reconfiguration of the Spanish-Moroccan border and its new role as a regulator of flows is characterized by what Anderson (2001: 3-4) describes as a 'selective permeability' of borders and their 'differential filtering effects'" (Ferrer-Gallardo, 2008: 309). This filtering corresponds to the West's categorical ascriptions of migrants, whereby one's perceived belonging to a particular racial, national, or ethnic group determines access to a society. Reinforced by the wall, bodies are spatially distributed according to such codifications. These codifications are what Bogard (2000: 279) refers to as 'marks':

> All these marks serve to differentiate bodies, group them, align them to other bodies according to status codes, which govern their distribution, the ways they 'fit' together. In the same way the lock and key are 'machined' to insure a smooth fit of surfaces, bodies are marked to insure that differences do not exceed the limit beyond which elements would no longer function as a social assemblage, i.e. would no longer constitute a heterogeneous yet consistent mix of 'social surfaces.'

These codes and filters have colonial undertones; the "social assemblage" is best preserved through excluding the 'uncivilized' – those hostile to the European way of life.

While European nations have most certainly permitted immigration, these flows are highly controlled and monitored in order to mitigate perceived 'risks.' This necessarily entails a degradation and criminalization of racialized migrants. Yasmin Jiwani (2002: 67), who explores the racialization of crime in Canada, establishes that the criminalization of particular racialized groups "has a long historical tradition grounded in colonialism." This can also be said for the Moroccans and other North Africans seeking passage to Europe. Reinforced by racist discourse, the security fences are part of a larger effort to reduce undocumented migration. Undocumented migration reduces the continent's capacity to monitor its population, which is necessary not only to maintain homogeneity, but also detect and control manifestations of resistance to structures of power.

When it was announced in September 2005 that a new fence would be placed around the exterior of the existing ones, some 700 migrants participated in a coordinated action in both cities to mount the fences (Shelley, 2007: 11). The actions took place over four weeks until sufficient Spanish defenses were rallied, ultimately resulting in several migrants wounded and five dead (ibid.: 13). This action was met with an increased militarization of the fences – a response that is best understood as pacification.

This event demonstrates that the security regime and its technologies will continue to be contested. Secondly, it illustrates that migrant workers and racialized others have not accepted the physical controls and subsequent subjectivities prescribed to them. Bogard (2000: 291) writes that "bodies, along the interface of their integration into the ordered grid of society, will continue to throw off their subjectivity and objectivity." A culture of security is accompanied by a culture of resistance (Rimke, 2011).

THE US-MEXICO SECURITY FENCES

In 1964, the US guest worker Bracero Program ended, causing formally legal migrant labor to go underground (Dunn and Nevins, 2008). In the early 1970s, the U.S. Immigration and Naturalization Service (INS) launched a highly effective public relations campaign highlighting the potential dangers of unauthorized immigration (ibid.). The following years witnessed increased funding for border regulation, eventually culminating in the construction of fences along border territories.

In 1990, the United States Border Patrol began erecting a 10-foot high fence, composed of welded steel, covering 14 miles of the San Diego border (Garcia and Nunez-Neto, 2007: 2). In the succeeding years, "the boundary-enforcement apparatus exploded with the emergence of geographically focused 'operations'" (Dunn and Nevins, 2008). Barricades were erected in Southern Arizona, Brownsville, and El Paso.

The Secure Border Initiative was announced on November 2, 2005, aiming to increase "physical layers of security," encompassing walls, fences, and barricades (ibid.). In 2006, the Secure Fence Act was signed into law, sanctioning the construction of 850 miles of at least two layers of reinforced fencing surrounding patrol roads. Multibillion dollar 'virtual fence' technologies have been deployed, outsourced to companies such as Boeing and its subcontractors. 98-foot towers were constructed in Southern Arizona, topped with cameras, sensors, radar and other surveillance equipment (ibid.). These are accompanied by biometric screening technologies at points of entry along the border, which recognize and register vocal, retinal and facial features. Interoperational databases collect, track, and coordinate information on individual movement (Brunet-Jailly, 2007: 198).

The US border infrastructure is one component of a wider anti-migrant regime that effectively criminalizes and excludes migrants. Civilian anti-migrant militias aggressively confront migration and threaten the safety of migrants. Arizona officials have revised local laws, transforming illicit border crossings from civilian offences to felonies – effectively criminalizing the act of migration. Proposition 200, legislation passed in 2005 in Arizona, denies undocumented migrants access to public social services and public education (Murphy Efani, 2007: 45). These policy measures exist parallel to the US border fences, which together pose as physical and immaterial modes of exclusion that target the movement of people alongside a national state agenda to liberalize the flow of commodities.

Many of the migrants traveling across the border are economic migrants. They are seeking out employment and better economic conditions. And while these migrant workers contribute significantly to the American economy as sources of cheap and exploitable labor, they remain targets of surveillance, hostility, racism, and repression. While the case of the London wall suggest that the capitalist security apparatus is concerned with constructing productive labor and securing private property, can the same be said for the US-Mexico wall?

While American employers clearly benefit from undocumented Mexican labor, capitalists that exploit labor in Mexico also rely on a cheap, expendable labor market. Regardless of increased economic ties between the US and Mexico since the establishment of NAFTA, the conditions within each country under which capital accumulates are distinct. As highlighted by Mathew Coleman (2005: 186), "if the border is criss-crossed by maquila-based flows of goods and capital, then at the same time it marks adjacent regimes of accumulation set firmly apart by wage, environmental, and labor regulations." Excluded from NAFTA were stipulations for cohesion in social and legal standards. Mexican markets were profitable targets for foreign investors specifically because the population was easily exploitable. In a sense, the wall creates a holding pen of easily exploitable labor for U.S. multinationals – a massive colonial labor camp where workers cannot receive the same benefits and compensation they would in the U.S. This has a twofold benefit for capitalists. It creates an immiserated, unprotected workforce in the South and an increasingly deindustrialized reserve army of workers in the U.S. willing to work for less and less. The more de-unionized, deindustrialized and exploited, the more statistically likely that public and private policing grow (Rigakos and Ergul, 2011). As a barometer of bourgeois insecurity, public and private policing employment growth is coupled with increased expenditures on all forms of physical security, from CCTV to walled estates. The wall amplifies this generalized sense of insecurity and social alienation. It produces the rationale for even more pacification. We build walls within walls – segregation within segregation.

The US border regime serves to provide security from 'social threats.' Coleman (2005: 187) suggests that the US, as a 'gatekeeper state,' provides "extraterritorial opportunities for national territory-based capital…while, somewhat paradoxically, providing security against the perceived social costs unleashed by globalization." Jason Ackleson (2005: 172) echoes this view, arguing that the US security initiatives of the 1990s reconstructed the border to respond to the 'threats' of social insecurity, including narcotics, undocumented economic migrants, social instability and poverty. He argues, "migration is partly spurred by an existing asymmetrical economic order which was further consolidated under neoliberal globalization" (ibid.: 267). Mexican migration challenges an international division of labor constructed around a regime of accumulation.

The US security wall physically prevents workers from engaging together in the same social sphere. Through the production of racist discourse, workers are alienated from other workers, and bonds are built around the construct of nationhood. In order to maintain power, rulers make concerted efforts to unite a population around a common identity; this also effectively suppresses class solidarity. The formation of a historic bloc, a term Gramsci borrows from Georges Sorel, requires the formation of alliances between an array of social classes – alliances not formulated purely on economic class. In the case of the United States, national unity necessitates the exclusion of 'foreigners' and migrants. The border security walls physically as well as symbolically distinguish 'us' and 'them.' These walls are to maintain a socio-economic hierarchy that is threatened by migration. "That which is outside both constitutes and threatens the integrity of the inside, and the decision to include/exclude both defines the population of the state and gives lie to the presumed homogeneity and stability of that community" (Salter, 2006: 172). Migrants are perceived as particularly threatening to a country's national image and political culture.

Yet industrialized states have sometimes facilitated migration to meet the needs of the labor market. Michael J.

Shapiro (1997: 6) notes that "While their representational practices have kept 'foreign populations' at a distance conceptually, other practices of industrially and economically advanced states have produced flows of such peoples across state boundaries." While some Mexican workers are allowed entry in the United States, the walls, through preventing illicit migration and ensuring that flows are documented, increase the state's capacity to manage these workers. If these workers should in fact pose a threat to the nation's social order, the state is able to appeal to nationalism and racism to pacify them.

Conclusion

The border security walls along the Morocco-Spain and US-Mexico borders are excellent examples of architectures of exclusion that also function as part of a broader race- and class-based pacifying mission. Just as colonization exported a culture, walls today work to preserve a distinct Western cultural composition. Walls, as biopolitical structures, carry out this civilizing mission through pacifying, homogenizing, and criminalizing. Codifying and filtering are central to this process, which William Petty was quick to establish in his theorized London wall. While the beginnings of the capitalist security regime were rooted in the securitization of property and the wage labor system, common functions of security today involve: ensuring exploitable labor; dividing the international working class socially as well as spatially; and securitizing an obedient, pacified social order. The management of populations is central to this regime, to which border security walls are an important facet.

As capitalist wars displace to secure geopolitical interests and economic resources, and as capital flows into the global North from the global South in the form of debt and interest repayments, the border security regime ensures that relations of exploitation and domination can continue to be mapped onto the desired people and spaces, all the while being ceremonially played out at summit after summit, reinforcing the connections between domestic and international pacification. They must be made part of the analysis of any anti-security project (Neocleous and Rigakos, 2011: 15-22).

Security walls, therefore, perform a number of important functions. First, they help to make labor more productive through practices of segregation, enshrining national competition and creating a generalized race to the bottom by convincing domestic workers that their interests are national and not international. Second, walls help reinforce a system that privileges the global protection of private property. It is a civilizing initiative, smoothing populations and vetting the deserving from undeserving by "reinforcing a circuit of cosmopolitan consumption" and making spaces "open for business and thus ripe for economic exploitation" (Rigakos, 2011: 79). Third, walls are "covers for war" in that they clearly signify that there is a binary 'dangerous' population and an oppositional population in need of protection. Outsiders are constructed as enemy hordes and the wall, in its military majesty, reinforces patterns of colonization and imperial domination by tying together in both tactical purpose and in the ideological imaginary scenes as disparate as U.S. Marine compounds in Iraq, French Foreign Legion garrisons in Morocco and pop-up security exclusion zones during the Toronto G20 summit. The metaphor extends even further such that border security walls keep outsiders on their own impoverished territory as much as they keep them from entering their neighbour's more economically abundant property. This is tantamount to a modern-day, international siege: slowly choking off populations until they are pacified into submission. In these ways and others, therefore, analyzing walls as a form of pacification can be a fruitful avenue of investigation.

References

Ackleson, Jason 2005. "Constructing Security on the US-Mexico Border." *Political Geography*, (2) 24: 164–184.

Beck, Ulrich 1999. *World Risk Society*. Malden, MA: Polity Press.

Bogard, William 2000. "Smoothing Machines and the Constitution of Society." *Cultural Studies*, 14 (2): 269–294.

Bronskill, Jim 2002. "Fence in all summits, RCMP says: 'essential' barricade made meeting in Quebec City 'a complete success.'" *Ottawa Citizen*, 25 February: A5.

Brown, Wendy 2010. *Walled States, Waning Sovereignty*. New York: Zone Books.

Brunet-Jailly, Emmanuel 2007. *Borderlands: Comparing Border Security in North America and Europe*, Ottawa: University of Ottawa Press.

Coleman, Mathew 2005. "US Statecraft and the US-Mexico Border as Security/Economy Nexus." *Political Geography,* (2) 24: 185–209.

Collyer, Michael 2007. "In-Between Places: Trans-Saharan Transit Migrants in Morocco and the Fragmented Journey to Europe." *Antipode*, 39 (4): 668–690.

Driessen, Henk 1998. "The new 'immigration' and the transformation of the European Frontier." In: T.M. Wilson and D. Hastings (eds.), *Border Identities*. Cambridge: Cambridge University Press: 96–116.

Dunn, Timothy and Joseph Nevins 2008. "Barricading the Border." *NACLA Report on the Americas*, 41 (6): n.p.

Enriquez, Carmen Gonzalez 2007. "Ceuta and Melilla: Clouds over the African Spanish Towns." *The Journal of North African Studies*, 12 (2): 223–238.

Fernandez, Luis 2008. *Policing Dissent*. New Jersey: Rutgers University Press.

Ferrer-Gallardo, Xavier 2008. "The Spanish-Moroccan border complex." *Political Geography,* 27 (3): 301–321.

Foucault, Michel 2007. *Security, Territory, Population*. New York: Palgrave Macmillan.

Garcia, Michael John and Blas Nunez-Neto 2007. "Border Security." *Library of Congress Washington DC Congressional Research Service.* May 23, at http://handle.dtic.mil/100.2/ADA469083 (accessed 26 January 2012).

Graham, Stephen 2010. *Cities Under Siege*. London: Verso.

Gramsci, Antonio 1971. *Selections from the Prison Notebooks* (edited by Quintin Hoare and Geoffrey Nowell Smith). New York: International Publishers.

Hagemann, Anke 2007. "Filter, Ventile und Schleusen." In: Volker Eick, Jens Sambale, and Eric Töpfer (eds.), *Kontrollierte Urbanität*. Bielefeld: transcript: 301–328.

Hall, Stuart 1996. "The Question of Cultural Identity." In: Stuart Hall, David Held, Don Hubert, Kenneth Thompson (ed.), *Modernity*. Oxford: Blackwell: 595–634.

Larrain, Jorge 1994. *Ideology and Cultural Identity*. Cambridge: Polity.

Hardt, Michael and Antonio Negri. 2001. *Empire*. Cambridge, MA: Harvard University Press.

Jiwani, Yasmin 2002. "The Criminalization of 'Race' and the Racialization of Crime." In: Wendy Chan and Kiran Mirchandani (eds.), *Crimes of Colour*. Peterborough: Broadview Press: 67–86.

Marx, Karl and Friedrich Engels 1994. "The Communist Manifesto." In: Lawrence H. Simon (ed.), *Karl Marx: Selected Writings*. Cambridge: Hackett Publishing: 157–186.

Murphy Efani, Julie A. 2007. "Whose Security? Dilemmas of US Border Security in the Arizona-Senora Borderlands." In: Emmanuel Brunet-Jailly (ed.), *Borderlands*. Ottawa: University of Ottawa Press: 41–73.

Mykkanen, Juri 1994. "To methodize and regulate them: Petty's governmental science of statistics." *History of the Human Sciences*, 7 (3): 65–88.

Neocleous, Mark 2011. "Security as Pacification." In: M. Neocleous and G.S. Rigakos (eds.), *Anti-Security*. Ottawa: Red Quill Books: 23–56.

Neocleous, Mark and George S. Rigakos 2011. "Anti-Security: A Declaration." In: M. Neocleous and G.S. Rigakos (eds.), *Anti-Security*. Ottawa: Red Quill Books: 15–21.

Petty, Sir William 1927. *The Petty Papers: Some Unpublished Writings* (Vol. 1, edited by Marquis of Lansdowne). London: Constable Press., orig. circa 1690.

Rigakos, George 2005. "Beyond Public-Private: Towards a New Typology in Policing." In: Dennis Cooley (ed.), *Re-imaging Policing in Canada*. Toronto: University of Toronto Press: 260–319.

Rigakos, George 2011. "'To extend the scope of productive labour': pacification as a police project." In: Mark Neocleous and George S. Rigakos (eds.), *Anti-Security*. Ottawa: Red Quill Books: 57–83.

Rimke, Heidi. 2011. "Security: Resistance." In: Mark Neocleous and George S. Rigakos (eds.), *Anti-Security*. Ottawa: Red Quill Books: 191–215.

Rose, William 2002. "Crimes of Color." *Journal of Politics, Culture and Society*, 16 (2): 179–205.

Salter, Mark B. 2006. "The Global Visa Regime and the Political Technologies of the International Self." *Alternatives*, 2 (31): 167–189.

Shapiro, Michael J. 1997. "Narrating the Nation, Unwelcoming the Stranger." *Alternatives*, 22 (1): 1–34.

Shelley, Toby 2007. *Exploited: migrant labour in the new global economy*. New York: Zed Books.

THE CORCORAN PROJECTS

Andreas Lohner

Corcoran, world leader.

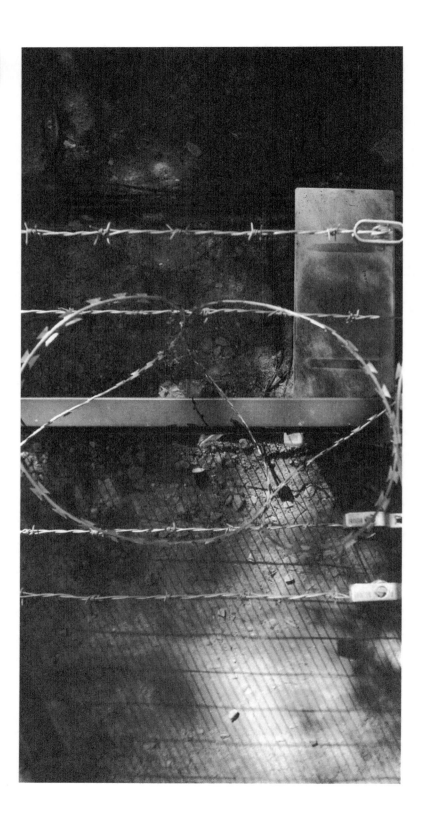

Corcoran, casa mia.

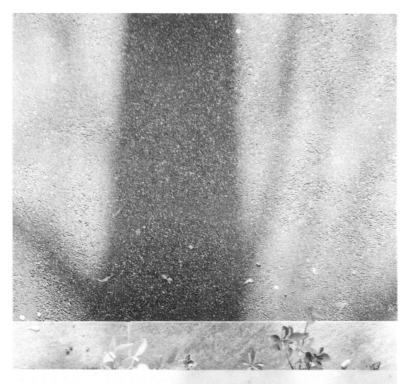

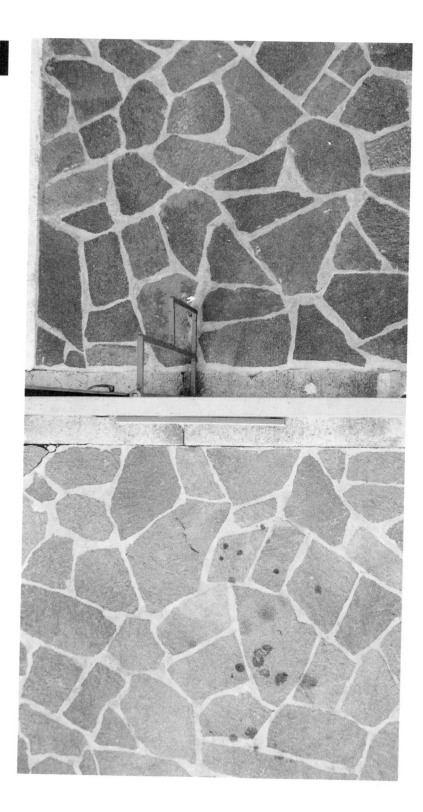

121

THE CORCORAN PROJECTS

Corcoran, multi purpose.

SECTION II
Policing as Urban Industry

Kendra Briken and Volker Eick

The commercial security industry is one of the fastest growing branches within the service sector. During the last decades, it has experienced a tremendous growth on a global scale. According to the Cleveland-based market research company 'The Freedonia Group,' the global market for private contract security services is expected to grow by 7.4 percent annually through 2014 and will generate a turnover of more than US$218 billion. Their 'World Security Services' report forecasts the largest market gains in the developing parts of Asia, Eastern Europe, Africa, and the Middle East. The US nevertheless will remain the biggest consumer of private contract security services accounting for 29 percent of the global demand in 2014. Contract guarding services is also expected to account for more than half of the total market's revenues in 2014:

> Factors such as rapid gains in economic activity, rising personal incomes, foreign investment activity, and the increasing belief that public safety forces are overburdened, corrupt or insufficient will boost gains,

as stated by the research firm (The Freedonia Group, 2012). Those who are interested in reading the 560 pages report on 'Demand and Sales Forecasts, Market Share, Market Size, Market Leaders' are required to pay US$6,100.

For those who would like to purchase only one selected page or table, Fredonia offers a discount – ranging from US$ 35.00 per page to US$ 60.00 per table.

In the words of the business world, we are to recognize 'a consolidating service industry.' The product 'security' has proved its value on the market, and several industry leaders, who previously were keen on avoiding the limelight, now start to push themselves to the fore. The related security value chain is characterized by two contradictory but complementary movements. While their 'successful' products cut through the market as a common (or global) good, growth rates of the industry are even higher compared to those within the service industry as a whole. Over the last ten years, the global security market has grown nearly tenfold from around €10 billion to a market size of more than €100 billion by 2011. Numerous studies show that "the European Union's as well as the worldwide security market will continue to have a growth rate which is beyond the average GDP growth" (European Commission, 2012: 2).

Beginning in the 20th century, the industrialization of security included the process of 'colonization' of space and people. The commercial security market today is characterized by the predominance of global players such as G4S, Prosegur and Securitas that invade national markets on a global scale by offering the so-called 'premium security' packages covering the full value-added chain both in terms of applied technologies and in the broad range of services provided.

Specialized high-tech goods are produced and services are provided (security consultancy; personal protection; critical infrastructure protection; surveillance equipment). At the same time, the traditional security services – known as 'no-brainers' like guarding or car patrol – turned into a customized service, and the consultancy industry and market research grab their share of the market. Thus, the commercial security industries' strategy is based on creating 'solutions' for the never ending and ever expanding problem called 'security.' In order to do so, the industry also 'invents' new threats to 'security' and claims not only to have identified deficits of state-led security providers but also to be capable of a better security provision than the police (Eick, 2008; Sterkl, 2012).

The 'consolidating service industry' though, still needs to be characterized as a SME-based industry with comparatively high numbers of companies entering and leaving the market. For the majority of companies, the national markets remain local in nature and their business is bound within the respective national borders. Interestingly, the same hold true with respect to the legal regulations of the industry which are either absent altogether or lacking international recognition.

Nevertheless, 'security,' formerly known as a state-granted service safeguarding a smooth capitalist development, has undergone a commodification process. It is now provided as a common service by human labor and increasingly by technology. Its widely accepted sale on the market as an ordinary good is reflected both by its growth in scale and scope and its success as a hardly contested good with a comparatively poor legal regulation.

Not surprisingly, such a successful *Landnahme* of the security landscape by the commercial security industry and the respective global consolidation processes are based on the exploitation of human labor. Yet, security work is characterized by a double movement as the 'success' of the industry creates two different occupations: On the one hand, skills that are required to produce, manage, promote and sell security concepts, known as knowledge-based work, call for a professionalization of the sector, and accordingly security companies and universities indeed started to offer B.A. and M.A courses in 'security management.'[40] On the other hand, working as an ordinary security guard on the beat – aside of specific tasks such as guarding atomic plants or military facilities – is still treated as unskilled labor, feasible even for the 'dump and dull.'

It is here, where the security industry still reflects all characteristics of a 'classical' precarious low-wage sector with bad

---

40   For the German context, cf. Briken (2011a)

working conditions. Therefore, the commercial security labor market is characterized by immense heterogeneity and fragmentation in terms of fields of activity, wages, competences, and reputation. Furthermore, union busting is common practice, and if workers' representatives exist at all, they have a hard time organizing security personnel. Of particular importance is the work environment characterized by flexible working hours and a high turnover of workforce. Given that security workers often perceive their situation as based on individual failure and feel stigmatized by their job, the management in turn is able to fall back on a comparatively powerless workforce.[41] The vast majority of security work is still done under the most precarious conditions with regard to wage, working hours and (lack of formal) qualifications, while the so-called soft skills are still widely ignored.

Surprisingly, even though it is well known that security work is largely done under bad (working) conditions and a low degree of union organization (unionization), most mainstream security studies still neglect one of the basic assumptions of political economy when researching commercial security providers – namely, the surplus-value production by exploiting human labor.

As several scholars have shown, commercial security provision dates back in the 19th century and therefore the industry is not entirely new. However, in times of glocal neoliberalism, commercial actors gain more influence in the decision-making concerning the mechanisms and the actors that would provide social control and security services. In particular, the 'entrepreneurial city' fueled a profit-oriented logic affecting law and order provision by commercial actors but also propagating the participation of nonprofit stakeholders. The next section explores the increasing influence of the commercial security industry with a focus on security in terms of work and employment. In this regard, the emerging new forms of cooperation, cooptation and conflict between state and non-state stakeholders in security

41   For the US, cf. www.standforsecurity.org; for Germany, cf. http://www.strikeinformer.com/germany/; for the worldwide struggle against union busting, cf. www.uniglobal-unions.org, (index 'Cleaning/Security').

provision, the different modes of regulating the industry as well as its impact on the stratification of the workforce are highly relevant issues. The contributors in this section discuss also the everyday life of commercial security officers on duty, their 'image' and the impact thereof on the industry and the workers. Further, the authors analyze the consequences of current labor market 'reforms' within the commercial security sector and related service sectors (establishment of workfare; extension of the low-wage sector; deregulation of labor agreements). Finally, the processes of neoliberalization also have impacts on the commercial security industry as an industry (intensified competition; subcontracting; de-unionization) and on the employees as individuals (working conditions; workload; self-perception) – a topic further explored in the next section of the book.

In his chapter on the variegated forms of policing, *Volker Eick* analyzes two fast-growing, yet crisis-prone sections within Germany's 'policing family' – the for-profit security industry and its nonprofit counterpart, i.e. third-sector organizations deploying long-term unemployed as 'security sentinels.' Understanding policing as a particular form of wage labor, Eick argues that these policing segments are neither meant to replace state police, nor are they undermining the state monopoly on the 'legitimate use of force' (Max Weber). These 'private' forms of policing are rather intended to supplement state-run law enforcement agencies with additional manpower and thus to extent the state monopoly on violence – though they are not necessarily successful in that. The extension of state-policing to the commercialized and nonprofit manifestations, together with their respective impact on the organization of state-policing, leads to particular forms of self-policing including what Eick calls 'protective prosumerism.' In contrast to police-private partnerships between the commercial security industry and the state police within the framework of a 'security architecture,' the prosumerist types of policing are less compelled to rely on the police.

Peter Gahan, Bill Harley, and *Graham Sewell* give a detailed account of Australia's private security industry focusing on the work and employment conditions of nightclub door staff or 'bouncers.' While they emphasize that there "is little doubt" that the poor image of the industry is "partially deserved" and that "low levels of training, relatively low wages, and high levels of turnover, do little to improve the prospects for the industry," they also highlight a "paradox at the heart of our attitudes towards the industry: at a time when everyone is demanding greater security and protection from risk no one appears to be happy to pay for it or to respect it as 'legitimate work.'" Despite their generally held view that the security industry in Down Under is a 'low road' industry, their findings reveal a potentially intriguing avenue for further research even though, as the authors conclude, "the industry is as effective as it is."

That such a perception of 'effectiveness' is not only embraced by a plethora of stakeholders but also highly contested became once again clear at the time when this introduction was in progress: Commercial provision of policing in the UK again came into the headlines of newspapers and websites. G4S and other commercial security companies were invited to take over the delivery of a wide range of services across England and Wales that previously had been carried out by the police (Sims, 2012). With a strong backing from the British Home Office, a joint transformation program by the West Midlands and Surrey Police Authorities "looks set to completely redraw the accepted boundaries between public and private and the definition of frontline and back-office policing," The Guardian revealed in March 2012 (Travis and Williams, 2012).[42]

In her chapter on Britain's 'extended police family,' *Alison Wakefield* brings up a painful aspect that, all differences abound, characterizes the larger part of the commercial

---

42   The 'transformation program' to be operative from February 2013 onwards and imposed by a budget cut of 20% on policing, includes the commercialization of investigating crimes, detaining suspects, developing cases, responding to and investigating incidents, supporting victims and witnesses, managing high-risk individuals, patrolling neighborhoods, managing intelligence, as well as more traditional back-office functions, cf. Grayson (2012), Sims (2012).

security service industry on a global scale: poor working conditions with long hours and low pay in a sector of intense competition and low profit margins. Instead of tackling these pressing issues, as she highlights, the UK further "delegated public services to the private security sector" and, with the Police Reform Act of 2002, promoted the creation of auxiliary, civilian patrollers, dubbed as "acceptable alternatives to police." Just as Briken (2011a, 2011b) twisted the knife in the wound of an only superficially considered integration of the German commercial security industry into the conservative government's so-called 'security infrastructure' in 2009, Wakefield pinpoints that in the UK, it was "under a Labour regime that the commercial security industry has been able to establish the wider political and social legitimacy it enjoys today."

Anibel Ferus-Comelo provides us with insights into the commercial security industry of India where over 5.5 million workers are employed – more than four times the number of the police officers across the country and more than five times the size of the national paramilitary forces. Large companies such as G4S control the Indian market – this is a company that "currently employs 150,000 guards nation-wide and will recruit an additional 50,000 by 2013," as Ferus-Comelo notes. Drawing upon evidence from the Indian state of Goa, she underscores that "bad jobs breed poverty, resentment, and disenfranchisement which can in turn lead to crime. Security guards have been reported by police in the local press to be involved in theft, sexual assaults, drug peddling, and even murder." She concludes that casual employment in the security industry erodes the traditional employer-employee relationship, generates insecure work and "paradoxically makes a society more vulnerable to crime."

The new cooperating collaborators, cooptation candidates, and/or competing colleagues of state police officers – private security guards and their nonprofit counterparts, the safety and security sentinels – are growing significantly in scope, scale and sway. Such growth might even be accelerated by the current financial and economic crisis, and might reshape (the understanding of) security in general: The "dangerous illusion" (Neocleous and Rigakos, 2011: 15) of security permeates every pore of the social. As noted elsewhere by Brenner and Theodore (2002), the "actual existing neoliberalism" is about regimes of coexistence and conflict that are evident within the urban environment. Developments in various policy fields (e.g. employment and labor market policy) show that the accomplishment of the neoliberal project is not only about the 'roll back' of the Fordist-Keynesian compromise but it is also about the search for, and proof of, new forms of capitalist regulation ('roll out'). As the following chapters show, the commercial security industry as an urban industry is both a service provider within the urban infrastructure – and part of it.

References

Brenner, Neil and Nik Theodore 2002. "Cities and the Geographies of 'Actually Existing Neoliberalism.'" *Antipode*, 34 (3): 349–379.

Briken, Kendra 2011a. "Suffering in Public? Doing security in times of crisis." *Social Justice*, 38 (1-2): 128–145.

Briken, Kendra 2011b. *Produktion von 'Sicherheit'?* Düsseldorf: Hans-Böckler-Stiftung.

Eick, Volker 2008. "Verlängertes Gewaltmonopol? Der kommerzielle Teil der 'neuen Sicherheitsarchitektur.'" *Bürgerrechte & Polizei/ CILIP*, 91 (3): 61–68.

European Commission 2012. *Security Industrial Policy. Action Plan for an innovative and competitive Security Industry* (SWD, 233 final). Brussels: EU.

Grayson, John 2012. "Britain as a private security state: first they came for the asylum seeker." *Open Democracy*, 9 March, at http://tinyurl.com/7jt255f (accessed 5 February 2013).

Neocleous, Mark and George S. Rigakos (ed.) 2011. *Anti-Security*. Ottawa: Red Quill Books.

Sims, Brian 2012. "Info4Security End User News: Plans unveiled for future regulation of UK's private security sector." *The Security Lion*, 21 November, at http://thesecuritylion.wordpress.com/2012/11/21/ (accessed 5 February 2013).

Sterkl, Maria 2012. "Wenn die Polizei mal Pause macht." *Die Zeit*, 10 June, at http://www.zeit.de/2012/24/A-Security (accessed 5 February 2013).

The Freedonia Group 2012. *Forecasts for 2016 & 2021 in 27 Countries*. Cleveland, OH: Freedonia Group.

Travis, Alan and Zoe Williams 2012. "Revealed: government plans for police privatisation." *The Guardian*, 2 March, at http://tinyurl.com/b6ock4u (accessed 5 February 2013).

VARIEGATED POLICING IN GERMANY
FROM POLICE-PRIVATE PARTNERSHIPS TO PROTECTIVE PROSUMERISM

Volker Eick

> "And you all know security
> Is mortals' chiefest enemy"
> *Macbeth*, III, 5[43]

I n recent years, Germany saw the mushrooming of new security agencies ranging from commercial security companies, significantly growing since the mid-1980s, to a 'civil society'-style of policing beginning in the 1990s. The latter's scope is defined by the extremes of armed militias protecting the eastern borderland of Germany against 'aliens' and the so-called crime prevention schemes which are organized, on the one hand, by concerned middle-class burghers and, on the other, by nonprofit organizations creating labor market (re)integration schemes for long-term unemployed. State police, in turn, have tried to adjust to these new conditions and to develop respective tactics und police units. While tactical responses to the new stake-holders ranged from sheer neglect, tacit admission and strict suppression to forms of guidance, support and participation, organizational reactions included the creation of new state police units such as Contact Constabularies and so-called

---

43   Shakespeare (1979: 56).

Operative Groups (both focusing on particular urban areas or ethnic groups) as well as voluntary police support units.

As ambivalent as the emergence of this pluralized policing *Kunden-Gemeinschaft* (customers' community) may seem, three general trends can be detected: First, a hardly controlled and diffuse division of labor emerged among the above mentioned stakeholders who, as should be noted, per se did *not* undermine the state monopoly on the use of force but indeed extended it. Second, in 2009 the federal and state governments intensified their attempts to regulate these shifts in policing by declaring the integration of the commercial security industry into a vaguely defined 'security architecture.' Third, what remains entirely unconsidered is the currently fastest growing section within the policing customers' community: voluntary (and involuntary) nonprofit policing agencies characterized by unspecified forms of cooperation, cooptation and competition and a significant lack of democratic oversight.

The argument developed in this chapter is based on and characterized by an understanding of policing as wage labor: Commercialization and commodification, thus the neoliberalization of policing, puts employees and their labor conditions under pressure. Consequently, policing is intrinsically connected with the struggle over wage labor as overseeing the (urban) poor is one of the core tasks of the police. Further, inasmuch as the distinctive forms of policing differ in significant ways, they are types of and meant to enforce wage labor. Until the mid-1980s the struggle between capital and labor in West Germany by and large could be safeguarded – to the advantage of the former – by a police apparatus[44] that was essentially public, universal, and reactive. But after the annexation of the GDR and West Berlin in 1989, policing changed not at least due to the end of the bipolar bloc confrontation (section 1). While a commercial security market was in place in Germany

---

44   Admittedly, police are not the only institution to guarantee for the (ever-contested) stability of capitalism. Yet, the further development of this point is beyond the scope of this paper.

already since 1901, it was only after the Wall came down that its market share started to grow significantly. In particular in the 'laboratory' of the former GDR – where, before the wall came down, commercial security companies were nonexistent – growth rates were outstandingly high from the 1990s onwards.

With the ongoing globalization and progress in technology the security *market* of the early 20th century turned into a security *industry* in the 21st century. Its advocates benefited even more, when, in 2009, the industry officially became part of what the German government now calls 'security architecture' (section 2). Further, nonprofit-organizations, voluntary services, citizens' grassroots associations, police-led security partnerships and neighborhood watch schemes emerged – displaying significantly rising growth rates – by providing 'their' respective neighborhood zones with what they understand as safety and security measures (section 3).[45]

Policing nowadays, therefore, is no longer a commodity only produced (Briken and Eick, 2011) and consumed (Rigakos, 2007) by the state and a commercial security industry but also, in a prosumerist manner, is a product of and for the 'civil society.'

The expression 'prosumer' denotes that the customer could fill the dual role of producer and consumer (Toffler, 1980) and, though such co-production is not new, what is new, "is the way that knowledge co-production with the customer expresses itself in role patterns and codes of interactivity" (Gibbert et al., 2002: 9). While, at first glance, police-private partnerships and self-policing endeavors could be subsumed under 'prosumerist policing,' the former differs from prosumerism in that prosumerism transforms customers into a co-value creators, endowing them with new competencies and benefaction opportunities. In other words, police-private partnerships are characterized by citizens' and

---

45   I am thankful to Elitza Stanoeva whose company in discussing issues, such as this chapter, I always appreciate.

commercial security providers' subjugation under police standards (Pütter, 2006; Eick, 2008), while self-policing tends to lack continuous interaction with other stakeholders (Short and Toffel, 2008) such as the police. Further, prosumerist policing is concerned with a moralized 'commodity,' turning engagement with policing into a (paid-for) 'duty' and 'gift' that shares characteristics of neocommunitarianism (Jessop, 2002; Eick, 2011b). Wage labor as the centerpiece of a capitalist economy increasingly refers to such a 'protective prosumerism' based on 'pre-law' and 'sub-order' rules and regulations provided and enforced even in decommodified forms, as paradoxical as this may seem.

> "'Wow,' I said. 'This was unexpected.
> You're like good cop and bad cop
> rolled into one.' 'Yeah, used to be
> they could afford two different guys.
> Now with all the budget cuts and shit
> they've got us doing double shifts'"
> *Motherless Brooklyn*[46]

'Our enemies in blue' turn colored[47]

Police, unlike commercial security providers with their economic reasoning (and unlike nonprofits, supposedly equipollent with brokering), are usually perceived to be acting within a bureaucratic logic (Emsley, 1983; Herbert, 1997; Knöbl, 1998). While German police still tend to follow the beaten track, new trails can be identified within federal and state police apparatuses. Such trails have been described by several scholars – though hardly mentioning Germany – with terms such as fragmentation, informalization, pluralization, and nodalization of policing (Bayley and Shearing, 1996; Crawford et al., 2005; Shearing, 2006; Button, 2008; Huey, 2008). In an

---

46   Lethem (1999: 114).
47   This subtitle is taken from William's (2007) book on the history of the US-American police.

attempt to briefly introduce the current changes within the German police, a look back into traditional understandings, logics, and strategies of policing is elucidating.

TRADITIONAL APPROACH TO INNER SECURITY IN GERMANY (1950s TO 1980s)

From the 1950s onwards, the main characteristics of what might be called the 'traditional approach' to policing in Germany are: Policing is 'public,' i.e. any forms of safety and security are provisioned by the state. Public provision, in turn, means a 'state police' organized in a federalist form, i.e. a respective separation of power between federal, state, and municipal scales applies.[48] Further, the police hold full monopoly in safety and security provision, i.e., police implies a 'universal,' or general, approach to law enforcement. Respectively, police work is understood as 'reactive' (not proactive); policing therefore is, first and foremost, a 'repressive' endeavor. Finally, the traditional approach until the 1980s treats the citizenry not as 'subjects' but as 'objects' and 'targets,' that is citizens, in essence, are not perceived as partners in or customers of safety and security provision.

Influenced by the mid-1960s social upheaval and the crisis of Keynesian capitalism in the early 1970s (Sklar, 1980; Hirsch and Roth, 1986), such an understanding of police no longer prevailed and, latest by the mid-1970s, evoked several lines of criticism (Busch et al., 1988; cf. table 1). By the mid-1980s, the state police, and along with them the cumbersome bureaucratic apparatus, started to come up with several packages of 'solutions,' though not in a linear manner. It was only from the early 1990s onwards that the assumption that the state should be *the* policing entity was called into question.[49] While, admittedly, this is a rather

---

48   In addition, it pertains to the *trias politica* principle – i.e., the state being divided into branches of an executive, a legislature, and a judiciary.

49   Though 9/11 definitely has had an impact on policing, it would be misleading to understand such an attack as the 'watershed' for the German government's (future) understanding of policing – it was rather a 'window of opportunity' for undermining democracy and human rights.

general picture, it nevertheless provides us with a starting point to better understand further developments within the emerging policing *Kunden-Gemeinschaft*.

Table 1: Challenges to the traditional approach of policing in Germany (1950s-1980s)

Traditional approach		Criticism (background)	'Solutions'	Examples
public	state-provided	financial limitations (neoliberalization)	non-state resources, local actors, technology	responsibilization, commercialization
police	state-run	limited scope and scale (*Rechtsstaat*, bureaucracy)	additional actors, extended scope (space)	extended 'policing family,' rent-a-cops
universal	indiscrete	neglect of specific contexts (individualization)	adoption/neglect of differentiated norms	Special Forces, 'state of exception'
reactive	repressive	lack of 'success' (dissent, crime rates)	preventive/proactive strategies, 'punitive turn'	community policing, 'zero tolerance'
citizens as 'objects'	subordinate	lack of democracy (citizens' demands/ protest)	citizens' participation, 'empowerment'	citizen patrol, police-private partnerships

Source: own account

As shown in table 1, the criticism of state policing and of its limits has been far-reaching and with wide implications: At the center of those critiques, based on the allegedly financial limitations of the state to further fund policing alone, are the limited capacities of the police to maintain an all-encompassing grid of control (noteworthy, such an aspiration remains in place). Furthermore, traditional foci of police work were perceived as lacking a sufficient grasp of a more individualized citizenry. In other words, the police failed to recognize a citizenry with a more 'complex' and so far unknown 'less conventional,' as distinct from 'unacceptable,' behavior. Subsequently, police were criticized by politicians to neglect specific contexts within which disorder and crime may occur. Its inability to adequately prevent crime and disorder, as the story goes, led to systemic failures in reducing crime rates.

The deepening and broadening dissent among the larger society from the late 1950s and early 1960s onwards (expressed by the movements against remilitarization and the so-called students' protests) led to intensified debates. Further, the government's failure to 'sustain' a peaceful, productive and consumerist society did not only end "the short-lived dream of permanent prosperity" (Lutz, 1989) but also led to the search for a 'techno-fix' against protest, alleged crime and 'terrorism' (Reiter and Weinhauer, 2007; Hanshew, 2010). In parallel, political and socioeconomic demands of the citizenry were partly taken up and canalized by the Social Democratic Party into the slogan '*Mehr Demokratie wagen*' ('Dare more democracy,' a phrase coined by the then-Chancellor and leading Social Democrat, Willy Brandt) in the late 1960s. While such a democratic departure came to a halt by the late 1970s, it meanwhile had stirred up reorganizational experiments within the police and beyond.

NEOLIBERAL EXPERIMENTING WITH 'SOLUTIONS'

This section intends to bring under scrutiny some of the dominant experimental types of policing. In the following sections, it proceeds with an empirical elaboration of the policing *Kunden-Gemeinschaft*. The intention, though, is not to describe and analyze empirically what state police are trying to achieve but to provide some background information for a better understanding of developments within the realm of for-profit and nonprofit policing.

Germany's complex 'search for security' and the fact that Germany is a federal state with 19 different police forces, reveals a quite multifaceted the picture (Busch et al., 1988; Lange, 1999; Groß et al., 2008). Nevertheless, some dominant trends within the German police apparatus can be summarized: An intensified orientation towards proactive crime prevention (including the selective integration of other policing stakeholders and the citizenry by responsibilization and economical means) was the first step taken up from US police experiences. It was paralleled, secondly, with the organizational specialization of the police apparatus (for instance, in certain ethnic groups and urban spaces). Third, a primacy of the executive authority against the legislature and judiciary emerged corresponding with the centralization of all security apparatuses by organizational and technological means (for instance, the 'dragnet investigation' of the late 1970s).[50] At the same time, police work began to be patterned after the intelligence service work and intelligence agencies to be patterned after police organizations while law enforcement embraced the upscaling of incivilities to crime (Busch and Pütter, 2004; Eick, 2006; Briken and Eick, 2011).

Inasmuch as public financial, administrative and human resources are said to be limited and respective limitations in productivity are to be addressed, strategies such as HR management, lean production and new public management also applied to the police (Gordon, 2005; Ritsert and Pekar, 2009). As another attempt to make wage labor in the realm of security provision more productive, security provision opened up to delivery by 'third parties' (Buerger and Mazerolle, 1998), i.e. by the corporate sector, by nonprofits, and by the voluntary sector.

In short, state-run (bureaucratic), for-profit (commercial) and nonprofit (brokering) policing stakeholders led to a 'pluralization of policing,' or policing by a customers' community. In so doing, for-profit and nonprofit stakeholders are deployed to help extending the scope and scale of policing (from local to cyber space; from pre-crime to 'terrorism'). Simultaneously, all stakeholders are to adopt understandings and indices enforcing productivity in the realm of prosumerist policing and are to neglect and/or to suppress those 'target groups' and 'undesirables' that do not subjugate under respective considerations of efficiency and effectiveness. Emphasis is laid on preventive and proactive

---

50   One expression of this centralization has been the setup of a comprehensive federal police (its reemergence being characterized by critics as a comeback of policing Third Reich-style).

strategies including those advertised by buzzwords such as self-management, self-responsibilization, citizen's participation, and empowerment.

As misleading as the wording of a "police family" (Home Office, 2001: IV) may be,[51] it needs to be highlighted though that such an "extended police family" (Home Office, 2001: 6) is not to be understood as a retreat of police presence[52] but as a rearrangement of security provision (Blair, 2002; Johnston, 2003; Eick, 2011b): the police are turning more into a protagonist rather 'steering' than 'rowing' on the ground (Osborne and Gaebler, 1992; Button, 2008; Eick, 2011b). By the same token, the other policing stakeholders – for-profit and nonprofit – are pouring forward, filling alleged voids left by the police (presence in public and semi-public space, i.e. mass private property; traffic control), entering new emerging markets (management of mega-events, i.e. festivalization of the city; workfare; IT surveillance) and do achieve some independence from police oversight.

As noted above, what is at stake here is not the fight against an alleged mushrooming of petty crime (even though this is one of the most popular headlines), an attempt to pave the way for gentrification (even though this is of growing significance), or a reaction to the fear of the 'Other' (even though migrants and 'aliens' remain the main targets). Rodenstedt *(this volume)* clarifies that even Sweden, formerly known as a *comme il faut* welfare state, increasingly rests upon 'Othering.' More generally, policing is not so much about addressing the lack of 'subjective feelings of security' (Klimke, 2008) but about the enforcement of particularistic norms for (urban) elites and the targeting of specific forms of behavior putting, in particular, wage labor in the line of fire.

---

51   On the respective use of the term 'family' within sports, international development, and the private security industry, cf. Eick (2011b: 30) and CoESS (n.d.).

52   "The fight against crime and disorder can only be won if there is an increased police presence in the community, matched by the greater public involvement of other agencies, groups and individuals. ... The Government is determined to do everything possible to support decent civil communities, and wishes to develop and support the 'extended police family'" (Home Office, 2001: 6).

Inasmuch as the neoliberalization of current capitalism goes with the intensified socioeconomic valorization and exploitation of hitherto neglected parts of the city, it goes with the mobilization of until then only latently and less considered opportunities for investment and profit generation (Harvey, 2005), plus with the 'reaping' of a potential workforce into wage labor. It is from the latter point that Gordon (2005: 55) argues,

> Law-and-order policing ... cannot be reduced to attempting to remove 'the other' from sight. It is, rather, an important part of the capitalist state form, an expression of the struggle over the wage relation between capital and labor which lies at the heart of capitalist society.

The German policing *customers' community*, in turn, represents what some have discussed as separated complexes under current capitalism – the penal state and welfare/workfare state, i.e. the 'iron fist' and the 'velvet glove.' Both or either are deployed to fight informal labor and to enforce labor market integration (Gilliom, 2001; Venkatesh, 2006; Wacquant, 2011). How much the wage relation and policing are intertwined becomes even more evident, if one takes into account that the German police not only perceive smuggling and trafficking but even shell games as 'Organized Crime' (Pütter, 1999) while a newly established branch of the customs deploys about 7,000 officers against informal labor (BMF, 2010: 20; cf. OECD, 2004a: chapter 5).

In the same line, current workfare schemes mobilize long-term unemployed as quasi-police forces in order to control the urban poor (see below). In a similar line, Spitzer (1975: 649) noted as early as in the mid-1970s,

> To a certain extent the expenses generated by problem and deviant populations can be offset by encouraging their direct participation in the process of control. Potential troublemakers can be recruited as policemen,

social workers and attendants, while confirmed deviants can be 'rehabilitated' by becoming counselors, psychiatric aides and parole officers. In other words, if a large number of the controlled can be converted into a first line of defense, threats to the system of class rule can be transformed into resources for its support.

Even the harassment and intimidation of striking laborers reemerges from one of commercial security's historical breeding grounds (Nelken, 1926; Shalloo, 1933), the latest examples in Germany being threats against hospital personnel in Berlin in the winter of 2011 (Schumacher, 2011)[53] and attempts to break a strike of commercial security workers in 2007.[54]

> "The private security companies
> do not shun the combat and feel up to
> the enemy, if only they are called
> to the battle ground in due time
> and in sufficient numbers"
> *Das Bewachungsgewerbe*[55]

Policing for profit: marketing insecurity

The German private security industry shares, at first glance, all the characteristics of a classical low-wage sector, including low levels of qualification, insecure and bad working conditions combined with poor promotion prospects (Briken, 2011b) – in sum, private security business is seemingly a 'low road' industry with dead end jobs (for Australia, see Gahan et al., *this volume*). A second look though, notably at

---

53   According to ver.di (United Service Union), contract workers were hired as strikebreakers and "square-shouldered private security guards snatched off strikers' placards" (Heine, 2011); respective attempts by private security guards to intimidate strikers occurred in Hamburg (Bremme, 2012) and Potsdam (Hohenstein, 2005).

54   The attempt failed though, as the more than 1,300 employees fighting for adequate wages at the Cash-In-Transit company *SecurLog* beat off the attack; in turn, union membership within the company grew from 16 to 60% in the very same year (Welsch, 2007).

55   Nelken (1926: 10).

the pay scale, reveals that not all jobs within the industry are cherished in the same (bad) manner; more over, wage levels differ significantly between regions. In particular affected by low wages are employees in East Germany and workers within those tariff regions, where 'yellow' or 'Christian' trade unions and employers negotiate with each other (Bispinck and Schäfer, 2004). In the case of commercial security services, this is true for negotiations between the *GÖD*[56] and the employers' representative, the *BDSW*[57] (Arning, 2012; Bremme, 2012). The following section gives an overview of the German commercial security market.

The commercial security market

For analytical purposes, statistics divide the German commercial security industry into three particular markets: mechanic, electronic security, and security services. In 2010, the respective annual turnovers amounted to €2.0 billion (mechanic security), €3.4 (electronic security), and €4.6 billion (services), the latter encompassing 3,700 commercial security companies with a workforce of about 170,000 employees.[58] In the following, the chapter focuses on security services and, in the subsequent section, provides further empirical background on working conditions of commercial security guards.

An additional specification may be helpful. In line with Nogala (1995: 250), who points to the fact that "commercial security companies ... owe their existence to a firmly profit mongering" and act "along an economic logic," this paper argues that security companies by definition are not 'private' but 'commercial,' i.e. concerned about profits and market shares (see also Wakefield, *this volume*). 'Private,'

---

56 The GÖD (Union for Civil Service and Public Services) is in favor of "sane coopera-tion, and not of class struggle," at http://www.goed-online.de/Allgemeine-Artikel/warum-christliche-gewerkschaften.html; for details see Bremme (2012).

57 The BDSW (Federal Association of the Security Industry) recently announced to focus on technology-prone subsections of the industry (Arning, 2012). Employers in the Cash-In-Transit branch are represented by the BDGW (Federal Association of the German Cash and Valuables Distribution Services).

58 Cf. "Statistiken," at http://tinyurl.com/ab5fpjm (accessed 19 January 2013).

to the contrary, are those initiatives that are not primarily interested in generating profits, such as, for example, militias, nonprofits, and crime prevention schemes in all their shades (Kury, 1997; Eick, 2011b). In short, if there is talk about 'privatization' with regard to the security business it is essentially about commercialization and commodification of "security promises" (Nogala, 1995: 252).

While the first German commercial security company (CSC) was founded already in 1901, the industry enjoys significant growths rates, in particular since the mid-1980s and early 1990s (for an overview cf. CoESS, 2004; BDWS, 2011; cf. table 2).

Table 2: Number of private security companies in Germany (1950s - 2011)

Year	1958	1966	1974	1984	1990	1994	1997	2000	2004	2007	2011
Companies	600	300	300	400	600	800	1,697	2,065	2,570	3,430	3,800

Source: Briken (2011b, updated)

The industrial structure of Germany's commercial security industry is SME-based, and of the 3,500 companies in 2009, 2,700 have had less than 20 employees. Of the remaining 800, only 3% employed more than 500 workers, while the ten biggest players had a workforce of about 51,000 (30% of the total workforce), thus representing an "oligopolistic market" (Eick, 2008: 61).[59] According to latest numbers, the ten largest companies, in 2010, employed 53,000 security guards with an annual turnover of roughly €1.6 billion (34,8% of the total turnover in this industry), an increase of 5.9% compared to 2009 (Lünendonk, 2011).

The constant growth of CSCs and employees alike does not, as several authors speculate, stem from a growing demand for a 'subjective feeling of security' throughout the populace (Kury, 1997; Klimke, 2008). Rather, the growth results from a redefinition of 'core tasks' by both commercial enterprises and state institutions (Osborne and Gaebler, 1992; Bachmann and Braun, 2011), influenced by the ideology and practice of neoliberalization, or 'actually existing neoliberalism'

---

59   All numbers refer to the workforce in Germany alone, i.e. not counting employees abroad.

(Brenner and Theodore, 2002). The respective concepts, promising increased efficiency through restructuring, entail as their leitmotif 'outsourcing,' and the first company divisions and administrative units affected were the respective service sections (Jann, 2003; Oschmann, 2005).

While the core activities of security provision – property protection (guarding), Cash-In-Transit, and alarm services – grew steadily over the years, they preserved a stable share vis-à-vis that of the new services. Even though new security markets emerged in the recent past (e.g. protection of so-called critical infrastructure; prisons and detention centers; mega events; IT security), about 40% of the workforce still work in property protection and additional 20% in reception services (cf. table 3).

Table 3: Areas of Activity by Private Security Companies, Germany (2010)

Turnover: €4.6 billion (*percentage of all turnover*)		
Property protection (60%)	Military property (6%)	Precinct control (5%)
Airport security (10%)	Alarm, emergency and control centers (5%)	
Cash-In-Transit (10%)	Protection of rail track construction work (4%)	
Employees: 170,000 (*percentage of all employees*)		
Property protection (36%)	Cash-In-Transit (5%)	Atomic plants' security (1%)
Reception (20%)	Military property (3%)	Emergency call centers (1%)
Event/Order service (7%)	Protection of rail track construction work (3%)	
Airport security (6%)	Public transport (2%)	Factory fire departments (1%)
Administration (5%)	Industrial, environmental, health safety (1%)	
Patrol security (5%)	City patrols/personal security (1%)	
Newer fields of activity (*selection*)			
City points	Criminal investigation	Critical infrastructure	Manhunt
Electronic monitoring	Facility management	Deportation centers	Prisons
Mega (sports) events	Psychiatric clinics	Forensics	Workfare
'Security architecture'	Security consulting, IT	Traffic control	War/peace

Sources: BDSW (2011); Eick (2006, updated)

Commercial security management perceives the protection of critical infrastructure (such as airports, atomic plants, electric utilities, and ports), of public transport and of urban mega events (such as FIFA World Cups, the Pope's visit, G8 and IMF summits) as emerging markets in the public and semi-public realm. At the same time, CSCs are heading into comprehensive consulting for the state and private companies ('holistic' analysis, and the respective provision of hardware, software, and humanware) including the related deployment of computer, cyber, and even DNA security analysis and protection.

In particular, three new developments are to be highlighted: Firstly, formerly sophisticated security technologies, including IT-based tools, transform into ordinary tool kits for mass-deployment (i.e. mobile phones, scanners for gate control). Paradoxically though, due to the growing complexity of security demands, socio-technological adjustments even create more complex challenges. Secondly, clients request and companies offer 'all inclusive' security packages with so-called systemic solutions. In particular, the market leaders within the commercial security industry nowadays advertise themselves as one-stop shops offering integrated, systemic, or so-called holistic security management solutions, including consultancy as an important pillar backed by facility management and IT security (O'Reilly, 2010; Briken, 2011a). Further noteworthy as the third new development is the institutionalization of police-private partnerships in what the German government calls 'security architecture.'

The term 'security architecture' dates back to 2004, when the then-Minister of the Interior, Otto Schily, demanded a massive centralization of the German law enforcement agencies. According to him, enabling the Federal Criminal Police (BKA) to direct the 16 State Offices of Criminal Investigations (LKÄ) and, accordingly, permitting the Federal Intelligence Service (BfV) to direct the State Offices for the Protection of the Constitution (LfV) are necessary steps to avert "overlaps, duplication of effort, frictional losses, and paucities of information" in the fight against terrorism (cited in Busch,

2008: 40). During the following debate all participants tried to outpace each other with proposals and demands for more 'security,' but disagreement remained about 'acceptable' degrees of centralization. In particular, the state authorities (*Länder*) insisted on keeping their own police and intelligence services. Resulting from the debate was the intensified integration of police and intelligence agencies, and the incorporation of civil protection and emergency services into the 'security architecture.' Attempts by the conservatives to also transform the *Bundeswehr* into a law enforcement agency failed as did efforts by the commercial security industry's lobby organizations to gain greater recognition. Nevertheless, the debate "was the first that took place under the headline of 'security architecture' in Germany" (Busch, 2008: 40).

As time went by though, the Interior's Minister Conference in November 2008 launched an updated version of the 1994 strategic paper *Programm Innere Sicherheit* and included the commercial security industry as an "important component of the security architecture" (Ständige Konferenz, 2009: 25). Since then, CSCs are officially recognized as part of this 'architecture,' while any meaningful 'construction plan' is still unknown (Briken and Eick, 2011; Stienen, 2011).

The German commercial security industry, well aware of both the important shift within traditionally state-led policing efforts[60] and the respective loopholes[61] left by the government, immediately took pride in the wording.

Its lobby organization, the Federal Association of the Security Industry (BDSW) right away translated this 'architecture' into demands for a security provision more independent from the state and for the self-regulation of the industry. The BDSW – in 2010, representing around 80 percent of the whole

---

60   For one, and unlike in many other countries in the 'developed' world, the number of private security guards in Germany is significantly lower than those of police officers (177,000 compared to 265,000).

61   A federal law overseeing the commercial security industry and any meaningful by-laws defining its role are unknown – thus pointing to the hitherto reluctance of the government to accept a 'second pillar' of security provision along with state police (Briken and Eick, 2011; Stienen, 2011). In line with this, Germany is among the very few European Union member states, together with Austria and Cyprus, not knowing a national law regulating the industry (CoESS and INHES, 2008).

industry in terms of turnover and 60 percent of the industry's whole workforce –, did not only agree on the government's call for the implementation of a hitherto non-existent certification system but instantaneously offered a draft. While, by the time of writing, in the winter of 2012/2013, such a system has still not seen the daylight, negotiations are underway. What is meant by 'certification' though seems to be clear, at least from the BDSW's point of view: blocking the market for newcomers and eradicating already existing, mainly small and micro companies.[62] While the BDWS remains silent on any further regulation of the industry in terms of do's and don'ts, the managing director of the BDSW recently clarified, "we almost have 4,000 companies on the German market, that's 3,000 too many" (Olschok, 2011: 15).

Inasmuch as the industry is under-regulated, there is a significant disequilibrium between claims and self-presentations of Germany's commercial security industry and the realities on the ground, in particular for the workforce.

The commercial security workforce

While it is true that technology plays an important and even growing role in the provision of safety, order and security on a global scale (OECD, 2004b; VDI and VDE, 2009), the commercial security workforce is growing as well (CoESS, 2004, 2012). Beyond the 'normal' growth rates of the security industry in the UK (Wakefield, *this volume*) and in Australia (Gahan et al., *this volume*), the BRIC states are outstanding examples of hyper growth: Brazil,[63] Russia,[64] India (Ferus-Comelo, *this volume*), China,[65] and South Africa[66] are the fastest growing security markets.

---

62   Micro companies, or 'own account workers,' can be defined as people working in their own business (officially) without employees.

63   Cf. "Introduction to the Security Industry in Brazil," at http://tinyurl.com/avg7k5z [accessed 28 January 2013].

64   Cf. "Welcome to the new world of private security," at http://www.economist.com/node/86147 [accessed 28 January 2013].

65   Cf. "Enter China's Security Firms" at http://tinyurl.com/byzavkg [accessed 28 January 2013].

66   Cf. "G4S," at http://www.corporatewatch.org.uk/?lid=339 [accessed 28 January 2013].

While Germany shares growth rates and other similarities with the European market (Button, 2008; CoESS and INHES, 2008) differences abound, among them cross-regional demographics. In 2008, a transnational comparative study showed that employees in Europe's commercial security industry on average are young, i.e. between 25 and 45 years old. Germany is an exception in that here more than 70 percent of the employees are older than 45 years (Cortese et al., 2008).

The reasons for these differences have not yet been evaluated, but the following explanations sound plausible. Firstly, the merging and significant shrinking of Germany's eastern and western armies in the 1990s left ten thousands of former soldiers without work opportunities after the Wall came down; the same holds true for the majority of, mostly low-ranking, East German former intelligence personnel edged out of business. Secondly and as in other countries such as Australia (cf. Gahan et al., *this volume*), the commercial security industry struggles with a bad reputation and an 'ambivalent image work' (Thumala et al., 2011; cf. Huey, 2008) which might lead jobseekers to refrain from applying for work in the industry. Another explanation might be found, thirdly, in the practice of the Public Employment Offices to put, in particular, older long-term unemployed and, to a lesser extent, low-qualified jobseekers in contact with the industry. According to interviews with unionists, demands for security services are always high and basically nobody is perceived of being inept to work as a security guard (Briken, 2011b).

Be this as it may, what remains uncontested is the number of commercial security guards working in so-called mini-jobs, i.e. jobs with a monthly earning of €400 outside the scope of national insurance: around 50,000 out of the roughly 170,000 security guards perform their duty under such conditions and many among them rely on additional benefits from the state to make a living (Briken, 2011b; Briken and Eick, 2011; Eick, 2011b, Bremme, 2012).

Even though the BDSW and the service union ver.di reached an agreement on a minimum wage in 2011 – €7.50 per hour by 2013, for all German employees and those from abroad working in Germany – the commercial security industry will remain a low-wage sector which hardly allows for sustaining a family (Bremme et al., 2007; Briken, 2011a). In addition to the mean working conditions and income situation, the treatment of employees sheds more light on the stability of the currently emerging 'security architecture.'

As Bremme (2012) highlights, managements' treatment of security guards even includes systematic wage fraud and thus tends to undermine any form of trust between management and personnel. Obviously, this also further destabilizes workers' identification with the company. Nevertheless, attempts to invoke loyalty are present as well. One way of doing so, as management representatives emphasized in interviews, are attempts to create a particular corporate culture and employee's ethos. One way to render the company attractive for the staff is appreciating their performance – if procurable, with limited material investment. "Appreciation, yes, but it may not cost money," as one respondent summarized.

> We try to show to our employees that we do acknowledge their performance [*How do you do that?*] Well, let's say, he needs new trousers, to make sure, he does not wait for them for four weeks; or, yes, each employee will receive a cup for Christmas (cited in Briken, 2011b: 36).

During the interviews, commercial security managers claimed that appreciation and recognition of the workforce are important ingredients for sustaining the company's success. Overall however, the interviews conveyed the impression that 'appreciation' is rather practiced on a symbolic level (providing 'freebees,' appointing 'employees of the month'). In the same way, meeting employees' work-related needs such as the provision of trousers (quoted above) is already rated as 'respectful' treatment (and not as the company's duty).[67]

---

67   Indeed, the provision with work clothing is part of employers' stipulated responsibilities.

Interviews with security managers are also abound with negative stereotypes about 'their' workforce. Bach (2008: 54), for instance, quotes an area manager, who considers his employees as being "all failed existences," and an operating manager, being asked about the reasons of subordinates for applying for a job within the security industry, is quoted as saying "they were unable to find anything else." 80 percent out of the 21 managers interviewed, perceive women of being "unable to convey what is expected, because their inhibition levels are just too high," and 19 percent of the respondents do not hire foreigners, because they lack a "sense for the state of law," or, as an attorney and area manager is quoted saying, "Turks are unable to deescalate" (cited in Bach, 2008: 32). Accordingly, Beste (2000: 352) talks about a poorly qualified workforce of a Cash-In-Transit company composed of "long-term unemployed, ex-convicts, and 'shattered existences'," while other scholars highlight the bad image, low reputation, and contested qualifications of both the management and the rank and file workforce within the industry (Huey, 2008; Thumala et al., 2011; Wakefield, *this volume*). Within Briken's (2011b) sample, the director of a HR department, being asked about the qualification background of her employees, somehow bashfully remarks:

> Let me put it this way, as for their IQ, they [the employees, V.E.] do not really have it. They are, well, let me put it this way, they are more like difficult people (cited in Briken, 2011b: 38).

In summarizing, three main developments should be high-lighted here: First, roughly 60 percent of a workforce of about 170,000 commercial security guards are operating in public space and are responsible for the maintenance of security and order provision. Therefore, they are constantly in contact with the public – not at least with its 'undesired' subsections (cf. table 3). Out of those 170,000 guards, around 30 percent neither hold a full-time nor a socially secured or otherwise safe and regular job. Second, even though this conclusion admittedly is based on a small number of interviewees (Beste, 2000; Bach, 2008; Briken, 2011b), security guards are expected to be all time work-ready and submissive to their 'masters' (Bremme, 2012) but are also perceived as more the less 'dumb and dull' by their respective management.[68] This in turn – as a third point in this argument – disturbingly resonates with the industry's self-perception of being ready to take over further tasks hitherto being perceived as sovereign duties of the state, including sophistical and ambitious missions demanding complex training and multifaceted experience. While commercial security guards are more the less accepted by rank and file police officers (as extra sets of 'eyes and ears'), this is not nessecarily true for the police management. In turn, the commercial security industry's management is accepted by the government and has been integrated by it into its 'security architecture.' Whilst it will be interesting to know who once will take the full responsibility for such a master stroke in 'architecture,' for now the chapter turns to an even more troubling policing stakeholder, (non)voluntary and nonprofit safety, order and security guards (SOS sentinels).

> "Some of the unemployed were sitting on park
> benches before and now can approach the others:
> 'Come on, take your bottle of beer with you.'
> For me that's a sociopolitical sign, too. That's much
> better than to continue to pay welfare and to have
> a debate whether begging should be allowed or not"
> *Kommunale Kriminalprävention*[69]

Nonprofit policing: for free and afield

An obvious question that emerges is what should be accounted for 'SOS sentinels' in either (non)voluntary or nonprofit appearance as many organizations provide safety, order and security personnel. A somewhat incomplete list includes

---

68   Importantly, all management personnel, by the time of the interviews, have been employed by private security companies being member organizations of the BDSW.

69   Schuster (1989: 24).

militias, ambassadors, civil wardens, security volunteers, neighborhood watch initiatives and crime prevention schemes (Kury, 1997; Eick, 2006; Pütter, 2006; Crawford, 2009). Such groups may occur with or without the support and/or participation of the police, and are thus either police-private partnerships or types of prosumerist policing.

It further encompasses long-term unemployed mobilized in workfare schemes based on the so-called German Hartz IV laws (Anderson, 2009; Knuth, 2009) who are to provide SOS services as so-called 1-Euro-Jobbers in projects that are deployed under fancy names, mirroring neocommunitarian endeavors, such as *Ortsdiener* (place servants), *Spielplatzkümmerer* (playground attendants) and *Wohngebietsaufsichten* (residential neighborhood supervisors) to name a few. What emerged in the early 1980s, became a relevant workforce with about 30,000 long-term unemployed operating as SOS sentinels in workfare schemes since the early 1990s (Briken and Eick, 2011).

As developed elsewhere (Eick, 2011b), 'nonprofit organization' is an ill-defined term. For the purpose of this chapter, suffice to emphasize that nonprofits are organizationally independent from the state and from for-profit business; they are formally structured, have a legally fixed constitution, lack a profit-maximizing orientation, rely on voluntary contributions and, by legal definition, should work in the public interest. Generally, they are perceived as those stakeholders, best suited to fill the gaps that either the state (neglecting particular parts of the population) or the economy (unable to identify meaningful profit options) leave unfilled – in short, they organize (wage) labor otherwise not profitable.

While similar deficits may apply in defining 'volunteers,' the understanding developed here rests on the understanding as first recorded around 1600, "one who offers himself for military service,"[70] its usage is still predominantly military

---

70   Cf. "volunteer," http://www.etymonline.com/index.php?term=volunteer [accessed 24 January 2013].

but also common in sports (see below) – in short, volunteers provide unpaid work.[71] In the following, three variegated forms of prosumerist policing are characterized.

From police-private partnership to protective prosumerism

As noted above, police-private partnerships are characterized by citizens' and commercial security providers' subjugation under police standards, while protective prosumerism allows for greater independence in decision making. The respective knowledge co-production does not rely on constant contact with the police and leads codes of interactivity characterized by larger autonomy. Further, police-private partnerships generally are not concerned with a moralized 'commodity' – the police by and large refer to law and order, the commercial security industry is interested in profits – while moralizing is of core importance for and a core 'competency' of prosumerist policing. Protective consumerism, in addition, allows for endowing its stakeholders with comparatively indefinite competencies and benefaction opportunities as they are providers and consumers of an uncontested good, 'security.'

Among the manifestations of protective prosumerism neighborhood watch schemes are standing out in that they represent self-policing endeavors without financial rewards and for own purposes. Such schemes take advantage of self-responsibilization strategies by the government and dissociate themselves from both society and state police; included is a moral undertone of self-empowerment camouflaging selfishness.

Security volunteers are also providing policing for free but not for themselves. Instead, they do so within a contractual framework based on a moral understanding of non-paid work as a 'gift,' the reward being, for example, the partici-

---

71   Expense allowances may be provided to volunteers though, such as in the case of volunteering police forces in Germany (Eick, 2008).

pation in mega-events. Both types of policing are based on a neocommunitarian understanding of self-determination while the third type is the imposed variation to the former.

Within workfare schemes long-term unemployed are required – if not forced to – to provide policing in the name of a 'moral order' suiting the interests of their masters and commanders, the nonprofit industry. For the former, non-paid labor no longer is associated with self-determination, a form of empowerment, or a 'gift' – but by all means with a 'duty.' For the latter, protective prosumerism creates competencies and benefaction opportunities transforming them into a new police force imposing their own moral values to the urban poor.

For the purpose of clarification, examples for prosum-erist policing are provided looking at neighborhood watch schemes organized by the more affluent sections of the citi-zenry, looking at volunteers policing sports mega-events, and looking at workfare schemes orchestrated by nonprofits.

In Berlin, notably a city with around 3 million foreign tourists annually,[72] police leaflets advice its burghers to "monitor slow-driving cars with foreign number plates" for own security purposes. In a "suspicious case" neighbors should write down the plate number and call the police. In addition, police offer yellow stickers that read, "Watch out! Vigilant Neighbor" to be placed on doors and windows (Zylla, 2009). Unlike in Sweden, where informal policing is tightly connected with the local administration and active participation (Rodenstedt, *this volume*), German neighbor-hood watch schemes rest upon self-policing and do only refer to the police in cases of emergency and as providers of information leaflets and related gadgets (Schneppen, 1994).

The same applies to parts of Bremen, Germany's tenth largest city with 550,000 residents, where the fancy yellow stickers, part of a coordinated federal and state crime preven-tion program, are already hanging on doors and windows,

---

[72]   Between January and September 2011 alone, Berlin statistics counted around 7.3 mil-lion overnighters, around 37% of them with foreign descendent – and many of them arriving with cars; http://tinyurl.com/3nopbv4 (accessed 29 January 2013).

signaling to passers-by and alleged burglars, *here does not yelp the dog, here straightaway the master yaps.*[73] Again, as in Berlin, prosumerist policing does not rest upon active participation but is a self-reliant defensive activity.

In a similar logic to neighborhood watch, the police and a local high-tech company provide technical equipment for self-defense to the more affluent citizens in the very same city a few streets further. A local savings bank, cooperating with the police and the company, promotes "Assault protection through DNA."[74] This model project provides citizens with artificial DNA to dab their valuables. The DNA-coded spray remains for weeks on items and on those touching them while allowing police officers on the beat to identify the substance with special torch lights (Ortspolizeibehörde, 2009); the police, the bank and the DNA-providing company are also running the local crime prevention council. These are just three examples of protective prosumerism, or prosumerist policing, based on the idea that the citizenry, provided with technical support of the police and local industry, should protect itself. A second type of prosumerist policing is volunteers 'hired' to protect mega-events.

In particular, sports has been the realm within which volunteerism emerged as both the paragon and paradigm for a new understanding of labor and security provision. A similar definition of 'volunteers' to that originating in the military context cited above is given by the International Olympic Committee (IOC): "the volunteer is a person who makes an individual, altruistic commitment to collaborate, ... carrying out the tasks assigned to him/her without receiving payment or rewards of any other nature" (cited in Moreno et al., 1999).[75] 12,000 FIFA volunteers were deployed in

---

73 I owe this phrase, and this subsection on Bremen, to my friend and colleague Kendra Briken.

74 Cf. "Diebstahlschutz durch DNA", at http://tinyurl.com/8283dxq (accessed 29 January 2013).

75 In the same vein the Union of European Football Associations has it that "Volunteer is someone who out of own's free will, choice and motivation undertakes without payment a voluntary activity to the benefit of other people or an organization, going beyond family or friendly ties" (UEFA, 2011: 3).

Germany in 2006, 15,000 served in South Africa during the World Cup in 2010, and more than 130,000 applied for participating at the World Cup in Brazil.[76] Not only the FIFA but also the IOC recruits volunteers: 70,000 in Sydney in 2000, 100,000 in Beijing in 2008, and around 70,000 for the 2012 London Games.

Sports provide a smooth entry into the world of unpaid work and workfare via the excitement of 'taking part is everything' and the respective 'gift' to participate – thus functioning as a role model. While neighborhood watch schemes allow for a distinctive freedom of choice, volunteers during mega-events are integrated into hierarchies while performing different types of prosumerist policing.

During the FIFA World Cup in Germany, for instance, per game between 900 and 2,300 rent-a-cops (called supervisors and stewards) and additional 300 volunteers secured the stadia and the security zones around them (Eick, 2011a). According to Bach (2008: 152-153), the 12,000 security volunteers were divided in sub-groups for information services outside the stadia and to provide information, guidance, safety and security services within the security rings around the stadia (entrance regulation, grandstand control, lost-property office). They were "integrated into a stringent hierarchy, organized in small groups with a team leader" and were "under control of the local FIFA security officer." In addition, FIFA developed guidelines to encourage cooperation between the supervisors and stewards and the volunteers that read: "The security and order staff is authorized to direct the volunteers and, depending on the situation, is allowed to integrate them into the security and order tasks" (cited in Bach 2008: 154). In other words, and as in the world of customer relations more generally (Gibbert et al., 2002), protective prosumerism does not go without hierarchies.

As noted, prosumerism allows for new competencies and benefaction opportunities without the necessity of

---

76   "Over 130,000 volunteer applications received", at http://tinyurl.com/bdlew2e [accessed 29 January 2013].

continuous interaction between the police and non-state policing stakeholders. In the case at hand, the nonprofit FIFA provides security and order guidelines, and on such a basis commercial security guards develop their own standards on the ground to direct volunteers. Whereas initiators of neighborhood watch schemes enjoy full independence in developing and putting into practice protective prosumerist activities volunteers have to apply for participation.

A more recent type of protective prosumerism emerged within workfare schemes and includes the imposition of sanctions. In the following, two examples are provided to illustrate this third type, leading to 'the poor policing the poor' (Eick, 2011b). Workfare schemes for long-term unemployed in Germany are organized by the nonprofit sector in order to enforce the key principle of the new approach to labor market (re)integration in Germany: *Fördern und Fordern* (support and stipulate), or 'no rights without responsibilities.' In order to do so, nonprofits create work opportunities next to the official labor market in so-called niche markets. Examples would be assistants for child care workers, for park maintenance, or long-term unemployed assisting school teachers. The unemployed would receive an allowance of 1 Euro per hour in return.[77] Given that such jobs should not replace already existing ones but should allow for re-acquainting long-term unemployed to the official labor market, nonprofits need to be 'innovative' to develop such workfare schemes as, according to the labor law, such jobs have to be additional, or *zusätzlich* (Eick, 2011b).

One of the more recent 'innovations' are the SOS jobs mentioned above. And one of the nonprofit organizations offering prosumerist policing on behalf of the Public Employment Office is BEQUIT; in 2008, the nonprofit company mobilized hundreds of long-term unemployed and generated an annual turnover of about €7 million for (re)integration measures into Berlin's labor market. In the

---

77   Part and parcel of the new workfare measures under Hartz IV are the so-called 1-Euro-Jobs. The employment relationships are not based on labor contracts but just allowances; such jobs are also not subject to social insurance contributions.

district of Neukölln, BEQUIT is the oligopolist in providing cleanliness, order and security. Under the headline "supervision projects," long-term unemployed are engaged as school and schoolyard attendants, as park inspectors, as supervisors of residential areas and of playgrounds. In the quarter Schillerpromenade alone, 24 long-term unemployed undertake such tasks as 1-Euro-Jobbers for a population of just 20,000; in addition, they "control underground parking lots, enforce public green space by-laws, are available as contact persons in emergency and conflict situations, and pay heed to cleanliness" (cited in Eick, 2011b).

Further, the 'support' for the poor ultimately means their suppression as a similar project, launched in 2005, shows. It attracted nationwide attention because of the sheer number of 1-Euro-Jobbers: Since then, 350 long-term unemployed control Neukölln's roughly 120 playgrounds as so-called *Spielplatzkümmerer*, or playground attendants. In order to defend the nonprofit against accusations by the service union ver.di that jobs on the regular labor market are substituted, a representative tackled this tender point with this telling answer:

> The easiest way to describe their duties is to clarify what [the 1-Euro-Jobbers] are not – namely police officers, trash collectors, or swing repairmen. Instead, it's their task, alone with their presence, to bar potential 'play ground disturbers' from drinking alcohol, from throwing garbage in the sandbox and to rampage (cit. in Leber, 2005: 9).

Such comments show in all clarity how much nonprofits are aware about the resulting crowding out of regular jobs by workfare measures and about the undermining of wage labor more generally. Nonprofits perceive themselves as customers and suppliers on an 'unemployment market.' The same holds true for providing protective prosumerism in particular: Prosumerist policing here is one type of workfare measures; the long-term unemployed are the 'tool' for its provision; and nonprofits produce and consume their 'innovative' products. With neocommunitarian wording nonprofits implicitly purport to be the policing force against the urban poor.

> "All fixed, fast-frozen relations ... are swept away, all new-formed ones become antiquated before they can ossify. All that is solid melts into air"
>
> *The Communist Manifesto*[78]

Conclusion

More than ten years ago, Joachim Hirsch (2002: 172) identified a specific ideological mélange "of neoliberalism, remainders of social-democratic state interventionism and libertarian trends, which won intellectual influx as disintegration products of the post-68 protest movement." He claims this mélange to be responsible for the widespread immunization against any meaningful critique of the "only seemingly paradoxical" form of "market-liberal etatism" in Germany. In concluding, this section applies this characterization to the variegated forms of policing analyzed in the sections above in order to reframe the empirical observations.

Under 'actually existing neoliberalism,' state policing is confronted with competing forms of security provision including the commodification but also neocommunitarization of policing. Nevertheless, remainders of social-democratic state interventionism are still dominant and policing by the state apparatus continues to be the prevailing form of policing in Germany. Also evident though is the growing impact of economically shaped market logics within the state-policing realm. New public management strategies are just one example for the transformation of police officers into service providers and of citizens into

---

78   Marx and Engels (1848).

customers. Despite this prevalence, the relative growth of commercial policing has been unprecedented in the recent decades.

Commercial security companies redefine and take over former 'core tasks' of the state and also develop new fields of expertise such as IT security provision. In addition, CSCs meanwhile are running more than 60 partnership contracts with the state police (Eick, 2011b). For commercial security providers such contracts aim at extending the market share to the detriment of the police apparatus. For the police, in turn, such contracts and the governments' initiative to integrate PSCs into the 'security architecture' are meant to guarantee for an extended state monopoly on the use of force.

The above mentioned transformations of policing are influenced by more general trends within the society (and vice versa), and it is thus not surprising that they neither emerge in a linear form nor without contradictions, but instead appear as a hardly regulated customers' community. In line with that, the state police also hold police-private partnerships with the populace but increasingly appeal to the citizenry to prosume 'security.' As for the latter, such a policing concept has been identified here as a neocommunitarian type of policing. Variegations include neighborhood watch schemes for self-protection and, in turn, self-production and -consumption of 'security' by choice. It also comprises types of policing organized around mega-events such as the Olympics or World Cup tournaments provided by contracted volunteers. Prosumerist policing though is not necessarily characterized by freely chosen decisions but may be enforced as in the case of workfare measures described above.

As for commercial security provision, a legal framework for the security industry as such is still missing. Despite this lack of regulation the government, in 2009, decided to advance the aforementioned 60 something police-private partnerships further into a nationwide and legally binding *Programm Innere Sicherheit*. None of the pillars on which this program rests – including the featureless term 'security architecture' – has been stabilized; a meaningful construction plan, most likely on purpose, has not yet been provided.

As for protective prosumerism, the police and government allow for self-determined policing activities within the customers' community based on selective and unquestioned interests of the respective stakeholders. Neighborhood watch schemes, sports-led security volunteers, and nonprofit-guided SOS sentinels cut themselves off from police oversight and are thus provided with the capacity to develop their particular moral understanding of policing one's community.

As unsavory as police-private-partnerships between the police and commercial and 'civil society' stakeholders have been in the past already, the current customer's community policing activities are inedible.

References

Anderson, Perry 2009. "A New Germany?" *New Left Review*, 49 (57): 5–40.

Arning, Oliver 2012. "Private Security Provision – Still a Highly Contested Terrain in Germany", at: http://tinyurl.com/adxyjjl [accessed 28 January 2013].

Bach, Stefanie 2008. *Die Zusammenarbeit von privaten Sicherheitsunternehmen, Polizei und Ordnungsbehörden im Rahmen einer neuen Sicherheitsarchitektur.* Holzkirchen: Felix.

Bachmann, Ronald and Sebastian Braun 2011. "The Impact of International Outsourcing on Labor Market Dynamics in Germany." *Scottish Journal of Political Economy*, 58 (1): 1–28.

Bayley, David H. and Clifford D. Shearing 1996. "The Future of Policing." *Law & Society Review*, 30 (3): 585–605.

BDSW 2011. *Marktanteile vom Gesamtumsatz*, at http://tinyurl.com/7o6a3uc (accessed 9 February 2012).

Beste, Hubert 2000. *Morphologie der Macht.* Opladen: Leske + Budrich.

Bispinck, Reinhard and Claus Schäfer 2005. "Niedriglöhne? Mindestlöhne!" *Sozialer Fortschritt*, 54 (1-2): 20–31.

Blair, Ian 2002. "Patrol Partnership." *Police Review*, 110 (5670): 30–31.

BMF. Federal Ministry of Finance 2010. *Die Bundeszollverwaltung. Jahresstatistik 2009.* Berlin: BMF.

Bremme, Peter 2012. "Private Security Provision – Still a Highly Contested Terrain in Germany", at: http://tinyurl.com/adxyjjl [accessed 19 January 2013].

Bremme, Peter, Ulrike Fürniß and Ulrich Meinecke (eds.) 2007. *Never Work Alone*. Hamburg: VSA.

Brenner, Neil and Nik Theodore 2002. "Cities and the Geographies of 'Actually Existing Neoliberalism.'" *Antipode*, 34 (3): 349–379.

Briken, Kendra 2011a. "Suffering in Public? Doing security in times of crisis." *Social Justice*, 38 (1-2): 128–145.

Briken, Kendra 2011b. *Produktion von 'Sicherheit'?* Düsseldorf: Hans-Böckler-Stiftung.

Briken, Kendra and Volker Eick 2011. "Recht und billig? Wachschutz zwischen Niedriglohn und Ein-Euro-Jobs." *Kritische Justiz*, 44 (1): 34–42.

Buerger, Michael E. and Lorraine G. Mazerolle 1998. "Third-party Policing: a theoretical analysis of an emerging trend." *Justice Quarterly*, 15 (2): 301–327.

Busch, Heiner 2008. "Neue 'Sicherheitsarchitektur' für Deutschland." *RAV-Rundbrief*, 28 (100): 40–46.

Busch, Heiner and Norbert Pütter 1994. "Operative Polizeimethoden." *Bürgerrechte & Polizei/CILIP* 49 (3): 6–15.

Busch, Heiner, Albrecht Funk, Udo Kauß, Wolf-Dieter Narr, and Falco Werkentin 1988. *Die Polizei in der Bundesrepublik Deutschland*. Frankfurt/M.: Campus.

Button, Mark 2008. *Doing Security*. London: Palgrave Macmillan.

CoESS (ed.) 2004. *Panoramic Overview of Private Security Industry in the 25 Member States of the European Union*. Brussels: Confederation of European Security Services.

CoESS (ed.) 2012. *Private Security Services in Europe. CoESS Facts and Figures 2011*. Wemme, Belgium: CoESS.

CoESS (ed.) n.d. "Definition of private security services (private security services family tree)," at http://tinyurl.com/7ut8xg2 (accessed 11 February 2012).

CoESS and INHES (eds.) 2008. *Private Security and its Role in European Security (White Paper)*. Paris: CoESS and INHES.

Cortese, Valter, Philippe Dryon, and Esteban Martinez 2008. *Die Modernisierung der Arbeitsorganisation im privaten Sicherheitsgewerbe in Europa*. Bruxelles: tef-ULB.

Crawford, Adam (eds.) 2009. *Crime Prevention Policies in Comparative Perspective*. Cullompton: Willan.

Crawford, Adam, Stuart Lister, Sarah Blackburn, and Jonathan Burnett 2005. *Plural Policing*. Bristol: Policy Press.

Eick, Volker 2006. "Preventive Urban Discipline." *Social Justice*, 33 (3): 66–84.

Eick, Volker 2008. "Verlängertes Gewaltmonopol?'" *Bürgerrechte & Polizei/CILIP*, 91 (3): 61–68.

Eick, Volker 2011a. "'Secure Our Profits!'" In: Kevin Haggerty and Colin J. Bennett (eds.), *Security Games*. New York: Routledge: 87–102.

Eick, Volker 2011b. "Policing 'Below the State' in Germany." *Contemporary Justice Review*, 14 (1): 21–41.

Emsley, Clive 1983. *Policing and its Context*. London: MacMillan.

Garland, David 2001. *The Culture of Control*. Oxford: Oxford University Press.

Gibbert, Michael, Marius Leibold, and Gilbert Probst 2002. *Five Styles of Customer Knowledge Management*. Geneva: University of Geneva, Switzerland.

Gilliom, John 2001. *Overseers of the Poor*. Chicago: The University of Chicago Press.

Gordon, Todd 2005. "The Political Economy of Law-and-Order Policies." *Studies in Political Economy*, 75 (1): 53–77.

Groß, Hermann, Bernhard Frevel, and Carsten Dams (eds.) 2008. *Handbuch der Polizeien Deutschlands*. Wiesbaden: VS.

Hanshew, Karin 2010. "Daring More Democracy?" *Central European History*, 43 (1): 117–147.

Harvey, David 2005. *A Short History of Neoliberalism*. Oxford: Oxford University Press.

Heine, Hannes 2011. "Arbeitskampf an der Charité" *Der Tagesspiegel*, September 12.

Herbert, Steve 1997. *Policing Space*. Minneapolis: University of Minnesota Press.

Hirsch, Joachim 2002. *Herrschaft, Hegemonie und politische Alternativen*. Hamburg: VSA.

Hirsch, Joachim and Roland Roth 1986. *Das neue Gesicht des Kapitalismus*. Hamburg: VSA.

Hohenstein, Erhart von 2005. "Streik: Weltkulturgüter in Gefahr." *Potsdamer Neueste Nachrichten*, May, 26.

Home Office 2001. *Policing a New Century*. London: HMSO.

Huey, Laura 2008. "'When it comes to violence in my place, I am the police!'" *Policing & Society*, 18 (3): 207–224.

Jann, Werner 2003. "State, administration and governance in Germany." *Public Administration*, 81 (1): 95–118.

Jessop, Bob 2002. "Liberalism, Neoliberalism, and Urban Governance: a state-theoretical perspective." *Antipode* 34 (3): 452–472.

Johnston, Les 2003. "From 'Pluralisation' to 'the Police Extended Family.'" *International Journal of the Sociology of Law*, 31 (3): 185–204.

Klimke, Daniela 2008. *Wach- und Schließgesellschaft Deutschland*. Wiesbaden: VS.

Knöbl, Wolfgang 1998. *Polizei und Herrschaft im Modernisierungsprozess*. Frankfurt/M.: Campus.

Knuth, Matthias 2009. "Path shifting and path dependence: Labour market policy reforms under German federalism." *International Journal of Public Administration*, 32 (12): 1048–1069.

Kury, Helmut (ed.) 1997. *Konzepte Kommunaler Kriminalprävention*. Freiburg/Brsg.: edition iuscrim.

Lange, Hans-Jürgen (ed.) 1999. *Innere Sicherheit im Politischen System der Bundesrepublik Deutschland*. Opladen: Leske + Budrich.

Leber, Sebastian 2005. "Im Einsatz auf den Spielplätzen." *Der Tagesspiegel*, June 2: 9.

Lethem, Jonathan 1999. *Motherless Brooklyn*. New York: Doubleday.

Lünendonk GmbH 2011. *Marktsegmentstudie 'Führende Sicherheitsdienstleister in Deutschland'*. Kaufbeuren: Lünendonk.

Lutz, Burkart 1989. *Der kurze Traum immerwährender Prosperität*. Frankfurt/M.: Campus.

Marx, Karl and Friedrich Engels 1989 [1848]. *Manifest der Kommunistischen Partei*. Berlin: Dietz.

Moreno, Ana, Miquel de Moragas, and Raúl Paniagua. 1999. *The Evolution of Volunteers at the Olympic Games*, at http://olympicstudies.uab.es/volunteers/moreno.html (accessed February 9, 2012).

Nelken, Sigmund 1926. *Das Bewachungsgewerbe*. Berlin: Verband der Wach- und Schließgesellschaften.

Nogala, Detlef 1995. "Was ist eigentlich so privat an der Privatisierung sozialer Kontrolle?" In: Fritz Sack et al. (eds.), *Privatisierung staatlicher Kontrolle*. Baden-Baden: Nomos: 234–260.

OECD 2004a. *OECD Employment Outlook*. Paris: OECD.

OECD 2004b. *The Security Economy*. Paris: OECD.

Olschok, Harald 2011. "7 Jahre BDWS (2004-2011)." *Der Sicherheitsdienst*, 63 (3, Special Issue): 15–17.

Ortspolizeibehörde Bremerhaven 2009. *Eigentumsschutz durch 'Künstliche DNA'*. Bremen: ms.

O'Reilly, Conor 2010. "The Transnational Security Consultancy Industry." *Theoretical Criminology*, 14 (2): 183–210.

Osborne, David and Ted Gaebler 1992. *Reinventing Government*. Reading, MA: Addison-Wesley.

Oschmann, Frank 2005. *Die Finanzierung der Inneren Sicherheit am Beispiel von Polizei und Sicherheitsgewerbe*. Köln: Heymanns.

Pütter, Norbert 1999. *Der OK-Komplex*. Münster: Westfälisches Dampfboot.

Pütter, Norbert 2006. *Polizei und kommunale Kriminalprävention*. Frankfurt/M.: Verlag für Polizeiwissenschaft.

Reiter, Herbert and Klaus Weinhauer 2007. "Police and Political Violence in the 1960s and 1970s." *European Review of History*, 14 (3): 373–395.

Rigakos, George S. 2007. "'Polizei konsumieren…' Beobachtungen aus Kanada." In: Volker Eick et al. (eds.), *Kontrollierte Urbanität*. Bielefeld: transcript: 39–54.

Ritsert, Rolf and Mirjam Pekar 2009. "New Public Management Reforms in German Police Services." *German Policy Studies*, 5 (2): 17–47.

Schneppen, Anne 1994. *Die neue Angst der Deutschen*. Frankfurt/M.: Eichborn.

Schumacher, Juliane 2011. "Erfolg für Streikende bei Charité-Tochter." *die tageszeitung*, December 6.

Schuster, Wolfgang 1998. "Kommunale Kriminalprävention." In: Innenministerium Baden-Württemberg (ed.), *Fachkongress Kommunale Kriminalprävention*. Stuttgart: LMinBW: 19–24.

Shakespeare, William 1979 [1623]. *Macbeth*. Bielefeld: Cornelsen-Velhagen & Klasing.

Shalloo, Jeremiah 1933. *Private Police*. Philadelphia: Rumford Press.

Shearing, Clifford 2006. "Reflections on the Refusal to Acknowledge Private Governments." In: Jennifer Wood and Benoît Dupont (eds.), *Democracy, Society and the Governance of Security*. Cambridge: Cambridge University Press: 11–32.

Short, Jodi L. and Michael W. Toffel 2008. "Coerced Confessions: self-policing in the shadow of the regulator." *The Journal of Law, Economics, & Organization*, 24 (1): 45–71.

Sklar, Holly (ed.) 1980. *Trilateralism*. Boston: South End Press.

Spitzer, Steven 1975. "Toward a Marxian Theory of Deviance." *Social Problems*, 22 (5): 638–651.

Ständige Konferenz der Innenminister und -senatoren der Länder (eds.) 2009. *Programm Innere Sicherheit. Fortschreibung 2008/2009*. Potsdam: IMK.

Stienen, Ludger 2011. *Privatisierung und Entstaatlichung der inneren Sicherheit*. Frankfurt/M.: Verlag für Polizeiwissenschaft.

Thumala, Angélica, Benjamin Goold, and Ian Loader 2011. "A tainted trade? Moral ambivalence and legitimation work in the private security industry." *The British Journal of Sociology*, 62 (2): 283–303.

Toffler, Alvin 1980. *The Third Wave*. London: Collins.

UEFA (ed.) 2011. *Frequently Asked Questions. UEFA EURO 2012™ Volunteers Program*. Nyon, Switzerland: UEFA.

VDI and VDE-IT 2009. *Marktpotentiale von Sicherheitstechnologien und Sicherheitsdienstleistungen*. Berlin: Verband Deutscher Ingenieure.

Venkatesh, Sudhir Alladi 2006. *Off the Books*. Cambridge, MA: Harvard.

Wacquant, Loïc 2011. "The Wedding of Workfare and Prisonfare Revisited." *Social Justice*, 38 (1-2): 203–221.

Welsch, Manfred 2007. "Lohntarifrunde 2007 in NRW." *sicherheitsnadel*, 7 (10): 3.

Williams, Kristian 2007. *Our Enemies in Blue*. Cambridge, MA: South End Press.

Zylla, Gabi 2009. "Kein Schloss ist hundertprozentig sicher." *Berliner Woche. Lokalausgabe Neukölln-Nord*, 22 (48): 16.

MANAGERIAL CONTROL OF WORK IN THE PRIVATE SECURITY INDUSTRY IN AUSTRALIA

Peter Gahan, Bill Harley, and Graham Sewell

rivate security is an increasingly pervasive part of life across many countries. Since the 1970s there has been large-scale growth in the industry (Prenzler et al., 2007/8). There has, however, been remarkably little research on the nature of work and employment in this sector (but see Briken, 2010). The little empirical evidence available suggests that security is a very labor intensive industry and characterized by relatively poor working conditions, low skill levels, low pay, and low job security (ABS, 2000).

Our aim is to develop a speculative argument, buttressed with some data, about the nature of work in the private security industry in Australia and, in particular, about employees' experiences of managerial labor control strategies. We are interested in security as an industry where, on one hand, employees commonly have high levels of autonomy and where service quality is critical but, on the other hand, formal management systems are underdeveloped and working conditions appear poor. Our central concern is with how compliance is elicited from employees in such a context.

In developing our argument we rely on two sources of data. First, prior research and our own analysis of official statistics are used to provide a general picture of the industry. Second, we utilize selected qualitative data drawn from our own interview-based research on the experiences of workers in the industry. The data are drawn from a small number of interviews with workers who predominantly work in crowd control and we make no claims about their representativeness, but our intention is not to develop a definitive account of workers' experiences[79]. Rather, we use the qualitative data to inform our preliminary, and somewhat speculative, theorizing about the nature of work in the industry and the ways that compliance is elicited.

The argument that we begin to develop in this chapter is that in important ways the private security industry resembles what might be termed 'low road' industries, characterized by a range of undesirable working conditions often ascribed to 'dirty work'. We suggest, however, that there are some important differences. First, it seems that workers in the industry enjoy quite high levels of autonomy and that they are required to deploy high level skills, although these tend to be 'soft' or tacit emotional and social skills. Second, it appears that conventional methods of surveillance and performance management may be difficult to implement in security. Third, in spite of the apparently poor working conditions and the lack of direct managerial control strategies, employees appear to comply with the needs of management. We put forward a number of speculative explanations for this employee compliance. The preliminary theorizing which we present in the chapter suggests that the nature of work in private security is rather more complex and difficult to categorize than that in many other 'low road' sectors and that this explains, in part, the reasons for employee compliance.

---

79   We recognise that 'security work' covers a wide range of quite diverse categories – guards in department stores, cash in transit operatives, armed bodyguards, airport passenger screeners, private investigators and so on. Our focus is chiefly on 'frontline' security staff – those whose work involves controlling crowds at private parties and public events such as music festivals – and accordingly we recognise that our findings may well only apply to some parts of the security industry.

The private security industry in australia: an overview

A key motivation for our own research on work in the Australian security industry is that there is so little known about this facet of the sector. In this section, we consider the evidence which can be gleaned from earlier research and report on an analysis of statistical information drawn from a number of surveys conducted by the Australian Bureau of Statistics (ABS). This detail is compared with earlier work undertaken by researchers relying on Census Data. Both sources of data have their limitations.

Previous studies

The most comprehensive analysis of the Australian private security industry to date has been undertaken by Tim Prenzler, Rick Sarre and their colleagues.[80] These scholars have tracked the growth of this sector over the last 30 years. Their findings show that the demand for private security has grown steadily over this period, such that by 2007, the sector contributed more than AUD1.4 billion, or approximately 2 percent of Australia's Gross Domestic Product. They find that this growth was driven by demand for private security services across all sectors, but notably in hospitality, retail services, banking and financial services, manufacturing and property and business services. This growing demand for such services is reflected in the relatively rapid growth in employment in the security industry. Drawing on national census data, Prenzler, Earle and Sarre (2009a) report that by 2006, there were over 50,000 workers who identified their main occupation as being security work, compared to only 45,000 police officers (Prenzler et al., 2009a: 3-4).

MANAGERIAL CONTROL OF WORK IN THE PRIVATE SECURITY INDUSTRY IN AUSTRALIA

---

80   This group of scholars has produced a significant number of publications. Those deal-
       ing specifically with developments in the Australian context include: Hardy and Prenzler
       (2002); Prenzler (2000, 2005, 2009); Prenzler, Earle, and Sarre (2009a); Prenzler and Sarre
       (1999, 2007, 2010); Prenzler, Sarre, and Earle (2008); Sarre and Prenzler (2009, 2011).

Using the same data source, Sarre and Prenzler (2011) provide a 'snapshot' of employment arrangements in the industry. The picture which emerges is one of 'low quality' work, characterized by precarious employment, low pay and limited training or career development. In 2006, just under half of all employees (47%) in the industry in Australia were employed on a casual basis (Sarre and Prenzler, 2011: 24) compared to a figure of just over 25 percent for the Australian workforce as a whole (ABS 2006).[81] Of those employed on a permanent basis, almost 27 percent were employed on a part-time basis.

Pay rates for security industry employees were also found to be considerably lower than in many other occupational groups. According to Sarre and Prenzler (2011: 25), 76 per cent of full-time security industry employees earned less than AUD800 per week (in 2006). This compares to a figure of only 33 percent of full-time workers in Australia earning below this rate of pay in their main job at the time (ABS, 2007: 26). The census data also reveal a relatively under-educated workforce when compared to the population overall, or to related occupational groups such as police officers (Sarre and Prenzler, 2011: 28). In 2006, around one-third (31%) of security guards reported that they had not completed high school, whilst a further 44 percent reported they had completed high school or undertaken some basic post-school certificate-level training.

Updating the industry overview

The general conclusions about the character of the sector that can be drawn from these previous studies remain largely the same today. In this section, however, we

---

81   Casual employment is a uniquely Australian phenomenon, which corresponds most closely to what the OECD calls temporary employment. It involves an arrangement whereby each period of employment is, in a legal sense, a one-off event with no expectation of future employment. As well as a lack of security casual employment is characterised by the absence of paid holidays and sick leave. Moreover, casual employment tends to be associated with less training, fewer opportunities for advancement and generally poorer working conditions than does permanent employment.

provide an up-dated snapshot of businesses in the sector and employment arrangements, based on survey data collected by the ABS.

The private security industry is characterized by the presence of a small number of large operators which dominate the market, and a large number of small operators with few or no employees (that is, businesses where the owner is the sole operative). Figure 1 reports the total number of businesses estimated to operate in the area of 'public order, safety and regulatory services' (the category which most closely corresponds to security) for selected years from 2004-2009. Figure 1 reports that in 2009, there were 8,369 businesses operating in the sector, compared with 7,395 in 2004 – a 13 percent increase in the number of firms operating in the sector over the five year period. Figure 1 also reveals that the majority of operators were self-employed contractors, although the proportion of operators in this category has fallen over the period to 2009. In contrast, very few businesses employed more than 200 workers. In 2009, of the 8,369 operators, 60 employed more than 200 workers, compared with just 9 of 7,395 operators in 2004 (for data on Germany, cf. Eick, *this volume)*. The most consistent trend over the period for which we have data relates to the growth of very small operators – businesses employing fewer than 20 workers. While this category represented less than 20 percent of all operators in 2004, by 2009 slightly more than 40 percent of all businesses in the sector employed fewer than 20 workers.

Figure 1. Number of Operators in the Public Order,
Safety and Regulatory Services sector, 2004-2009

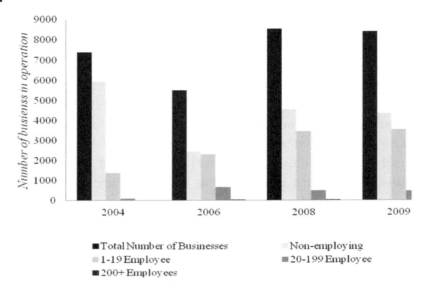

Source: *ABS Cat. No. 8165.0 - Counts of Australian Businesses, including Entries and Exits.*

The small size of most operators is reflected in the relative vulnerability of these operations. Figure 2 reports survival rates of all business in operation in June 2007, and reports on the proportion of these firms that remained in business in 2008 and 2009. It compares businesses based on the number of employees engaged and the annual turnover. Of the 7,470 operators in business in 2007, slightly more than 20 percent had ceased operation just one year later, whilst more than one-third had ceased operations within two years.

Not surprisingly, smaller operators were found to have a significantly lower probability of survival. Of those businesses that did not report engaging any employees, slightly less than half had ceased operations within two years. This compares with just 20 percent of operators employing more than 200 employees leaving the sector within the same period. A similar pattern is evident when survival rates are compared on the basis of annual turnover. Again, of the 2,430 operators who reported a annual turnover of less than AUD50,000 in 2007, around 55 percent had ceased operations within two years. In contrast, around 85 percent of operations who reported a turnover of AUD2 million or more remained in operation in 2009.

The diversity of firm operations – notably the predominance of small firms – is reflected in the pattern of employment arrangements in the sector. Figure 3 reports the total number of security guards employed for the period August 1996 to March 2011. These data cover the broader occupational group of 'security officers and guards' for which we have collected interview data. These include persons employed as front desk security in large corporate officers, 'bouncers' in night clubs, through to persons employed to as armed escorts, the protection of sensitive infrastructure or 'important persons.'

Figure 2. Survival Rates of Australian Businesses Operating in the Public Order, Safety and Regulatory Services, 2007-2009a

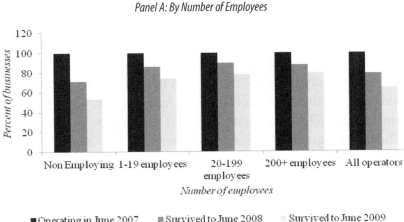

Panel A: By Number of Employees

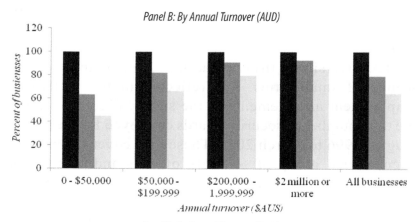

Panel B: By Annual Turnover (AUD)

Panel B: By Annual Turnover (AUD)

Source: ABS Cat No. 8165.0 - *Counts of Australian Businesses, including Entries and Exits.*

a.   The figure reports all businesses included in the Australian Business Register for the ANZSIC sub-division, 77 Public Order, Safety and Regulatory Services.

Panel A in Figure 3 shows a breakdown of these figures for individuals working full-time and part-time. These figures include security guards reporting themselves as engaged as employees, as well as contractors, 'own account workers'[82] and managers and owners of businesses in the sector. This figure shows a steady increase in employment over the period. In March 2011, the ABS Monthly Labour Force Survey estimated that around 53,000 persons were in employment as security officers and guards, down from a peak of 57,000 in 2007. Of these, around two-thirds reported being in full-time work.

Panel B in Figure 3 shows a breakdown of employment by gender. This figure indicates a steady increase in total employment in this sector has not altered the gender distribution of employment. In August 1996, of the 32,000 persons employed as security officers or guards, around 5,000 (15%) were women. By March 2011, women account for around 8,000 of the approximately 53,000 workers in this occupational group – or approximately the same proportion of total employment.

---

82   'Own account workers' are defined by the ABS as 'people working in their own business without employees' (ABS Cat No. 1321.0 - *Small Business in Australia, Explanatory Notes*).

Panel A: Employment Growth by Employment Status

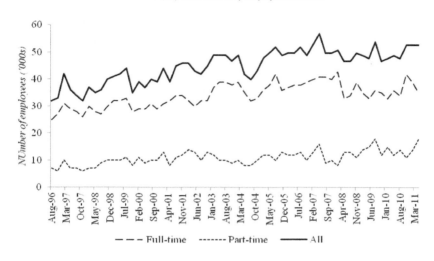

Panel B: Employment Growth by Gender

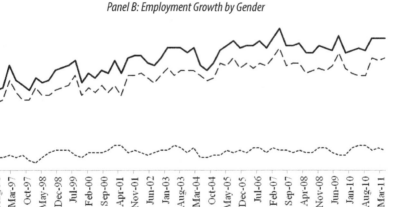

Source: ABS, Catalogue Number 6291.0. 0.55.003 *Labour Force, Australia, Detailed, Quarterly, May 2011.*

a.   Employment figures are at the disaggregated occupational unit level (Security Officers and Guards).

Figure 4 reports average weekly working hours worked by full-time and part-time security guards for the period August 1996 to March 2011. This figure shows a relatively stable pattern of hours over the period for which we have data. In March 2011, security officers and guards reported working an average of 34 hours per week, compared with average weekly hours of 37 in August 1996. The difference between full-time and part-time average weekly hours also remained relatively stable. In 2011, full-time workers on average reported working 41 hours, compared with an average of 20 hours among part-time workers. This compared with 41 and 19 hours, respectively in August 1996.

Figure 4. Average Weekly Working Hours for Security Officers and Guards (Full-time and Part-time workers), 1996-2011

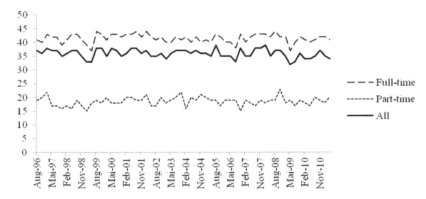

This relative stability in average working hours is not evident when we compare men and women workers. Figure 5 reveals that, for most periods for which we have data, men worked, on average, more hours than women. Whilst the pattern remained relatively stable for men over this period, average weekly hours for women are significantly more variable (standard deviation: men=1.61; women=3.43), suggesting a different pattern of attachment to paid work among women working in the sector compared with men.

Figure 5. Average Weekly Working Hours for Security Officers and Guards (Men and Women), 1996-2011

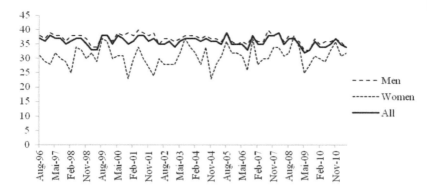

Source: ABS Cat. No. 6291.0.55.003 - *Labour Force, Australia, Detailed, Quarterly.*

An even more marked pattern of variability is evident in Figure 6, which graphs average working hours for individuals working in different forms of employment. Here we are able to compare working hours of individuals who report being engaged as employees with those who report running a business and those working as independent contractors.

Variability of working hours provides one immediate measure of job security. Employees appear to have the most stable working hours arrangements of the three groups. At the start of the period for which we have data, employees reported working, on average, 36 hours per week. This compares with an average weekly work of 34 hours in March 2011. In contrast 'own account' workers' hours vary, on average, between 54 hours (in May 2002) and 18 hours (February 1999). As Figure 6 reveals, this high degree of variability in average weekly working hours is even more pronounced for persons identifying themselves as employers (i.e., employing at least one worker, whether as an employee or independent contractor). Again, this is consistent with international evidence which highlights the growing insecurity associated with many different types of routine service work as a major factor in generating greater insecurity (see, for example Allen and Henry, 1997).

Figure 6. Average Weekly Working Hours for Security Officers and Guards (by Form of Employment), 1996-2011

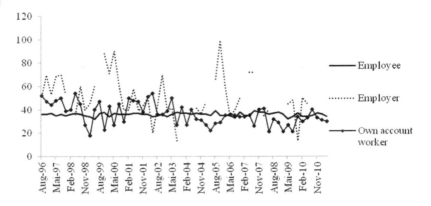

Source: ABS Cat. No. 6291.0.55.003 - *Labour Force, Australia, Detailed, Quarterly.*

Figure 7 reports hourly pay rates (including both ordinary hours and overtime) for selected occupations – including prison and security officers – and all employed persons in 2010. It shows hourly pay rates separately for men, women and all persons. Broadly speaking, the selected occupations represent jobs of similar skill and entry requirements and, for this reason, might be seen as alternative occupational comparisons for persons employed as security officers and guards. Of the group of occupations included, a number of observations can be made in relation to pay for prison and security officers. First it is noteworthy that of all the occupations included in our selection, it is the only occupation in which there are virtually no gender differences in average hourly rates of pay. Second, compared with the other selected occupations, prison and security guards receive hourly rates of pay commensurate with call centre workers and personal service workers; and significantly higher hourly rates of pay than hospitality workers, checkout operators, cleaners or food process workers. The most obvious point to note is that all selected occupations receive hourly rates of pay below the average for all occupations – in some cases, around two-thirds the mean hourly rate of pay for all occupations. In the case of security guards the mean hourly rate of pay is 20 percent less than the mean hourly rate for all occupations.

Figure 7. Hourly rates of pay, selected occupations, for men, women and all persons (May 2010)

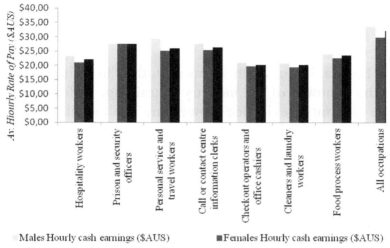

Males Hourly cash earnings ($AUS)   ■Females Hourly cash earnings ($AUS)
■All persons Hourly cash earnings ($AUS)

Source: ABS Cat. No. 6306.0 - Employee Earnings and Hours, Australia.

The pattern of employment described so far would indicate a difficult environment for unions to operate in. Whilst is not possible to obtain reliable data specifically on security guards, the anecdotal evidence from those unions that do organise security guards would indicate that unionization is low. This was certainly confirmed in our interview data, where interviewees when asked reported little knowledge of unions in the sector. For example, when asked about the role of unions, one interview responded that:

> Well, I didn't know about them and I've been - like I said, I've been doing this 20 years. I didn't know about them. I really don't think that they would - I can't see how they could help in any way, I really can't.

Other interviewees reported some involvement, but typically saw their role as limited, especially by the high level of turnover in the sector:

> Well they could do a better job... That's why I say we had an issue last year where we were going to go

out on strike - protected action and the people I was working with in Clayton wouldn't and the whole thing just fell apart... A lot of them joined up for the fight then and they've left it now.

The final issue which seems important to us in mapping out the contours of the industry is training. Unfortunately, there is limited evidence concerning the extent to which individuals or employers engage in training beyond that formally required by licensing arrangements in specific jurisdictions. In the Australian context, regulation of the security industry has been the responsibility of state governments. In recent years, however, there has been a growing willingness among states to co-ordinate and harmonise training requirements. This has led to the introduction of National Training Package for the industry and the establishment of common training standards across all states for different types of security work.

In one of the few studies intended to examine this issue, Prenzler and Sarre (2011) conducted a survey of security operators and managers to ascertain, among other things, perceptions of training requirements for security officers. This survey indicated that most operators felt the standard of entry level training was adequate for most types of security work (such as knowledge of the relevant law), but indicated training was generally inadequate in 'soft skills' associated with the job (communication skills, conflict resolution, handling physical confrontations and self-defence).

The picture which emerges from the admittedly partial evidence on the industry is one characterized in large part by irregular employment, relatively low pay and a lack of training. This would suggest that the security industry tends towards what might be called a 'low road' approach to employment and that it would not be an attractive destination for employees. This picture is reinforced by the responses of employers in the industry whom we interviewed as part of the research which led to this chapter.

One employer told us:

> Turnover's fairly high. We've got our fair share of unscrupulous employers and we attract our fair share of fairly lazy employees...you get paid $20 an hour flat rate...we're not attracting the right people...My view is that people become security guards because they're too lazy to be cleaners or taxi drivers.

As well as being an unattractive industry when assessed in objective terms, it is clear that the industry in Australia has a poor public image and is not regarded as somewhere that most people would choose to work. Regular media reports highlight the negative side of the industry, usually in terms of violence by 'bouncers' employed by pubs and nightclubs (Prenzler and Sarre, 2008). Indeed, one could make a case that at least some types of security work could be regarded as 'dirty work' in the sense that there is stigma attached to working in the industry (see Ashforth and Kreiner, 1999). As one might expect, the work can also be dangerous, with security staff being more likely to be injured at work than members of other occupational groups (Sarre and Prenzler, 2011: 124).

In a recent review of the state of the sector internationally, van Steden and Sarre (2010: 14), for example, note the 'tragic quality of security guards':

> The tragic quality of contract guards, in short, is that everybody needs private security, but nobody really wants it. No matter how well entrepreneurs are organized and how well they try to distance themselves from unsavoury "cowboy companies," their private security industries are bound to be beset with enduring tensions and difficulties.

All of this would suggest that the experience of working in the service sector would be expected to be overwhelmingly negative. We would expect jobs to be characterized by low pay, irregularity and lack of training, but also by the low levels of discretion and direct forms of managerial control which tend to go hand in hand with low-skill service work. At the same time, however, other researchers have noted the more contradictory *experience of work* in service sectors such as security (Sengupta, Edwards, and Tsai, 2009; Wakefield, 2008; Korczynski, 2003). In the next section we begin to explore the question of what it is like to work in the security industry and, in particular, how managerial control is exerted.

The nature of work in the private security industry

It seems highly likely that in important ways the private security industry resembles what might be termed 'low road' industries, characterized by low pay and unattractive employment conditions (Sengupta, Edwards and Tsai 2009). This view is supported in important ways by comments from security guards whom we interviewed for this chapter. Our respondents frequently commented on the low pay characteristic of the industry, often mentioning that the risks associated with the work justified higher levels of remuneration.

> I don't think you're ever paid enough. It's a bit like being in the military. You're getting paid to be shot at and shoot people. How much do you put on that? You risk your life. I - from - depending on the different companies - some of the pay is shocking but they employ monkeys.

> Well, I'll tell you 15 years ago, maybe 13 - my daughter's 15 so it must've been 14 years ago I was getting paid $22 an hour. The rate now is $25. I get about $25. Sometimes I'll get $30. But if you look at - 14 years have gone by... It should be more, and it's way more dangerous now. The amount of threats and people - smash your lights in; get out of my way you [unclear].

Every night you work there's a possibility that you're going to go home injured. Not enough money.

...you've got to remember that they're not the ones - management aren't the ones - that are at risk. It's the poor bunny out there that's carrying the cash and it's a real risk. You should be renumerated for the fact that you are taking this risk, far more so than most people. We don't get much more in real terms than some bunny operating out of the MCG [Melbourne Cricket Ground] at the football.

As van Steden, Sarre, and others, have noted, the very character of security work has been associated with a pervasive stigmatization as 'dirty work' (Kriener, Ashforth, and Sluss, 2006). These aspects are clearly an important element of how security officers and guards experience work:

if we're talking about a crowd control activity, having to deal with an intoxicated person yelling in my face and me having to keep cool, calm and collected all the way through. It's not the remaining cool, calm and collected that I have a problem with, what I have is a problem is with their saliva spitting all over my face.

It's the invasion of space and that becomes a little bit - the hygiene aspect of it I guess. It's an OH & S issue and I think every security operative needs to ensure that they always have their backup with them and when I mean backup, I mean other security operatives with them when approaching persons and never working on their own.

Driving, stopping, checking buildings, so forth and it's reasonably dangerous. I've had bricks thrown at my car, I've been approached by two or three youths and - wanted to have a fight. Fortunately for me I carry a baton so when you produce that they tend to break off a bit because they're intoxicated and you bring it to the next level. Ninety per cent of the time they want to take a run.

As we have noted, these features of the industry would suggest that the security industry is generally not somewhere most people would choose to work if they had other options available. Certainly our respondents frequently reported having come into the industry almost by accident. One interviewee reported that she had been working out in her gym, when a fellow gym member, who owned his own security business, suggested she get her license to operate as a security officer and he would make work available to her:

> I said girls don't do security work, and he said, yeah, they do, we need girls. So I said okay. I was twenty. I did it, and never meant to be doing it for this long. I don't know how it happened, but here I am [twenty years later]... Before that I did a bit of bar work, I was a dance teacher. My very first job was at a supermarket. I was fifteen.

Others report various events in their lives which made security work an attractive option. Examples of the paths people followed are provided below.

> I was working at [...]. I was working as front house, just an usher. They offered me – to send me to get my security license because they do in house. I liked how it worked in there so I decided why not and they paid for it and I've been doing that up until – for five years.

> When I left the police force I bought my own company. It was actually a security company and I was doing all right... I had a car accident, a very serious one and I was out of action for years. I got involved in

local government... I left local government and an opportunity opened up with the Commonwealth Games to get in to be trained at [...]'s] expense to work at the Commonwealth Games. So I did and I've worked for them ever since.

Well to be honest with you I had been working in the cosmetics industry for quite a while and was interested in the training rung. Initially I thought, mmm, do I become a trainer within the cosmetic industry? I thought, oh no, really I don't want to do that. I might look at something totally different and at that point in time I was married and realized that no, I need to get a part time job because I need to move on. So it was a decision that I had made to work evening hours, as well as my day time job. Things weren't looking too well in the marriage so I thought bugger it, I'll just go and do some extra security work.

According to Prenzler and Sarre's (2011: 56-58) survey of employers and managers, the view that security is an unattractive destination that attracts 'undesirables' is widespread, with a significant proportion of operators reporting existing systems did not adequately screen individuals entering the industry, or remove disreputable or criminal elements from the industry. Overall, the majority of respondents indicated that the current regulatory arrangements were largely ineffective in raising the level of professionalism in the sector. Our respondents frequently made similar comments, with one being:

...there are a lot of people who, in real terms, should never have got a security license.... the license and provisions are quite strict but people can get around that and that's where the problem is. The regulations are there, they're not being enforced properly... But until the licensing is sorted out, until there's some sort of oversight body that has some real teeth into things like training and organizations and their ability to contract out it's never going to change.

So far, the picture which we have painted is of a typical low-road industry, but our argument is that this would be far too simplistic a reading of the reality of the industry. Of course, we do not deny that many of the features of the industry are consistent with other low-level service sectors, but there are also some important differences.

First, in many security industry jobs, notably crowd control and mobile patrols, workers by necessity have a fairly high degree of autonomy. That is, they work alone or in small groups, and often in situations where employees must make decisions and solve problems using their own resources, albeit bound by specified routines and procedures. This was a feature of working in the industry, which came up repeatedly in our employee interviews and, moreover, was identified as an aspect that made the job appealing.

You control your own - which is what I like - you're controlling your own work environment. You're controlling your own abilities and it's where you get your experience.

I'm not a power tripper, but my experience enables me to make decisions that, as far as I'm concerned, are the best decisions for my safety and everybody else's safety that's around me. I need to know that everyone's safe and everyone's looked after.

Security's the kind of work where if you pause and second guess yourself or have some reason why you're holding back - it's potentially your safety. The security role is one where you're the one in charge; you need to be able to make those decisions then and there. You can't be oh hang on, wait a second and I'll just go see. That just doesn't make sense.

In practice, the scope for decision making may often be limited. For example, one respondent noted:

> There'll be certain issues like the traffic is buggered here today so if we were doing a run in towards the city you might want to take some of the other jobs outside the city first and then come to the city after the traffic's died down. But the run is set and then you can modify it. But the main issue is if you perceive a threat or an issue just leave. You've got to make that decision. If there's a problem that's an issue for you, a potential threat, you just don't do the job, just drive away.

Nonetheless, we would suggest that the inherent autonomy of some forms of security work marks a qualitative difference from many other forms of service sector work.

> I'm not afraid of any frontline work, because as I said earlier on, it's all about communication skills and giving good customer service and ensuring that you've always got your team around you to back you up and making sure that you're able to risk assess every situation and if you're able to assess every situation to the best of your capabilities, that's going to help to minimize any risk that's imposed on you. So really at the end of the day, you know what, I could be doing this at least for another 15, 20 years I'm sure.

> ...the biggest issue is that not everybody has that sort of ability. I mean to really operate within security, as I've said, you've got to be able to assess risk, make split second decisions and carry them through. ... You've got to be able to assess what's happening and then make a decision on what action you take and so forth. Very few people can do that and it doesn't matter whether they're in police or whatever.

Second, although much security work is typified as having low levels of technical skill with limited formal training, it seems that many jobs in the industry require higher levels of other skill, which tend not to be formally recognized and involve 'soft' skills of a tacit, emotional and social character.

[What do you think are the most important skills for you to do your job properly?] Communication skills... if you don't have communication skills and you're not able to converse, you're not able to have those skills required in order to get the best out of a situation, you're going to have problems... you need to know how to defuse situations and if you can't negotiate, you've lost the battle already. That comes hand in hand with being able to communicate and be able to get the point across...

You know what, at the end of the day, if I was going to be employing somebody I would want them to be mindful of their fitness, but having said that, you can't use that against someone. If they've got great communication skills and they've got the knowledge and the experience there, then you're hoping that they're going to be able to do their job effectively.

Negotiation ...and being able to read people's demeanor is extremely important because you can gauge their reaction to what you're going to say. You've got to have a very good judgment of somebody's - what do they call it - their - you've got to be able to read their - can't think of the words for it - their body language, because a person that's sober acts very differently to somebody that's intoxicated or on drugs.

See, it's a judgment thing. Extremely important is your judgment, I believe, anyway, within that - and again you don't overstep your own abilities. It comes back to abilities, I believe, and your - which is experience.

Experience in judging and negotiation skills are extremely important.

We do not claim that the preceding conjectures and supporting quotes by any means represents a definitive picture of the nature of work in the industry. What it does tell us, however, is that in at least some cases the experience of work in the sector is more complex than might be expected. In particular, it suggests that we should take seriously the claim that some security work, while taking place in a 'low road' service industry, may be characterized by higher levels of skill and autonomy than would be expected in this type of work. In the next part of the chapter we begin to develop an argument about what this means for managerial control strategies in the security industry.

Managerial Control Strategies in private security

In other parts of the service sector, routine workers are commonly subject to managerial control strategies which emphasize broadly Taylorist approaches – tightly constrained and 'scripted' job roles, direct monitoring and simple performance-pay systems – bolstered by job insecurity and the absence of superior alternative employment (Ritzer, 2008; Thompson and van den Broek, 2010). In some parts of security, and to some extent, no doubt such approaches are applied. The picture that we have begun to paint above, however, suggests that in some cases this is simply not going to be viable.

Our preliminary research in the sector provided some indication of the limits of surveillance and performance management. In some parts of the industry these tactics appear to be quite viable. For example, an armored car guard told us:

> [How does your employer know that you're doing a good job? How do they keep tabs on what you're up to?]
> Well there is a paper trail. So supposing you wanted to

help yourself to some of the money. We've recently just had someone do just that. Worked out a very cunning scheme and eventually got caught. Because there is a paper trail, everything should be accounted for and if it's not well then they start following through and finding out what's happened. The other thing they do have is that they do have a team of security investigators. Don't know how good they are but they do follow the trucks around to pick up issues where the operators are in breach of company procedures.

In crowd control, which is characterized by higher autonomy and more remoteness from the employer, it would seem likely that such an approach would be very difficult to implement. This can be illustrated by this excerpt from an interview.

Facilitator: So how do they know whether you're doing a good job or not?

Interviewee: They'll soon hear from the client. If you're an idiot, pretty soon you'll get that call. The clients are actually pretty good, they do like to give feedback on whether they like you or not, so they'll ring. If they do like you they'll ring and say yeah, they were good, please send them back, because it is actually hard to find guards who are good.

Facilitator: Is there any sort of formal system of monitoring evaluation. If you go to a restaurant or you stay in a hotel or anything like that, you always have to fill in a little satisfaction survey. Do the people you work for do anything like that or is it just...

Interviewee: No.

Facilitator: It's just that they might have a chat with some of the clients and see how things are going?

Interviewee: Yeah. I think the client is the only way, really, that they can find out.

A further barrier to such approaches is the relative under-development of systematic management in the industry, in conjunction with the fact that much of the industry operates on low profit margins. A respondent told us that:

> I think it's limited by the dollar and I think it's limited by the level of incompetence right the way through the industry and that starts from training and it goes right the way through management procedures. ... Because there's no money in it. No one wants to pay for it.

If, as we speculate, routine and direct managerial control strategies are not widely applied in the industry, then an obvious question is why employees who have considerable autonomy, yet have relatively poor conditions of employment, comply with managerial requirements to do their jobs, especially as the industry is not an obvious place to find employees exercising self-discipline based on widespread norms of professional conduct. Of course, the fact that many who work in the industry do not have attractive alternative options is likely to be a factor in fostering a sense of self-discipline and it may also be the case that actual levels of discretion are quite low. Nonetheless, employees do their jobs, apparently largely in the absence of direct forms of managerial control. A number of possible explanations can be put forward for this.

First, it may be that employers are, against the odds as it were, able to elicit a degree of employee loyalty and self-discipline (see Townley, 1993). Our preliminary research does not allow us to deduce a great deal about this possibility, but the low rates of pay and relatively high rates of turnover in the industry are not suggestive of high levels of mutual commitment between employers and employees. One of the few comments on this general topic made by one of our employee respondents is suggestive of a low-loyalty environment.

There are a few [companies that actually look after their employees] but there really aren't many, and some of them are that bad that I've been disgusted with the way that they've treated their staff. When I was rostering[83] manager at the last company, one of the guards, who was a fantastic guard, really hard worker, always did his job to the best of his ability - he twisted his ankle when he was walking down the steps at the site that he was working and he broke his ankle, really badly broke it... Then the boss said okay, sack him. He'd been working for them for over 10 - he was one of their first employees - over 10 years. I think it was over 15 years. He was one of their first employees, and that's what he did. I thought, you bastard.

Where respondents expressed loyalty to their employer, it tended to be in terms of personal loyalty, based more on having worked closely in small organization than on loyalty to the employer per se. For example:

I do, actually, yeah [feel a sense of commitment to the company]... Well, because - actually, I've been friends with them now for - I think it's because when you work with other people in the security industry, they become like your family because you look after them and they look after you. Because of that, because of the close team work that's involved, you do end up getting involved in their lives and them into yours. So you do kind of end up - I've got friends from 20 years ago that I worked with.

A second possible explanation is that systems of peer surveillance within teams of employees perform the role which would otherwise be taken by direct managerial surveillance and control (see Barker, 1993; Sewell, 1998).

---

83   The rostering manager is the person with responsibility for allocating employees to shifts.

Our preliminary investigation suggests that there is some monitoring by peers in the form of 'team leaders'. Generally, however, our respondents framed these mechanisms as being about team ethos, support for colleagues, 'watching your partner's back' or similar. This seemed to be more about self-policing than about deliberate managerial strategy. Comments from respondents included:

> You rely on each other [co-workers]. There's so many times when you've got their back and they look after you and you look after them. When they do look after you, you think wow, that - it's a protective thing and in a way they become like your family because that's what family does. So family's got your back, they make sure that you're okay. When you need help, they help you. It's on a more basic level but it's the same thing.

A third explanation which we suggest should be entertained is that staff in the industry, in some cases at least, do indeed develop a quasi-professional service ethic (see Anderson-Gough et al., 2000) and sense of satisfaction and pride in their work. This may well be part of the way that staff seek to construct positive identity in the context of dirty work.

Illustrative examples of comments made by respondents are presented below:

> if you're working for an employer and you've got pride within yourself and your performance, you're going to want to ensure that you're perceived in the right fashion whilst you are out there working in the industry.

> Well it's all customer satisfaction. It's all ensuring that you're satisfying the client's needs. It all interlinks...

> I enjoy doing what I do. I find it easy because I've been doing it for so long. Like water running off a ducks back. So look, there are opportunities available to me

out there and I'll certainly look at those. As I get older and feel that maybe I need to take a little bit more a back step, I'm sure I'll certainly be able to do that.

I have, I think, a commitment in the way that my commitment is that I will do the best job that I can do, but I will always do that no matter what job I do. I'll do it to the best of my ability. As far as loyalty to the client, I wouldn't say there's a whole lot of loyalty as such.

I do actually have a strong sense of [commitment to the public] - I think I have a personality that I'm kind of a protective person, especially of people that can't protect themselves. I'm really protective of women who are out in - the clientele, the patrons who are out there, because it is dangerous. Guys are just - it's dangerous for girls, especially young girls because I see them, they're fresh out of school, they get blind drunk, drugs, and I think oh my God, this could be my daughter in a few years. It could be. So I do have very strong protective feelings for anyone who can't take care of themselves.

Finally, we also found evidence suggestive of the fact that some employees in the sector experience intrinsic motivation. That is, in spite of its perceived 'dirty' nature, there are elements of security work which are inherently satisfying and motivating. Again, these comments may be part of an attempt at positive identity construction, but we would argue that we should take seriously the possibility that for some employees the work is indeed intrinsically motivating.

You've always got to think on your feet and you've got to keep your wits about yourself. You don't just go there and switch off. You can't. That's why - I like that sort of thing, I like to stay active and keep myself going that way.

Look, I love watching people. I'm a people watcher and you need to be able to pick up people's body language and some of time you'll be standing there and you'll see people do the most ridiculous things and you think, surely they've got no idea of what they've just done. [Laughs]... They might just decide to scratch themselves in a particular spot... Right there. It's like, everybody else is standing here and have you not noticed what you've just done. Just the stupidest of things you know.

The particular people I work with I like working with. Within - if I'm not happy within any job I do I leave. It's my philosophy and if I'm enjoying my job I'll stay there and I like a challenge. I like to be thinking on my feet like that all the time I - we do a varied array of things and we interact with people a lot and it's good. You - people come up and talk to you wherever you're standing and we're always hi, how are you and all that sort of thing. The pleasantries, the PR work. I've always liked doing that sort of thing so I just enjoy the different aspects of the - of working within the industry.

The picture that we have begun to sketch out above suggests to us that there is considerably more going on in the private security sector than might at first be supposed. We have started to develop an argument that work in security industry may well be more varied and complex than the industry-level data and our knowledge of 'low road' industries would suggest. In particular, there is evidence of higher levels of skill and autonomy than we would expect associated with such work. Importantly, these factors in conjunction with the nature of much of the work in the sector mean that the kinds of managerial labor control strategies we would expect to see are also not present. In part this may reflect the lack of well-developed management systems, particularly among small employers, but it also reflects the unique nature of work and employment in this industry.

Conclusion

When reflecting on the state of employment practices in the Australian security industry it is always advisable to consider it in its social, political, and economic contexts. In this way the industry is not that different to its counterparts in other developed countries where important trends like an ideological preference for private rather than public service provision or the development of 'night-time' service and leisure economies to replace traditional manufacturing activity (Hobbs et al., 2005) have transformed the economic landscape. To these, however, we would proffer a further sociological explanation for the broadening and deepening of private security in Australia by drawing on the observation, common among sociologists of a certain stripe (e.g., Giddens, 1999), that it is but one manifestation of our preoccupation with risk that itself is a form of anxiety about current technological and social predicament. Things like globalization, the roll-back of the welfare state, scaremongering about immigration or the rise of an "underclass," global warming, "off-shoring" of high paid manufacturing jobs and a "rebalancing" of developed economies towards (usually lower paid and insecure) service jobs, the dangers of "nano-technology", and so on (for the list is potentially endless). It's not so much that these things make life any more hazardous than it was in the past; rather, they are things about which our previous experiences can teach us little as we seek ways of avoiding certain future states (be individual or societal material) while making others more likely. At the same time we have come to expect that everything – from the smallest and simplest organic particles like disease-causing viruses through to largest and most complex social systems like global financial markets – can be controlled (or, at least, ought to be controllable). So, when there is a failure to mitigate risk and our personal or collective safety is compromised it is attributed to our failure of "risk management." This gives rise to an obsession with the anticipation of adverse outcomes and the need for risk mitigation of one form or another. In this context the presence of security personnel in an increasing array of social settings sends the message that "something is being done" about the uncertainties of modern life. We mention these things in passing to support our claim that developing a better understanding of the growth of the security industry in Australia is not solely an economic matter.

Despite this increasing importance it is nevertheless an industry that is still struggling for legitimacy; a struggle that is not made any easier by the stubbornly poor image it has in the mind of most people. Add to this concerns about the poor regulation, high profile reporting of fatal incidents involving security employees, and the apparent infiltration of criminal elements (Hobbs et al., 2003; Prenzler and Sarre, 2008), and we can begin to appreciate the challenges facing the industry. There is little doubt then that this poor image is partially deserved and we would further contend that many of the things we identify in this chapter, such as low levels of training, relatively low wages, and high levels of turnover, do little to improve the prospects for the industry. There appears to be a paradox at the heart of our attitudes towards the industry: at a time when everyone is demanding greater security and protection from risk no one appears to be happy to pay for it or to respect it as 'legitimate work.' This leads to a vicious circle where an unwillingness to invest in training and a refusal to pay attractive wages will mean that the industry continues to underperform. This is because, as service industry, its performance is largely determined by the quality of its workforce.

Despite our confirmation of the generally held view that the security industry in Australia is a 'low road' industry our preliminary findings did reveal a potentially intriguing avenue for further research. As we noted earlier, given the absence of attractive working conditions and direct managerial control it is perhaps surprising that the industry is as effective as it is. It has become fashionable in recent years to explain employee self-discipline as the internalization of the norms underlying things like performance measurement. Thus, there is less need for employees to be disciplined as *objects* of managerial control because they have become self-scrutinizing and self-regulating *subjects*. Hobbs et al. (2007), however, offer an alternative account of, what we called earlier, 'intrinsic motivation.' Based on extensive ethnographic work over many years, Hobbs and his colleagues have developed the view that security workers develop a distinctive *habitus* which, while not necessarily being edifying to outsiders, does form the basis for camaraderie and mutual obligation in the face of danger. Although Hobbs et al's research was conducted within one specialized community within the security industry – nightclub door staff or 'bouncers' – it is suggestive of an interesting possibility that we have underestimated an important normative and social dimension to security work which warrants further investigation.

References

Allen, John and Nick Henry 1997. "Ulrich Beck's Risk Society at Work." *Transactions of the Institute of British Geographers* (New Series), 22 (2): 180–196.

Anderson-Gough, Fiona, Christopher Grey, and Keith Robson 2000. "In the Name of the Client: the service ethic in two professional services firms." *Human Relations* 53 (9): 1151–1174.

Ashforth, Blake and Glen Kreiner 1999. "'How Can you Do It?' Dirty work and challenge of constructing a positive identity." *Academy of Management Review*, 24 (3): 413–434.

ABS. Australian Bureau of Statistics 2000. *Security Services: Australia*, Canberra: ABS.

ABS. Australian Bureau of Statistics 2006. *Year Book Australia, 2006* Canberra: ABS.

ABS. Australian Bureau of Statistics 2007. *Employee Earnings, Benefits and Trade Union Membership, August*, Canberra: ABS.

Barker, James R. 1993. "Tightening the Iron Cage: concertive control in self-managing teams." *Administrative Science Quarterly*, 38 (3): 408–437.

Briken, Kendra 2010. *Producing Insecurities: security work and labour precarization*. ISA World Congress, Gothenburg.

Giddens, Anthony 1999. "Risk and Responsibility." *Modern Law Review*, 62 (1):1–10.

Hardy, Samantha and Tim Prenzler 2002. "Legal Control of Private Investigators and Associated Private Agents." *Australian Journal of Law and Society*, 16 (1): 1–20.

Hobbs, Dick, Philip Hadfield, Stuart Lister, and Stuart Winlow 2003. *Bouncers: violence and governance in the night-time economy.* Oxford: Oxford University Press.

Hobbs, Dick, Philip Hadfield, Stuart Lister, and Stuart Winlow 2005. "Violence and governance in the night-time economy." *European Journal of Crime, Criminal Law and Criminal Justice,* 13 (1): 89–102.

Hobbs, Dick, Kate O'Brien, and Louise Westmarland 2007. "Connecting the Gendered Door: women, violence and doorwork." *British Journal of Sociology*, 58 (1): 21–38.

Kalleberg, Arne L., Barbara F. Reskin, and Ken Hudson 2000. "Bad Jobs in America: standard and nonstandard employment relations and job quality in the United States." *American Sociological Review*, 65 (2): 256–278.

Korczynski, Marek 2003. "Communities of Coping: collective emotional labour in service work." *Organisation*, 10 (1): 55–79.

Kreiner, Glen E., Blake E. Ashforth, and David M. Sluss 2006. "Identity Dynamics in Occupational Dirty Work: integrating social identity and system justification perspectives." *Organization Science,* 17 (5): 619–636.

Prenzler, Tim 2000. "The Privatisation of Policing." In: Rick Sarre and John Tomaino (eds.), *Considering Crime and Justice.* Adelaide: Crawford House: 267–296.

Prenzler, Tim 2005. "Mapping the Australian Security Industry." *Security Journal*, 18 (4): 51–64.

Prenzler, Tim and Rick Sarre 1999. "A Survey of Security Legislation and Regulatory Strategies in Australia." *Security Journal*, 12 (3), 7–17.

Prenzler, Tim, Karen Earle, and Rick Sarre 2009a. "Private security in Australia: trends and key characteristics." *Trends and Issues in Crime and Criminal Justice,* 374: 1–6.

Prenzler, Tim, Karen Earle, and Rick Sarre 2009b. *Private Security in Australia: trends and characteristics.* Canberra: Australian Institute of Criminology.

Prenzler, Tim and Rick Sarre 2007. "Private Police: Partners or Rivals?" In: Margaret Mitchell and John Casey (eds.), *Police Leadership and Management in Australia.* Sydney: Federation Press: 50–60.

Prenzler, Tim, Rick Sarre, and Karen Earle 2008. "Developments in the Australian Private Security Industry." *Flinders Journal of Law Reform*, 10 (3): 403–417.

Sarre, Rick and Tim Prenzler 2009. *The Law of Private Security in Australia*, 2nd edition, Pyrmont: Thomson Reuters.

Sarre, Rick and Tim Prenzler 2011. *Private Security and Public Interest*. Adelaide: University of South Australia.

Sengupta, Sukanya, Paul K. Edwards, and Tsai Chin-Ju 2009. "The Good, the Bad, and the Ordinary: work identities in 'good' and 'bad' jobs in the United Kingdom." *Work & Occupations*, 36 (1): 26–55.

Sewell, Graham 1998. "The Discipline of Teams: the control of team-based industrial work through electronic and peer surveillance." *Administrative Science Quarterly*, 43 (2): 397–428.

van Steden, Ronald and Rick Sarre 2010. "The tragic quality of contract guards: a discussion of the reach and theory of private security in the world today." *The Journal of Criminal Justice Research*, 1 (1): 1–19.

Thompson, Paul and Diane van den Broek 2010. "Managerial control and workplace regimes: an introduction." *Work, Employment and Society*, 24 (3): 1–12.

Townley, Barbara 1993. "Foucault, Power/Knowledge, and Its Relevance for Human Resource Management." *Academy of Management Review*, 18 (3): 518–545.

Wakefield, Alison 2008. "Private Policing: A View from the Mall." *Public Administration*, 86 (3): 659–678.

PRIVATE POLICING IN A NEOLIBERAL SOCIETY
THE NEW RELATION IN BRITAIN'S 'EXTENDED POLICE FAMILY'

Alison Wakefield

Through the 1980s and early 1990s, the United Kingdom's social democratic state was fundamentally reformed under Margaret Thatcher's Conservative government. The Conservatives resurrected ideas of economic liberalism to drive forward a distinctive 'neoliberal' agenda characterised by market liberalisation, deregulation, privatization, forms of public sector marketization, promoting the internationalization of markets and reducing direct taxation (Jessop, 2003). By 1995, McLaughlin and Murji (1995: 124) were to observe how market principles had become embedded in the culture of the country's public sector to the extent that "the image of the central or local state as the monolithic provider of all people's needs and wants is passing into distant memory." For the police, they argued, the development of internal or quasi-markets was promoting a "creeping privatisation" (ibid.: 125) associated with growing private sector involvement, the consolidation of policing functions and hiving off of certain tasks, and expanding community self-policing.

A subsequent Labour government maintained this trajectory with its own brand of neoliberalism, continuing much of what had been set in motion, but redirecting any savings in public spending towards a redistribution of income to the very poor, rather than tax reductions (Jessop, 2003). Jessop describes their stance as encompassing a very different conception of the problem of growing social polarisation and exclusion, that is, as an obstacle to economic growth, as opposed to a problem that economic growth would ameliorate. This led to a number of labour market reforms such as the introduction of a national minimum wage, a package of taxation and benefit reforms and social policy programmes to target poverty. Other distinctive features he identifies include an "enhanced disciplinary role for the state" (ibid.: 23), with respect to the public and private sectors and the citizenry, and in terms of which we might interpret a number of distinctive policy measures concerning public and private policing.

Since this process began, and with the Conservatives now back in power in the UK, the country's policing has been transformed, both in terms of how it is actually delivered, and importantly the wider social and political expectations of how this should be done. The country's 'neoliberalization' has relied on growing partnerships between the public and private sector, presenting substantial opportunities for a commercial security industry afforded a new degree of legitimacy through a number of key measures, most notably the introduction of a framework of statutory regulation. The purpose of this chapter is to review these changes with reference both to the changing political and policy context and the actual delivery of commercial security, in the latter case drawing on the author's empirical research to illuminate the distinctive features of 'private policing.' The discussion then turns to the current UK security context, in which the ongoing threat of terrorism has provided an important further *raison d'être* for private security, affording it an increasing role in the national security strategy.

Neoliberal policing in the UK

UK policing is distinctive when compared with other countries in the sheer extent to which it has been shaped by neoliberalization. Such policies have fallen short of outright privatization of operational policing, however, and such an outcome is unlikely: neoliberal societies rely on effective state agencies of security to ensure the wider social order is maintained, including the effective functioning of the capitalist system. Furthermore, police numbers have long been a politically charged issue in the UK and significant threats to police resources are considered an electoral liability. Yet the observations of McLaughlin and Murji (1995: 125) of a "creeping privatisation" echo Johnston's (1992: 51) earlier commentary on the government's "privatisation mentality" from the 1980s onwards, in which he identified three main ways in which neoliberal policy had already impacted significantly on policing by the time of writing.

The first of these Johnston referred to as 'load shedding,' as certain areas of policing came to be supplemented or replaced by commercial or voluntary provision. A central aspect of this was, he argued, the growing recourse of organisations and individuals to commercial security, but he also employed the term to include the active encouragement by police of third party provision. His examples ranged from police initiated Neighbourhood Watch schemes to situations whereby some police functions were effectively being 'usurped' by voluntary action such as street patrol initiatives. More substantial developments of this nature have occurred in the last decade, as a result of legislation introduced by the Labour government after 1997.

Statutory requirements to drive more active forms of partnership between the police and other agencies – primarily local authorities but extending to other stakeholders including the corporate sector – were put in place through the Crime and Disorder Act 1998, reflecting a new conviction at the heart of government that other public and private bodies had a greater role to play in local crime control. Subsequent to this, as detailed further below, the Private Security Industry Act 2001 afforded the commercial security sector the means to improve its credentials by legislating for a framework of statutory regulation for the industry. In the same year, a new acknowledgement that non-police operatives could play a more active role in policing began to be expressed by the government in talk of the 'extended police family' (Home Office, 2001), and provisions to facilitate this were enshrined in law through the Police Reform Act 2002. The most far-reaching aspect of this legislation was the creation of auxiliary, civilian patrollers known as 'police community support officers' (PCSOs), subsequently introduced in all UK police forces, and similar to the Dutch *politiesurveillanten* (police patrollers), reinforcing the message that there were acceptable alternatives to police officers. With specific regard to 'load shedding', the Act also granted authority to chief police officers to confer limited powers on third party operators (commercial security personnel or street wardens employed by local authorities) carrying out patrols in public places by means of what are known as Community Safety Accreditation Schemes. These were reported by the Home Office, the government department responsible for policing in England and Wales, to be present in 23 out of the 43 police forces in those regions by 2008.

The second trend identified by Johnston was the rise of 'contracting out' or outsourcing, whereby police forces enter into contracts with third parties to purchase goods or services. This has seen such practices extended from uncontroversial functions within the police organisation such as the procurement of goods ranging from stationery to police equipment, and of ancillary services such as cleaning, catering and maintenance, to 'back office' elements of policing, specifically custodial and prisoner escort services, and technically specialised areas including forensic services and information technology development and delivery. Such has been the scale of these developments that the UK is described in a report by the Confederation of European Security Services (CoESS, 2008) as a special case within Europe in the extent to which it has delegated public services to the private security sector. Notably, recent events in the UK have shifted the prevailing public mood towards privatisation from one of quiet acceptance, to disquiet over the prospect of its further substantial growth. Following the government's announcement in late 2010 that central government police funding would reduce by 20 per cent in real terms by 2014/15, two police forces, the West Midlands and Surrey, invited bids for the largest ever police outsourcing contract at a value of £1.5 billion (Guardian, 2012a), invoking a brief media storm in the spring of 2012. Surrey, however, suspended its plans a few months later following a considerable furor over G4S, the world's largest security company, which failed to meet the terms of its substantial contract to provide the security officers for the London Olympics, with respect primarily to the number but also the quality of personnel they were able to mobilise for such a large event (Guardian, 2012b).

Johnston's third category covers the levying of charges for certain police services that can be sold to other public and private sector organisations. One element of this is the sale of patrol services (now including the cheaper option of PCSOs) to other public institutions such as local authorities, or commercial operators of public venues such as football clubs and shopping malls. Permissible since the Police Act 1964, today such a practice sees the police effectively engaging in active competition with other service providers such as local authority wardens or commercial security personnel. Also distinctive in the UK's 'extended police family' is the financing of the British Transport Police, responsible for the policing of the railways and underground rail systems, provided mainly through the charges for its services made to the private franchises of the rail network.

Outright privatization of the police, the transfer of government owned assets or services to private companies either wholly or in part (Wakefield and Prenzler, 2009), looks likely to remain the stuff of fantasy and fiction, the 1987 film *Robocop* offering a dystopian vision of neoliberal measures taken to extremes at a time when such policies were gaining momentum in the US under Reagan's presidency. Yet, as Tim Prenzler and I have previously argued, a *de facto* privatization of policing can nonetheless be seen in the UK and elsewhere, which has driven a revolution in the structure and delivery of contemporary policing (Wakefield and Prenzler, 2009). This has occurred largely through rising demand for private security, resulting in the sector's phenomenal growth. Such expansion can be attributed not only to political developments but to a host of social and economic forces, including increasing prosperity, with more private property and consumer goods to protect; an accompanying rise in crime in many countries, especially from the 1970s to the 1990s; the expansion of privately controlled, publicly accessible spaces ranging from hypermarkets to airports; a general growth in the sub-contracting of security functions within both the public and private sectors to limit spending and gain from the economies of scale achieved by specialist providers; and increased safety concerns on the part of companies, public institutions and private individuals. All of these factors have promoted a growing governmental and social acceptance of private security, as it has become increasingly recognized that the commercial sector has a role to play in the security of citizens and organizations, and the British government has taken steps to support this. At the same time, a growing security sector has been able to develop products and services better tailored to the needs of its customers, capitalizing on benefits ranging from economies of scale to technological advancement. As we have previously asserted, these developments are a key element of a more general, worldwide trend whereby law enforcement and crime prevention services are expanding and diversifying (Wakefield and Prenzler, 2009).

The UK security sector

Partnerships between government bodies and other agencies are a fundamental aspect of neoliberal policy as a means of 'doing more with less', and the term itself has become a buzzword in UK government policy. One example is the 'public private partnership' (PPP), an explicit policy area with its own dedicated team in Her Majesty's Treasury tasked with supporting joint working between the public and private sector to deliver policies, services and infrastructure, and promoting private sector investment in public provision through a Private Finance Initiative (PFI). In UK policing, partnership takes many forms and is becoming ever more a priority in the contemporary security environment, discussed later on, with the corporate sector and commercial security industry expanding their role in wider national and local security arrangements.

The commercial security industry's relationship with government and the police has not always run smoothly in the UK. Despite their commitment to promoting private enterprise, successive Conservative governments resisted calls from industry bodies such as the British Security Industry Association (BSIA) for the establishment of a statutory system of regulation. From their perspective, this was necessary to improve service quality and thus the industry's legitimacy, enhancing opportunities for growth as well as driving out some of the competition from the lower charging, less scrupulous operators. Such demands were, however, incompatible with the government's political preferences for *de*regulation, and for the industry to manage its own self-regulatory system. Yet in the absence of statutory regulation, the industry remained especially vulnerable to media criticisms about poor operating standards on occasions when cases of poor practice or criminal behaviour came to light, and able to do little to challenge concerns, while there were a number of cases through the 1990s of senior police officers publicly denouncing the sector.

The situation began to change after the Labour government gained power in 1997, the Party's support for a regulatory system having long been championed by the senior MP Bruce George, and complementing the wider package of policing and criminal justice reforms that were introduced over a five year period. Labour's longstanding commitment to the statutory regulation of commercial security was delivered in the passing of the Private Security Industry Act 2001, which allowed for the creation of a new regulatory framework for the industry through the establishment of a Security Industry Authority (SIA). This brought the UK more into line with the rest of Europe, being one of the last European countries, along with Greece and Ireland, to introduce such a system (cf. de Waard, 1993, 1999; CoESS, 2008) while as Eick (*this volume*) outlines, Cyprus, Austria and Germany still lack specific legislation.

The SIA framework is based primarily around the licensing of individuals employed by contract security companies, a process that began with the issuing of security guarding licences in 2005, and extended to the cash-in-transit, close protection, door supervision, public space (closed circuit television) surveillance, key holding and vehicle immobilization sectors. The SIA also requires those employing, managing or supervising licensable personnel to hold 'non-front line' licences. Licences are awarded on the basis of applicants achieving specified training qualifications, coupled with evidence of a clean or minimal criminal record, with decision making in the latter case being based on the time passed since sentence restrictions have ended, number of convictions and seriousness of offence(s). There is also a voluntary Approved Contractor Scheme for companies operating in the industry sectors regulated by the SIA, following a similar approach to that employed by industry associations the BSIA and the International Professional Security Association (IPSA) in the preceding era of industry self-regulation. This involves the assessment of such elements of company practice as 'fit and proper' organisation and management, the company's complaints record, and the percentage of deployed personnel holding a licence. Individuals whose applications have been accepted and are being processed by the SIA are allowed to be deployed, but a majority of a company's personnel being fully licensed is deemed an indication of a more proficient and stable workforce. The SIA does not regulate the in-house security sector, which has so far been deemed to present no substantiated risk to the public, while presenting significant resource implications should it be included in the regulatory arrangements since it is estimated that up to five million further licences would be required (SIA, 2009: 7). Plans to extend licensing to the private investigations sector are, at the time of writing, on hold, with the UK's current regulatory framework now being reassessed in the current fiscal climate. A forum of key security industry bodies, the Security Alliance, recently formed to establish a collective voice in favour of continued statutory regulation and formulate proposals for a new solution, and this new body is actively engaged with the SIA in reviewing options for the future.

As previously noted, and as the leading stakeholders in the commercial security industry had wanted, the Labour government reforms contributed to a widening social acceptance in the UK that the private sector has an active role to play in the delivery of security. Consequently, the UK's commercial security industry has continued to grow and evolve. Although it is difficult to estimate the industry's scale with any great accuracy, both nationally and globally, four years ago the UK's security industry was estimated to have a net worth of between £3 billion and £4 billion per annum and to be experiencing continued growth (CIPD, 2007: 4). The BSIA (2012a) more recently claimed that the total turnover of its member companies, reported to supply 70 per cent of UK security products and services, is £4.33 billion.

What might be termed 'security goods and services companies,' represent the most substantial as well as visible sector of the commercial security industry. These are companies selling manned and/or physical security goods and services, as summarised in Table 1. They tend to be multi-functional and indeed the larger security goods and services companies are increasingly becoming 'one stop shops' for security products and services, G4S (2008) for example having expanded its business into developing markets with the 2008 purchase of Armorgroup, capitalising on the growing market for security in hazardous environments. Today there are few functions undertaken by police forces that the commercial security industry does not also fulfil.

Table 1: Services provided by the security goods and services sector

Cash handling services	Cash-in-transit (CIT)	ATM maintenance
	Cash processing	
Crowd management	Event security	Door supervision
Electronic security	Alarms	Closed circuit television (CCTV)
	Access control	
Guarding	Static	Security checks
	Mobile	Close protection
	Reception	Alarm response
	Key holding	
Information security	ICT security	Document security
	ID security	
Monitoring and alarm receiving	Alarm receiving (and dispatching)	
	Electronic surveillance and positioning	
	Operational remote control	
	Guard safety control	
	CIT remote control	
Physical and mechanical security	Locks	Lighting
	Barriers	Safes
	Seals	Strong rooms/vaults
Security consultancy and training		

Source: adapted from Hakala (2010)

It is, however, what is known as the 'manned guarding' sector of the industry, and its growing profile as well as scale, that most visibly demonstrates the industry's growing ubiquity, with commercial security officers now a common sight in the UK protecting communal and corporate spaces alongside their police counterparts. The BSIA (2012a) claims that the total annual turnover for its member companies in the guarding sector is £1.58 billion, although in practice it is impossible to distinguish clearly between the guarding companies and other market sectors, given the wide range of security products and services being offered by many firms in response to the growing market for integrated security solutions. Today's so-called guarding companies range from small, locally oriented firms through to the global operators, the largest of which are the Swedish firm Securitas, operating in 50 countries and dominating the US and European markets (Securitas, 2012), and the Anglo-Danish firm G4S (2012), which operates in a wider spread of countries, stated to number over 125 at the time of writing.

Pan-European research has demonstrated that market dynamics differ considerably from country to country. One means of comparison is the size of private security workforces, measured in a 2004 study by CoESS and Uni-Europa (a European trade union federation) and summarised by CoESS (2008: 22). It was estimated that, on average, 237 security personnel can be found in Europe for every 100,000 inhabitants. Yet the ratio varies markedly, with six of the 25 member states belonging to the EU in 2004 (there are now 27) having ratios above 350, Hungary's ratio being exceptionally high at 791, and Poland falling second at 524. Conversely, five countries were found to have ratios below 120, including Denmark (97), Italy (95) and Austria (83). The ratio for the UK was found to be fairly average, at 251, although it is observed that these differences are difficult to explain other than as a result of market dynamics in each country, since there are no apparent patterns relating to national cultures or policies. There are similarly wide variations in the numbers of police officers per head in different European countries but no clear relationship between the two sets of figures can be discerned: for example, in those three countries with the lowest numbers of security personnel per head, the number of police officers per head was estimated at 194 in Denmark, 562 in Italy and 333 in Austria (ibid.: 24).

The delivery of private policing

In police studies and the wider criminological discipline, interest in commercial security has tended to concentrate on activities traditionally associated with the police that are today increasingly being delivered by a growing manned guarding industry, as well as piecemeal elements of private security that raise particular controversies. Thus, security products and services such as open space CCTV monitoring, gated communities or armed private security may reflect the inevitable inequalities associated with an increasingly market based system in relation to citizens' personal feelings of security and insecurity, their access to security measures, or their experiences on the receiving end of others' security procedures. Notably, those most likely to experience genuine insecurity are least likely to be able to afford the measures that will protect them, while inhabiting a social position that places them under greater levels of scrutiny and control by public and private security interventions alike. Other concerns have related to the standards of service prevailing in what remains a sector of low profit margins, and the industry's failure to prevent occasional instances of outright criminality (cf. Wakefield, 2003); or wholesale discomfort about private bodies being allowed to deliver policing related services without substantial oversight by public authorities, associated with an intrinsic belief that policing should be conceived as a public good (Loader and Walker, 2001).

Some of these issues were the initial motivating factors behind an ethnographic study of private policing that I commenced in the UK just prior to the election of a Labour government in 1997 (Wakefield, 2003, 2008). In the absence of much empirical research into private security at that time, the research contributed a detailed insight into its objectives and operating practices in three research settings. It generated findings that remain relevant today despite the subsequent policy changes detailed above and other developments in the political and economic environment. The study drew on case studies of security provision at three publicly accessible, commercial facilities in England, selected as being typical of the private security interventions that many of us, and particularly those of us residing in urban areas, routinely encounter in our daily lives.

The first of the research sites I referred to as the 'Arts Plaza,' was a cultural centre in a major city that housed visual and performing arts facilities as well as restaurants and bars.

The second was the 'Quayside Centre,' a large shopping centre situated in a northern coastal town. The third, the 'City Mall,' was a retail and leisure complex located in a northern urban centre, containing retail outlets for daytime shopping, as well as pubs, restaurants and nightclubs. The methodology combined a total of 60 days' observations whereby I accompanied the security personnel in the course of their work (20 days at each site); 59 semi-structured interviews with many of the security officers, management personnel from the centres and the security companies that supplied the officers, and representatives of the local police forces; and the analysis of supporting documents such as duty sheets and log books that related to the observation periods. The research findings, outlined in more detail elsewhere (Wakefield, 2003, 2006, 2008), highlighted many of the distinctive features of private policing, covering its objectives, organisation, image, functions, working conditions and accountability. These six elements are discussed in turn.

OBJECTIVES

There are fundamental differences between the police and private security which frame their respective objectives in terms of the masters they serve and the territorial, functional and legal scope of their mandates, but for many it is the symbolic role of the police that distinguishes it from private security and other alternative policing bodies (cf. Loader and Walker, 2001). For Manning (1997: 319), for example, policing by the police "is an exercise in symbolic demarking of what is immoral, wrong, and outside the boundaries of acceptable conduct." Thus, "It represents the state, morality and standards of civility and decency by which we judge ourselves" (ibid.) Private security objectives, by contrast, emanate from contractual relationships determining the instrumental needs of those purchasing security services.

At the three centres in the study, management representatives were asked to describe the objectives underpinning the deployment of security personnel. For the manager of the City Mall, these were, quite simply, "to protect the company's property," while at the other two centres a greater emphasis was placed on satisfying the needs of the customer, where the duties of the security personnel were tied in more explicitly with the broader commercial objectives of the organizations. The deputy manager of the Quayside Centre explained:

> The public is our key thing, I mean, making sure they have an enjoyable time. If it means changing security directives and doesn't mean it's going to endanger anyone else whatsoever, we will quickly change them.

In all three cases, unsurprisingly, the security personnel delivered a service whose very character was driven by the 'end user' (as the purchaser or client is more commonly known in the trade within the UK), oriented towards the commercial objectives of the business, and quickly adaptable to the requirements of the marketplace.

ORGANIZATION
Similarities between the police and private security were more apparent in aspects of their organizational arrangements: the hierarchical structures of the contract security companies supplying security officers at two of the three sites, and the organization of the work by means of shift systems. The personnel at the Arts Plaza and the Quayside Centre were supplied by contract security companies, with the exception of the control room staff at the Quayside Centre who were employed 'in-house,' while the City Mall team were all directly employed by the property company that owned the Mall. Their end users saw contracting as a significantly cheaper way of gaining a similar service, as the deputy manager of the Quayside Centre explained:

> The advantage [of contracting] is very simple, I mean we've seen it ... so many times where companies like Birds Eye, ICI ... had in-house security ... but at the end of the day when they had to get rid of them there

were gatehouse guardsmen earning £21,000 a year because their pay rise and incentive had to be linked with what was on the factory, and then they realized they could call in a company and get it for eight thousand a year, for the same benefits.

The organizational structure underpinning contract security at the Arts Plaza and the Quayside Centre differed considerably to the in-house arrangements at the City Mall. Similar to a police or military organization, each of the contract security firms was hierarchical in structure and, depending on the size of the contract, these companies could supply end users with teams of personnel comprising up to five operational 'ranks' headed by a 'site manager.' The organization of personnel in this way possibly reflected the transition of many police and military personnel into the industry (Shearing et al., 1980) and thus the influence of these sectors on private security, exemplified in the fact that the managing directors of both companies had pursued prior careers in the police service, as had their site managers at the Arts Plaza and the Quayside Centre.

The research also highlighted the way in which, in common with police work, time plays an important role in structuring security work by means of a shift system, an approach that 'tends to bind officers together' (Holdaway, 1983: 116).

The police 'relief' system in the UK, described in early ethnographies by Banton (1964) and Holdaway (1983), involves teams of officers rotating through a pattern of 'early,' 'late' and 'night' shifts and rest days of approximately seven to nine hours in length, as part of a forty hour working week (PA Consulting Group, 2001). As outlined in detail below, the daily and weekly working hours of the security personnel varied between the centres and between contract and in-house security work, but similarly revolved around teams of officers operating on rotating shift patterns.

IMAGE

Another relevant feature of private policing was the officers' uniforms (or 'working clothes' from the perspective of continental European readers, for whom the word 'uniform' is associated with sovereign power), because they appeared to have an association with the officer's demeanour and the character of the service being delivered. Holdaway's (1983) police ethnography introduced the concept of 'body territory' conveyed through the police uniform, which he portrayed as drawing attention to the taboos associated with touching a police officer. This has pertinence to security work, since uniform *style* appeared to be a contributing factor in the manner of policing adopted. At the Arts Plaza and the Quayside Centre, the management team had opted to replace the police-style security uniforms previously issued in favour of less formal 'blazers and slacks,' designed to make the security officers appear more approachable to visitors as part of the emphasis on 'customer care' at these centres:

> ... the customers, we were aware, didn't like the official 'I'm nearly a policeman' look, so we actually changed image totally at the beginning of this year into blazers and slacks. Up until then that look was ideal because the Centre was quite wild ... and now it's all calmed down ... you can bring the image down into the softer look ... people come up and talk to them quite happily when they didn't before ... (deputy manager, Quayside Centre)

The growing preference for more casual uniforms for customer facing security officers has been conveyed in the UK's two main trade publications in subsequent years, reporting guarding companies to be 'chucking out their tunics and peaked caps and going casual' (Info4security, 2000; cf. Info4security, 2002, 2004), while later articles refer to a wider range of styles including high visibility jackets employed in car parks and town centres (Professional Security, 2006, 2007, 2009). Yet at the time of the research the City Mall officers retained the more authoritarian looking 'police-style' uniforms, including tunics and peaked caps, and this demeanour fitted with their more detached style of policing. At intervals during their patrols, the security officers positioned themselves on the Mall's mezzanine balcony to oversee the public from a distance, as though seeking to deter troublemakers rather than welcome and assist customers. While always willing to respond to customer queries, their apparent constructions of 'body territory' through uniform and manner were very different to the approach employed at the other centres, allowing them to preserve their personal space.

WORKING CONDITIONS

My fieldwork was conducted just before 1998 when the UK implemented a national minimum wage, which has had a positive impact on wage levels in the lower paying regions of the country (at the time of writing, £6.08 per hour for workers aged 21 or over),[84] as well as the European Union Working Time Regulations limiting the working week to 48 hours. The latter policy change has had less impact on the commercial security sector since employees commonly sign a declaration opting out of the directive in order to make up their weekly wages (Professional Security, 2008). For the contract security officers in the study, their earnings were low and their hours were long. The hourly wages of the London-based contract security personnel at the Arts Plaza at the time of the case studies was £5.11, while at the Quayside Centre, located in a northern region of the country with much lower average wage levels, the contract security staff and in-house security staff received £3.50 and around £5.00 respectively. The wage at the City Mall, also in the north of England, was £5.10, and these in-house employees received 50 per cent additional pay for each hour of overtime and 100 per cent extra for hours worked on public holidays.

---

84   £1.00, by the time of writing, equals U$1.56 and €1.19, respectively.

Security officers at each of the centres reported that their wage rates exceeded local averages for the security industry, although they differed in their perceptions as to whether the reward levels were fair. One pertinent complaint was made by an officer from the Quayside Centre, who argued that their pay did not reflect the dangers that the security officers faced in their day-to-day roles: 'It's really bad with shoplifters, fights, you get a fight every day and you can get hurt and that, and for £3.50 an hour it's rubbish.' Her view was shared by an officer from the City Mall, who argued for more pay on the grounds that '... the violence means we're practically police without badges.'

Notably there were no fringe benefits for contract security officers. A director from the security company employed at the Arts Plaza acknowledged:

> ... until the individual reaches or completes his first year, his terms and conditions of employment don't really improve that much. I am talking about holiday pay and so on – you are working in an industry where there is no sick pay or guaranteed sick pay. We all base ourselves on, and I speak for the majority here, statutory sick pay conditions.

At the City Mall, by contrast, the more generous wage levels were supplemented by sick pay, three weeks' paid holiday, free parking, company pension arrangements and shares in the company after a year's service.

The hours of employment at all three centres were structured around shift systems, although the arrangements varied. Most of the security officers at the Arts Plaza performed 12-hour day and night shifts with shift changes at 7am and 7pm, working an average of 60 hours per week. In addition, a number of officers covered the public opening hours on 11am to 11pm shifts, working up to seven days a week. Many of the security officers on the day shift were the transient workers, seeking to save as much money as possible, and therefore usually grateful for the extra time.

At the Quayside Centre, the security officers who patrolled the malls worked an average of 50 hours per week made up of ten- and 12-hour shifts. The in-house control room staff worked fewer weekly hours, with the supervisor performing a 40 hour week of eight to four shifts, and his two colleagues working blocks of five 12-hour day shifts and averaging 42 hours a week. At the City Mall, the four officers on the day shift worked 40-hour weeks and took turns in carrying out additional Sunday shifts, while the night security officers performed 13-hour shifts in three-day blocks interspersed with three rest days, working an average of 40 hours a week. There was, therefore, a marked difference in the total working hours of the security officers at the three sites, with the in-house employees at the Quayside Centre and City Mall working considerably fewer hours than their counterparts in contract security, in which overall working conditions were considerably more challenging.

ACCOUNTABILITY MECHANISMS

Stenning (2000) argues that the mechanisms of account-ability for private security are more extensive and complex than the security industry has often been given credit for (South 1988; Johnston 1992; George and Button 1994, 2000; Button 1998), made up of a host of processes laid down by the industry itself, the security companies and the end users, as well as informal processes related to the commercial priorities associated with their roles (such as comments and complaints from visitors to the centres). The contract security companies delivering services to the Arts Plaza and the Quayside Centre were accredited by means of the system of self-regulation that was the only basis for standard setting in the UK industry prior to the implemen-tation of a statutory regulatory framework, its parameters including minimum standards in the vetting and training of contract security staff and the general operating standards of the company. The former are set out in the British Standards Institution (BSI) standards BS 7499 (code of practice for static guarding, mobile patrol and key holding services) and BS 7858 (code of practice for security screening of personnel employed in a security environment), and the latter in International Standards Organisation standard ISO 9002 (quality management), with companies inspected and accredited by bodies such as the Inspectorate of the Security Industry (now the National Security Inspectorate). Compliance with such standards was, and still remains, a condition of membership of the primary trade associations for the UK security industry, the BSIA, which claims to represent over 70 per cent of the UK security market (BSIA, 2012b), and IPSA.

The insurance policies of the security companies (e.g. public liability insurance, employers' liability insurance) provided a further check on their employee vetting, while placing constraints on the actions of the security personnel, who were covered for accident in the line of duty only within the confines of the centres. The absence of such restrictions on the recruitment and training practices for the in-house staff members at the Quayside Centre and City Mall (who continue to fall outside the current regime of statutory regu-lation) was a potential area for concern, particularly for the personnel at the City Mall who patrolled among members of the public, since there was scope for the passing on of misin-formation and bad habits from one officer to the next. The better working conditions of the in-house security personnel were likely to have had a positive effect on staff loyalty and standards of working, however, perhaps reflected in the ten or more years' service of four of the ten men employed at the City Mall. The management and disciplinary structures for the security personnel at each site provided another layer of oversight, extending for example to controls on the storage and use of closed circuit television (CCTV) footage (at the time of the research there was no explicit legisla-tion or regulation in the UK governing the use of CCTV or those operating such systems, only governmental guide-lines). It should also be recognised that the high visibility of their work placed the security personnel under continuous informal scrutiny – from members of the public, the staff employed in tenant companies such as shops and bars in the three centres, and other staff members within the client organisations, as well as the gaze of the CCTV cameras, so that the combined range of checks on their actions was extensive. A final constraining factor for the contract security companies was the pressure of competition – should they not be seen to be doing a good job by the purchaser of their services, they could readily be replaced after the next tender process.

Yet despite their breadth, it should be emphasised that these various formal and informal accountability processes served primarily to protect the end user as opposed to the visitors to the centres who might form targets for policing. While, by operating in the public eye, the opportunities for malpractice by security personnel were limited, there were no formal means of redress for visitors to the centres who might have complaints about their treatment: these would need to be resolved informally by the end users, at their own discretion. Subsequent to the research, a web based reporting system for illegal activity by private security operatives has been implemented by the SIA. With respect to CCTV, measures that have since been put in place to promote responsible use of such systems comprise specific legislation within the Data Protection Act 1998, a *CCTV Code of Practice* (Information Commissioner's Office 2008) and the licensing of public space surveillance operatives. Such regulation remains minimal, however, and proposals to extend it are, at the time of writing, being considered in a new Protection of Freedoms Bill.

FUNCTIONS
Banton's (1964: 21) early ethnography of the police drew attention to the heterogeneity of police work. Recording tasks in the police officer's daily routine as diverse as serving a summons, "receiving a wallet that someone found," "collecting particulars about a motor accident" and responding to "a complaint about a dog barking at night" (ibid.: 25), he observed, "One of the most striking features

of this account is the great variety of tasks performed by policemen" (ibid.). The observation periods at the three research sites revealed a similar diversity of tasks undertaken by the security personnel in the course of their continuous patrols of the buildings, or their monitoring from control rooms of cameras and radio communications. These tasks, detailed in Wakefield (2003), were divided into six categories that embodied the core functions of the security personnel in the three centres:

- 'Housekeeping' (helping to maintain safe and well-kept environments within the buildings in a similar way to a caretaker);
- 'Customer care' (serving as contact points for customers needing assistance);
- 'Preventing crime and anti-social behaviour' (consisting of preventative patrols or escorting of staff, as well as the monitoring of the visiting public);
- 'Enforcing rules, and administering sanctions' (telling people to desist from prohibited behaviours and asking non-compliers to leave);
- 'Responding to [crime and non-crime] emergencies and offences in progress'; and
- 'Gathering and sharing information' (including CCTV recording and report-writing).

In spite of the acknowledged differences in emphasis and style of security across the three centres, there were few variations in the nature and range of guarding duties that were carried out. It was evident that the multi-faceted roles of the security personnel had as many similarities with the work of a warden or caretaker as that of the patrolling police constable, and involved much more than simply 'policing.' The first two functions reflected an emphasis on keeping the buildings safe and providing a comfortable and welcoming environment for the visiting public, highlighting the mundane aspects of security as well as its association with commercial interests. The customer care function in particular emphasized how even the most obscure of tasks could be assigned to the security officer if they served the purpose of keeping customers satisfied, with security personnel routinely being diverted to such activities as fetching wheelchairs or even – at the Quayside Centre – donning a padded bear costume and entertaining visiting children. A similar practice was evident in my subsequent research with Martin Gill into the use of retail security officers, in which the diversion of security officers to retail tasks such as shelf stacking was found to be commonplace, and viewed by participants as undermining their effectiveness in delivering security (Wakefield and Gill, 2009).

The rest of the functions, associated more closely with the officers' 'policing' role, illustrate their preventative approach to the activity, involving concentrated surveillance by means of foot patrol and CCTV monitoring, and a readiness to respond instantly to any signs of disorder, crime or non-crime emergency. Their ability to do was made possible by the legal rights they held (as bestowed by the property owners) to impose the instant sanction of exclusion against any perceived miscreants, so that the problems of crime and disorder could be displaced outside the boundaries of the centres. Elsewhere (Wakefield, 2000, 2003), I discuss the manner in which this was undertaken, and the wider implications of such exclusion from communal spaces. Notably, at the time of the research, only the Arts Plaza placed a significant emphasis on countering terrorism within its wider policing objectives but, as discussed below, this has become a much more prominent aspect of private security in the UK in a post 9/11 environment.

SUMMARY

The empirical research offers a valuable insight into how commercial objectives shape the day-to-day delivery of private policing, as well as its similarities and differences when compared with state provision. Even before statutory regulation was introduced in the UK, it substantiated Stenning's (2000) observations that private security is in many ways more accountable than commonly thought, particularly in communal spaces where individual workers are especially visible. Yet it also highlighted the challenging working conditions in the guarding sector that have only improved marginally with the UK's implementation of a national minimum wage, a factor that is bound to limit professional standards far more than the absence of an effective regulatory framework.

The new security context

It is clear that private policing has flourished in the UK in the thirty years of neoliberal policy, and shaken off much of the widespread social concern about its practices that was present in the 1990s. In the future the private sector is likely to cement its position in policing still further: the social and economic forces that have promoted its expansion show no sign of abating, while global events in the new millennium have heralded a new era of security in which established assumptions about the undesirability of private interests playing such a significant part may have to be put to one side.

Terrorism is not a new problem for the British, our nation having operated in the shadow of the IRA campaign for many years and continuing to face a threat from dissi- dent groups. Yet 9/11, the 7/7 bombings of the London Underground and buses (2005) and the ongoing threat of Al Qaeda-inspired terrorism has ensured that measures to counter an increasingly sophisticated and brutal terrorist threat will be a national priority for the foreseeable future. Many of its typically mass casualty, civilian targets have been corporate assets, including the World Trade Center, major hotels and airlines. The threat of terrorism to the corporate world is illustrated in figures from the US State Department indicating that 85 per cent of the world's terrorist attacks are against the private sector (cited in Briggs, 2005: 13). In a study by Briggs and Edwards (2006: 28), 9/11 was seen to have served as "an important turning point in corpo- rate security" that "focused minds, worried staff and made boards ask questions about how their security was being managed."

The terrorist threat is listed as the first of four primary risks to the UK in the country's national security strategy (HM Government, 2010), in which the importance of a multi-faceted response underpinned by international alliances and partnerships, as well as national and local level collaborations, is heavily stressed throughout the document. One key dimension of this, it is noted, is the government's relationship with the corporate world: the strategy emphasises the need to "take account of the activities of others: the positive contributions of allies and partners and of the private sector" (ibid.: 10). This is seen to be critical not only with respect to terrorism, and the need to protect corporate targets, but with regard to all types of emergencies that may affect the national critical infrastructure, so that the country is not only "prepared" for the unexpected, but also "able to recover from shocks and to maintain essential services" (ibid.: 33). Briggs (2005) points out how, as a result of neoliberal economic policies from the 1980s onwards, the nation has become much more reliant on the private sector in order to function effectively. Much of what is has come to be termed the 'critical infrastructure' in a post 9/11 world – its essential utilities, such as gas, electricity and water – was under state ownership until a comprehensive privatisation programme was introduced by Margaret Thatcher's Conservative government. Since that time, we have become more reliant on other services that are primarily controlled by the private sector and underpinned by information technology, such as electronic money transfer and communication. As a result, in the delivery of national security, as Briggs (2005: 16) observes, "What was once a relatively straightforward system now requires the coordination of many hundreds of organisations across public and private sectors and across different parts of the economy."

It is now well recognised that today's interconnected world is inhabited by diverse and complex risks that defy national and agency boundaries, and that partnership working has become a critical aspect of the delivery of security. The UK's national security architecture is therefore adapting in a number of ways. The restructuring is occurring less visibly than in the United States, which responded to the 9/11 attacks and the prospect of future threats by establishing a new central government department, the Department of Homeland Security, as a means of improving co-ordination across the country of statutory agencies and other actors playing a part in protecting the nation. In the UK, among the new structures and strategies to engage the private sector are the Centre for the Protection of National Infrastructure, an inter-departmental body reporting into the Security Service, with a mission to disseminate security information to businesses, and Project Griffin, a police-led initiative that involves the public and private sectors working more actively together. This was launched by the City of London and Metropolitan Police forces in 2004, bringing the police together with local authorities, corporate security, the emergency services and other stakeholders to deter and detect terrorism and crime, and work together in the event of a serious threat or emergency. Since its launch, the Project has been extended around the country, and the model exported to a number of other countries, including Canada and Australia. Its approach is to train private security officers to provide their own companies with better protection against terrorism, as well as to assist the police and other organisations through information sharing and securing cordons in the event of an emergency (City of London Police, 2012).

Stenning (1989) presented a typology of reactions by the Canadian police service to the growth of private security, presenting seven distinguishable stages which can equally be applied to the British situation. Progressing through (1) 'denial,' (2) 'grudging recognition,' (3) 'competition and open hostility,' (4) 'calls for greater controls,' (5) 'mutual suspicion and ambivalence,' (6) 'active partnership,' and (7) 'equal partnership,' it can be said that the shift towards stage six is getting increasingly close with ventures such as Project Griffin coming to be recognised as an important dimension to the country's national security. At the time of writing, however, the UK's new Conservative government has been vague in its position with respect to the relationship between the police and private security. One of their early green papers, setting out a new vision for policing, commented overtly only on the need to enhance co-operation with the community (as opposed to the corporate) sector, plans to allow more flexibility in inter-agency partnership working by removing regulations about its format, and the possibility of elevating such collaboration to a force-wide level (Home Office, 2010).

A useful insight into current and prospective future relations between the two sectors is provided in a study by Gill et al. (2010), in which the authors emphasise the growing size and status of private security, and today's mounting challenges for policing, ranging from countering terrorism to planning the security for the 2012 London Olympics. Their efforts to explore the barriers and opportunities to effective partnership working comprised a literature review, interviews with 43 representatives of police and police-related organisations (including 32 at assistant chief constable level or above) and 25 representatives of the corporate and commercial security sectors, and an online survey of police superintendents.

Their research suggested that there is a lack of mutual understanding between the police and business community, the former prioritising the prevention, detection and prosecution of crime, and the latter treating crime as a risk to be managed to the degree and in the manner that makes most economic sense, even if this allows a certain amount of crime to be tolerated. The study participants emphasised the need for better quality interactions between the two sectors to enhance understanding and trust, and allow for better sharing of resources and expertise.

With respect to relations between the police and the commercial security sector, it is similarly suggested that a better police understanding of its private sector counterparts needs to be fostered if the police are to make more effective use of them. This aspect of the research, summarised in Table 2, focused on the possibilities for more police outsourcing of functions to the private sector, and uncovered a range of barriers relating to the types of role that might be suitable, lack of knowledge about the capabilities of the private sector as well as its regulation, concern about the possible threat to policing associated with its profit-making orientation, and lack of police confidence in how to undertake effective procurement (Gill et al., 2010: 112-118).

Table 2: Barriers and opportunities to policing partnerships

Barriers	Opportunities
• *Lack of leadership from official bodies such as the Association of Chief Police Officers and the BSIA on the opportunities, benefits and methods of closer working;* • *Lack of accountability/regulation of the private security industry and lack of awareness of the current regulation regime;* • *Concern about the differing principles under-pinning public and private security, and how these could be reconciled in an outsourcing arrangement;* • *The nature of front-line policing (emergency response, patrolling and investigation) not seen to be conducive to outsourcing;* • *Resistance to reducing police numbers associated with public relations and national resilience requirements;* • *Shortage of the necessary business skills to develop and manage contracts, with civilianisation perceived as an easier option than outsourcing;* • Reservations about the skills, competence and capacity of the private security industry to deliver the required level of service; • *A lack of case study or evaluation evidence that outsourcing provides value for money*	• Efficiency drives in the public sector (with the possibility of greater police outsourcing of functions to the private sector); • Support for closer partnership working; • Workforce modernisation initiatives promoting more openness to alternatives to full time police officers; • Building on the success of sub-contracting in areas such as IT support, custody suites and security of police stations to extend this to other areas

Source: own account

The report's authors see scope for much more effective partnership working between the two sectors. They relate this not only to the new crime and security imperatives referred to above, but also to the pressures on police forces associated with continued rising demand for service, and the need to find new efficiencies in the face of reductions in public spending. Their recommendations propose some of the steps needing to be taken for the UK's police to move closer to realising Stenning's (1989) sixth stage of acceptance of private security more fully, and to shift a step closer to that of 'equal partnership.'

Conclusion

'Neoliberalization' has had a profound impact on policing in the UK in many ways, the growing profile of private policing being a significant element of this process. It has been shown how, despite the neoliberal agenda having taken shape in Thatcher's Conservative government in the 1980s and early 1990s, it has been under a Labour regime that the commercial security industry has been able to establish the wider political and social legitimacy it enjoys today, and achieve a significant and accepted presence within what has come to be regarded as the 'extended police family.' With the country now in the control of a Conservative government once again, it is unlikely that this tide will turn, and the contribution the private sector must play in helping to protect the nation in today's more complex threat environment is being increasingly acknowledged. Events of 2012, namely the controversial announcement by two police forces of a £1.5 billion outsourcing contract, and the failure by G4S to meet the terms of its substantial guarding contract for the London Olympics, have had a negative impact on social attitudes to privatisation. It remains the case, however, that financial austerity measures could well lead to further recourse to outsourcing and partnership working by police in the drive to 'do more with less.'

What is perhaps most notable about the picture in the UK, then, is the degree of public and political acceptance of the substantial private sector penetration of policing that has occurred under successive governments. Yet a matter of significant concern that continually escapes notice is the challenging working conditions in the lower ranks of commercial security, characterised by long hours and low pay in a sector of intense competition and low profit margins. Given their growing presence in the communal spaces of Britain's cities, at a time when national security concerns are substantial and security workers' commitment to their task has never been more important, improving the prospects for, and in turn the calibre of, workers in the manned guarding sector needs to remain one of the priorities for the British security industry's development.

References

Banton, Michael 1964. *The Policeman in the Community*. London: Tavistock.

Briggs, Rachel 2005. *Joining Forces: From National Security to Networked Security*. London: Demos.

Briggs, Rachel and Charlie Edwards 2006. *The Business of Resilience: Corporate Security for the 21st Century*. London: Demos.

BSIA 2012a. *Facts and Figures*. Worcester: British Security Industry Association, at http://www.bsia.co.uk/our-industry/facts-and-figures (accessed 1/19/12).

BSIA 2012b *Welcome to the British Security Industry Association*. Worcester: British Security Industry Association, at http://www.bsia.co.uk/ (accessed 1/19/12).

Button, Mark 1998. "'Beyond the Public Gaze.' The exclusion of private investigators from the British debate over regulating private security." *International Journal of the Sociology of Law*, 26 (1): 1–16.

CIPD 2007. *Introduction to Purchasing Security*. Stamford: Chartered Institute of Purchasing and Supply, at http://www.perpetuityresearch.com/publications.html (accessed 1/19/12).

City of London Police 2012. *Project Griffin*. London: City of London Police.

CoESS 2008. *Private security and its Role in European Security*. Paris: Confederation of European Security Services/Institut National des Hautes Études de Sécurité.

CoESS and UNI-Europe 2004. *Panoramic Overview of Private Security Industry in the 25 Member States of the European Union*. Wemmel, Belgium: Confederation of European Security Services and UNI-Europe.

de Waard, Jaap 1993. "The Private Security Sector in Fifteen European Countries: size, rules and regulation." *Security Journal*, 4 (1): 58–62.

de Waard, Jaap 1999. "The private security industry in international perspective." *European Journal of Criminal Policy and Research*, 7 (2): 143–174.

G4S 2008. *G4S Completes Acquisition of ArmorGroup International plc*. Crawley: G4S, http://www.g4s.com/en/ (accessed 11/27/11).

G4S 2012. *History*, at http://www.g4s.com/en/ (accessed 11/27/12).

George, Bruce and Mark Button 1994. *The need for regulation of the private security industry. A Submission to the House of Commons Home Affairs Select Committee.*

George, Bruce and Mark Button 2000. *Private Security*. Leicester: Perpetuity Press.

Gill, Martin, Katy Owen, and Charlotte Lawson 2010. *Private Security, the Corporate Sector* and the Police. Leicester: Perpetuity Research and Consultancy International.

Guardian 2012a. "Revealed: government plans for police privatization", at http://www.guardian.co.uk/uk/2012/mar/02/police-privatisation-security-firms-crime, (accessed 30/9/12).

Guardian 2012b. 'Surrey police shelve privatisation plan after G4S Olympic failure' , 12 July, http://www.guardian.co.uk/uk/2012/jul/12/surrey-police-privatisation-g4s-olympic (accessed 30/9/12).

Hakala, Jorma 2010. Definition of Private Security Services. Confederation of European Security Services.

HM Government 2010. *A Strong Britain in an Age of Uncertainty: The National Security Strategy*. London: The Stationery Office.

Holdaway, Simon 1983. *Inside the British Police*. Oxford: Basil Blackwell.

Home Office 2001. *Policing a New Century: A Blueprint for Reform*. London: HMSO.

Home Office 2008. *Community Safety Accreditation Schemes National Audit*. London: Home Office.

Info4security 2000. "Security stitch-up" *Info4security*, July 1, http://www.info4security.com/story.asp?storyCode=18816&section code=10 (accessed 11/27/11).

Info4security 2002. "Security's image is all-important" May 31, *Info4security*, http://www.info4security.com/story.asp?storyCode=1028634&sectioncode=10 (accessed 11/27/11).

Info4security 2004. "Stitch in time" *Info4security*, October 1, http://www.info4security.com/story.asp?storyCode=3051253&section code=10 (accessed 27/11/11).

Information Commissioner's Office. 2008. *CCTV Code Of Practice*. CheshireWilmslow: Information Commissioner's Office.

Jessop, Bob 2003. "From Thatcherism to New Labour." In: Henk Overbeek (ed.), *The Political Economy of European Unemployment*. London: Routledge: 137–153.

Johnston, Les 1992. *The Rebirth of Private Policing*. London: Routledge.

Loader, Ian and Neil Walker 2001. "Policing as a Public Good." *Theoretical Criminology*, 5 (1): 9–35.

Manning, Peter 1997. *Police Work: The Social Organization of Policing*, 2nd edn. Cambridge, MA: MIT Press.

McLaughlin, Eugene and Karim Murji 1995. "The End of Public Policing?" In: Lesley Noaks et al. (eds.), *Contemporary Issues in Criminology*. Cardiff: University of Wales Press: 110–127.

PA Consulting Group. 2001. *Diary of a Police Officer*. Police Research Series Paper 149. London: Home Office.

Professional Security 2006. "In Heart of London." *Professional Security Magazine Online*, October 26, at http://tinyurl.com/bhn8kxs (accessed 29 January 2013).

Professional Security 2007. "Looks count." *Professional Security Magazine Online*, November 6, at http://tinyurl.com/bdmh7ne (accessed 29 January 2013).

Professional Security 2008. "Guard call." *Professional Security Magazine Online*, March 10, at http://tinyurl.com/bcrer97 (accessed 29 January 2013).

Professional Security 2009. "Norfolk Marshals." *Professional Security Magazine Online*, June 10, at http://tinyurl.com/ak9xja7 (accessed 29 January 2013).

Securitas 2012. *Our History*, Stockholm: Securitas, http://www.securitas.com/en/ (accessed 27/11/11).

Shearing, Clifford D., Margaret B. Farnell, and Philip C. Stenning. 1980. *Contract Security in Ontario*. Toronto: Centre of Criminology, University of Toronto.

SIA 2009. *In-house Licensing Review – Outcome Report*, London: Security Industry Authority, at http://www.sia.homeoffice.gov.uk/Pages/licensing-in-house.aspx (accessed 27/11/11).

SIA 2012 *Reporting Illegal Activity*, London: Security Industry Authority, http://tinyurl.com/7hmt74s (accessed 19/1/12).

South, Nigel 1988. *Policing for Profit*. London: Sage.

Stenning, Philip C. 1989. "Private Police and Public Police." In: Donald J. Loree (ed.), *Future Issues in Policing*. Ottawa: Canadian Police College: 169–192.

Wakefield, Alison 2000. "Situational Crime Prevention in Mass Private Property." In: Andrew von Hirsch, David Garland, and Alison Wakefield (eds.), *Ethical and Social Perspectives on Situational Crime Prevention*. Oxford: Hart Publishing: 125–146.

Wakefield, Alison 2003. *Selling Security: The Private Policing of Public Space*. Cullompton, Devon: Willan Publishing.

Wakefield, Alison 2006. "The Security Officer." In: Martin Gill (ed.), *The Handbook of Security*. Basingstoke: Palgrave Macmillan: 383–407.

Wakefield, Alison 2008. "Private Policing: A View from the Mall" *Public Administration*, 86 (3): 659–678.

Wakefield, Alison and Martin Gill 2009. "When Security Fails: The Impact of Human Factors on the Deployment of Retail Security Personnel." *Journal of Policing, Intelligence and Counter Terrorism*, 4 (2): 9–23.

Wakefield, Alison and Tim Prenzler 2009. "Privatization." In: Alison Wakefield and Jenny Fleming (eds.), *The Sage Dictionary of Policing*. London: Sage: 243–245.

PRIVATE SECURITY, PUBLIC INSECURITY
THE CASUALIZATION OF EMPLOYMENT AND ITS EFFECTS IN INDIA

Anibel Ferus-Comelo

T*his paper*[85] examines the working conditions of security guards in Goa, a coastal state in India, within the context of privatization and growing contractual employment in the country and beyond. The exponential growth of the private security industry in India can be traced to two concurrent trends: (1) the onset of the era of global terrorism which became an enduring feature on the public radar-screen in India post-November 2008; and (2) the abdication by the state of its responsibilities to protect the life and property of its citizens through a well-equipped and adequately staffed police force. As a consequence, the private security industry has become one of the largest employers of youth and the rural poor around the country. Its business and employment practices have been largely overlooked in the absence of a regulatory framework. The research addresses questions related to the role of the state in regulating contract work and ensuring social protection for low-wage workers. Besides the quality of employment generated by the security industry, the study also raises concerns about the quality of security the

---

85   This paper is based on a study conducted in association with the V.M. Salgaocar College of Law, Panaji and the Centre for Workers Management, Bangalore. The author would also like to acknowledge funding support from Hivos Foundation.

private contract agencies provide to the local community. The paper argues that contractual employment in such a sensitive industry as security has implications for the public beyond the workforce, and therefore, the two issues of employment and security need to be treated more seriously as inter-related by the state.

This argument is based on a survey of 101 security guards which was conducted over 2.5 months from October to December 2009. The workers were engaged through more than 30 different security agencies operating in Goa, representing the experiences of a total workforce of at least 3,000 associated with these agencies. The study included focus group sessions with security workers, semi-structured interviews with owners and managers of private security agencies, and informational interviews with governmental officials. Primary data were complemented by information obtained under the Right to Information Act, 2005. Interviews with workers were conducted in Hindi, the dominant language in India, and Konkani, the official language of Goa.

This chapter proceeds in three sections. The first discusses the extent of privatization of security in India accompanied by the growing investment of multinational corporations. This is followed, in the second section, by a description of the informalization of employment within the industry and its implications for the predominantly migrant workforce. The third section explores the limited role played by the state in regulating the industry, followed by an examination of possible reasons for gross lapses in the regulatory system. Finally, the conclusion draws out the implications of privatization of the security industry and the associated casualization of employment which leave both workers and the general public unprotected.

The privatisation of security

A deep sense of insecurity vis-à-vis global terrorism since 2001 was aggravated within India with the terrorist attacks in Mumbai in November 2008, industrial unrest, and bomb blasts in important economic centers of the country. With the general feeling among large enterprises, banks, hospitals, governmental units and private households alike that the existing police force and public national security force are inadequate to meet the challenges of terrorism, industrial espionage and incidents of crime and violence, there has been a boom in the private security industry in India. The private security industry has had a phenomenal growth rate tripling in value in the last five years to over Rs. 14,000 crore[86] [US$ 2.729.775] in late-2010, and is expected to continue expanding rapidly in the coming years (Kaushik, 2010).[87]

The shortage of security personnel was most acutely felt after the Mumbai blasts when anxiety about similar attacks arose in hotels, hospitals, retail centers, malls, and other commercial and trading sites across the country. Such an environment has fuelled a tremendous growth spurt in the private security business with powerful corporate players. Group 4 Securicor, for instance, is a London-based $11 billion company with operations in more than 100 countries. It is the largest employer listed on the London Stock Exchange with close to 600,000 employees and is the second-largest private employer in the world.[88] Group 4 Securicor India (G4S) is a national leader in integrated security cover. The company currently employs 1.5 lakh [hundred thousand] guards nation-wide and will recruit an additional 50,000 by 2013, while Tops Security which has 85,000 on its payroll plans to add another 36,000 workers in the next two years, and Chennai-based SDB-CISCO has 20,000 guards (Kaushik, 2010; Oberoi, 2008; Toms, 2007).

'Man guarding' is nearly 90 percent of the security industry (Kaushik, 2010). The big players have focused on scaling up their operations in order to meet the growing demand by recruiting millions of Indian job seekers, especially rural youth, who turn to the security industry for first-time employment. With over 5.5 million workers, the

---

86   1 crore = 10 million.
87   At the current exchange rate of 1 US$ = 51.30 (http://www.xe.com, accessed November 18, 2011).
88   Cf. the G4 Securicor website: www.G4S.com as well as UNI (2008).

private security industry in India employs more than four times the number of police across the country (around 1.4 million) and more than five times the size of the central paramilitary forces, or 1 million (Kaushik, 2010).

Despite its size and the rising demand for security, the industry is plagued by a major challenge, that of well-qualified staff. According to the Chairman of Securitas, which employs 15,000 workers and is expected to add another 8,000 in 2011, only one in 100 applicants meet the company's eligibility criteria of physical built (height and weight), education (completion of schooling) and communication skills (Kaushik, 2010). One of the growth strategies adopted by the industry therefore, has been to focus on workforce training in order to equip security personnel with basic as well as specialised skills, e.g. to deal with emergency situations or provide what is known in the industry as 'executive protection' (Kumar, 2009). Executive protection is security cover for government bureaucrats, politicians, celebrities, diplomats and company executives, which yields about 20 percent profit margin in comparison to the 12 percent profit margin generated by the regular guarding segment (Kaushik, 2010). Building up the skill sets of their workforce to match the range of services demanded by clients is a top priority for large security firms aspiring to a larger chunk of the market.

Since the passage of the Central Industrial Security Force (Amendment) Bill by the Parliament in February 2008, the paramilitary force has been approved to provide security to private industrial enterprises which reimburse the state for the costs. Professionalisation and specialisation in certain skill-sets are critical to the success of the well-established industry leaders and aspirants which are subsequently made to compete with the paramilitary Central Industrial Security Force (CISF) to provide security to large companies. The CISF is perceived to be well-trained and well-equipped but is sorely short-staffed. Deployment of CISF personnel also requires military clearance of the company seeking security provision from them, something that is rarely granted (Kaushik, 2010).

Yet the possible decrease in market share for the private sector has spurred the industry association into action. The Central Association of Private Security Industry (CAPSI), which has representatives in each state, is setting up 2,000 security training centres to be funded by state governments with counter-terrorism training of security personnel to be provided by Ultimate Tactical & Combat Pvt. Ltd. Individual players have likewise established their own training facilities to be position themselves strategically for the growth spurt that is expected.

The Security and Intelligence Services (SIS), a private security firm, has embarked on a Rs 50-crore expansion plan across the metropolises of Delhi, Mumbai, Chennai, Ahmedabad, Kolkata and Bangalore. The Rs. 1,500 crore [15,000 million] Delhi-based company has also signed a memorandum of understanding (MoU) with the government for training and placement of rural youth under its Swarn Jayanti Shahri Rozgar Yojna, which is a scheme "to provide gainful employment to the unemployed and under-employed in urban areas by encouraging self-employment ventures, or by the provision of wage employment."[89] SIS has an ambitious target of identifying, training and certifying 100,000 youth over two years through its subsidiary, the Security Skills Council of India, which offers a diploma course based on 320 hours of training in collaboration with the state-sponsored Indira Gandhi National Open University.[90] It plans to employ nearly 60% of these state-certified and trained youth and assist the others in obtaining jobs through other agencies.

Along a similar vein, the Swedish security company Securitas, which launched its India operations in 2008, has opened six training centres in Bangalore in order to tap the growth potential in the industry. Securitas, which operates in 38 countries, plans to focus on recruitment and training in order to equip its workforce with skills in specialised guarding, executive protection, and transport security.

---

89   Cf. http://delhigovt.nic.in/dept/district/da2b.asp, accessed April 29, 2010.
90   Cf. http://www.sisindia.com/features.htm, accessed April 16, 2010.

Informalization of employment

Having set out the growing power of the security industry above, this section focuses on the working conditions of the people who are at the frontlines of this rapidly expanding service industry. A noteworthy feature of employment in the security industry in Goa as in the rest of the country is its casual nature. Almost forty percent of the national market is served by the unorganized sector of the security industry (Kaushik, 2010).[91] Workers are increasingly hired through middle-agents or contractors rather than directly by the principal employer, who needs them. Only two of the workers interviewed in this study were employed directly by the employer. All others worked through private agencies on a contract basis. By eroding the traditional employer-employee relationship upon which most labor laws are predicated, contract employment undermines workers' rights and makes it virtually impossible for workers to gain the protection afforded by collective bargaining (ILO, 2010).

A significant feature of security work in Goa besides contractual arrangements was the composition of the workforce. Only 19% of the workers surveyed were Goans and an overwhelming majority (81%) was migrants. The chart below illustrates the places of origin of workers who have come to Goa from elsewhere.

Table1: Places of Origin

Nepal	23%
Assam	23%
Orissa	17%
Maharashtra	16%
Uttar Pradesh	6%
Bihar	4%
Others	11%

Source: own account

---

91   The unorganised sector refers to small-scale enterprises whose activities fall outside the purview of existing legislation, within which labour relations, if any, are based mostly on casual employment, and kinship, personal or social relations rather than contractual arrangements with formal guarantees (Harriss-White and Gooptu, 2000).

Of the security guards who were not of Goan origin, the highest percentage was Nepalese and Assamese with 23 percent in each category. The rest were from Orissa (17%), Maharashtra (16%), Uttar Pradesh (6%) and Bihar (4%). The remaining 11% were from nine different states including Meghalaya, Rajasthan, Jharkhand, Andhra Pradesh, Karnataka, Madhya Pradesh, Jammu and Kashmir, Kerala and West Bengal. The combination of contract labor and a migrant workforce is associated with poor working conditions in the security industry for all workers regardless of ethnic origin.

One of the most notorious working conditions in the security industry is the long work day and the lack of a regular weekly day off duty. Three-fourths of the workers (75%) surveyed regularly worked 12 hour shifts without over-time wages for the additional half-day (4 hours) over the legal 8-hour shift. Only 12 percent of the workers worked a regular 8-hour day, while 3 percent of the workers worked between eight and twelve hours each day, without over-time wages. Interviews with workers suggest that it is not uncommon for workers to put in two 8-hour shifts during the same day in two different locations, thereby working 16-hours in a day for two single wages, not over-time. Many workers did not consider this wholly negative because they were able to earn more money. Only one worker expressed his fear of the effect of such long hours on his health. It was also evident from worker interviews that a security guard typically works a 7-day work week with no weekly off-day.

Another feature of security work is the sheer monotony of the work throughout the year. Only 17 percent of the workers surveyed received paid leave. An overwhelming majority of the security workers surveyed (83%) did not receive any paid leave during the year. Many were able to arrange a week to a month off work per year in order to visit their native villages, but this leave was un-paid. It was evident throughout the study that the workers appreciated having the time off, even though it was unpaid, in order to attend to family matters. Several of the migrant workers interviewed had not visited their family in their home villages for more than five years. There were some, however, who made it a point to take (unpaid) time off each year to visit their families with a tacit agreement with their supervisors that they could have their post back when they returned. These were workers who had built a positive reputation for themselves through years of service and had demonstrated their loyalty to the company as well as a self-disciplined work ethic and reliable nature.

Among those who reported receiving paid leave, a few said that this was sick leave upon mutual understanding with the supervisor or manager. One said he received eight casual days per year and nothing else. One confused 'paid leave' with a weekly off day (or a regular 6 day work week) for which he did not receive payment. This made it obvious that the workers had a very low expectation of their contract agencies and paid holidays were seen as an inaccessible luxury.

Besides the long work hours and seven-day week without holidays, workers were paid subsistence wages. Under the Minimum Wages Act, the daily wage of an unskilled worker was Rs. 103 (US$ 2) based on an 8-hour day and four days off per month. Since security work is considered unskilled, the basic salary at the time of the survey should have been Rs. 2,678 (US$ 53) in a 30-day month for those who worked 8-hour days, six days of the week.

Of the workers surveyed, 19 percent of the total respondents earned sub-minimum wages and may have worked daily for more hours than the legal 8-hour shift, upon which the minimum wages are based, for no additional wages. The security guards were paid on the basis of a full month of work without a single day off. Most of the workers interviewed said that they were paid as daily wagers; regardless of the number of hours overtime they worked each day. In other words, if they worked for 25 out of 30 days in a month, they are paid only for the 25 days. Many workers employed by different agencies reported that if they missed a day of work, their monthly earnings were cut by one, and in some cases, two days' wages.

The average monthly wage of those who worked a daily, 12-hour shift (75% of the sample) was Rs. 4,034 (US$ 80), when in fact they should have been earning Rs. 7,004 (US$ 139) per month if the wages were calculated on the basis of an 8-hour shift for a 30-day month, plus double rate for overtime.[92] This gives a difference of Rs. 2,970 (US$ 59) per month between the legal minimum wage and the average monthly wage earned by the workers. The average monthly earnings of the guards who worked an 8-hour shift (22% of the sample) was Rs. 4,130 (US$ 82), when in fact they should have been earning Rs. 4,914 (US$ 98) if the wages were calculated on the basis of double wage for the seventh day of work each week. This amounts to a difference of Rs. 784 (US$ 16) each month or Rs. 9,408 (US$ 187) in a year.

One of the reasons why workers are unable to pursue their claims for the legal minimum wage is the casual mode of payment adopted by the contract agencies. A majority of the workers (77%) received payments in cash without receiving a pay-slip or signing a wage register. All of the cash payments to workers were made either by the owner or by an agency supervisor, without any oversight by a representative of the principal employer, as mandated by the Contract Labour Act.

One of the most frequent complaints of security guards who participated in the study was unpaid and late payment of wages for work they had done. Section 5 of the Payment of Wages Act specifies that wages should be paid before the end of the 7th day of the following month in a workplace employing less than 1,000 people, and before the end of the 10th day of the following month in a workplace employing more than 1000 workers. However, this is commonly violated as the date often varies for security workers and is typically not before the 10th of the following month. There were numerous stories of workers being denied their wages for work they had already done and end up losing

---

92   This includes four Sundays per month paid at double rate since the Minimum Wages
      Act stipulates four days off per month.

significant amounts of money as a result of this unethical and illegal practice. The usual reason for resigning from one contractor and joining another was either low wages or late and unpaid wages.

Security work implies many occupational risks. Two of the most reported risks that the security workers faced were verbal or physical abuse by supervisors and agency owners, and assault or battery in burglary attempts that the guards try to prevent. About 17% of those surveyed had personally experienced harassment from their supervisors and the public during the course of their duty. They commonly got insulted, shouted at, and had foul language directed at them by the supervisors and managers.

The lack of social protection for the unorganized workforce in India is a cause for major concern, confirmed by the research findings in this study. Although most of the workers surveyed were entitled to be enrolled as members of the statutory Provident Fund to which workers and employers contribute,[93] nearly half of them were not. In fact, they received nothing beyond their wages, typically paid in cash as discussed earlier, and were not even aware that they were entitled to anything more.

Among those who were enrolled in the Provident Fund, not everybody knew how much was being deducted from their wages as their own contribution to the Fund, nor how much was being contributed by their employer. Many did not receive the annual statement (typically sent to the employer who is then responsible for distributing them among the employees), and so had no idea what their account number was or how they could access these funds when needed.

The situation was similar in the case of the Employees' State Insurance (ESI), which provides certain benefits to employees earning Rs. 15,000 (US$ 298.60) per month or

---

93   According to the Employees' Provident Funds and Miscellaneous Provisions Act, 1952 the employee and the employer each contribute 10-12% of the wages (inclusive of dearness and retaining allowances). Members can access these funds with accrued interest in order to cover their retirement (or old age) needs, medical care, housing, family obligations, education of children, and financing of insurance policies. For details, see http://www.epfindia.com.

less in case of sickness, maternity and employment injury, and related matters.[94] ESI is an essential not a 'fringe' benefit for security workers since physical fitness is a job requirement and physical assault is an occupational risk. Just over half of the survey respondents did not receive ESI. Instead, they ended up paying out of their meager earnings for their own medical expenses and those of their families, if their ailments were perceived as serious enough to warrant professional care in the first place.

In spite of the modest earnings from jobs which are their (families') lifelines, security workers are also deprived of the annual bonus to which they are entitled. The Payment of Bonus Act, 1965 states that a minimum bonus of 8.33 percent of the wage or salary earned by the employee or one hundred rupees, whichever is higher, be paid once annually to those employees who have worked for the employer for no less than thirty days of the same accounting year. However, nearly four-fifths of the survey respondents reported that they did not receive an annual bonus from their employers. The number of workers who had not worked for the same employer for longer than one accounting year (and therefore, may have missed the timing of the bonus paid in their agency) was negligible.

In sum, the study shows that there are many exploitative practices which are common within the industry. These include: the long work days and lack of weekly days off; a lack of paid holidays; low payment, late or no payment for work already performed; verbal and sometimes physical abuse; and a lack of social security provisions. How can such a situation persist when there are laws that are supposed to protect workers? The next section examines the response of the state.

94   The Employees State Insurance (ESI) is "a self-financing social security scheme ... of health insurance that provides comprehensive medical cover and cash benefits in the contingencies of sickness, maternity, disablement and death due to employment injury to the Insured Persons and their dependants." For details, see http://esic.nic.in/.

Regulation and enforcement by the state

Goa is not only the smallest state in India with an area of just 3,702 sq. km., it also stands apart due to its colonial history. Goa was a Portuguese colony for about four centuries, two hundred years longer than most of the rest of India which was under British rule. After its independence in 1961, it became a union territory governed by the central government in New Delhi until 1987 when it was officially recognized as the 25th state of India. Although Goa boasts some of the highest indicators of development, such as a literacy rate of 82 percent in comparison to the national average of 65.38 percent, this socio-economic profile belies a level of poverty and deprivation that is a growing issue of concern. The state's economy is dominated by two major industries, mining and tourism, which have come under heavy criticism for their negative social and environmental effects. Goa's population of nearly 1.5 million is multi-lingual with a 70-30 ratio of Hindus and Christians. The state plays host to nearly two million tourists each year and an additional transitory population of workers from other parts of the subcontinent. Thus a huge influx of people amidst a sudden spike in inward investment in real estate development has been associated with a radical transformation of community life in Goa, heightening a sense of insecurity among residents.

Goa has seen the mushrooming of security agencies since 26/11 with over 500 existing agencies.[95] According to the leaders of the Security Association of Goa (SAG), the industry is "thriving without any regulations" (Fisher, 2009). By law, employers are required to register their staff with the police, get their backgrounds checked and the guards should carry on their person a valid photo ID issued by the police in its jurisdiction. However, these procedures are often not followed. Instead, SAG representatives point

---

95   This figure is an estimate provided by the Labour Commissioner's office as there is no exact figure available.

out that with increasing demand for security personnel, "anybody is being employed as a guard" thereby compromising on the quality of security provided. SAG has been lobbying the government to provide it with land to set up a registered training institute under the guidance of the Goa police (Fisher, 2009). One reason that it has not been successful in this venture may be attributed to the fact that less than 10% of the security agencies operating in Goa are members of SAG (NT, 2009).

At the same time, the industry's record elsewhere serves as a warning against the lack of proper oversight of private security agencies in Goa. Group 4 Securicor (G4S), the world's largest security firm with a leading presence in Goa and India, has been criticized by Human Rights Watch for violating workers' freedom of association, national labor law, and its own business ethics policy in the United States of America (HRW, 2010).

Preliminary evidence from other parts of India indicates that a cut-throat business environment has also taken a toll on the quality of employment that the industry has generated. The President of the Central Association of Private Security Industry (CASPI) has estimated that nearly ninety percent of private security workers in India are below the poverty line (UNI, 2008). Workers reportedly do not receive their payment, suffer physical abuse at the hands of the agency owners or managers, have no access to toilet facilities, receive no training even by the agencies which claim that they have rigorous programs in place, and receive minimum wages at best, except in violence-prone areas where the agencies claim to pay a slightly higher salary. Another issue that gets highlighted is the fact that uniforms have to be purchased by the guards at a cost collected up-front or in wage deductions in order to prevent guards from leaving with the uniform (Oberoi, 2008). Such conditions point to the need for a proper regulatory framework and enforcement mechanisms.

Even though security is a highly sensitive industry, it has not been regulated under any special provisions which ensure industry-specific standards. So far security companies have registered with the state authorities under the broader Shops and Commercial Establishments Act that covers all industry. In 2005, the Indian government enacted the Private Security Agencies (Regulation) Act (hereafter referred to as 'the Act'). The purpose of the Act was to regulate a highly disorganized industry and set industry-wide norms with regard to hiring practices, background checks, training, wages and other statutory benefits. Specifically, the Security Act stipulates that every security agency should be registered with the state government and provides 160 days training to its staff before deployment to the worksite. It lays down specific pre-conditions for security guard training institutes including infrastructure requirements and emphasis on skilled manpower.

There have been several calls from industry representatives to all security agencies to register themselves under the Act, but so far there has been little effort on the part of the government to pursue this matter, partly due to bureaucratic inertia and partly due to the lack of concerted pressure from business and civil society. Once implemented, the Act may lead to a consolidation of the industry with the edging out of the fly-by-night operators while threatening the survival of small players with limited finances, which may have to depend upon larger operations for their training needs (Venkat, 2007).

Registering under the Security Agencies Act would also mean that security firms would have to be accountable to the central government under the Home Ministry, and not the labor commissioner's office within the state government. By taking away the authority to approve and regulate security agencies in their states, the Security Agencies Act may reduce local bureaucrats' vested interest, political paternalism and corruption (see UNI, 2006), thereby creating an impression that it would not be in the interest of state governments to notify or implement the Act. Instead, security agencies continue to be registered under the aforementioned Shops and Establishments Act and are able to maintain their invisibility to regulatory bodies.

In 2008, Maharashtra and Goa were the only two states in the country to have notified this Act. Currently, ten states have adopted, but none, including Goa, has implemented it. The International Institute of Security and Safety Management (IISSM) argues that this central law would go a long way to streamlining the industry and make it more effective by forcing professionalism and holding them accountable to industry-wide standards achievable through accredited training institutes. The Union government had issued instructions to implement the Act by March 15, 2007. However, the Act remains un-implemented and the lack of proper regulation of the industry prevents it from gaining the level of respect and legitimacy to which it aspires (Costa, 2008).

Although the Act covers the security industry, there is a substantial body of legislation and policy frameworks that pertain to the operation of enterprises more generally. Two of the most important roles of the state with regard to employment and the protection of workers' rights are the registration and licensing procedures and the enforcement of existing laws. Research findings in the security industry indicate that both of these are problematic as discussed below.

Any principal employer (including governmental establishments), engaging more than 20 employees through one or more contractors, has to obtain a registration certificate from the state Labour Commissioner under the Contract Labour (Regulation & Abolition) Act dating back to 1970. If a contractor employs 20 or more employees then that contractor should have obtained a license to engage employees on contract basis. This license (issued to the Contractor) is renewable every year while the Registration obtained by the principal employer need not be renewed.

In Goa, security agencies are predominantly registered as commercial enterprises under the Shops and Establishments Act, 1973.[96] Registration under this Act is done at

---

96   Security agencies may also be registered under the Companies Act, 1956 and the
       Private Security Agencies (Regulation) Act, 2005. However, this is not yet the practice
       in Goa.

the appropriate centre of the Labour Commissioner. Agencies are also required to register under the Contract Labour Act, if applicable, which is done District-wise.

The Labour Commissioner's office estimates that more than 500 private security agencies are licensed under the Shops and Establishments Act at its seven centers in Goa. There are 97 security contractors registered with 2,100 employees in the Deputy Labour Commissioner's office in South Goa. Due to the decentralization of registration and the lack of an electronic network among the centers, it is difficult to obtain a complete list of licensed security agencies in the state. It is also difficult to ascertain when a particular agency may have been registered because the Registers of 'Commercial' Establishments (and others) under the Shops and Establishments Act are organized by the date when the agencies were originally registered and there is no separate register of renewals or the possibility of attaching an addendum to existing records when an agency renews its license. It would be virtually impossible to identify the establishments that are operating on lapsed registration certificates. As an official in one of the Labour Commissioner's offices stated: "If it is detected by the Inspector (during an inspection) then the establishment can be issued a penalty." The implication here is that an enterprise can continue to operate without a renewal certificate until it is inspected or is asked for it by a potential client.

The licensing procedure under the Shops and Establishments Act at the Labour Commissioner's office involves submitting the requisite forms and paying the fees which, depending upon the number of employees, range from Rs. 60 (US$ 1) for agencies having no employees to Rs. 5,000 (US$ 100) for those having 20 or more employees, at the time of registration. Police clearance is required of all agencies operating in the state. Exact information on the number of agencies or workers who have been cleared by the police is not available as there are 26 police stations which have jurisdiction to carry out such work.

There is one effective safeguard for workers if a contract agency obtains a license at the Labour Commissioner's office. Under Rule 24 of the Contract Labour (Regulation and Abolition) Act, the contractor has to pay a security deposit of Rs. 500 (US$ 10) per worker (according to the number s/he registers as employees), which will be refunded once the contract ends provided that the contractor obtains a Certificate of Completion or termination of contract from the principal employer along with proof of salary payment to workers. In this way, a small amount of money is theoretically made available by the contractor in advance in order to cover his/her wage obligation to the workers. This money can be distributed among workers in case the contractor does not pay them for any time period before moving on.

In practice, there may be some shortcomings of this otherwise sound measure. For example, Agency X may register a minimum number of workers (say, 2) and pay the required security deposit, i.e. Rs. 1,000 (US$ 20), but may in reality have ten (implying a deposit of Rs. 5,000, or US$ 100) or more workers whom s/he does not pay during a month before moving on to another principal employer or simply disappearing. The deposit paid does not even cover the monthly wage of one worker at the minimum wage rate, leaving the other nine (or more) cheated of their earnings. The nominal deposit can be seen as a small price to pay for operating in disregard of the law.

It is also possible that the agencies registered under the Shops and Establishment Act in the security industry, are not claiming their security personnel as employees. For example, an agency's registered office may have just two to four employees, e.g. a peon, clerk/receptionist, sweeper and a supervisor, but the agency may deploy thousands of security guards at different sites of its clients. None of these security guards may be covered as an employee of the establishment under the Act.

In sum, the study shows that many security agencies in operation do not have the requisite registrations and licenses to operate legally. This is a concern even though the registration process required of security agencies (and other companies) appears to be a straight-forward administrative procedure. However, the registration and licensing process is not a sufficient measure of legal compliance nor is it a standard by which employers can be judged as 'responsible.' The study has found that even registered companies employ workers off the books and that un-registered companies sometimes pay workers higher than average salaries. In fact, as discussed next, there is very little oversight of the private security agencies which operate legally in the state of Goa.

Off the books, off the hooks

Although essential to ensure that the law gets implemented on the ground, the enforcement system is extremely weak and fails to hold employers accountable to the labor standards set by law. It must be noted at the outset that Indian labor law and the enforcement process are extremely complex, making regulation a theoretical concept rather than a practical reality. Logistically speaking, the number of labor inspectors in Goa is woefully inadequate to handle the large number of establishments that operate in the state. There are 43 pieces of labor legislation and the inspectors cover about 10 to 12 Acts in daily inspections. The inspections are conducted according to check-lists on forms that correspond to different Acts. The enforcement officers or inspectors interview the managers/owners and examine the paperwork at hand. For many reasons explained below, it is not surprising that violations of the law are not detected and errant employers can continue cheating their workers with impunity.

First, in the private security industry, the offices of some of the agencies were apparently just office shells and may have only been used as postal addresses and payment centers. A list of registered security agencies obtained from the Labour Commissioners' offices indicated only the general locality in which the company was based, such as Cavorim, Chandor or New Delhi, without any other details as part of the address, even though these were specifically requested under the Right to Information, 2005. This could mean that the companies were registered with incomplete or vague addresses, making it difficult for any postal correspondence. During field research, the managers and owners were difficult to contact both in person at the office and on the phone. This may be due to the fact that many run other businesses or work somewhere else and run these 'agencies' on the side. This would make inspections a tedious affair for time-constrained inspectors who need to 'chase' the employers for the inspections to take place at all.

Next, by examining the paperwork in the offices and not speaking directly with workers, the inspectors would miss many irregularities. It is important to talk to the workers in a scattered workforce such as security workers or construction workers, as it is hard to get a sense of the situation for workers in different locations from just office visits. For example, an inspection would not indicate that the security guards have not been issued identity cards, unless the inspector visits the guards at their work-sites.

Interviews with security guards revealed that the enforcement system does not catch the tricks of the trade used by contractors to circumvent the law and to generate huge amounts of profit. One of the most obvious ways in which contractors manipulate the loop-holes in the system is by deploying workers for 12-hour shifts or more in situations where 24-hour security coverage is needed, while claiming wages and benefits from the principal employer for a workforce that is engaged for an 8-hour shift on paper. This allows the contractor to pocket the wages of the 3rd shift worker(s). This can easily be practised undetected as the security guards are not personally known to the principal employer, who is also not concerned about the detail of the contractual arrangement as long as its need for security coverage is met. Whether or not the principal employers' (PE) facilities are really secure is an open question.

Security agencies may have contracts with several different institutions at the same time and are able to negotiate different rates with their clients for their services. They shift workers from one post to another depending upon where they are needed (in case another worker resigns or is absent, and if more workers are needed at a site). They may keep the workers' pay constant even if the new post is at a work-site where the PE has paid a higher rate to the contractor for more job responsibilities of the guards. Such an irregularity goes undetected unless the security workers uniformly receive sub-minimum wages. The case story below illuminates the ways in which workers get cheated of their earnings due to the non-compliance and the multiple identities of contract agencies, and equally due to the faulty enforcement system.[97]

Box 1: Multiple Employers and Namesake Rectification

"Manoj" had worked for a security agency since 2007 but did not receive any appointment letter or identity card as proof of employment. At the start, he did not get paid for about four months at a stretch. Each time he asked for his payment, he was told that it was coming. Eventually, he received a lump sum that amounted to three months salary, not four as he was owed. He did not dare to ask about the missing month's salary and optimistically thought that it would be paid to him. Soon his salary began to be deposited in his bank account but the amount would vary from month to month despite his regular presence on duty. Since he did not receive a pay-slip each month, he did not know why the amount was different and whether or not any deductions were being made and if so, for what purpose.

At some point during the year, he received an Employees' State Insurance (ESI) card which named his employer as another entity than the one in whose name his salary was being deposited into his account. Again, he asked no questions for fear that he would be considered too meddlesome. In about January 2009, his agency was investigated by some government officials from Delhi and was made to take some corrective measures. A few security guards were called in to the office and told to sign some papers, which they did not fully understand. Even some who had already resigned from the agency for some time were summoned to the agency's office to collect their Provident Fund payment. Soon after, the name of the agency changed and the guards were told by way of explanation that the two agencies had divided their jurisdiction between Mapusa (North Goa) and Panaji (the capital), even though they were owned by the same person. The agency still does not provide all the workers with their identity cards (which the workers have paid for) or a monthly pay-slip which explains how much they are earning and how much is being deducted in social security benefits, if at all. Some do receive their pay-slips, which also show that there is a monthly deduction of Rs. 5 for "Labour Union" membership, about which the workers know nothing.

---

97   As recounted to the author over several visits in January and February, 2010.

According to the worker who recounted this case, the agency's number of contracts has greatly reduced over the last two years. This may be due to the fact that the principal employers gradually become wise to the wily ways of the agency. More importantly, the narrative above indicates a few ways in which the workers are cheated and the government tricked (with or without the knowledge of the inspectors involved). When inspected, the company was given some time to correct its mode of operation. At the agreed time, the company showed that all back-wages and PF accounts of former workers had been settled.

A focus group session with workers revealed that they have caught on to the tricks played by the agencies. For instance, when the agency in the story above was inspected, it may have registered a new company under a different name, manipulated its past paperwork and paid part of the money owed to some of the workers in order to show that it is fulfilling its obligations as an employer. One of the workers interviewed shared that this may be done with the full knowledge and even in connivance with the government official/inspector.

This section has highlighted some reasons why existing labor legislation is not being enforced despite such a desperate situation for security workers. It points to some of the structural weaknesses that exist within the enforcement system itself such as the lack of political will to invest time and energy to identify and pursue errant employers on the part of inspectors within an under-resourced, lumbering system. It also sheds light on some of the ways in which the security agencies evade detection by frequently changing their names or locations, and even operating with 'shell' offices. There was enough evidence to suggest that a lenient nexus between the government and private players, which could possibly include corruption, is also part of the vexing lack of enforcement of labour legislation.

Conclusion

This chapter has documented the bad working conditions which relegate security workers to the ranks of the working poor and the inadequate regulation on the part of the governments. Drawing upon the evidence in Goa as a microcosm of India, the paper argues that the negative effects of contract labor are not limited to individual workers but also for the general public.

One way in which public security is compromised by the employment practices of the private security industry is the lackadaisical recruitment process and the name-sake vetting procedures undertaken before engaging new hires. Research shows that by and large security workers are recruited casually through newspaper advertisements, word of mouth or family, village, and caste-based connections. Basic requirements of age, physical fitness, and training for security jobs are ignored, presumably because some agency owners consider a part of the demand for security guards as just 'ornamental,' to show the presence of a watchman who keeps an eye on the human traffic. The role of the security guard in preventing crime must nevertheless not be under-estimated. Registration and police clearance needed prior to hiring personnel are sometimes neglected as a time-consuming and costly procedure for a big agency. In the face of a high labor turn-over, an agency which has adopted a short-term approach does not place much importance on what appears to be a cumbersome administrative procedure. Agency owners thus fail to acknowledge the professional nature of the occupation, under-value the guards and depress wages.

However, bad jobs breed poverty, resentment and disenfranchisement which can in turn lead to crime. Security guards have been reported by police in the local press to be involved in theft, sexual assaults, drug peddling, and even murder. It is much harder to track down burglars, rapists and murderers through their jobs if there are no records of them easily available. Security agencies could contribute positively to crime prevention by following the legally mandated procedures for registration and police clearance of new hires. It would also be advantageous to the principal employers and the agencies to have the workers registered as they would be properly vetted in advance. A long-term strategy for reducing crime committed by security guards and others, would involve motivating security guards to invest themselves in their jobs. This would require higher wages, quality benefits and better facilities made available to workers.

On the contrary, casual employment through contracts without the statutory registration process translates into a depression of wages and benefits in the local labor market, especially when the pool of available workers keeps expanding with in-migration. This means that casual employment in the security industry not only generates insecure work but paradoxically makes a society more vulnerable to crime.

References

Costa, Glenn 2008. "Govt still not utilizing private security agencies for policing." *Navhind Times*, November 14.

Fisher, Michael 2009. "Security market growing at 20%." *Navhind Times*, July 29.

Harriss-White, Barbara and Nandini Gooptu 2000. "Mapping India's world of unorganised labour." *Socialist Register 2001*: 89–118.

HRW 2010. *A Strange Case: Violations of workers' freedom of association in the United States by European multinational corporations*. Geneva: Human Rights Watch.

ILO 2010. *Global Employment Trends, 2010*. Geneva: International Labour Organisation.

Kaushik, Manu 2010. "A force to reckon with." *Business Today*, October 31.

NT 2009. "Security agencies asked to register under Security Act." *Navhind Times*, October 2.

Oberoi, Radhika 2008. "Private guards have no set selection criteria." *The Times of India*, December 7.

Toms, Manu P. 2007. "Private security industry set to enter high-growth trajectory." *The Hindu Businessline*, December 12.

UNI 2006. "SAI for implementation of Pvt Security Agencies Regulation Act." August 4.

UNI 2008. *The Inequality beneath India's Economic Boom: G4S Security Workers Fight for Their Rightful Place in a Growing Economy.* London: UNI Property Services G4S Alliance.

Venkat, Archana 2007. "Industry demand places private security guards in new roles." *The Hindu Businessline*, November 12.

SECTION III
Policing the Urban Battleground

Volker Eick and Kendra Briken

Some years ago, Pierre Bourdieu (1991: 30) observed that "domination of space ... is one of the most privileged forms of executing power ..., manipulation of the spatial distribution of groups has always been used to manipulate these very groups;" therefore, the spatial distribution of social classes and the use of space can be seen as a result of social confrontations for "space profits" (ibid.: 31). One might read "space profits" as space/social control capacities for domination over space keeping at a (physical) distance people or places that are claimed to disturb or bring discredit upon the ruling classes. We are referring here to a concept of space in the sense of a social relation – producing and being reproduced by the built environment.[98] Therefore, space is always a contested terrain.

Obviously, contestation can take different forms: Looking at the "militarization of urban space" by politicians, real estate agents and the police in the 1990s in Los Angeles, Mike Davis (1992: 180) observed "moves to extinguish [the] last real public spaces, with all their democratic intoxications, risks, and undeodorized odors." Some twenty years later, Stephen Graham studied urban

---

98   Thus, space is not a simple 'container.'

conflicts on a global scale and identified a "new military urbanism" growing in scope and scale. By highlighting that by 2007 "*Homo sapiens* had precipitously become a predominantly urban species" as half of the world's 6.7 billion people today are city-dwellers, and since then "1.2 million people were added to the world's urban population each week" (Graham, 2010: 1-2), he underlines a soaring enthusiasm among urban elites with high-tech weaponry and the deployment of both police and the military in order to control these urban masses.

Such attempts to secure the urban battleground especially apply to the poverty-ridden parts of the urban environment increasingly perceived as jungles or 'zoos' (Schweer et al., 2008), and particularly to the metropolises in the Global South labeled as 'feral cities' (Norton, 2003). However, policing the urban battleground does not target only the urban poor but it also encompasses policing of protest movements especially as the last decade saw the worldwide growth of (transnational) protest movements in scope and scale, among them the alterglobalization movement, the 'Right to the City' movement, and Occupy Wall Street (see Mayer, *this volume*). Transnational protest in particular and the staged counter-summits against the 'globacracies' (Luis Fernandez) are an example of the adaptations that urban and social movements undergo in response to the shift in decision-making power from the nation state to supranational institutions (EU, IMF, World Bank, etc.) and even networks (G8, G20, World Economic Forum, etc.).

In times of an ongoing retrenchment of the welfare state, the neoliberalized city does not only entail serious hardship for the urban populace but also brings about new policing strategies. More particularly, so-called distressed neighborhoods and their surplus populations – long-term unemployed, migrant youths, and other 'undeserving poor' – are under continuous control by a plethora of social control agencies, above all the police. Inasmuch as social services, sustainable and affordable healthcare services, adequate wages and proper living conditions are no longer on the agenda, the social decline of neighborhoods, the growth of zones of poverty and deprived areas intensify, while social protest, civil unrest and political dissent might arise and then need to be put under control. On the one hand, what is at stake then is no longer the fight against poverty but rather the fight against the urban poor. On the other hand, policing the urban battleground also refers to policing strategies targeting those urban dwellers who actively contest the global neoliberalization and its outcomes by initiating political actions.

While section II has shown that commercial security personnel is part and parcel of such attempts, the next section is concerned with the far-reaching endeavors of police and local administrations to secure the urban battleground. In this framework, the individual chapters deal with case studies from North America, Lithuania, Sweden and France, and provide us with examples of variegated forms policing strategies. Examples range from attempts to criminalize and thereby pacify the alterglobalization movement in the US context, to break the anti-austerity mobilizations in a post-communist country, to policing strategies of 'Othering' by informal and semi-formal social control groups in a Swedish neighborhood, and to the articulation of spatial conflicts between the French police and the Banlieue youths as their 'alienated counterpart.'

Based on their ethnographic work in the last decade, *Luis Fernandez* and *Christian Scholl* argue that the criminalization of global protest movements today is more similar to insurgency control tactics than to traditional models of protest policing. The protests of the alterglobalization movement saw one of the first waves of what some scholars call 'strategic incapacitation' (Noakes and Gillham, 2007; Gillham and Noakes, 2011), while, beginning in 2011, Occupy Wall Street was the second movement to be confronted with a heavily policed 'globopolis' (Bowling and Sheptycki, 2011). Fernandez and Scholl show that insurgency control occurs within a longer time-frame and across mobilizations, goes beyond national borders and has much larger financial resources. For the purpose of securing the urban battleground, the police rely on a comprehensive set of instruments based not only on repression but also on preemptive and network-based approaches aiming not at one particular protest event but at entire movements and their respective mobilizations. 'Networking' is no longer an exclusive tool for social movements to organize responses against neoliberal globalization but became also a tool of the police.

When in 2011 cities across the US evicted the encampments of the Occupy Wall Street movement, similarities in the timing, talking points and tactics among metropolitan mayors and police chiefs have led critics to suspect possible coordination moves on the federal level. Indeed, it was a nongovernmental organization, the 'Police Executive Research Forum' (PERF), which attempted to crack down the Occupy movement in the US (Gaynor, 2011). In March 2012, President Obama signed H.R. 347 which allows for suppressing "lawful protest by relegating it to particular locations at a public event," as the American Civil Liberty Union highlighted in a statement, clarifying that "These 'free speech zones' are frequently used to target certain viewpoints or to keep protesters away from the cameras" (Rottman, 2012; cf. US Government, 2012).

While H.R. 347 directly targets protesters by legal means (see below), PERF exemplifies those security complexes that Boyle (2011: 170), when referring to sports mega-events, calls "security knowledge networks." The way this knowledge becomes 'sturdy' on the ground is revealed by Fernandez and Scholl's chapter which leads them to the conclusion that reactions to and strategic incapacitation of the alterglobalization movement can no longer be subsumed under protest policing but should be understood as counter-insurgency, because "movements and mobilizations are targeted even before they fully emerge."

Referring to two of their case studies – the 2003 protest against the Free Trade Area of the Americas summit in Miami, and against the G20 meeting in Toronto in 2010

–, Fernandez and Scholl make the point that manipulating the law is one of the governments' additional tools to criminalize dissent. Modified city codes in Miami redefined public assemblies to gatherings of eight and more people and parades to an organized participation of two or more people, while the 'Public Works Protection Act' in Ontario allows for blocking public space surrounding public buildings and expanded law enforcement powers based solely on the decision of the Lieutenant Governor of Ontario. By similar legal means, the Occupy Wall Street movement across the US is confronted with anti-camping ordinances and curfew regulations – originally developed against homeless people – that allow the police to raid and evict protesters from public parks. While also looking at police media teams before, during and after political mega-events such as the G8 summit in Germany in 2007, Fernandez and Scholl trace how, by diffusing false media reports, a 'terrorist' threat is created, which in turn seemingly allowed for arbitrary violence of coercive state power against protestors even beyond the constraints of the law.

Intimidation by state police is also one of the topics in the chapter of *Arunas Juska* and *Charles Woolfson* who chart the eruption of popular protest in the Baltic State of Lithuania in response to crisis-driven government austerity measures. They paint a rather bleak picture of Lithuania's protest movements and the unionized working class in particular where austerity, as they emphasize, "confronts the individual in the form of growing state and increasingly supra-state (reified 'financial markets') authoritarianism." At the beginning of the 1990s, all three Baltic States adopted neoliberal 'open market' policies of economic and social reconstruction designed to promote foreign direct investment. Ensuing protest coordinated by trade unions – but "against a background of weak social ties and an absence of solidarity in civil society in general" – led, in January 2009, to the deployment of police dressed in full body armor, wearing black balaclavas and tear-gas masks, armed with truncheons, shields and rubber bullet rifles and accompanied by dogs. As they point out, "nothing like this had been seen since the days of an abortive Soviet military intervention in January 1991 which cost the lives of thirteen demonstrators." Such a recourse to an even greater authoritarianism with the deployment of repressive policing strategies and technologies led to 22,000 Lithuanians leaving their country (2.5% of the workforce) in 2009 alone; between 2009 and 2011, more than 153,000 people also left Lithuania. As Juska and Woolfson highlight, police repression in the name of the new 'kleptocracy' together with the consequences of the neoliberal 'smash and grab' capitalism lead to the expulsion of the protesting populace and "exactly conforms to the conjunctural needs of austerity."

While Juska and Woolfson highlight the brute force of neoliberal 'reforms' and police brutality, *Anna Rodenstedt* analyzes how since the 1970s trust in the Swedish state as an enforcer of urban security has steadily declined, and commercial companies, private organizations and 'committed' individuals have simultaneously assumed an increasing role in crime prevention and maintenance of security. As Rodenstedt clarifies, the Nordic countries with their robust tradition of preventive social policy used to pursue crime prevention first and foremost through welfare institutions and programs (schools, youth activities, maternity welfare, etc.). Today they increasingly rely on policie forces, commercial and other on non-state security providers. Referring to Garland's (2000, 2001) 'responsibilization strategy' of society, Rodenstedt argues that the rational individual and the physical characteristics of places have become more important to crime prevention in Sweden, whereas social measures are increasingly seen as costly and inefficient. Her chapter investigates how security is practiced in a suburb in Stockholm – alleged to be unsafe and crime-ridden – on the basis of increasing "social control of parents over youths," and additional informal and semi-informal control agencies. Referring to 'Othering' processes and 'banal Orientalism' that both informed the understanding of newcomers in the neighborhood and of youths identified as 'annoying,' Rodenstedt states that "improving social control was brought forward as an important challenge, and several 'semi-formal control groups' have thus been created over the years" in order to target "the 'bad' forces." Stockholm's district Rinkeby was the first to "arrange security walks" in order to support the "good forces" and to secure a particular urban battleground by informal and semi-formal policing means.

'Good' and 'bad' forces are also a topic of *Mélina Germes*. Based on interviews with police officers in France, she analyzes how spatial conflicts are articulated, creating the 'Other' and the respective 'enemy territory.' By breaking down these articulations into particular speech acts, she also shows that (post)colonial understandings are widespread within the French police. Inasmuch as walls are both physically functioning as and symbolically representing a race- and class-based pacifying mission (Ponting and Rigakos, *this volume),* the denomination of particular parts of a city as 'badlands' (Dikeç, 2007) is meant to accomplish a similar mission. The Banlieues, as Germes shows in her chapter, are such a 'badland' for the French police and especially for its special police units (cf. Fassin, 2011). Germes identifies the "discursive construction of a conflict-prone territory" by the police "in a context where the increasing enforcement of the penal State is a response to advanced marginality." She reads the intensified socio-spatial segregation and crisis policing of the *Banlieues* under France's 'actually existing neoliberalism' in the context of emerging post-industrial cities, ongoing discrimination in postcolonial societies paralleled by the shrinkage of the welfare state and the shift to more law-and-order approaches in policing. Policing the urban battleground within the French context is based on appropriations of contested space. The police perceive the socioeconomic problems in a place as problems of the place, and the respective 'gangs' of the disconnected *Banlieues* are described as the unnamed 'Other.' An important difference though, as identified by Germes, is the fact that the municipal police try to avoid entering the 'enemy territory,' while the national police identify the territory as something to be recaptured from the 'Other.' Stemming from such an understanding, domination through space (narratives) is what guides policing strategies and tactics that nevertheless might play out differently: either in containment strategies or, to use Neil Smith's (1996) term, in 'revanchist city' policing – an attempt of reconquesta.

References

Bourdieu, Pierre 1991. "Physischer, sozialer und angeeigneter Raum." In: Martin Wentz (ed.), *Stadt-Räume*, Frankfurt/M.: Campus: 25–34.

Bowling, Ben and James Sheptycki 2011. "Policing Globopolis." *Social Justice*, 38 (1-2): 184–201.

Boyle, Philip 2011. "Knowledge networks: mega-events and security expertise." In: Colin J. Bennett and Kevin D. Haggerty (Eds.), *Security Games*. New York: Routledge: 169–184.

Davis, Mike 1992. "Fortress Los Angeles: The Militarization of Urban Space." In: Michael Sorkin (ed.), *Variations on a Theme Park*. New York: Noonday Press: 154–180.

Dikeç, Mustafa 2007. *Badlands of the Republic*. Oxford: Blackwell.

Fassin, Didier 2011. *La Force de l'ordre: Une anthropologie de la police des quartiers.* Paris: Seuil.

Garland, David 2000. "Ideas, Institutions and Situational Crime Prevention." In: Andrew Von Hirsch, David Garland and Alison Wakefield (eds.), *Ethical and Social Perspectives on Situational Crime Prevention*. Oxford: Hart: 1–16.

Garland, David 2001. *The Culture of Control*. Oxford: Oxford University Press.

Gaynor, Shawn 2011. "The cop group coordinating the Occupy crackdowns." *San Francisco Bay Chronicle*, 18 November, at http://tinyurl.com/7qb8qe4 (accessed 3 February 2013).

Gillham, Patrick F. 2011. "Securitizing America: Strategic Incapacitation and the Policing of Protest Since 11 September 2001." *Social Compass*, 5 (7): 636–652.

Graham, Stephen 2010. *Cities Under Siege. The New Military Urbanism*. London: Verso.

Noakes, John A. and Patrick F. Gillham 2007. "Police and Protest Innovation since Seattle." *Mobilization*, 12 (4): 335–340.

Norton, Richard J. 2003. "Feral Cities." *Naval War College Review*,

LVI (4): 97–106.

Smith, Neil 1996. *The New Urban Frontier: Gentrification and the Revanchist City*. New York: Routledge.

Schweer, Thomas, Hermann Strasser, and Steffen Zdun (eds.) 2008. *Das da draußen ist ein Zoo, und wir sind die Dompteure*. Wiesbaden: VS.

US Government 2012. *Federal Restricted Buildings and Grounds Improvement Act of 2011 (H.R. 347)*, at http://tinyurl.com/7p3djpm (accessed 3 February 2013).

THE CRIMINALIZATION OF GLOBAL PROTEST
THE APPLICATION OF COUNTER-INSURGENCY

Luis A. Fernandez and Christian Scholl

In 2010, UK activists uncovered the undercover police officer Mark Kennedy (alias Mark Stone), who spent at least seven years infiltrating radical environmental and alterglobalization networks in the UK and 21 other countries. It was shocking to many activists, but not a surprise for those studying protest policing. In the months that followed the discovery of Mark Kennedy, more cases of deep surveillance were uncovered (in the UK, Germany and Switzerland) corroborating the suspicions that Kennedy was part of a larger effort of state authorities to come to terms with alterglobalization protest in dubious ways (cf. Monroy, 2011). As activists and scholars, it is unsettling to know one has shared many meetings, conversations, drinks or a tent with a person who was paid to spy on you and other activists.[99] It also raises many questions: What were authorities doing here? How were they operating? And what does this mean for radical movements in the Northern world organizing internationally against neoliberal globalization? In this chapter, we argue that the criminalization of global protest points towards a developing trend that

---

99   Rob Evans and Paul Lewis, "Former lovers of undercover officers sue police over deceit," *The Guardian*, December 16, 2011, http://www.guardian.co.uk/uk/2011/dec/16/lovers-undercover-officers-sue-police; Tom Whitehead, "Undercover police not banned from sleeping with targets," *The Telegraph*, February 2, 2012, http://www.telegraph.co.uk/news/uknews/law-and-order/9055209/Undercover-police-not-banned-from-sleeping-with-targets.html (both accessed February 4, 2012).

is more similar to insurgency control tactics than to traditional protest policing models. Generally speaking, protest policing models assume that a protest is discrete phenomena, with scholars focusing on each individual protest. We argue that insurgency control occurs in a longer time-scale, across mobilizations, and goes beyond national boundaries, all of it supported by increasingly larger resources. Below we make the case that "protest policing" is now more akin to pacification and insurgency control aiming to reduce uprisings. We base our findings on our ethnographic work, which expands through a decade of participation and examination of alterglobalization protests. Yet, in this chapter we focus mainly on the broader argument, inserting examples where appropriate.

Shifting social control

Hoping for more evidence about the functioning of undercover officers, one lesson is instructive: repression is not only what happens on the streets. It is not only police beating up, tear-gassing, pepper-spraying, erecting fences, or other measures to build no-protest zones (which are only the most evident forms of repression; see also Juska and Woolfson, *this volume*). It also includes monitoring and surveying, following and undermining, threatening and pervading, chronicle and indexing: the subtle forms of social control (Fernandez, 2008). Instead of repression, we therefore like to speak of social control to capture these subtle and less overt operations (cf. Starr, Fernandez, and Scholl, 2011).[100] In the Northern world, these operations have shifted tremendously in the past decades, also in response to alterglobalization and other large protests (Scholl, 2012). We expect that a

---

100   The authors intentionally use the term *social control* as a critique of the concept of *repression*. We argue, both here and in several recent publications, that the concept of repression often leads scholars to erroneously ignore important aspects of how policing affects social movements. To that end, the authors have made this case clear in at least two recent books: *Policing Dissent* (Fernandez) and *Shutting Down the Streets* (Starr, Fernandez, Scholl). Both of these works contain a much longer treatment of this issue. The reader can find the full reference to these works at the end of this chapter.

further shift will occur in North America in response to the
Occupy Wall Street Movement. However, for now we can
already describe trends, some that resemble regular protest
policing and others that are more like insurgency control
tactics.

When looking at repression, social movement scholar
generally focus on the policing of protest, examining the
way movements are shaped and defined through how law
enforcement reacts to their actions. In contrast, counter-
insurgency operations are tactics used during war, deployed
against enemies involved in an armed rebellion. These tactics
can include armed suppression, mixed with tactics of divide
and rule or wining the "hearts and minds" of the population.
Generally, these second set of tactics aim at placing a wedge
between the insurgents and the general population, seeking
to minimize public support. We argue that when looking at
policing of large mobilizations, they increasingly appear
more like insurgency control rather than the protest policing
described in the literature.

Central to this shift toward insurgency control is its
preemptive and networked character. Combined with newer
tactics (e.g. Internet surveillance, cell phone tracking), the
age-old practice of infiltration advances the focus of control
to before concrete actions occur, even before concrete risks
emerge. Risk management is seen as a pivotal feature of
the general tendency of securitarization (or the process of
convincing people that they must be protected from a threat),
focusing on the calculation of probabilities (de Goede, 2008).
That is, instead of just repressing a movement, these tactics
seek to reduce the probabilities of larger movements developing into the future. Thus, movements and mobilizations
are targeted even before they fully emerge, aiming to reduce
their full bloom. For police, this means focusing on information gathering and on monitoring individuals, activist
groups, networks, and mobilizations in the months before a
mobilization, through tactics that include police raids. In the
United States, one might see the targeting of local organizers
through grand jury and more raids.

The networked character stems from the increasing (international) cooperation of various security agencies, as well as from increased links between police departments within national boundaries.[101] New laws for data exchange on various levels have been established, new agencies for security cooperation created, and, as the case of Kennedy proves, undercover officers are exchanged. Especially within the EU and between the EU and the US, security ties have been thickening since September 11 (9-11). The networked character makes social control more diffused and more pervasive, but also hard to study and to trace because the currents of communication between police departments are submerged and information is being transferred laterally.

One may wonder what the purpose is of preemptive and networked forms of social control. Vitale (2007) points out that recent shifts aim at the avoidance of disruption. The power to disrupt routine affairs is perhaps the most important tool of social movements, as pointed out by scholars more than thirty years ago (cf. Piven and Cloward, 1977). At the turn to our millennium, mass mobilizations to disrupt the summit meetings of WTO, World Bank, or the G8 made the power of social movements palpable to global elites. Shifting forms of control of alterglobalization protest have to be seen as a response to this.

In this chapter, we examine one of the most serious consequences of the shifting social control: the criminalization of alterglobalization protest and the use of insurgency control tactics. Thereby it is important to remember that, because of its preemptive character, it is not only on the street that protest is controlled, but in advance *and* afterwards. 9-11 happened only two months after the major G8 protests in Genoa and changed the political context for alterglobalization movements. However, we believe that, by that moment, many of the developments we describe were well

---

101   The increase in internal policing networks is particularly poignant in the United States, where information system sharing is changing policing generally, and protest policing more specifically. For instance, Fusion Centers are changing the way that police gather and share information between police departments across the U.S.

underway. Thus, preemptive and networked forms of social control are not a result of post-9-11 anti-terrorist legislation, but rather an intensification of them. Moreover, current shifts in controlling protests in the context of the financial-economic crises can be considered equally worrisome, since their intensification resembles a counterinsurgency model.

The theoretical and typological formulation we present in this chapter come from our ethnographic experience within the alterglobalization movement. Together, we participated in no fewer than 15 large mobilizations, including protests in Mexico, the United States, Canada, France, The Netherlands, and Germany. The conceptual framework presented here derives from our experience. To that end, we will discuss three key aspects of the criminalization of alterglobalization protest since the 1999 WTO protests in Seattle: the manipulation of laws, the creation of terror, and the legal consequences for activists. All of them show the preemptive, subtle, networked, and pervasive character of shifting social control, demonstrating an insurgency control style of policing. Manipulation of laws and legal restriction on public assembly and the freedom of speech have become habitual tools for national and local authorities to shift the boundaries of legal and criminal protest. The creation of 'terror' amongst the local population is also accompanying all summit protests, and spin-doctor operations criminalizing (potential) protesters have become a standardized police repertoire. Last but not least, activists have to face legal consequences. Legal prosecution and political litigation are another key aspect of turning alterglobalization protesters into criminals, and sometimes so-called terrorists. None of these three key aspects, however, goes uncontested. Where possible, our analysis fleshes out the responses and counter-strategies of activists.

In the final section of this chapter, we reflect on how the shifting social control mechanisms of protest translates and transforms again in the light of recent crisis-related protests. Recently, in Northern countries such as Greece, Spain, the UK, and the US, major mobilizations and social unrest are facing highly overt police repression and violence. And it is easier to see the insurgency potential in these demonstrations. It might be too early to fully grasp these recent shifts, but many developments point to a shift towards insurgency control. Insurgency control seeks to move beyond the immediate control of a single protest or mobilization and toward the control of uprisings. What we see in the U.S., in Occupy, is not just a series of protest but an uprising (see demonstrations in Oakland as the most obvious example). Instead of studying the policing of a single protest, which is what scholars generally do, we suggest that scholar shift to an insurgency control framework that examines control across protests and national boundaries.

Manipulation of laws toward the criminalization of dissent

In the summer of 2010, the G20 met in Toronto, Canada. Protesters were there to 'welcome' the G20 leaders and their delegates. To prepare for any possible disruption, the local police retained approximately 4,000 local law enforcement officers. The Royal Canadian Mounted Police brought in approximately 5,600 officers to work throughout the duration of the G20 gathering. An additional 1,000 private security agents were present to provide security. In all, over 10,000 different types of police officers were ready to secure the event, including SWAT teams, intelligence personnel, motorcade escorts, and bike police.[102] In addition, a Canadian federal government hired private contractors to provide airport-style security at several checkpoints throughout the city of Toronto, performing pedestrian screening with hand-held metal detectors, X-Ray scanners, and Magnetometers. This level of expense alone indicates a shift in policing away from traditional forms to something resembling insurgency control. That is, the

---

102   http://www.theglobeandmail.com/news/national/toronto/small-army-to-protect-toron-to-during-g20-summit/article1525511/ [accessed December 10, 2011].

concentration of officers, the pooling of resources and the increase in budgets suggest a blurring of the lines between order maintenance policing and the suppression of ongoing mass mobilization. These resources are not aimed at one protest, but rather at a movement and sets of mobilizations that spread across different events.

As you can deduce from the description above, the City of Toronto was briefly transformed into a high security zone, perhaps similar to a war torn area. However, we contend that to really understand the insurgency control, we need to go beyond the physical aspects that precede repression. That is, while we need to carefully examine the militarization of protest policing, we also need to examine the wide array of other control tactics that lead to insurgency control.

One such control tactic is the use of regulatory codes to prevent protestors from mobilizing large groups of people. Scholars and activists alike have noticed how difficult it is to use public space for democratic purposes, such as holding meetings, rallies, gatherings, or camp (Amster, 2008; Mitchell, 2003). This is not a coincidence, rather a situation that developed after several decades of regulating space, in some instances targeting the homeless populations and in others aiming to control the power of mass demonstrations. Let us provide just three examples of regulatory control, each showing how laws developed for one purpose are appropriated and implemented against dissent. These examples come directly from our ethnographic experience in the movement.

Our first example takes us back to the 2003 FTAA protest in Miami. At that time, U.S. activists were protesting the creating of an international economic zone that would open markets across North and South America. In an attempt to directly target alterglobalization protesters, the City of Miami modified city codes defining a public assembly as 8 or more people gathering in a public space. They also redefined a parade as two or more people walking in the streets with the intent to promote a point of view. Generally, it would not matter much how a city defines a term. However, in this case it meant that all the regulatory codes that apply to an 'assembly' and a 'parade' now applied to almost anybody in protesting FTAA (Fernandez, 2008). This means that the police now could use all the laws requiring permits and insurance to prevent people from demonstrating. That is, if activists walked down the streets in groups of two or more, the police could legally stop them, inquire about a "parade" permit, and cite them if they could not produce them.

Similar use of city regulations has been reported in other protests in the U.S. and Europe, where law enforcement use laws to restrict the streets to activists. For instance, police used laws against wearing masks in public assemblies to attack 'masked' anarchists. In 2007, the German authorities tried to use anti-masking laws against the Clandestine Insurgent Rebel Clown Army. Activists must be aware of theses tactics, doing research before hand to see what police will try to unleash on them.

Our second example brings us back to the 2010 G20 protest in Toronto, Canada. Adding to the large numbers of law enforcement officers in the streets, the City of Toronto also invoked the *Public Works Protection Act*[103] in an effort to further control the public space surrounding the gathering location for the G20 delegates. The origins of the *Public Works Protection Act* date back to 1939, when the Ontario city government sought to protect public buildings and construction from potential saboteurs. As such, the law protected such "public works" as railways, canals, highways, bridges, or any public unity that is either owned or operated by the Government of Ontario. In addition, a "public work" can also include any site that the Lieutenant Governor in Council designates as such. That is, the Act gives the power to designate any public location in Ontario as a "public work," making this a useful city code to the state.[104]

---

103 To read the entire Public Works Protection Act, go to http://www.e-laws.gov.on.ca/html/statutes/english/elaws_statutes_90p55_e.htm [accessed December 10, 2011]. To see the changes done in June 2010 go to: http://www.e-laws.gov.on.ca/html/source/regs/english/2010/elaws_src_regs_r10233_e.htm [accessed December 10, 2011].

104 See the footnote above for the link to the Public Works Protection Act. In it, you will find the descriptions of who is allowed to define a public work.

More importantly, accompanying the "public work" designation are the expanded law enforcement powers. The powers include the ability to arrest anybody who does not identify him- or herself and is entering or attempting to enter any public work area. The Act also grants police the power to search, without warrant, any person entering or attempting to enter a public works area, either on foot or in a vehicle. Finally, it allows law enforcement to use any force necessary to prevent any unauthorized person from entering the public work area. Thus, when Toronto designated the area in and around the G20 meeting location a "public works," it brought with it a slew of police powers.

The point here is that the reapplication of the law not only extended police powers, but also transformed the type of activities of activists in and around the G20 gathering. It drastically changed how protesters would approach this mobilization, making it more difficult to engage in creative disruption. In the days leading to the G20 protest, local media often reported that law enforcement would require identification and would search anybody who approached within six feet from the fence erected to separate protestors from the G20.

After the 2010 G20 protests in Toronto, it was clear that the actual police powers granted through the act were never completely clear to local law enforcement. Civil liberties organization proclaimed this unconstitutional. Regardless weather or not the designation of the G20 area as a public work was legal; the effects on protesters were palpable. That is, the media reports left protesters unsure of what the police could or could not do, producing a state of confusion.

Our last example of criminalizing dissent through the use of legal regulation comes from the Occupy Wall Street (OWS) movement. OWS originated in September 2011, when a group of activist, following a call by *Adbusters* magazine, occupied Zuccotti Park, primarily because it was private property, which made it harder for police to force protestors to leave. That is, the public regulatory laws that are described above were not applicable, given that the property owners were not working with the police. The Occupy sentiment then spread throughout the United States, with hundreds of other occupied locations. Unlike New York City, the majority of the occupied areas were in public parks, rendering activist susceptible to city codes and regulations. In the end, it was these codes that allowed police to evict activist gathering in parks and other public spaces. This also demonstrates a net-widening effect, where tactics developed against one movement over time widen to affect another set of mobilizations.

We provide three examples of the types of laws used against the OWS activists. One of the most used regulations deployed against OWS are anti-camping ordinances. One can find such ordinances across the nation, from city to city, including in smaller towns. Originally, these ordinances were developed to target homeless people, aimed at "cleansing" city parks from the "inconvenience" and "blight" produced by the down-trodden (Amster, 2008). The ordinances arrive in local city council based on the Broken Windows Theory, which argues that police must eliminate minor offences (like j-walking or graffiti) to prevent bigger ones. To that end, cities across the United States placed laws targeting sleeping in public, seeking to push homeless people out of sight.

These laws targeting homeless are now used against activists who seek economic justice. For example, in Phoenix, Arizona, OWS protesters are allowed to be at Cesar Chavez Plaza as long as they do not fall asleep in their camps. In turn, the police made several arrests one night, taking away activist who were sleeping, who turn out to belong to the anarchist tent. In Los Angeles, California, protesters had to move their tents every night to the sidewalk, just outside of the public park. In Chicago, OWS activists took turns going to the car to sleep. As you can see, the ordinances make dissent a little more uncomfortable, as well as it makes illegal the act of sleeping in public to protest economic inequality.

Equally problematic for OWS protesters are the curfew regulations. Similar to the anti-camping laws, public parks are subject to curfews that make it illegal to be in a given area past specific times. For example, in Denver, Colorado, the police used the curfew laws to raid and evict protesters from a public park, leading to 21 arrests. The state parks in Colorado allow for an 11 pm to 5 am curfew, making it instantly illegal to be in a park between those times.

Our last example of criminalizing Occupy protester activity is the prohibition of semi-permanent structures. Generally, the term "semi-permanent structures" is interpreted as erecting tents, tarps, or using sleeping bags as shelters. In Phoenix, Arizona, law enforcement officials used this code to arrest several Occupy protesters who were sitting under a tarp. Coincidently or not, the police later identified the arrested individuals as anarchists, leaving other protesters in peace. More absurd yet, the Seattle Police Department warned protesters not to "have an umbrella open unless you're standing and holding it," because an open umbrella is a semi-permanent structure. Reportedly, Seattle city officials were concerned that protesters, intentionally skirting the no-camping rule, could be using umbrellas as makeshift shelters.[105] Indirectly, then, this city code served as a tool to keep protesters under control.

The criminalization of dissent continues. In a strange twist of events, the City of Ashville, in North Carolina, is using the Occupy movement as the primary excuse to propose urban camping laws that place park curfews, include the prohibition of enclosed shelters, and makes illegal the storage or leaving of equipment, bags, parcels, or other personal items in city property.[106]

In sum, the criminalization of dissent involves the manipulation of laws that target the use of public space. Because dissent generally requires the use of public space, these tactics point to an important aspect of dissent: demo-

---

105   "Umbrellas banned at Occupy Seattle Protests," *RT*, October 11, 2011, http://rt.com/usa/news/umbrellas-outlawed-occupy-seattle-585 [accessed December 10, 2011].

106   "Council will vote on camping ban, aimed at Occupy Asheville," *Mountain Express*, September 12, 2011, http://www.mountainx.com/article/38249/Council-will-vote-on-camping-ban-aimed-at-Occupy-Asheville [accessed December 10, 2011].

cratic practices require location where people can gather. As such, the laws that aim to regulate these practices not only decrease the potential for disruption, but also the emergence of democratic forces that challenge the status quo. These laws also suggest a trend towards insurgency control. The criminalization of dissent, or the presenting of protesters as individuals disrupting the public order, can result in a wedge between the protesters and the local population. In the next section we discuss the use of 'terror' to decrease participation.

The creation of 'terror'

Scare tactics are an old phenomenon of police and counterinsurgency work. They can be addressed at activists, potential ones, and the general public. The preemptive functioning is to intimidate, to keep people away from protest. After the successful blockades of the 1999 WTO summit in Seattle, many observers compared subsequent summit meetings to 'war zones.' Entire city centers were fortified, border controls reintroduced, shops barricaded, thousands of police and often even military officers present. Government officials and police asked the local population to leave the city or otherwise stay at home and make no contact with protesters. Who can tell how many people have not joined those protests for these intimidations?

Before the 2001 G8 protests in Genoa, rumors about 'terrorist' attacks and prepared bags made the news and Italian authorities reported 60 cases of bomb scares (Federici and Caffentzis, 2001). These operations do not stop during the protests. Juris (2008) vividly describes how, during those days, Genoa transformed from a protest site to a space of control, at times inducing feelings of terror. Terror here means that activists felt exposed to the arbitrary violence of coercive state power acting beyond the constraints of the law.

However, as overt creation of terror, Genoa has not found real imitation afterwards. Creation of terror is applied more subtly, often in advance, by spin-doctor operations in the media. Examining the case of the 2007 G8 summit in Heiligendamm, Stad (2007) shows how police media teams systematically diffuse false reports about protesters dressed as clowns confronting police with toxic acid in their water pistols, or hundreds of police being injured during street clashes.

Authorities and police know that the media are a site of struggle about the representation (and legitimacy) of summit protests. The head of the police operations during the 2005 G8 in Scotland, Brian Powrie, praised the German police organization for the 2007 G8 summit, Kavala, for their extensive in advance press work (BAO Kavala, 2007: 9). The Komitee für Grundrechte und Demokratie (2007) doubt in their report that such police tactics, crossing the boundary to opinion making, are in line with democratic principles.

Next to intimidation of (potential) dissenters, the creation of terror also stigmatizes and marginalizes. The media play a crucial role in this. Labeling alterglobalization activists as (potential) criminals, and bringing summit protests in connection with terrorism, the media creates sticky images that separate the protesters from the "common sense" of the rest of the population. Criminalization marginalizes social movements and activists often internalize their marginalization. Enlarging the social networks that nurture social movements (Melucci, 1989) becomes a difficult task under such circumstances.

Another form of stigmatization is the division of protesters into 'good' and 'bad' ones. 'Good' protesters refrain from violence and disruptive actions, obey the laws and follow police orders. Such media classifications are easily reproduced in internal movement debates and can drive a wig in the movement. Moreover, it gets hard to make wise tactical choices for protests, when most tactics are stigmatized or criminalized in advance.

House searches and raids on activist projects are another tactic for creating terror. Weeks before the 2007 G8 protests, 9,000 police officers raided 40 houses and projects under suspicion of being part of a "formation of a terrorist association with the goal to prevent the G8 summit." None of

URBAN (IN)SECURITY: POLICING THE NEOLIBERAL CRISIS

the searched persons, however, was convicted afterwards. The German criminal investigation police even admitted to just have "shot in the bush to see what is moving."[107] Authorities often raid houses in advance and this nurtures the idea that there are criminal persons and activities in alterglobalization networks. Moreover, it intimidates the activists concerned and other activists who anticipate that the police might knock on their door any time soon.

The 2008 raid of the small village Tarnaq, France, with 150 heavily armed riot police officers and helicopters is another telling example. Nine persons were arrested as part of anti-terrorist investigations because they allegedly had sabotaged train tracks aiming at destabilizing the state by violent actions. One of the arrestees was held in custody for six months without initiation of a trial. None of them was convicted, but the stigma of leftwing terrorism was imprinted, a type of divide and conquer strategy often seen in counterinsurgency campaigns.

Activists have a hard time in countering the creation of terror. Not only intimidation but also the criminalizations of the protests in general are effects difficult to balance. One strategy has been to scandalize the spin-doctor operations of authorities and to provide quick and factual counter evidence with press releases of activist media teams. Activists involved in activist media groups during the 2005 and 2007 G8 protests told us how they struggled to find time to react adequately to each of the false reports and how this, in turn, distracted them from focusing on the actual message they wanted to get out. Alterglobalization activists are forced to react to a hostile and suspicious context.

To counter the intimidation of the local population, activists have recently engaged more systematically in building up direct ties and to embed summit mobilizations more in the local context. One year in advance of the 2007 G8 summit in Heiligendamm, activists held an interna-

---

107   See http://www.spiegel.de/politik/deutschland/0,1518,482222,00.html [accessed March 27, 2010; own translation].

tional preparatory camp close to the summit's venue and started house-knocking engaging locals in their ideas and action plans. The 2010 G20 mobilization in Toronto was embedded in a local mobilization trying to bring together different grassroots movements from the region. According to Wood (2010) however, such efforts were fraught with tensions around different strategies and identities.

Stigmatizing, intimidating, and marginalizing alter-globalization activists, the creation of terror reduces the participation in these networks and makes it more difficult for activists to diffuse their substantive messages. As we have shown here, spin-doctor operations are not only a battle about minds. It is also a battle about social networks, trust, and the building of collectivity in social movements. Scaring people is a good way of keeping them from the streets. But scare tactics do not need guns to work, only fear.

Legal consequences

The year-long trials after the 2001 G8 protests in Genoa showed how spin-doctor operations can go hand in hand with legal prosecution. In a trial against 25 activists concluded in 2007, the state prosecution claimed that, next to criminal acts, the activists had polluted the image of the city of Genoa. Legal prosecution and political litigation are another key aspect of shifting social control. But whereas anti-terrorist legislation may be mobilized for criminal investigations, it is rarely applied to convict activists. In fact, looking at the number of arrests made during summit protests (usually at least several hundred if not thousands), the number of convictions is relatively low. Nevertheless, anti-terrorist legislation has consequences for alterglobalization activists (Aksyutina and Maeckelbergh, 2012). In many countries, legal circumscriptions of terrorist acts came to include direct action or even civil disobedience tactics. The 2002 *European Council Framework decision* (European Union: Council of the European Union, 2002) defines terrorism as acts that:

"given their nature or context, may seriously damage a country or an international organization where committed to the aim of: seriously intimidating a population; or unduly compelling a Government or international organization to perform or abstain from performing any act; or seriously destabilizing or destroying the fundamental political, constitutional, economic or social structures of a country or an international organization."

Such a definition relegates blockades of summit protests to the realm of terrorism, and the very suspicion of plans thereto gives police and criminal investigation agencies extended powers.

The most outstanding case of anti-terrorist legislation applied is the FBI's Operation Backfire, a major federal prosecution project aimed against environmental property crimes committed during the 1990s, such as damaging biotechnological field trial crops, burning SUVs at automobile dealerships, and freeing animals from fur farms. In the end, fifteen people were convicted and activists dubbed this FBI project "the Green scare" (Potter, 2011). Although in none of the incidents human life was under threat, authorities categorized them as "eco-terrorism" and "domestic" terrorism. The extensive investigations created widespread distrust in activist spaces, networks and relationships (cf. Starr, Fernandez, and Scholl, 2011: 87-88).

Legal measures can also work preemptively, for example in the case of the arrest of eight activists who were planning to participate in the 2008 protests against the Republican National Convention in Minneapolis. They were charged with conspiracy to riot and conspiracy to damage property with terrorism enhancement. In the end, the terrorism charge had to be dropped entirely, the charges against three of the activists were dropped, and four of the others accepted plea agreements for gross misdemeanor convictions.

The biggest charges for conspiracy occurred after the 2010 G20 protests in Toronto. Seventeen people were charged with conspiracy to resist and planning to disrupt the summit, but the charges for 11 of the 'conspirators' were eventually dropped. Three of them have been convicted so far to 3 to 5.5 months in jail. And also out of the other more than 1,000 detainees 300 were facing a trial.[108]

In Europe, activist work against legal prosecution and other forms of social control is typically called "anti-repression." In many countries anti-repression projects include leftwing lawyers supporting activists and some-times documenting mass protests, legal teams consisting of law students, legal practitioners, and other volunteers, documenting police behavior, arrests, and the ensuing legal consequences (for a German example, cf. RAV and Legal Team, 2008). There are also a number of groups organizing solidarity with imprisoned people, and others who support activists in political trials financially.

To be prepared for legal consequences is an important aspect of activist work. More complicated it is to push legal consequences for the measures and the behavior of police and authorities: After the 2001 G8 protests in Genoa, a series of trials was speared against the Italian police. High-rank police officers responsible for the G8 security operations were not convicted. And of the 45 police officers accused of torture in the so-called Bolzaneto trial, 15 got convicted, but will never have to serve jail time, due to the long time since the crime.[109]

Proactive political litigation can focus either on individuals (or groups of individuals affected in a similar way) or on class-action suits alleging violations of civil rights. In the light of the systematic infringement on civil rights and alter-globalization movements, the latter way is used relatively little. We do not want to project too much hope here on the judicial apparatus. However, it might be worthwhile to think more strategically about how to protect social movements as a vital context for people to exercise their right to (public) assembly, freedom of speech, and dissent.

---

108   For updates on the 2010 Toronto arrests see web page: http://fightyourtickets.ca/g20-litigation.

109   See "Remember Genoa 2001?" at: http://prenzlauerberger.wordpress.com/tag/bolzane-to-trial/ [accessed January 18, 2013].

From summit protest to insurgency control

So far, we provided several examples of the move from protest toward insurgency control, focusing specifically on how law enforcement criminalizes protest.In this section, we want to draw attention to the limits of the "protest policing" concept, while also showing that framing police tactics as counterinsurgency helps us better understand the spectrum of strategies that police deploy against protesters.

We first noticed problems with the concept of protest policing when examining the total costs for securing G8/G20 summits.[110] Despite the limited amount of information available, we were able to discern a great deal about what states spend on security. When analyzed across time, the trend upwards is evident. For example, Germany spent $124 million to secure the G8 in 2007, while Japan spent $280 million in 2008 for a similar operation. However, expenditure reached a zenith in 2010 when the Canadian government spent approximately one billion dollars to secure the G20 meeting in Toronto.[111] The money was spent mostly on personnel and police equipment, with estimates suggesting involvement of over 40 different law enforcement agencies. For us, the high investment and increasing coordination across police agencies suggest a qualitative shift. That is, we argue that the level of effort is more similar to low intensity warfare than what scholars term protest policing. Let us explain these terms.

Generally, the concept of protest policing refers to the way that police maintain order at various public political events. Usually, this involves either a single protest or perhaps a few days around a single event. Traditionally, police actions are also thought of as internal to the nation-state and aim at order maintenance. Yet, the more we examined the tactics, costs, and communication of law enforcement agencies, the

---

110   Chapter Three in our book *Shutting Down the Streets* contains a deeper analysis of the security costs for G8 meetings.

111   Office of the Parliamentary Budget Officer, *Assessment of Planned Security Costs for the 2010 G8 and G20 Summits. Ottawa, Canada.*

more it seems that the concept of counterinsurgency is more useful in grasping the phenomenon we are witnessing.

In contrast to protest policing, counterinsurgency or Low Intensity Operations (LIO, also called Low Intensive Warfare) involves governmental actions designed to contain or quell an insurgency or an insurgent group. In war areas, the insurgents attack the political authority of the state, while the authorities seek to maintain their power and eliminate the threat from the insurgents. Counterinsurgent operations are common during occupations and armed rebellions. The tactic involves the armed suppression of rebellion, along with other strategies designed to "win the hearts and minds" of the local population by dividing the insurgents from the local population. There is a long history of these tactics that expand from Algeria to Vietnam to Iraq (Neocleous and Rigakos, 2011).

Counterinsurgency, then, includes military actions external to the nation-state and aim to eliminate and destroy the enemy. It involves military-style deployments without a declaration of war, coupled with diplomatic and media efforts. In sum, Low Insensitive Operations fall short of full-scale warfare because the insurgents are difficult to distinguish from the general populations. Thus, it often involves the use of less-than-lethal weapons, public relations campaigns, and the extensive gathering of intelligence. Moreover, it seeks to intimidate sympathetic observers from joining the targeted social movement.

When looking at the policing of summit meetings (such as those for the G8/G20, WTO, etc.), we see events that are multidimensional. They include police coordination across nations, across agencies, and between law enforcement and the military. They include not only crowd control, but also extensive surveillance operations that extent to the control of border flows. In addition, they also involve carefully designed media campaigns launched in coordination with the institutions being protested. To us, all this points to what we term a counterinsurgent effort.

Why is this terminology important? It's important because, if we are correct that we are dealing with a counterinsurgent strategy, then we are witnessing a serious attack directed at social movements that have traditionally been a force of social change. We must conclude, then, that dissent in these instances is being treated as insurrection. The new wave of activists must take this fact into account as they create strategies to contend with it. Least the reader think this is a gloomy picture, we remind them that counterinsurgency measures have not always succeeded.

Conclusions

In this chapter, we revisited alterglobalization protests over the past decade, demonstrating a trend away from protest policing and toward insurgency control. Starting with the unsettling news about an apparent network of undercover police officers spying for years on alterglobalization networks in Europe (and the US), we presented examples of the less overt, but nevertheless pervasive forms of social control, pointing out a shift towards preemptive and networked forms of control that are aimed at reducing potential insurgency.

In understanding this shift, it is important to note that we see protest policing and insurgency control not as two separate and distinct strategies. Rather, they are part of a continuum of social control that extends from order maintenance (or "regular" policing functions) through protest policing and into insurgency control. Thus, police can, at any given time or protest, deploy any of these approaches. What is particularly important here is that in the examples we provided, it appears that police tactics are increasingly more likely to tend towards the insurgency control section of the continuum.

Throughout Europe and the United States, protest events are also shifting in important ways. What were large gatherings targeting institutions such as the World Trade Organization, International Monetary Fund, or NATO, new mobilizations are gaining strengths against the economic collapse and austerity measures (e.g., the protest in Greece and Spain, as well as the Occupy Movement in the United States). Further, these mobalizations seem to have more potential for general insurrection in the population. As such, police in these nations will likely have to respond with tactics that may further develop the insurgency control aspect of law enforcement. Only time will tell which direction this will develop.

Finaly, in trying to make sense of the shifting social control of global protest in the past decade, we have to acknowledge the often systematic approach of authorities and the exorbitant costs and efforts. Therefore, we suggest to frame these control activities as counter-insurgency operations than as protest policing. Most of the operations described above only make sense if they are not only seen in the context of a single protest or mobilization, but in the context of an emergent uprising, a continuous threat for global rulers. In the past decade global revolt has been joined by global counter-insurgency.

The activist reader may ask: Where do we take it from here? Well, knowing what the opponent does is an important step towards developing new tactics in the struggle for global justice. We hope this chapter helps to understand and further investigate counter-insurgency operations. Last but not least, we need to better protect social movements as key vehicles for social change. We cannot let governments criminalize popular non-institutional forms of organization.

Literature

Aksyutina, Olga and Marianne Maeckelbergh (eds.) 2012. *The Criminalization of Protest: Using 'terrorism' to suppress dissent.* Oakland, CA: PM Press.

Amster, Randall 2008. *Lost in Space: The criminalization, globalization, and urban ecology of homelessness.* New York: LFB Scholarly Pub.

BAO Kavala 2007. *Kavala Report 2.* Rostock: BAO Kavala.

Caffentzis, George and Silvia Federici. 2001. "Genova and the Antiglobalization Movement," http://www.commoner.org.uk/01-1groundzero.htm [accessed November 28, 2011].

de Goede, Marieke 2008. "The Politics of Preemption and the War on Terror." *European Journal of International Relations*, 14 (1): 161–185.

European Union: Council of the European Union 2002. *Council Framework Decision 2002/475 on Combating Terrorism* , 13 June 2002, 2002/475/JHA, at http://www.unhcr.org/refworld/docid/3f5342994.html [accessed 6 February 2012]

Fernandez, Luis A. 2008. *Policing Dissent.* New Brunswick: Rutgers University Press.

Juris, Jeffrey S. 2008. *Networking Futures. The movement against corporate globalization.* London: Duke University Press.

Komitee für Grundrechte und Demokratie 2007. *Gewaltbereite Politik und der G8-Gipfel.* Köln: Komitee für Grundrechte und Demokratie.

Melucci, Alberto 1989. *Nomads of the Present: Social movements and individual needs in contemporary society.* Philadelphia: Temple University Press.

Mitchell, Don 2003. *The Right to the City.* New York: Guilford Press.

Monroy, Matthias 2011. "Using false documents against 'Euro-anarchists': the exchange of Anglo-German undercover police highlights controversial police operations." *Statewatch Journal*, 21 (2): 1–16.

Neocleous, Mark and George Rigakos (eds.) 2011. *Anti-Security.* Alberta, Canada: Red Quill Books

Piven, Frances Fox and Richard A. Cloward 1977. *Poor People's Movements.* New York: Pantheon Books.

Potter, Will 2011. *Green is the New Red Format: Trade Paper.* San Francisco: City Lights Publishers.

RAV. Republikanischer Rechtsanwältinnen- und Rechtsanwälteverein/ Legal Team (eds.) 2008. *Feindbild Demonstrant.* Berlin: Assoziation A.

Scholl, Christian 2012. *Two Sides of a Barricade. (Dis)order and summit protest in Europe.* New York: State University New York Press.

Stad, Kees 2007. "Spin and rumor at the G8", at http://www. spinwatch.org/-articles-by-category-mainmenu-8/62-international-politics/4260-spin-and-rumour-at-the-g8?format=pdf [accessed 20 November 2011].

Starr, Amory, Luis A. Fernandez, and Christian Scholl 2011. *Shutting Down the Streets*. New York: New York University Press.

Vitale, Alex S. 2007. "The command and control and Miami models at the 2004 Republican National Convention: new forms of policing protests." *Mobilization*, 12 (4): 403–415.

Wood, Lesley 2010. "Bringing together the Grassroots: A strategy and a story from Toronto's G20 protests." *Upping the Anti*, 11: 85–100.

AUSTERITY ERA POLICING, PROTEST AND PASSIVITY IN LITHUANIA

Arunas Juska and Charles Woolfson

Introduction

As a number of European governments imposed drastic austerity measures in the aftermath of the global economic and financial crisis, social unrest occasioned by austerity became a major issue of policy throughout European Union. The economies of new EU member states such as Lithuania had already experienced the pain of radical austerity measures and seemed to provide some pointers to the beleaguered governments facing rising popular discontent elsewhere. The Lithuanian Prime Minister, Andrius Kubilius, interviewed by Steve Forbes, the editor-in-chief of *Forbes Magazine,* defended the raft of severe austerity measures which his government had adopted since the beginning of 2009 in response to the fiscal crisis facing his country. Kubilius was visiting the US to talk-up his country's prospects for economic recovery from one of the worst-hit economies in the European Union. The economic and, in particular, the social costs of the crisis and the socially harmful impact of the austerity measures adopted by his government had been recently detailed in an article on the front page of the business section of the *New York Times* (Thomas, 2010).

Kubilius was in the US to repair any reputational damage and re-assure potential investors that Lithuania was a good place in which to do business. Lithuania (along with neighbouring Latvia) was duly characterized by *Forbes* as among 'Europe's unsung heroes'. "Not every recession-hit country in Europe is like wayward Greece, Portugal and Spain," enthused its eponymous editor Steve Forbes, noting "amazingly, Lithuanian unions went along with the government's policies. There were no street riots *à la* Greece (*Forbes*, 2010)." The truth is rather more complex, and tells us much both about *'policing the crisis'* in neo-liberal times in the context of post-communist Eastern Europe.

In order to contextualize austerity era governance, and to understand policing responses in particular, we provide a broader outline of the severe socio-economic and political downturn which began in Lithuania in late 2008 with the "burst" of stock and real estate markets. Such a description is important because it allows us to trace the developments that led to a large scale protests in early 2009, including a particularly violent mass protest demonstration in the capital Vilnius. Since then, as political protest began to decline rapidly, Lithuania experienced a wave of emigration from the country, unprecedented in scope. We argue that political demobilization and its transformation into mass "exit" can only partially be explained by purely economic factors such as dramatic increase in unemployment and drastic wage cuts. We point instead to an unacknowledged drift towards authoritarianism in governance as one of the responses to increasing political and social unrest in the region, including the criminalization of protest and the centralization and militarization of policing, in particular (see Fernandez and Scholl, *this volume*). Such austerity era policing strategies not only have imposed restrictions on "voice," but also have facilitated the transformation of protest into emigration. Thus, we highlight the need to analyse both protest and policing, in order to understand political acquiescence and emigra-

tion as mutually co-dependent and reinforcing responses
to austerity. In this regard, the attempt to draw reassuring
lessons (*a la Forbes* magazine) from Baltic states such
as Lithuania that seemingly successfully imposed severe
austerity measures on their populations without provoking
destabilizing social unrest, may be misplaced.

The contours of the crisis

Since the collapse of the Soviet Union at the beginning of
the 1990s, all three Baltic states have adopted neo-liberal
'open market' policies of economic and social reconstruction designed to promote foreign direct investment (Bohle
and Greskovits, 2007; Aidukaite, 2009). By the middle of
the previous decade, the Baltic States collectively dubbed
'tiger economies', had received a special accolade for their
efforts in introducing free market reforms from the World
Bank (World Bank, 2005). The successful economic transition was marked by steadily high growth levels of GDP from
the beginning of 2000, and particularly since joining the EU
in 2004 until 2008. In Estonia and Latvia, the average yearly
growth of GDP exceeded 8% and in Lithuania it reached
around 7.5% during 2000-2007, while EU27 average was
less than 2.5%. The unwelcome corollary of higher GDP
growth rates was that it was largely based on the development of unsustainable economic sectors such as speculative
property development and personal consumption, financed
by external liquidity. When the economic downturn finally
arrived in 2008, the relative sharpness of the decline
occasioned by the crisis was significantly greater than the
average for the EU.

Previous growth in the Baltic economies had been largely
based on 'bubble' economics. Property acquisition and an
orgy of profligate personal consumption, fuelled by cheap
foreign credits courtesy mainly of Swedish banks, rather
than investment in productive industries, produced much of
the spectacular GDP growth of the early and mid-2000s.
As a result, the Baltic States were economically vulner-

able to a 'hard landing,' contingently exacerbated by the systemic problems of the global financial system. All three Baltic countries subsequently experienced sharp economic downturn with the onset of crisis, with collapsing output and a severe 'correction' in property prices. This occurred most sharply of all in Latvia closely followed by Lithuania. Thereafter rapidly declining income and consumer consumption levels emerged as widespread unemployment gripped all three Baltic States, including the previously prospering Estonia.

By the spring of 2009, the European Commission economic forecast for the Baltic states was gloomy, with the economic downturn predicted to be "deeper and more protracted than previously assumed" (European Commission, 2009: 80). Already in 2008 compared to 2007, Estonia, Lithuania and Latvia had witnessed decreasing GDP. By the 4th quarter of 2009 compared to the previous year, GDP had decreased by 17.9% in Latvia, 13.2% in Lithuania and 9.4% in Estonia (the three most significant declines in the EU). The EU27 average decline for this period was 2.7% (Eurostat, 2010a). An economic shock of this scale has had its impact on labour market. In 2009, official unemployment rates in Baltic countries equalled the highest in the EU after Spain, reaching 17.6% in Latvia, and 14% in Lithuania and in Estonia (Eurostat, 2010). Youth unemployment reached over 30% in Latvia and Lithuania, and 28.5% in Estonia (Eurostat, 2009b). In all three Baltic countries, the situation in labour market was still deteriorating in the spring of 2010 with unemployment rates continuing to rise.

As such, the Baltic region has had the unwelcome distinction of suffering the economic effects of the crisis in perhaps the most acute form within the European Union, with their currencies, banking systems and economies verging on collapse (*The Economist*, 2009a). It should be noted, however, that not all the Baltic countries were in an equally difficult situation, and that the measures taken to adjust their economies to the impacts of the crisis were to some extent different. Estonia, for example, had exercised more prudent expansion policies than its neighbours during the boom years, moderating the kind of 'over-heating' most drastically experienced in Latvia, and to a slightly lesser extent in Lithuania from the early 2000s onwards. Again, in contrast to neighbouring Latvia which had been forced to seek a €7.5-billion bailout from lenders led by the International Monetary Fund, Lithuania and Estonia attempted to resolve their budget deficits without reliance on external support which would have made their domestic economic adjustment packages subject to even more stringent policy measures.

Each of the Baltic States was presented with a dilemma: how to construct a national policy response, being small nations in the context of a financial and economic storm that was global in scope and with a past pattern of economic expansion based on speculative investment and a 'business-friendly' flat tax regime that had left them especially vulnerable. The lessons of economic interdependency were particularly unpalatable for these three former Soviet republics which had experienced the massive industrial dislocations of transition to the market in the 1990s, only now to discover that expectations of uninterrupted growth and prosperity were misplaced. The 'hard landing' in the Baltics became all the harder as foreign investors in the form of Swedish banks through their local subsidiaries, having significantly overexposed themselves to potential defaults, exercised their vested interest in securing early loan payments on borrowers, with resultant widespread defaults and bankruptcies. These loans had been mostly denominated in Euro (up to 90% of the total) which simultaneously had the effect of drying up the credit market for investments in the productive sector. Currency devaluation, one potential response option of the Baltic governments, posed a threat not just to lenders and foreign investors, but to domestic borrowers. In the event of widespread defaults, both personal and corporate, the worrisome prospect of a wider 'contagion' existed, potentially affecting other banking systems like those of the UK and the Netherlands

(*The Economist*, 2009b). As a result, the entire European financial system could potentially unravel. The European Central Bank asserted the necessary precautionary warning in order to forestall any parliamentary (i.e. 'democratic') interference with the operations of the subordinate national central bank in Lithuania (the Lithuanian Litas being 'pegged' to the Euro), arising as a result of popular resistance to budgetary cuts from a disgruntled population (European Central Bank, 2009).

With currency devaluation ruled out, an 'internal devaluation' in terms of radical reductions in wages, especially in the public sector and a massive retrenchment of public expenditure, was the preferred option of government. Thus, in response to unfolding events, including the threat of 'excessive debt procedures' from the European Central Bank, the recently formed centre-right ruling coalition, proposed a series of draconian measures to address a budget deficit of 4.8 billion Litas (€1.4 billion) accounting for up 4.8% of GDP. These crisis measures included swinging financial cuts, general increases in value added tax (VAT) on certain products up to six times, reductions in state pensions and other forms of social support and substantial wage reductions across the board amounting to up to 30%. The strategy of 'internal devaluation' was in sharp contrast to the initial pump-priming counter-recessionary expenditures of the governments of the US and the older EU member states. Lithuanian government policies thus resulted in radical changes in the labour market conditions. The question was how far would it be possible for such sacrifices to be imposed, without disrupting 'social cohesion' in society, a question that was to have European-wide resonance as the economic crisis unfolded.

Criminality and post-communism

A discussion of social trust and cohesion in post-communist societies such Lithuania is helpful in order to understand the subsequent pattern of events. In the literature of post-communism it is frequently asserted by policy agents such as the European Union that a functioning 'civil society' in the form of non-state voluntary organisations is an intrinsic necessity in the construction of 'new democracies' in Eastern Europe (Lane, 2010). Usually, the difficulties in establishing a viable civil society are ascribed to the 'atomisation' of social and political life due to the experience of statist totalitarian suppression under communist rule (Howard, 2003). Less often acknowledged is the ongoing fragmentation of social solidarities in the new democracies of Eastern Europe by the baleful and often criminal process of transition to the market.

The new market economies present in unvarnished detail, a picture of business-led and organized crime reaching to, and in some cases orchestrated at, the highest levels of the state and government (Rutland, 2000; Satter, 2003). Take Lithuania as one example. Here, pervasive criminality impregnated the entire fabric of post-communist society. In recent times, Lithuania distinguished itself in initiating the first impeachment of a serving president of an EU member state, with his advisors accused of links to Russian organised crime, eager to acquire the last as yet unprivatized 'blue-chip' assets of the state (Valentinavicius, 2004: Paulikas, 2004a, 2004b, 2004c). Privatisation, the economic engine of the transition process to the market, according to its proponents, was supposed to make workers "co-owners" and fulfil "social justice" and equity objectives (Lithuanian Free Market Institute, 2000). Yet, within a matter of sometimes months, the majority of privatisation vouchers handed out to workers in former state enterprises, as elsewhere across the former communist world, were sold on the black market for cash and ended up in the pockets of enterprise managers on extremely favourable terms. This flawed privatisation jarred with "public expectations... strengthened by propaganda, promising high dividend rates, high profitability of the shares and higher living standards" (Maldeikis, 1996: 3). So great was public unrest in Lithuania concerning "corruption and the influence of organised criminal groups" over the process of privatisation that it was temporarily halted (Maldeikis, 1996: 16). The distribution of assets before auctions, via "payments to organised criminal groups for the right to acquire particular assets, selling of 'insider' information by officials and their participation in privatisation process" had a significant impact in producing a popular negative view of the whole process.

The stripping of business assets, insider-dealing, the creation of 'daughter firms,' organized theft and nepotism thus rapidly produced profound social disenchantment among those sectors of the population excluded from the new 'kleptocracy.' Economic reconfiguration was a violent "smash and grab" process (Fearon and Laitin, 2006: 20). The majority of the population has experienced the trauma of transformation to the market system as coercive economic dispossession. Such coercion and gangsterism was accompanied by the 'capture' of the institutions of government by the new (old) elites, laying the foundations in Lithuania for a "symbiosis of politics and crime" (Juska and Johnstone, 2004). The local press unblushingly observed that "many of the 340 or so national legislators in the three countries are pocketing bribes is common knowledge and, when mentioned, fails to raise an eyebrow at any conference or sowing circle" (*The Baltic Times*, 2004a). The chief commissioner of police in Lithuania's second-largest city, Kaunas, accused mafia bosses of directly financing a number of deputies in parliamentary elections, carefully choosing candidates who had no previous criminal record, as well as providing funding for both the country's traditional and new political parties. "Kaunas is a state within a state with its black business" the police chief was reported as saying (*The Baltic Times*, 2004b). Not without reason, the World Bank noted a high degree of "conquering" of parliaments in this region by "economic interest groups" (Jacobsen, 2001).

This corrupt reconstitution of society has undermined social trust and belief in the basic fairness of the new form of society and its institutions (Kornai, 2004). The corruption of the elites translated into a pervasive social pessimism, a popular alienation from the institutions of state, judiciary

and government, and from the political process in general.
Symptomatically, authoritative survey evidence consistently
pointed to Lithuania as among a group of European countries
in which people reported "particularly low life satisfaction,
happiness and life fulfilment" (Anderson et al., 2009: 22; see
also Eurobarometer, 2007). Using a more qualitative approach,
Reiter (2007, 2010) has perceptively explored the sociological
dynamics of contemporary alienation in Lithuanian society,
characterised by what he terms the "de-solidarisation" of
society and "citizenship uncertainty." An important aspect
of this process has been an explicit "*de*-legitimation" of an
independent working class voice which has found almost no
public space in post-communist rhetorical landscape. The
sociologist Rasa Balockaite (2009: 16) describes the process
of marginalization in which the dispossessed 'new poor' have
been rendered 'voiceless':

> These people did not master the new language of
> power – the market economy and political liberalism
> – and were left adrift outside of the public discourse.
> Their pauperization was reinforced by the shift in
> ideological guidelines; while socialist ideology was
> based on collectivist righteousness and pride of the
> working class, the new liberal regime emphasized
> personal ability and individual success. The very term
> 'working class' became disgraced and discredited
> (2009: 16).

It is against this background that the obstacles to the
mobilisation of trade union resistance against austerity
measures must be assessed.

The exclusion of trade union 'voice'

The voice of resistance to austerity in many European countries has been the organised trade union movement whose
members' jobs and livelihoods have been directly threatened by cuts in public expenditure. The situation in the

Baltic states is rather different, due in part to the weakness of the trade unions, itself a legacy of the communist era. In all three Baltic countries in the post-communist period, there has been a high degree of employer resistance to union organization, especially at enterprise level, with very few sectoral agreements being negotiated covering wages and working conditions (Vatta, 2001: 129-130). The majority of smaller enterprises, major foreign multinationals and many of the larger companies play little or no part in the affairs of employers' confederations. Thus, firstly, the trade unions represent a very small fraction of employees, and the decline of union membership that started with the transition process has steadily continued. Second, the low level of membership does not permit the servicing of a large union apparatus which could be effective in representing employees on the one hand, and enable competent participation on wide array of policy and employment issues, on the other. Third, the fragmented structure of union representation, a legacy of transition, with several confederations splintered between rival organizations, further depletes the already limited organizational and financial resources. In total, there are three separate trade union confederations representing 7.6% of employed people in Lithuania. Such trade union presence as exists is mainly concentrated in the public sector and among older workers. Trade union density in the three Baltic countries is the lowest in the EU and in recent years has declined more sharply than in most other EU member states (European Foundation, 2009: 10).

Faced with the tsunami of the crisis which struck Lithuania in the latter half of 2008, the anti-crisis measures of the new government were hastily devised and unilaterally pushed through parliament in day and night sessions during December of 2008, in order to be in place before 1 January 2009, the date of the new taxation year. These measures were to be implemented over the succeeding months. The trade unions, over a period of the three previous months, had repeatedly requested the continuation of the social dialogue established with the previous administrations. Their successive letters and entreaties over proposed fiscal measures received no response. As a result, for the first time in the post-independence period, the notoriously fractious Lithuanian trade union confederations publicly united around a common set of demands designed to mitigate the impacts of the crisis and called for a popular demonstration in the form of a warning strike in late January 2009.

The protest demonstration, held in Vilnius on 16 January 2009 took place one week after a similar demonstration in Riga, capital city of Latvia. The Riga demonstration had ended in social disorder and riot – the first such occurrence of social unrest in a new EU member state. In Vilnius, some seven thousand persons, both young and old, gathered in freezing temperatures and heavy snowfall in one of the largest popular gatherings since independence. Co-ordinated trade union-led protests also took place in at least half a dozen smaller towns and other cities, such as Klaipeda, Siauliai and Panevezys, places that had rarely or never seen trade union demonstrations before on this scale. In Vilnius the mass assembly outside the parliament began in an orderly enough fashion with the leaders of the various trade union confederations addressing their supporters. After respectfully listening to their leaders, the demonstration proceeded down the main thoroughfare, Gedimino Avenue, to the government headquarters where a petition was to be handed in relaying the trade union demands.

A sizeable crowd remained outside the parliament building. There were repeated calls for government ministers to speak with the demonstrators. Angry shouts could be heard of – *'We are waiting!'* The embattled and dispirited police officers guarding the parliament doors were taunted by calls from the crowd: *'You live for our money. What are you doing? You are protecting thieves!'* Chants began to swell up of *'Why? Why? Why?'* and *'Away with thieves! Away with thieves!' 'The parliament are thieves!'* Enraged demonstrators began pelting the parliament windows with eggs and stones. Finally, there was a surge forward as demonstrators attempted to enter the parliament building which the regular police officers guarding the doors found increasingly difficult to contain.

Within minutes formations of riot police had appeared and taken up positions in front of the parliament. They were dressed in full body armour, wearing black balaclavas and tear-gas masks, armed with truncheons, shields and rubber bullet rifles and accompanied by dogs. Nothing like this had been seen since the days of an abortive Soviet military intervention in January 1991 which cost the lives of thirteen demonstrators. The riot police were also supported by a khaki-clad paramilitary unit, the Public Security Service, answering to the Ministry of Interior, and comprising about a thousand hand-picked officers with a remit that included the suppression of riots and civil unrest (King *et al.*, 2007: 432). One demonstrator shouted, *'When we elect them, they shut the doors and call in the army and don't come out to speak.'* Someone in the crowd threw a smoke flare, and the phase of riot began. For the next few hours, pavements were torn up to provide ammunition, and police and rioters hurled missiles and tear-gas canisters at each other in running battles. In an attempt to force demonstrators away from the parliament building, the main thoroughfare was sealed off. Thick clouds of tear gas drifted across Independence Square adjacent to the parliament. One protestor accused:

> We are living in a criminal world and a world of lies. But the worst thing is when Lithuania completely collapses, the old generation and the new generations will be buried together under the ruins.

And another continued this theme with eloquent outrage:

> We need to change the system because the only people who are doing well now are a bunch of arrogant parasites. We are run for the last nineteen years by garbage, and it should be the other way. Because the really good people, who can actually do something, are on the bottom, because trash managed to take over Lithuania.

The perception that the livelihood of people had been *stolen* was ubiquitously present in chants of demonstrators: *'The parliament are thieves.'* It imbued their discourses with an accusatory tone that challenged the basic legitimacy of the political system.

The 'demonstration-cum-riot' as the local press liked to describe it, saw some acts of wanton hooliganism including attacks on vehicles, as well as casualties on both sides, and over a hundred and fifty arrested, with several dozen subsequently sentenced to periods of imprisonment. Following this event, the leaders of the three trade union confederations appeared in court, charged with failing to ensure public order during the demonstration. In post-communist Lithuania there has been an imperceptible line between legitimate social dissent and perceived subversion. In any event, to forestall further such unwelcome occurrences, the government immediately authorised the purchase of more traditional technologies of repression. Lithuanian law enforcement now had at its disposal its own 'anti-riot control vehicles' fully equipped with high power water cannon.

As the crisis unfolded further sporadic but increasingly 'muted' social protests led by organized workers, mainly in the public sector, or by particular hard-hit groups of the population such as pensioners, students and others, took place. In each case the law on assembly in public places was applied assiduously, either to prevent protest actions being held in the first place, or to confine them to out-of-the-way locales where they could be easily contained by the authorities. Thus young mothers and fathers concerned about reductions in child benefit requested permission to demonstrate outside government headquarters, but the numbers of those eventually permitted to do so was restricted, while supporters were consigned to on-looking from a prescribed distance. The black masking tape over the mouth of one protesting father (a prominent television personality) spoke volumes about the perceived lack of freedom to express dissent.

Centralization and militarization of policing

Social unrest of early 2009 significantly speeded up the centralization of the police force, as locally accountable and more community-oriented municipal police units came under the direct control and supervision of the national police headquarters. This allowed for the re-distribution and re-direction of limited and shrinking police resources towards the strategic management of potential social unrest in the capital, Vilnius, and, to some degree, in other large cities. As resources from other regions were shifted towards the capital, policing in Vilnius was increasingly seen as being provided at the expense of public safety and security in other areas of the country (BNS, 2009).

Centralization of command and control went hand in hand with policies strengthening the military ethos of police officers, especially in their interaction with citizens, publicly manifested in military-style deployments with the goal to attack and destroy 'the enemy.' Critics dubbed such tactics as a drift towards the 'Belarussification' of policing, likening the increasing use by authorities of repressive strategies and tactics to those employed by authoritarian leader Alexander Lukashenko in neighbouring Belarus (Paulauskas, 2011; Vasiliauskaite, 2011). Even at small-scale demonstrations of labour unions or marginal political groups numbering in the few hundreds, police now routinely established barricades with entry posts to check the rucksacks and hold-all luggage bags of demonstration participants. Mounted police and special riot units tended to be present, dressed in bullet-proof military apparel with (anti-barricade) battering rams and with accompanying police dogs; extensive visible surveillance and video-recording were also conducted (see also Fernandez and Scholl on similar tactics in policing the alterglobalization movement, *this volume)*. In early 2011 police created a special fenced-in area near the *Seimas* with manned security checkpoints and command and control headquarters from which the police command and interior ministry leadership were able to watch live video feeds from multiple surveillance cameras. At times, policing of political protest acquired an eerie resemblance to Soviet era policing tactics when intimidation by overwhelming force and extensive surveillance was used against small groups of protesting dissidents. This represented a very worrisome shift towards policing by threat of violence rather than policing by consent. Virtually absent from such practices of austerity policing was the core democratic acknowledgement that protesters were not 'the enemies' of the state and that demonstrations and rallies were not 'enemy operations' to be either disrupted or prevented altogether, far less that these were citizens exercising their constitutional rights in a democracy.

Similarly, there was a clearly pronounced trend, especially in the capital Vilnius, towards an increasing number of arbitrary administrative prohibitions and restrictions on political protest that in some cases resembled a virtual bureaucratic sabotage of rights to free speech and public assembly by citizens. As a result, contesting bureaucratic obstructionism by raising legal challenges in the courts became an almost routine way for civic groups and political parties to obtain permits for public rallies. Municipal authorities routinely delayed, dragged out, restricted, and prohibited demonstrations (Ignatavicius, 2011; Kranauskas, 2011). Even when the courts overruled municipal authorities, new administrative manoeuvres were invented such as seemingly arbitrary restrictions on the number of protesters: in once case to 300 for a coalition of groups 'For high quality and affordable higher education in Lithuania' (Delfi, 2009); in another to 2,249 participants in the permit issued to labour unions (ELTA, 2011a).

As the acquiescence of the public to austerity policies (at least for the time being) was secured by growing restriction of and militarized responses to political protest, the ideological justification of austerity measures imposed by the government was increasingly framed in terms of a necessary response to an unforeseen natural calamity similar to that of a hurricane or earthquake. If the banking crisis was interpreted as a natural calamity, then the only politically relevant question that could be asked was how better or more efficiently to respond to it; i.e., to ask the potentially system-threatening question 'who is benefiting and who pays the price for austerity measures?' becomes "irrational." This to a large degree explains why from Prime Minister and the Speaker of the *Seimas* down to local municipalities localized anti-austerity protest actions were treated as disturbances, as annoyance, as superfluous noise, or something negative which should be pushed out of sight to remote suburbs. There was also a tendency to demonize protesters who by the very fact of gathering in public had declared 'a war' on authorities or to characterise them as easily manipulated simpletons (ELTA, 2011b). Finally, the charge of "irrationality" of protest actions and the "naturalisation" of the character of the financial crisis to some degree explains the difficulty that an alternative discourse had in gaining political traction. Austerity was simply a 'given' and therefore issues of social justice were simply not on the agenda of public debate.

'Exit'

Denied 'voice,' the other main channel for 'dissent' has taken the form of individual withdrawal from society, in the form of emigration. Such 'exit' on an unprecedented scale may also be viewed as process of silent (or 'silenced') protest. 'Exit' surpassed all previous migrations, even those in the period of two or three years which immediately followed EU accession (Figure 1). In 2009, the total of persons officially declaring 'departure' from Lithuania (by official estimates, more than half did not declare) surpassed the post-accession peak migration in 2005 by over 40% (*Statistics Lithuania, 2010a*). In 2009 alone, almost exactly 1% of the total population exited within a twelve month period, or if calculated on the basis of working age emigrants, approximately 2.5% of the workforce (*Statistics Lithuania, 2010b*). Over two-thirds of these migrants departed to other EU member states, Britain, Ireland and Spain being the leading favoured destinations (Migration department under the Ministry of the Interior, 2010). Since these countries were also faced with unemployment and recession, the choices reflect some measure of the desperation of those leaving.

However, the real acceleration of outward migration had only just begun. In 2010, the numbers of recorded departures increased to 10,000-12,000 per month, eventually totalling over 83,000 persons, nearly four times the rate of 2009. In part, these figures reflected changes in the reporting requirements for those departing who wished to avoid social insurance liability in Lithuania. Although by 2011 emigration had declined to 53,800, it was still about 2.5 times higher than in the pre-recession period. Overall, between 2009 and 2011 about 153,000 people left Lithuania, an enormous number for a country of just over 3 million. More than 65% of those who departed were 35 years of age or younger and over 70% had high school level of education or higher qualifications (Januskeviciene, 2012). Because of deteriorating socio-economic conditions, already very low birth rates in the country declined even further. Such intensified emigration began to threaten the demographic viability and survival of the Lithuanian nation.

Figure 1. Emigration, Emigration Rate, and Immigration in Lithuania, 2003-2012.*

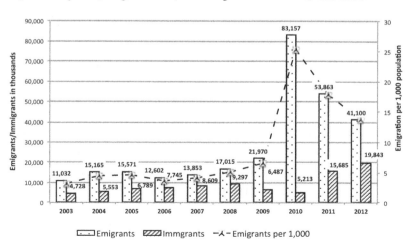

*Source: Statistics Lithuania at http://web.stat.gov.lt/lt/pages/view/?id=1298

*Based on Department of Statistics of Lithuania at www.stat.gov.lt/en/pages/view/?id=1392. The data is only for emigrants who had registered their departure with the Migration Department.

AUSTERITY ERA POLICING, PROTEST AND PASSIVITY IN LITHUANIA

Faced with this extraordinary hemorrhaging of the population, the country's new president, Dalia Grybauskaite, a hard-headed former EU Commissioner for Finance, admonished government to intervene to regulate prices in order to protect more vulnerable sections of the population from the 'unreasonable appetites' of the oligarchs. Threatening to veto legislation, implementing further cuts in social spending and 'irresponsible tax rises,' imposed by government, Grybauskaite, a cold and austere Brussels bureaucrat, became a 'tribune of the people.' Prefacing her first 'State of the Nation' address with the stark observation that Lithuania had "come to the breaking point," Grybauskaite articulated the dynamic of disillusion and migratory 'exit':

> The decision to leave your homeland is a difficult one. But the number of those who decide to take this step is growing. ... We console ourselves by saying that it is a natural consequence of the downturn. However, the countries where our fellow citizens emigrate are also challenged by the crisis. ... And it is not only those without a job who are leaving. So, let us look the reality in the face and admit that people are emigrating not only for economic reasons. They are moving abroad because they feel alien at home (Tracevskis, 2010).

The central theme of this extraordinary address – the loss of trust and confidence in the institutions of the state and the collapse of participation in civic and political life – was no less than a blistering attack on the perceived consequences of "extreme economics", "the lack of justice and solidarity" in society, and rampant corruption orchestrated by individual "special interest groups."

Austerity and its prognosis

Forecasts of a number of international organizations suggest that the Baltic economies are unlikely to attain growth at pre-recession levels (European Commission, 2009: 86; IMF, 2010: 55).

For the foreseeable future therefore, unemployment will probably remain high and wage rates depressed as GDP struggles to recover. Consider the most recent trends in unemployment. Unemployment in Lithuania had more than tripled from 5.8% in 2008 to 18.3% in the second quarter of 2010. Since then unemployment began to decline and in the second part of 2012 reached 13.3%, mostly because of large-scale emigration, but in the last 12-18 months also because of an export-led economic recovery, which led to an uptick in creation of new jobs. However, despite positive and encouraging signs of recovery serious concerns persist about its capacity to reduce outflows of emigration and sustain longer-term economic growth.

Thus, increasing competitiveness of Lithuanian exports, especially vis-à-vis China and other low labour cost producers, was achieved to a large degree because austerity policies significantly reduced wages (to the third lowest in EU – about €5.5 per hour in 2011) and left those in employment increasingly 'unprotected,' and pressured to accept lower labour standards in terms of working conditions. Skyrocketing Asia-Europe shipping costs that increased by about 80% in 2012 alone (see Damas, 2012: 14), growing labour costs in China and quality control problems with Chinese imports (at least in some categories of merchandise such as furniture) also contributed to growing competiveness of the Lithuanian producers (July 2012 interview with the president of the Lithuanian furniture manufacturing firm engaged in production for export to Germany, France and Scandinavian countries). Therefore some Lithuanian economists began to argue that Lithuania had now become "an European China (or more precisely, yesterday's China), therefore we are able to be competitive with real China in the European Union markets" (Cicinskas, 2012).

Decline of wages occurring in conditions of high levels of unemployment had also led to a significant increase in poverty. If in 2008 there were 420,000 or 12.7% of the population living in poverty, by 2009 the poverty rate increased to 20.6%. Although by 2010, there was decrease in the number of poor this was caused mostly by a downward revision of the income poverty measure from 1,746 Lt (€505) in 2009 to 1,472 Lt (€426) per month for a four-member family in 2010 (IQ.lt, 2011). Thus, despite modest recovery, growing poverty and widening wage differentials with EU core countries (e.g., in Sweden 7 times more than in Lithuania) tend only to strengthen these "push" factors in emigration.

When in the second quarter of 2010 the Lithuanian economy grew by 1.1% for the first time since contracting by 14% in 2008-2009, a number of commentators asserted the success of internal devaluation policies in stabilizing financial systems in the region (Duxbury, 2010; Looby, 2011; Samuelson, 2011). Accolades to austerity policies only became louder when in 2011 all three Baltic countries registered significant (in Lithuania 5.9%) annual growth. Estonia, Latvia and Lithuania were praised as examples to be followed by other countries, first of all the deeply indebted Eurozone 'P.I.I.G.S' (Portugal, Italy, Ireland, Greece and Spain). There were claims of the supposed "maturity" of the electorate in the Baltic region in quietly accepting draconian cuts in living standards implying "vibrant" democracies that took in their stride the hardships of recession and endured them in order to implement the necessary market "corrections" (Aslund and Dombrovskis, 2011). Characteristically, in these pro-austerity accounts relatively little attention was paid to social costs of such policies because it was assumed that renewed economic growth would remedy negative impacts produced by the recession.

Despite positive signs, export-based recovery in Lithuania proved to be extremely vulnerable to the on-going sovereign debt crisis and the rapidly slowing economy within the Euro zone. As a result, the Lithuanian economy by the second quarter of 2012 decelerated to 2.1%, while economic forecasts were being continuously downgraded, most recently to about 2.7% growth for the whole year (Klyviene, 2012). This indicates that economic recovery will probably remain sluggish at best and at least a decade or more will be needed to return to pre-recession levels of economic activity (Krugman, 2011a; Weisbrot, 2010b). In fact, by 2015 according to IMF projections, Lithuanian

GDP as measured in $US is projected to remain 12% less (as measured in current prices) than in 2008, with unemployment at 8.5% (Figure 2).

So far the trends seem to confirm the position taken by critics of internal devaluation policies who had used a number of metaphors to juxtapose the paucity of austerity gains with the disproportionally high social costs such that "where they make a desert, they call it peace" by Tacitus (Krugman, 2011b); or the proverbial medicine that cured the disease, but killed the patient. Comparisons were also made between internal devaluation in the Baltics with the brutal 19th century type pro-cyclical economic policies in the UK (Weisbrot, 2010a; 2010c). Jeffrey Sommers and Michael Hudson most notably have argued that the austerity policies amounted to a bailout of Scandinavian and other banks for their legacy of bad mortgages and other loans at the expense of average wage earners and pension savers. Internal devaluation in this view could be compared to imposition of "a kind of debt serfdom" (with the active cooperation of national governments) by the European Union, European Central Bank and the International Monetary Fund (Hudson and Sommers, 2010a; Sommers and Hudson, 2011).

Figure 2: Lithuanian GDP and Unemployment, 2008-2015*

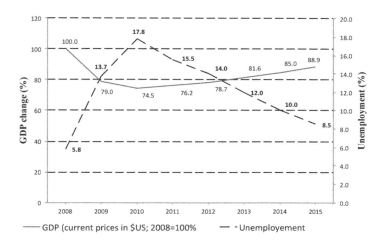

*Source IMF World Economic Outlik Database. September 2011 Report

Of particular interest to commentators was the question why austerity policies imposed on the Baltic countries of "a 19th century level of brutality" (Weisbrot, 2010c), provoked no social upheavals, especially when compared to massive social unrest in Greece, Spain and Britain? As Hudson and Sommers (2010b) have pointed out, there were indeed protests in both Latvia and Lithuania. However in the absence of any significant labour movement in the region, protests soon fizzled out and instead Latvians, Lithuanians and to a lesser extent Estonians, chose emigration as the path of the least resistance.

Although lack of strong labour movement and emigration are very important factors in understanding social and political acquiescence, other commentators also pointed out that the severe economic crisis had accelerated centralization and a growing authoritarianism in post-communist countries. For example, Sippola (2011: 14) argues that the economic crisis has facilitated a rise of authoritarianism which reflects a shift from democratic to technocratic values, more interested in efficiency than in democracy. In the Lithuanian context, the attainment of efficiency in crisis management also included calls for strengthening "law and order." Especially following the January 2009 street riots, the authorities resorted to increasing surveillance, restrictions, constraints, and, in some cases, suppression of political protest, while policing was progressively centralized and militarized to deal with the potentiality for large-scale social unrest.

Conclusion

In the altered world of austerity, new EU member states such as Lithuania now face even more challenging dilemmas so far as policing in society is concerned, in terms of an intensification of an already-present impaired moral and political legitimacy. Criminality tacitly sanctioned and built into the very foundations of the new order raises paradoxical challenges for the issue of policing. What is the role of policing in an unfair society in which the rule of law has been manifestly perverted in the interests of a few and the justice system itself is in general disrepute? Such challenges, not new, have been intensified by the onset of the crisis. The absence of "voice" and deep malaise, fatalism, resignation and "exit" are being fed by a number of developments. These are not only grievances against domestic "kleptocracy." A pervasive sense of powerlessness is also fed by the lack of social and legal protection from and vulnerability to pressure (or whims) of employers and the fear of losing one's employment. There are also accumulated grievances against politicians and government bureaucrats who are not only failing to protect the society and favour the interests of the rich, but are also perceived to be shielding themselves from austerity and benefiting themselves either semi-legally or through outright illegality, due their positions of authority and power. Finally, there is also a sense of vulnerability and powerlessness vis-à-vis anonymous international financial institutions and banks that can to a large degree dictate policies to the Lithuanian government, and over which not only ordinary people in Lithuania, but even the domestic business and the political elite have very little control.

Austerity thus confronts the individual in the form of growing state and increasingly supra-state (reified "financial markets") authoritarianism. This only strengthens perceptions of powerlessness against a background of weak social ties and an absence of solidarity in civil society in general. It is expressed not only in the lack of strength of the labour movement, but also in deep interpersonal feelings of mistrust. Thus the pervasive sense of social injustice in the country is mixed with the grievances of powerless victimhood imposed by an oppressive state and by anonymous global forces. Excluded here are alternative possibilities of mediating relationships between individuals vis-à-vis the state through a variety of interest groups or collectivities that would enable individuals to organize, pool resources, provide representation and solutions, thus influencing state policies as well as providing social space to mobilize for action in the realms beyond the state. In such a fraught context, recourse to a greater authoritarianism and the deployment of repressive policing strategies and technologies exactly conforms to the conjunctural needs of austerity. In terms of the wider political significance of these developments, it is worth reflecting that 'successful' austerity management, and Lithuania is a prime case in point, does not rely on popular acquiescence or even tacit acceptance of policies which are overtly harmful to working people. On the contrary, 'success' if such is the appropriate term, has rested on a mixture of state repression of popular protest and a government prepared to contemplate the haemorrhage of its disaffected population in the name of 'necessary economic adjustment.' Far from being, in the words of *Forbes* magazine, among 'Europe's unsung heroes', for Lithuania today, those who have imposed such harsh policies on its population are among the expanding list of 'Europe's unlamented villains' for whom a day of reckoning still awaits.

References

Aidukaite, Jolanta 2009. "Transformation of welfare systems in the Baltic states: Estonia, Latvia and Lithunia." In: Alfio Cerami and Pieter Vanhuysse (eds.), *Post-Communist Welfare* Pathways. Basingstoke, UK: Palgrave Macmillan, 96–112.

Anderson, Robert, Branislav Mikuliç, Greet Vermeylen, Maija Lyly-Yrjanainen and Valentina Zigante 2009. *Second European Quality of Life Survey: Overview*. Dublin: European Foundation for the Improvement of Living and Working Conditions.

Aslund, Anders and Valdis Dombrovskis 2011. *How Latvia Came Through the Financial Crisis*. Washington, DC: Peter G. Peterson Institute for International Economics.

Balockaite, Rasa 2009. "Can you hear us? The lower class in Lithuanian media and politics." *Problems of Post-Communism* 56 (1): 12–20.

Baltic Times 2004a. "Opinion, Spineless," no. 415, 15 July.

Baltic Times 2004b. "Police Chief: Kaunas mafia bosses eyeing parliamentary seats," no. 425, 23 September.

BNS (2009) "Policija skundziasi, kad del mitingu nukencia saugumas kitose vietose," *Lietuvos Rytas*, December 14, at http://tinyurl.com/abvanl9 (accessed 18 January 2013).

Bohle, Dorothee and Bela Greskovits 2007. "Neoliberalism, embedded neoliberalism and neocorporatism." *West European Politics* 30 (3): 443–466.

Cicinskas, Jonas. 2012. "Veiksmai ekonominiam augimui skatinti." *Atgimimas*, Vilnius, August 26, at http://verslas.delfi.lt/stock/veiksmai-ekonominiam-augimui-skatinti.d?id=59379255 (accessed 27 August 2012).

Damas, Phillip. 2012. Drewry. Container Shipping Market Outlook, Freight rates, and Index-linked Contracts. Birmingham, May 2, 2012, at http://www.tradeextensions.com/multimodal2012.asp (accessed 27 August 2012).

Delfi. 2009. "Dideliems mitingams Vilniuje – Raudona sviesa," *Delfi.lt*, February 24, at http://tinyurl.com/apqj3gg (accessed 18 January 2013).

Duxbury, Charles. 2010. "Irish should look to Baltics, not Iceland." *Wall Street Journal*. New York, NY. December 10, at http://tinyurl.com/aa56e24 / (accessed 18 January 2013).

Economist, The 2009a. "No panic, just gloom," 14 May, at http://tinyurl.com/bcr26l4 (accessed 18 January 2013).

Economist, The 2009b. "Briefing, Ex-communist economies, the whiff of contagion", 26 February, at http://tinyurl.com/bjlw7dc (accessed 18 January 2013).

ELTA, 2011a. "Anuliavus leidima, profsajungos ruosiasi nesankcionuotam mitingui," *Delfi.lt*, February 17, at http://tinyurl.com/b4u568j (accessed 18 January 2013).

ELTA, 2011b. "Protesto kulturos nebuvimas uzkerta kelia tikrosios demokratijos link," *Atn.lt*, February 10, at http://tinyurl.com/atlcnso (accessed 18 January 2013).

Eurobarometer 2007. *European Social Reality. Special Eurobarometer 273*, at http://tinyurl.com/2hjx2w (accessed 18 January 2013).

European Central Bank 2009. *Opinion of the European Central Bank of 20 July 2009 on the procedure to change the official litas exchange rate* (CON/2009/61), at http://tinyurl.com/ar66qfp (accessed 18 January 2013).

European Commission 2009. *Economic Forecast Spring 2009,* Brussels, Directorate-General for Economic and Financial Affairs, May 4, at http://tinyurl.com/dd4872 (accessed 18 January 2013).

European Foundation 2009. *Trade Union Membership 2003-2008*, Dublin, European Foundation for the Improvement of Living and Working Conditions.

Eurostat 2009a. Newsrelease, euroindicators, 121/2009, 24 August, at http://tinyurl.com/m23arb (accessed 28 January 2013).

Eurostat 2009b. Newsrelease, euroindicators, 112/2009, 31 July, at http://tinyurl.com/lrjdar (accessed 28 January 2013).

Eurostat 2010. First estimates for the fourth quarter of 2009, euroindicators 34/2010 - 4 March, at http://tinyurl.com/acpjs3z (accessed 28 January 2013).

Fearon, James. D. and David. D. Laitin 2006. Lithuania. Draft working paper, Stanford University, at http://tinyurl.com/aakk89u (accessed 28 January 2013).

Forbes, Steve 2010. "Europe's Unsung Heroes," *Forbes Magazine* online, June, at http://tinyurl.com/bdodrgb (accessed 18 January 2013).

Howard, Marc. M. 2003. *The Weakness of Civil Society in Post-Communist Europe*. Cambridge: Cambridge University Press.

Hudson, Michael and Jeffrey Sommers 2010a. "Latvia's road to Serfdom." *Counterpunch edited by Alexander Cockburn and Jeffrey St.Clair*. February 15.

Hudson, Michael and Jeffery Sommers 2010b. "Latvia provides no magic solution for indebted economies." *Guardian*. London. December 20, at http://tinyurl.com/26h765s (accessed 18 January 2013).

Ignatavicius, Tadas 2011. "I busimus mitingus - tik su bilietu?" *Lietuvos Rytas*, February 9, at http://tinyurl.com/barrs75 (accessed 18 January 2013).

IMF (International Monetary Fund) 2010. *World Economic Outlook - Rebalancing Growth April 2010*. Washington DC, IMF, at http://tinyurl.com/a7hksp8 (accessed 18 January 2013).

IQ.lt 2011. "Mazejo skurstanciu, bet didejo priklausomybe nuo pasalpu," Vilnius. August 12, at http://tinyurl.com/ab2pwap (accessed 18 January 2013).

Jacobsen, Christen. B. 2001. *Adaptation of the Legal Systems of Candidate Countries – The Case of the Baltic States*. DUPI Working Paper 2001/8, Danish Institute of International Affairs.

Januskeviciene, Liudmila. 2012. "Didele emigracija - prarasta darbo jega ir nususe ekonomikos raumenys." *Lietuvos Rytas*. Vilnius, April 25, at http://tinyurl.com/aa4fnnu (accessed 18 January 2013).

Juska, Arunas and Peter Johnstone 2004. "The symbiosis of politics and crime in Lithuania." *Journal of Baltic Studies* 35 (4): 346–359.

King, Mike, Arianit Koci and Antanas Bukauskas 2007. "Policing social transition: Public order policing change in Lithuania." *Policing*, 1 (4): 428–437.

Klyviene, Violeta. 2012. Lietuvos ekonomikos augimas letejo labiau nei prognozuota. *15min.lt*. Vilnius, August 1, at http://tinyurl.com/a6edfpw (accessed 18 January 2013).

Kornai, János, Bo Rothstein, and Susan Rose-Ackerman (eds.) 2004. *Creating Social Trust in Post-Socialist Transitions*. London: Palgrave Macmillan.

Kranauskas, Linas 2011. "Mitingu menuo (ne)patekejo," *Atgimimas*, Vilnius. February 18, at http://tinyurl.com/bya6wg7 (accessed 18 January 2013).

Krugman, Paul 2011a. "Bully for the Baltics?" *The Conscience of a Liberal*. September 24, at http://krugman.blogs.nytimes.com/2011/09/24/bully-for-the-baltics/ (accessed 5 November 2011).

Krugman, Paul 2011b. "Can Europe be saved?" *The New York Times.* New York, NY. January 12, at http://tinyurl.com/bjqvqld (accessed 18 January 2013).

Lane, David 2010. "Civil society in the old and new member states." *European Societies* 12 (3): 293–315.

Lithuanian Free Market Institute 2000. *Privatization in Lithuania, Analysis*, at http://www.freema.org/Research/Privatisation.phtml (accessed 8 August 2010).

Looby, John 2011. "A Latvian solution to an Irish problem?" *Business and Finance.* February, at http://tinyurl.com/bl28w63 (accessed 18 January 2013).

Maldeikis, Eugenijus. 1996. *Privatisation in Lithuania: Expectations, Process, Consequences,* CERT Discussion Papers, 96/3. Edinburgh: Herriot-Watt University.

Matonyte, Irmina 2006. "Why the notion of social justice is quasi-absent from the public discourse in post-communist Lithuania." *Journal of Baltic Studies* 37 (4): 388–411.

Migration Department under the Ministry of the Interior 2010. *Migration Yearbook 2009*, Table 3.3. Number of citizens of the Republic of Lithuania and aliens who departed for residence to foreign states in 2009, by states. Vilnius, 25.

Paulauskas, Donatas (2011) "Protestas ar Gedulas?" *Delfi.lt*, January 19, at http://tinyurl.com/bfahh76 (accessed 18 January 2013).

Paulikas, Steven 2004a. "Ugly details of MP corruption come to light." *The Baltic Times* no. 416, 22 July.

Paulikas, Steven 2004b. "Seimas sheilds MPs from prosecution." *The Baltic Times* no. 415, 15 July.

Paulikas, Steven 2004c. "Vilnius Major dragged into corruption scandal." *The Baltic Times* no. 417, 28 July.

Reiter, Herwig 2007. "The Post-Communist Triangle of (Non-) Solidarity and beyond." In: Lars Magnusson and Bo Stråth (eds.), *European Solidarities.* Brussels: P.I.E. Peter Lang: 193–217.

Reiter, Herwig 2010. "Towards a concept of biographical alienation." *XVII ISA World Congress of Sociology*, 13 July, Gothenburg, Sweden.

Rutland, Peter (ed.) 2000. *Business and the State in Contemporary Russia.* Boulder: Westview.

Samuelson, Robert 2011. "What we can learn from Latvia's economic recovery." *Washington Post.* Washington, DC. July 17, at http://tinyurl.com/axjjqre (accessed 18 January 2013).

Satter, David 2003. *Darkness at Dawn. The Rise of the Russian Criminal State.* New Haven and London: Yale University Press.

Sippola, Markku 2011. "Internal devaluation and the Baltic labour market." In: *3rd International Conference Economies of Central and Eastern Europe.* Tallinn, Estonia.

Sommers, Jeffrey and Michael Hudson 2011. "Latvia and the disciples of 'internal devaluation'." *The Guardian*. September 16.

Statistics Lithuania 2010a. International Migration, at http://tinyurl.com/6c7vchr (accessed 18 January 2013).

Statistics Lithuania 2010b. Migration: Declared und undeclared flows by age, statistical indicator and year 2009, at http://tinyurl.com/bf5xtmy (accessed 18 January 2013).

Thomas, Landon Jr. 2010. "From Lithuania, a View of Austerity's Costs." *New York Times*, 1 April, Business supplement: 1.

Tracevskis, Rokas 2010. "Grybauskaite's first state of the nation address." *The Baltic Times*, Riga, 16 June, at http://www.baltictimes.com/news/articles/26428/ (accessed 31 July 2013).

Valentinavicius, Vytautas 2004. "All the President's Men." *Transitions OnLine*, 24 March.

Vasiliauskaite, Nida (2011). "Apie viesas erdves, Sajudi ir Nauja Kaire," *Delfi.lt*, January 31, at http://tinyurl.com/bl33at6 (accessed 18 January 2013).

Vatta, Aleissa 2001. "The Enlargement of the European Union and Social Dialogue in Central and Eastern Europe." *Perspectives on European Politics and Society*, 2 (1): 127–146.

Weisbrot, Mark 2010a. "A Baltic future for Greece?" *The Guardian*. April 28, at http://tinyurl.com/2v7kwoc (accessed 18 January 2013).

Weisbrot, Mark 2010b. "Greece should look before it leaps." *The Guardian*. May 18, at http://tinyurl.com/b5938pm (accessed 18 January 2013).

Weisbrot, Mark 2010c. "Latvia's EU handcuffs." *The Guardian*. February 15. http://tinyurl.com/y885my9 (accessed 18 January 2013).

World Bank 2005. *Doing Business in 2006: Eastern European and Baltic Nations Encourage Businesses with Aggressive Regulatory Reforms*. Washington, D.C.: World Bank.

CREATING SECURITY AND FEARING THE OTHER IN RINKEBY, SWEDEN

Ann Rodenstedt

Over the last couple of decades, urban fear has become an increasingly important issue to address in Western crime policies. Today, it is in fact seen as a problem of the same magnitude as actual crime rates as it is believed to have similar negative effects on the urban population. Fears as well as crime levels are often seen as increasing, and this is frequently reported on by the media. The notion of growing fear, and unequally divided fears between women and men, has since the 1960s created an academic interest in studying the development of fear in the city (Heber, 2007: 11).

Crime prevention is today seen as a way to affect fear and during the same time period as urban fear has been seen as becoming a more vital problem, prevention and policing measures targeting the physical environment and trying to increase social control in public space have received increasing attention. The expectation is that fear can be reduced if the physical environment is neat and tidy and if citizens take responsibility in caring for and controlling the neighbourhood (see for instance Wilson and Kelling, 1982).

However, as will be elaborated upon in this text, fears should not only be seen as individual experiences but rather as collective phenomena affected by discourses and power structures. When fears are attached to lacking welfare as well as prejudice and Othering processes, they pose a difficulty to security measures aimed towards physical space. These processes can be directed towards a minority population by the majority but, as this study will show, they can occur between minority groups as well. The challenge for the local municipalities is thus to tackle these fears in ethnically mixed urban areas.

This chapter is about Rinkeby, a district north of Stockholm often portrayed as a segregated and unsafe area. The aims of the text are twofold: First, to see how fear is experienced and created in Rinkeby, and second, how security is practised in the area in relation to the perceived fears and the general development of crime prevention policies in Sweden over the last 50 years. In order to investigate this, eight people (four women and four men) whose jobs are connected to security initiatives in the area were interviewed in 2009. As a complement to this, shorter interviews were conducted over the telephone and by email. These interviews focused on details of the security work being undertaken in Rinkeby and were conducted a bit later in 2011; one interview was conducted with an earlier interviewee and two were made with officials at the district administration.

Since much research on this topic is dominated by Anglo-Saxon theories, there is a need for an overview of the research on fear, security and crime prevention in light of the Swedish context. Security and social control have become increasingly important within the neoliberal state, as will be elaborated upon in the upcoming section about the development of crime prevention policies during the 1990s. In comparison to countries such as the USA and the UK however, Sweden has maintained strong welfare ideals during the last century. This makes Sweden an interesting case to study given the growing predominance of neoliberal security approaches.

Fear, security and the creation of the crime problem

The concept of *fear* is not easy to define; as an emotional state, it is experienced in different ways by different people. This study will use a broad definition where fear is seen as a concept describing a range of related feelings such as insecurity, risk, worry, danger, intolerance, anger and vulnerability (Heber, 2007). Similarly, Pain (2001: 901) characterises *fear of crime* as the "wide range of emotional and practical responses to crime and disorder made by individuals and communities." But even though fear is an emotion played out inside individuals, these fear-related feelings should not be seen as appearing in a vacuum. Rather, the feelings of fear and other emotions are tightly connected to discourses and power structures in society. As Pain and Smith (2008: 9-10) write, fear can be seen as a collective experience in a "moral geography" which is an effect of power relations determining both moral codes and behaviours in our everyday lives as well as in international affairs. Feminist scholars have provided much theory on female fear over the last couple of decades, and many stress that fear is more than a reaction to specific incidents or events. Instead, fear is often the result of harassment, discrimination or other encounters in everyday life, which creates a "generalised state of insecurity."[112] Koskela (2010: 389-390) writes that fear both reflects social relations as well as influence them. Fear is socially produced, and the experiences an individual has of other people in surrounding spaces are important to fear-related feelings. Fear and insecurities can create an Other by targeting specific people or groups which are seen as threatening. This is also highlighted by Yarwood and Gardner (2000: 403-404) who assert that when perceived cultural differences are seen as a threat to local values, "the cultural can become the criminal."

---

112   Koskela (1997) however makes an important statement in pointing out that even though women tend to report higher levels of fear than men, fear should never be seen as an innate quality of women. On the contrary, women are often challenging fears and claiming urban space.

Strongly related to fear is the concept of security, and Zedner (2003: 154-158) defines security as both a subjective and objective "state of being" as well as "a means to that end" (the latter referring to the pursuit of security by, for example, the local community or the security industry). Objective security as a state of being means being exempt from danger, which is more of a utopia as the concept of security itself often implies the presence of some kind of threat. Subjective security is more related to fear, as security in this case is founded on feelings and apprehensions of threats. Crime prevention, on the other hand, deals with security as well as fear. As practices carried out by, for example, local communities, housing companies and private security companies, crime prevention is not just about obstructing criminal acts from occurring. A substantial part of practising crime prevention today is about preventing fear of crime as well as increasing the likability of various urban places. The Swedish National Council for Crime Prevention (BRÅ), created in 1974 by the Swedish government, distinguishes between "social crime prevention" and "situational crime prevention" to describe crime prevention activities in Sweden. Social crime prevention constitutes those efforts directed towards the primary causes of crime and individuals' tendencies to commit criminal acts, and is often executed by different welfare institutions (Andersson, 2001). Other kinds of behaviour which are legal but considered deviant are also targeted, like substance abuse, as well as different structural problems such as economic disparities and segregation (Sarnecki, 2004: 24-26). In other words, the concept of social crime prevention as it is used by BRÅ is very broad and can lead to many different measures; they can be directed towards welfare related problems and, as will be clear further along in the text, measures can also be directed to target a perceived worsening in social control.

While social crime prevention focuses on the individual, situational crime prevention is more directed towards the scene of the crime and the opportunities to commit crime within certain environments. Possible measures include technical tools in order to prevent stealing and different kinds of surveillance (ibid., 2004).[113] It has however been claimed that there are considerable differences between the theoretical backgrounds of situational and social crime prevention. While social crime prevention is based on the notion that criminal behaviour lies within the individual due to innate or structural factors such as poverty, situational crime prevention assumes that crime is a rational behaviour. The offender is assumed to compare the advantages of committing the crime with the disadvantages, a perspective which has been criticised for ignoring the underlying causes of crime (Takala, 1997).

Garland has outlined the rise of situational crime prevention strategies, which are included in what he terms "the new criminologies of everyday life." Social crime prevention used to be more dominant in policy and research during the beginning of the 20th century, but the development of situational crime prevention and related strategies marked a break with previous criminological thought. These new ways of thinking were inspired by an increasingly popular view that high crime rates were a normal part of contemporary life and reflected a decreasing faith in the criminal justice state. There was also a pessimistic view on the ability of the state to rehabilitate offenders and control crime. As a result, governments started to reallocate their responsibilities to other actors, and the private security industry, local communities, organizations and the everyday individual became new partners in policing and preventing crime (see Eick on similar trends in police-private partnerships in Germany and Wakefield referring to the 'extended police family' in the UK, *both this volume*). Garland stresses that situational crime prevention is very much associated with the market as it assumes that humans

---

113   According to Listerborn (2002) a variety of theories are seen as included in situational prevention in Sweden today. For example "Fixing Broken Windows" (Wilson and Kelling, 1982), "Defensible Space" (Newman, 1972), "Crime Prevention Through Environmental Design"(Jeffery, 1971) and the work of Jane Jacobs (1993) and Bill Hillier (1996).

make choices by economic reasoning, rather than the social reasoning typically associated with the welfare state. This focus on everyone's responsibility in fighting crime and a belief in short-term measures that keep costs down are often connected to governments with post-welfarist and neoliberal approaches (Garland, 2000, 2001).

Neoliberalisation processes have also been noticed in Sweden since the 1980s. Because of its strong social democratic welfare state with good economic growth, industrial development and low unemployment levels, Sweden became known after World War II for the so called "Swedish model." During the 1980s, however, the Social Democratic Party started to adapt to neoliberal economic doctrines, which according to Schierup et al. (2006: 202) had "exceedingly disruptive economic effects."[114] After the financial crisis in the beginning of the 1990s the Swedish social democratic regime changed and started to share some similarities with the "Third Way," even if the changes were not as extensive as in the UK. "The New Swedish Model" still emphasises social welfare and solidarity, but Schierup et al. (2006: 206) assert that this change from the old model to the new has led to "a rising number of 'working poor'" and the labour market has become increasingly "workfare-like." These processes of neoliberalisation also affected the crime policy. Sahlin (2008) describes how Swedish crime policy changed by adapting to different models from the 1970s until today. In the 1970s it was more common that crime preventive measures targeted what were perceived as structural problems, such as social and economic security. These were however increasingly criticised during the 1980s as they were seen as decreasing the power of families and individuals. More focus was thus given to the individual rather than the structure. Efforts were also taken by the state and municipalities to make institutions more efficient by coordinating formal and informal control by,

---

114   The increasing neoliberalisation of Swedish politics during the 1980s has also been noted by Boréus (1994).

for instance, sharpening legislation and creating local crime prevention councils. In response to these changing policies, the previously mentioned Swedish National Council for Crime Prevention (BRÅ) was founded during this time. Eventually in the 1990s social control became one of the most important issues for crime policy and so called "night walkers" (groups of adults walking the streets at night), Closed Circuit Television (CCTV), guards and patrolling police were identified as efficient in preventing crime. It was during this time that crime prevention became conceptually divided into "social and situational crime prevention" and Sahlin (2008) points out that the former should not be confused with the more structural welfare efforts directed towards inequalities as a source of crime. Instead, social crime prevention as it is practiced today was developed together with the concept of situational crime prevention and is more concerned with increasing the social control of parents and schools over youth.

During the 1990s the government also accepted a new national crime prevention program fittingly named "Allas vårt ansvar" ("Everyone's responsibility"), which coincided with cut downs in welfare services and welfare infrastructure such as youth centres as well as increasing income disparities and residential segregation. The program gives local communities a key role and stresses the importance of regaining social control that has been lost over the last couple of decades. Citizens are therefore expected to practise surveillance in the local community in order to promote good norms and spread good values. Tolerance towards deviant behaviour such as disturbances of public order should also be reduced among the general population (Lidskog, 2006; Sahlin, 2008). Crime prevention is often described as an apolitical phenomenon as there is often a wide consensus that crime prevention issues transcend the boundaries of political parties (Listerborn, 2002), but crime prevention is anything but apolitical. Instead, crime prevention is governed by political aims, choices and decisions and should therefore not necessarily be seen as dealing with the causes of crime. In fact, it could even be argued that crime prevention is *constructing* the causes of crime. Those defining what are perceived to be problems regarding crime and its causes are those in power, such as government authorities, and the discourses around what needs to be prevented and which goals should be strived for are thus constantly changing (Sahlin, 2008). These discourses are also reproduced by media, voters and citizens who are constantly striving for objective and subjective security from the threat of "crime problems."

After this brief presentation of central concepts and the development of crime prevention policies in Sweden, an introduction to Rinkeby as a stigmatized and Otherised area is in place.

Rinkeby and its inhabitants as the Other

Rinkeby is a suburb of about 15,600 inhabitants in the northern part of Stockholm. It is an area which onlookers often deem as segregated, crime ridden and generally unsafe. It was constructed during the late 1960s and early 1970s as a result of the social democratic government's campaign to fix the housing shortages of the time by building one million housing units in ten years. Since 2007, Rinkeby has been administratively merged with three of the neighbouring districts and is therefore a part of the new district Rinkeby-Kista.

The structure of the area is characteristic of the time period as the area is planned in accordance with the ideal image of "the neighbourhood" which was supposed to stimulate activity and community through the inhabitants' social relations (Franzén and Sandstedt, 1981: 37). There is a city centre with shops and a few restaurants and cafés as well as access to the metro system and buses nearby. Pedestrians and cyclists are separated from vehicular traffic and the residential area (consisting of 100% rentals where 57.5% constitutes public housing units) is encircling the city centre. The area has a high number of immigrants coming from a relatively broad range of countries in comparison to the rest of the districts in Stockholm; in 2009 the inhabitants with "foreign background"[115] constituted 89.6% of the total population in Rinkeby. 19.9% of the total population received social welfare benefits and in 2008 the average income of the population in the age category of 20-64 years was 164,300 SEK (€18,256), which can be compared to the merged average income of all the city districts in Stockholm which, during the same time, was almost double: 319,800 SEK (€35,533).[116]

Rinkeby has been exposed to extensive media reporting since its construction. Discourses of Rinkeby as well as the surrounding suburbs often portray a picture of a "problem area" or a "ghetto" that is dangerous and dirty and has high levels of crime and other social problems (Ericsson et al., 2002: 15-18). These stereotypes also apply to other areas constructed during the same time period as Rinkeby, and have not gone unnoticed by academics (see for instance Ålund, 1997). However, it is not only Rinkeby as an area that is depicted as a "spatial Other" (Molina, 1997: 210). It is common in Sweden to speak in terms of "immigrants" and "Swedes," and to make divisions between "immigrant culture" and "Swedish culture." These terms are used by politicians, institutions, the media and in everyday discourse. What is perceived to be Swedish signifies normality. The "immigrant characteristic" is a label that carries a negative meaning, but as Molina points out it is nothing but a social construction. The view of "the Immigrant" suggests that there is a homogenous "immigrant culture," and that the reason why so many immigrants live in particular areas is because immigrants want to live together with others of "the same"

---

115   The concept of "foreign background" is often used in Swedish statistics, and is defined by the Stockholm Office of Research and Statistics (USK) as those individuals who are either born abroad or born in Sweden with both parents born abroad. Asylum seekers are excluded in this definition as they do not have a residence permit, and are therefore not nationally registered in Sweden, at http://www.usk.stockholm.se/internet/omrfakta/definitioner2009.pdf (accessed 29 October 2011).

116   See http://www.uskab.se/index.php/omradesvis-statistik.html (accessed 17 March 2011).

culture. Instead, the ethnic segregation in Rinkeby and other immigrant dense areas is part of a racialisation process where immigrants with limited means are often placed together in particular urban areas as a result of decisions made by institutions and policy makers (Molina, 1997).

Connected to Molina's critique, Ålund writes that social inequalities in contemporary Sweden are increasingly interpreted as the product of cultural differences. In turn, this conception becomes tied to fixed ideas about what characterises different ethnicities and races. This makes the social aspects of ethnicity, such as hierarchies based on class and status, invisible. Ethnicity should, just like culture, not be seen as a constant, but rather as something that is constantly being reproduced and renegotiated depending on the social relations in society. But as it is today, "immigrants" tend to be associated with violence, exotism and extremism which are characteristics believed to be inherited from their cultural backgrounds (Ålund, 1997). This way of creating "the Swedish Self" and the "Immigrant Other" relates to Said's concepts of the Occident and the Orient in "Orientalism" (Said, 2000). The concept of "banal Orientalism" (Billig, 1995) is used by Haldrup et al. (2008) in order to describe how global images of "Muslim Others" or non-Europeans are reproduced in everyday practices and experiences, and is taken for granted as the truth. Characteristics that signify difference are often seen in stereotypical ways and they become objects of fantasy and fear. Orientalism is thus created in the practises and encounters of unknown bodies in public space.

As noted previously in the text, feelings of fear arise in relation to what is perceived as the Other, which is also elaborated upon by Sibley (1995: 32). Boundaries and stereotypes are created between different categories or groups in order to create security and comfort, but at the same time also define the Self by making clear what the Self is not: The Other. As long as you stay on the familiar side you may feel safe, but when you cross over you will feel anxious. The establishment of boundaries and categorisations are a way to "make sense of the world." The Other is thus an important factor for urban fear, just as Koskela (2010: 390) points out: "Collectively, fear plays an important role in the process of 'Othering'. If there was no Other there would be no reason to be afraid. Fear *needs* the Other" as "fear has an unholy alliance with prejudice, hate and anger" (*italics* in original).

Security and fear in Rinkeby

The people interviewed for this study[117] in this study all worked with issues relating to security in Rinkeby, and they were asked how they experienced the security work in the area, as well as what the measures were aimed towards: What (and who) was seen as threatening the security of Rinkeby? The interviewees are thus both respondents and informants, as they describe how they experience fear and security in Rinkeby from a personal point of view, while also providing an official assessment of security work from the perspective of their work positions. Even though Rinkeby is often portrayed in negative ways from the outside, the participants give a positive picture of the area and stress that they generally feel safe in the area as they know their way around. Many of them expressed strong resentment at the ways in which Rinkeby has been portrayed as a violent and unsafe place in the media, and that it is unfair as bad things happen everywhere. If there is something positive to report about Rinkeby, the media does not show any interest.

Many interviewees talked about Rinkeby as a small village where all kids know each other no matter which background they have.[118] In this village, there is a certain

---

117 The interviewees names have been changed in this text, even though none of the participants requested anonymity. They are thus referred to as Ahmed, Najma, Marianne, Riitta, Branko, Erik, Isidora and Mustafa.

118 This notion is confirmed by Listerborn (2005). In the suburbs, "the Other" has the ability to create its own space without the judgemental looks from the majority population. See also previous research on Rinkeby and the neighbouring area Husby by Listerborn (2005), Ålund (1997) and Olsson (2008) where the positive aspects of glocality, microcultures, diversity and creativity is elaborated upon.

"Rinkeby spirit" which, according to them, made them feel more secure. Some participants also highlighted other areas as worse than Rinkeby and one interviewee, Riitta who works as a "field assistant" (and is thus a part of the "semi-formal control groups" which will be explained further in the next section of the chapter), explained that she thought one of the neighbouring areas was more frightening as she does not know it as well as Rinkeby. This is a clear example of how lack of personal experience of an area creates a place of fear, at the same time as it illustrates how stigmatization affects the perception of space even for people living in a similarly stigmatised neighbourhood. Fear and insecurity in Rinkeby was however also reflected upon by the interviewees. Erik, who is in charge of crime prevention on behalf of the district administration, mentions that it is often older members of the population who know Swedish who tend to be fearful in the area. They have witnessed the turnover of residents in the last couple of years and may know the area physically, but they do not feel like they know the people in the area anymore.

The participants generally agreed that there are aspects of the security in the area that need to be improved. Ethnic mix was by the participants seen as one of Rinkeby's good qualities, but segregation in terms of language barriers, poverty and high residential density were presented as problems. Those interviewees who had lived in the area since the beginning of its construction felt that the integration of immigrants has become increasingly difficult to accomplish over the years. One interviewee explained how Rinkeby started to receive "waves" of new ethnic groups in accordance with the active conflicts in the world: In the 1970s the Turks started coming, in the 1980s people from South America and Syria arrived, in the 1990s the new inhabitants were mainly coming from Somalia and Yugoslavia and in the 2000s the dominant immigrant groups have become Iraqis and Somalis. Branko, who works at the youth centre, feels that income disparities is a problem to security as some of the kids who come there sometimes do not have any money and use drugs, which creates an unsafe atmosphere which is transmitted to the children. Isidora, who works at one of the local schools, mentions how she thinks that security in Rinkeby can never be perfect due to the "shoving together" of different cultures with different views of morality. This means that the inhabitants' situation can only be "relatively safe."

One specific place that was mentioned by the interviewees as frightening or unpleasant was the public square and the streets and alleys immediately surrounding it. The public square is the heart of the area, located in its absolute centre, where transportation networks meet and connect the area to the rest of Stockholm. Many people walk through here every day but despite that the square is perceived as being dominated by specific groups at specific times, making the participants feel ill at ease. One group that stands out is the boys that hang around the metro station especially during evenings and nights, where they are perceived as loud and mischievous. A couple of the interviewees mention how the kids have been seen setting of rockets and fire crackers close to the exits of the metro and on the platforms, which affected their feelings of security. Ahmed, who works for a local Islamic organisation, explains that the reason why the youths are hanging out around the metro is because the dwellings are often overcrowded. There is simply no way for some of the kids to bring friends home and they have to find ways of entertaining themselves on the streets instead:

> The lack of living space. I think that's perhaps the obstacle that contributes to the youths not growing up in a safe environment. They have to get out in order to get any air whatsoever.

Branko finds the square problematic as it is today because he thinks that the public square's neutrality is threatened by religious activities which are practiced in the vicinity. This, according to him, makes the place feel unsafe for many younger women:

I know a lot of Turkish girls who are not Muslim, but they are nice good looking girls who like wearing jeans and show their hair and perhaps also some skin. Gorgeous girls. Of course they should dress up, they are going into town. But they choose to take a different path and another entrance to the metro because they don't want to walk through the centre. If they do they will be looked at and hear comments and such ... So there are very, very, very strong conservative and strong religious powers in Rinkeby, there really are.

Many of the participants in this study stressed that women do not have the same opportunities to claim urban space in Rinkeby as men; the modernist city planning seems to not only create divisions in physical space, but actually makes it more difficult for women to socially participate in public areas. The public square is seen as a male space, mainly due to the fact that there are many unemployed men standing there socialising with each other and who, in addition to the mischievous boys, add to the feelings of insecurity. Najma, who comes from Somalia and works with girls at the community centre, has a lot to say about the situation of women in Rinkeby. She claims that the men on the square are used to being the providers of the family and now when they do not have a job they are depressed and have nothing better to do. Because of these men she finds it very uncomfortable to be at the square; she feels like the men are just standing there in a group, talking to each other and watching her every move.

The home was also brought up as an unsafe place by two of the participants: Erik who was up to date on the latest statistics on domestic abuse in the area and Najma, who is also volunteering as a contact person for women who are victims of abuse. Najma stresses that domestic violence is a serious problem, as women come to her on a daily basis to show her their injuries. The women are often reluctant to involve the authorities and she sometimes feels that she does not dare to be home sick from work in case someone needs her help urgently. Another thing that Najma is upset about is how boys' activities tend to receive more funding in the area than girls' activities. She is hosting a girls' night at the community centre once a week, but it is sometimes difficult to convince the parents to let the girls come. Najma cannot understand why the municipality is not doing something about this as she feels that it is very unfair that girls are not allowed to have the same social life as boys of the same age. The lack of activities for girls in the area is mentioned by several of the participants, and it has also been brought up in Listerborn's research about the neighbouring area of Husby (Listerborn, 2005).

It is not only women who highlight how the men on the square negatively affect their feelings of security. A few of the male interviewees also expressed their concerns. When talking to the participants of the study, the Somali nationality of the men was brought up as a particular characteristic. One person described the men as just hanging around and chewing the drug khat, waiting for some war to end so that they can go home, and referred to the Somali women as ghosts who scare the children. This stereotypical image of the Somali group in Rinkeby was presented to me several times and can be related to the previously mentioned concept of "banal Orientalism": The interviewees mention that several inhabitants in Rinkeby find them frightening, loud, taking a lot of space, being up to mischief and oppressing women. Interestingly, a very similar picture is painted in Ålund's work from 1997 about youths in segregated suburbs, only the group depicted this way by the interviewees in her work was the Turkish (Ålund, 1997). Since the time of Ålund's work, it would seem that the image of the Turkish population as the Other in Rinkeby has changed. The quote above by Branko suggests that the Turkish woman is now described as liberated and a victim to a conservative Muslim gaze. Erik describes the fear towards different groups this way:

> It is always the latest group to arrive that tends to make people feel unsafe, and the latest group to

arrive in Rinkeby is the Somalis. So then you feel unsafe with the Somalis. And that is the general apprehension among the people living there. Before the Somalis came here it was the second to last group of immigrants which became very large... back then it was the Turks. So it is probably the new ones that you feel unsafe about...

One conclusion that can be drawn from this is that there are Othering processes going on between different groups of immigrants as well, which should not be very surprising as there is no homogenous "immigrant culture." Othering processes exist between different groups and the fears related to the Others tend to change as the Others become more known to the Self. The boundaries that separate different categories, like depicted earlier when referring to Sibley (1995), could therefore be seen as constantly under negotiation.

The proliferation of semi-formal policing and situational crime prevention

Most of the participants of the study were working with issues described as contributing to the social crime prevention in the area. The school and youth activities were highlighted as important in teaching children and youths the Swedish language and ethics as well as working against violent behaviours.[119] For instance, Najma explains how she organises activities for girls and tries to help abused women, and she is also engaged in other youth activities where she, among other things, shows documentaries about sex, alcohol and fear. Apart from this, she is working with the social services to help youths who have been to juvenile jail to get back to a crime-free life. Another interviewee, Branko, stresses how important it is that the youths in the

---

119   Most of the interviewees were working with children and youths. For example Marianne worked at a day care, Isidora at one of the schools, Najma with girls at the community centre, Branko at the youth centre and Riitta as a so called "field assistant."

area have a place like the youth centre to spend their spare time. Youths are open to change, and if they are heading in the wrong direction there is good chance that they can be helped. Branko is also involved in a project called "the Rinkeby Academy," which is run by people living in or coming from Rinkeby who have some kind of academic education. The goal is to increase the youths' motivations in school in order to improve their grades, which is sometimes difficult if their parents have not had the chance to get an education themselves. The staff is supposed to assist with daily homework as well as help the youths to get in touch with companies for employment and internships.

All interviewees working with these more structural approaches towards crime, fear and alienation felt that they were doing an important job that had positive effects. However, the participants expressed serious concerns regarding how the financial support for social work have diminished over the last couple of years; support they are completely dependent upon in order to carry out their work. For instance, Ahmed mentions that his potential to improve security through the Islamic organisation is hindered by a lack of funding, which he believes is a result of the negative label that has been placed upon the Islamic faith. He would like to have the same abilities as the churches to carry out social work, but without money there is no possibility. Branko also feels that more resources should be given to the youth centre as they now have more youths than ever but less staff than in the 1980s. Also, some of the participants expressed discontent over the fusion of Rinkeby into the new city district Rinkeby-Kista,[120] which has resulted in the relocation of many social service institutions. Thus, the civil servants and the inhabitants do not meet on the square or in the shops in the same way as before, a development that is

---

120 The reasons for the merge were indistinct according to the interviewees. According to one of the additional interviews with a district administration official in 2011, it was a political agreement which was decided upon by the municipal council in central Stockholm. Other districts apart from those included in Rinkeby-Kista were also merged, which resulted in cut downs in staff and tax expenses.

breaking with the neighbourhood ideal which inspired the construction of Rinkeby. One of the interviewees gives his view of the development:

> The social welfare office has moved away from here. There is nothing left in Rinkeby. The social insurance office moved away. The employment office moved away. There is nothing left. It is no fun for all the other businesses, there are restaurants going bankrupt. They are all moving to Kista.

Even though structural approaches towards reducing crime and fear have a strong tradition in the area, the district administration has started to direct increasing attention and financial support towards so called "semi-formal control groups." This is coherent with the general development in Sweden over last 40 years, elaborated upon by Sahlin (2008), where welfare infrastructures such as youth centres are receiving diminishing financial support at the same time as crime policies are starting to put more efforts towards increasing social control. The issue of social control and behaviour in public space seem to be important to feelings of fear in Rinkeby, as shown earlier in this study. With this comes the notion that children and youths lack values, leading to a conclusion that an increase in social control is necessary. Several of the participants stressed that it seems like many parents have no idea what their children are doing when they spend time outside the home. The disturbances of social order is probably seen as the biggest "crime problem" in Rinkeby, even if deviant behaviours like those carried out by youths and men at the square are not always classified as illegal.

Erik, who is in charge of the crime prevention on behalf of the district administration in Rinkeby, explains how this perception of poor social control gave rise to the "semi-formal control groups." With this expression he means the various groups, initiated and governed by the district administration and the municipality, who are patrolling the streets in Rinkeby but do not have any more authority to enforce the law than any average citizen. He also refers to these groups as 'the good forces' of Rinkeby.

Table 1: The semi-formal control groups patrolling Rinkeby

Group	Number on the streets	Initiated by	Financed by	Payment (in €)[1]
Field assistants	2 (minimum)/ day and night	City of Stockholm	District administration	2,667-2,822 /month
Citizens' hosts	2/day and night	District administration	50% by external actors 50% by District administration	2,111-2,444 /month
Youth hosts	5-20/every weekend and school holiday (depending on the season)	District administration	District administration	11-12 /hour
Night wanderers	10-15/ every weekend and at special events	District administration and parents	Voluntary, but office financed by public transportation	Free

1   At the time of writing, the exchange rate was 1 EUR = 9,00 SEK.

Source: *own account*

The *field assistants* are employed by the social services and are required to have a degree in social work or equivalent. They walk around Rinkeby during days and nights (until 01.00 at the latest) and talk to the youths in order to prevent crimes, drug use and social problems. The field assistants also inform the youths about tobacco, drugs, values and the law. They often communicate with the parents of the youths, and sit down with kids under 15 and their parents if a crime has been committed for the first time. There are local field assistants working in most of the districts in Stockholm, and they are thus slightly different from the other groups which are executed by the Rinkeby-Kista district administration, external actors and voluntary citizens.

The *citizens' hosts* were created on Erik's initiative in 2001. They collaborate with housing companies, real estate agents, local companies and the district administration. According to an interviewee, their task is to serve the citizens and visitors of Rinkeby and "disturb the criminal forces that are active in the area." The citizens' hosts were established as a reaction to studies showing that the inhabitants of Rinkeby felt most unsafe in the area's centre. The hosts all live in Rinkeby and act as informal guards; they always stay informed on where the 'problems' are, report on vandalism, talk to the youths if they 'behave badly' and try to stop fights before they actually happen. The financing actors can always ask them to keep an extra eye on their grounds and interests, but the citizens' hosts walk all over Rinkeby during their shift. They are not required to have any previous higher education or work experience, but should have a good reputation and be 'well established' in the area.

The *youth hosts* were initiated a few years ago by the district administration and are supposed to increase the likeability of Rinkeby. They consist of youths, between 18-25 years old, who are supposed to communicate with the other youths in the area and pose as role models (they have not been punished by law or have committed minor crimes but since then changed their way of life). They should also inform youths about leisure activities offered by the district administration during holidays.

The *night wanderers* consist of parents and other civilian adults who voluntarily patrol the streets until about 01.00 at night, walking up to kids and checking what they are up to. They report to the field assistants and have their own office in the Rinkeby metro station which, according to the website of the National Network of Night Wanderers in Sweden, is a good place for controlling the youths moving in and out of the area. In the metro there is also a glass case displaying photos of the youths; it is a way for parents to keep track of where their kids have been and what they have been up to.[121]

The semi-formal control groups in Rinkeby bear certain resemblance to the security "ambassadors" studied by Stenson and Lippert (2010) in Canada. The role of the ambassadors, and the semi-formal control groups, is to

---

121   Cf. http://www.nattvandring.se/nv/Om_natverket/Reportage/Valkommen_till_Rinkeby (accessed 18 January 2013).

perform certain aspects of informal policing such as being the "eyes and ears" of the police, target nuisance behaviour and perform their work in accordance with a "clean and safe" rationality. As Svenonius (2011: 24, 42) writes, policing cannot be separated from the concept of surveillance and it should not merely be referred to as solving crimes. Rather, policing can be seen as a central form of social control in urban environments. These groups, or "good forces," are also collaborating with the emergency services as they meet every Friday at 7.30 p.m. together with the guards patrolling the public transportation to discuss the potential "problems" of the weekend.

According to Erik, the semi-formal control groups are mainly taking part in social crime prevention but since most of them strive to obstruct crimes from happening at specific locations, they could also be considered as having a situational crime preventive effect. The citizens' hosts are especially responsible for reporting on vandalism and disturbances in the physical environment, which is also the goal of the security walks initiated by Erik in 2001. These walks are performed once per year by a group of people (including representatives from the district administration, the police, housing companies, field assistants and voluntary residents). Together they comment on things that need to be improved in the physical environment, and the information is documented and forwarded to the property owner. Rinkeby was the first district in Stockholm to arrange security walks, and it is clear that Erik finds the situational crime prevention measures very important to the security work in the area. He explains that Rinkeby has become a lot better at developing these measures over the years and is doing this to a larger degree than other districts in Stockholm. Erik stresses that social crime prevention in the shape of semi-formal control groups has received more financing from the district administration, but he claims that this also holds true for schools and social services. According to him, even if social crime prevention can improve certain individuals' tendencies to commit crimes, people are mobile and can move away from the area. The situational crime prevention is on the other hand more long-lasting and affects everyone, no matter who you are. As an example he mentions how situational crime prevention can be aimed towards specific crime problems, such as installing benches of concrete on the public square outside shopping windows in order to affect so called "crash and grab-robberies."

Much of the work on crime prevention and improving feelings of security targets the everyday maintenance of the physical structure of Rinkeby which is carried out by the caretaker Mustafa, another interviewee. Mustafa believes just like Erik that cleaning up the environment and making it look nice increases the likability of the area, which in turn reduces feelings of fear. Erik stresses he is inspired by Wilson and Kelling (1982) and that keeping Rinkeby clean and unbroken is an important part of the security work of the district administration in order to affect crime and feelings of fear. In this sense, the housing companies are important collaborating actors. As previously mentioned the interviewees portray the area as a little village with a special "Rinkeby spirit" which gives pride to the neighbour-hood and contributes to feelings of security. However, it is obviously seen as problematic that not all residents share this spirit, which is reflected in the new measures trying to strengthen the social control in the area. Littering and mischievous behaviour are described as the consequence of how some people in Rinkeby lack pride of the area. Mustafa, however, believes that littering is the result of "immigrants" not feeling like they belong in the area, and that they just continue to litter no matter how many bins he puts up.

The interviewees working with youths report decreasing finances in welfare infrastructure, which is partly inconsistent with Erik's notion that the district administration has invested more money into social crime prevention *as well as* schools and social services over the last couple of years. When talking to the interviewees it is clear that traditional welfare structures are still seen as important in the crime prevention work, but the results of this study also show that efforts targeting physical space and involving other actors in order to enhance policing and social control are increasingly seen as vital to improving security in Rinkeby. This development raises important questions: How do the new methods of creating security by increasing social control and improving physical space actually deal with the fear of the Other which is prevalent in the area? And if it is true, like Mustafa claims, that the 'immigrants' are littering because they do not feel like they belong and in turn affect the sense of security in a negative way, are more bins the best solution to the problems or would structural approaches be more appropriate?

Conclusions

To conclude, it can be noted that the participants in the study generally thought that Rinkeby was a safe place. When asked to identify security problems in Rinkeby, they started to reflect on experiences of fear and these were often related to issues regarding social domination in space by men and youths at the square, and behaviours that are seen as threatening the social order of urban space. It also becomes evident that the Somali group is depicted as different and problematic to security; they are described as the Other in an area that already carries the burden of being a spatial Other (cf. Germes, *this volume*, on 'Othering' in the French banlieus).

Much of the security work is described as social crime prevention, where efforts in the shape of 'good forces' are directed towards youths and changing their values and behaviours. Improving social control was brought forward as an important challenge, and several semi-formal control groups have thus been created over the years. However, while the participants worry about the lack of social control they also speculate that the reason why youths are up to mischief in the metro is because of lacking welfare. They hang out in public space because of residential crowdedness and they are up to mischief because they do not care for the area; they are not seen as embracing "the Rinkeby spirit" and could perhaps be seen as the 'bad' forces towards which the 'good' forces are targeted. In addition, the men standing on the square are there due to unemployment and depression. Ethnic mix is seen as a positive thing, but segregation is not. There also seems to be a hierarchy in which some cultures are seen as embracing the ruling social order and norms, something that changes as successive groups move in to the area. Analysing the interviewees' statements, the biggest threats to security in Rinkeby seem to be the spatial domination of the Other, decreasing welfare and a worsening of social control.

The district administration stresses the importance of situational crime prevention and keeping the area clean, but the question is how maintenance of the physical environment affects fear in the area. As Koskela and Pain (2000) claim these kinds of measures are more likely to affect certain qualities of life rather than actually increase feelings of security. It is not the physical environment in itself that people fear, but the social relations played out in the physical environment. This seems to be the case in Rinkeby as well: The fear is connected to power relations and social behaviours in space as well as to welfare problems such as segregation, unemployment and poverty.

Interviewees suggest that structural welfare efforts are important for preventing crime and mitigating fear and they perceive that social work receives less funding than before. At the same time, other semi-formal control groups are taking on more responsibility in preventing crime and policing the residential area. This shows that Sweden constitutes an interesting example of how neoliberal approaches on crime prevention are applied in a context where the welfare ideal is still viewed as important to the practitioners. Similarly, Rinkeby is with its social characteristics a special case when studying how the development of Swedish crime policy plays out on a local level. But at the same time, some of the findings cannot be seen as exclusive to Rinkeby. The fear of Others is always present to some extent: Rinkeby is perceived as a homogenous Other to larger Stockholm while there are Othering processes and "banal Orientalism" at work within Rinkeby as well. Othering processes and social hierarchies targeting different groups exist everywhere. Rinkeby should thus not be seen as an exceptionally fearful or intolerant place. The problems mentioned in Rinkeby regarding clashes in norms and values should not be viewed as static but rather as constantly changing, just like the view of the Other is also changing when it becomes more known to the Self. It is difficult to come up with a perfect solution for how to mitigate fear and Othering processes. However, it is not farfetched to claim that structural and social efforts are important to increase welfare and to promote meetings and understandings between different groups, and that security measures targeting social control and physical space definitely have their shortcomings when fears arise due to discourses of the Other.

The author would like to thank her colleagues at The Institute for Housing and Urban Research, especially professor Irene Molina and professor Terry Hartig, as well as the reviewers of this text for invaluable comments. Special thanks also to Melissa Kelly for proof reading.

References

Andersson, Tommy 2001. *Kriminell utveckling: tidiga riskfaktorer och förebyggande insatser.* Stockholm: Brottsförebyggande rådet (BRÅ).

Billig, Michael 1995. *Banal nationalism.* London: Sage.

Boréus, Kristina 1994. *Högervåg: nyliberalismen och kampen om språket i svensk debatt 1969-1989.* Stockholm: Tiden.

Ericsson, Urban, Irene Molina and Per-Markku Ristilammi 2002. *Miljonprogram och media: föreställningar om människor och förorter.* Stockholm: Riksantikvarieämbetet.

Franzén, Mats and Eva Sandstedt 1981. *Grannskap och stadsplanering: Om stat och byggande i efterkrigstidens Sverige.* Uppsala: Sociologiska institutionen, Uppsala Universitet.

Garland, David 2000. "Ideas, Institutions and Situational Crime Prevention." In: Andrew Von Hirsch, David Garland and Alison Wakefield (eds.), *Ethical and Social Perspectives on Situational Crime Prevention.* Oxford: Hart: 1–16.

Garland, David 2001. *The culture of control.* Oxford: Oxford University Press.

Haldrup, Michael, Lasse Koefoed and Kirsten Simonsen 2008. "Practising Fear: Encountering O/other Bodies." In: Rachel Pain and Susan J. Smith (eds.), *Fear.* Aldershot: Ashgate: 117–128.

Heber, Anita 2007. *Var rädd om dig!: rädsla för brott enligt forskning, intervjupersoner och dagspress.* Stockholm: Kriminologiska institutionen, Stockholms universitet.

Hillier, Bill 1996. *Space is the machine: a configurational theory of architecture.* Cambridge: Cambridge University Press.

Jacobs, Jane 1993. *The death and life of great American cities.* New York: Modern Library.

Jeffery, C. Ray 1971. *Crime prevention through environmental design.* London: Sage Publications.

Koskela, Hille 1997. "'Bold Walk and Breakings': Women's spatial confidence versus fear of violence." *Gender, Place & Culture,* 4: 301–320.

Koskela, Hille 2010. "Fear and its Others." In: Susan J. Smith, Rachel Pain, Sallie A. Marston and John Paul Jones III (eds.), *The SAGE Handbook of Social Geographies.* London: Sage: 389–407.

Koskela, Hille and Rachel Pain 2000. "Revisiting fear and place: women's fear of attack and the built environment." *Geoforum,* 31: 269–280.

Lidskog, Rolf 2006. *Staden, våldet och tryggheten: om social ordning i ett mångkulturellt samhälle.* Stockholm: Daidalos.

Listerborn, Carina 2002. *Trygg Stad: Diskurser om kvinnors rädsla i forskning, policyutveckling och lokal praktik.* Göteborg: Chalmers Tekniska Högskola.

Listerborn, Carina 2005. *Kvinnors liv i Husby: en skildring av kön, plats och etnicitet.* Lund: Lunds Tekniska Högskola.

Molina, Irene 1997. *Stadens rasifiering: etnisk boendesegregation i folkhemmet.* Uppsala: Uppsala Universitet.

Newman, Oscar 1972. *Defensible space: crime prevention through urban* design. New York: MacMillan.

Pain, Rachel 2001. "Gender, Race, Age and Fear in the City". *Urban Studies,* 38: 899–913.

Pain, Rachel and Susan J. Smith 2008. *Fear.* Aldershot: Ashgate.

Sahlin, Ingrid 2008. *Brottsprevention som begrepp och samhällsfenomen.* Lund: Arkiv.

Said, Edward W. 2000. *Orientalism.* Stockholm: Ordfront.

Sarnecki, Jerzy 2004. *Kunskapsbaserad brottsprevention: teoretiska utgångspunkter för brottsförebyggande arbete i Stockholms* stad. Stockholm: Stockholms stad.

Schierup, Carl-Ulrik, Peo Hansen and Stephen Castles 2006. *Migration, citizenship, and the European welfare state.* Oxford: Oxford University Press.

Sibley, David 1995. *Geographies of exclusion.* London: Routledge.

Sleiman, Mark and Randy Lippert 2010. "Downtown ambassadors, police relations and 'clean and safe' security." *Policing and Society*, 20 (3): 316–335.

Stockholm Office of Research and Statistics 2011. At: http://tinyurl.com/as86zzr; http://tinyurl.com/actb5pn (both accessed 18 January 2013).

Svenonius, Ola 2011. *Sensitising urban transport security.* Stockholm: Department of Political Science, Stockholm University.

Takala, Hannu 1997. "Social brottsprevention och nordisk välfärd." *Apropå,* 5-6.

The National Network of Night Wanderers in Sweden. *Välkommen till Rinkeby*, at http://tinyurl.com/au329r2 (accessed 11 April 2011).

The Swedish National Council for Crime Prevention 2011. *Statistikdatabasen över anmälda brott*, at http://statistik.bra.se/solwebb/action/index (accessed 10 April 2011).

Wilson, James Q. and George L. Kelling 1982. "Broken Windows." *The Atlantic*, at http://tinyurl.com/3azl6k8 (accessed 18 January 2013).

Yarwood, Richard and Graham Gardner 2000. "Fear of Crime, Cultural Threat and the Countryside." *Area*, 32 (4): 403–411.

Zedner, Lucia 2003. "Concept of Security: An Agenda for Comparative Analysis." *Legal Studies*, 23: 153–176.

Ålund, Aleksandra. 1997. *Multikultiungdom: kön, etnicitet, identitet.* Lund: Studentlitteratur.

URBAN (IN)SECURITY: POLICING THE NEOLIBERAL CRISIS

WORKING FOR THE STATE
A READING OF THE FRENCH POLICE
DISCOURSES ON "BANLIEUES"

Mélina Germes

During the course of an interview I was conducting, a policeman made the following comment about one neighborhood in the poor French suburb where he was working: *"Here is a neighborhood which it seems is not really under the laws of the French Republic anymore; it is now under boss rule..."*[122]. With this statement, he wanted to give me an idea of how easily confrontations and acts of violence could occur there, how hard it was to work as a policeman in this district, and that it was necessary to adapt one's procedures and methods to the area's particular demands. Such "no-go zones" (as they are commonly called, for example in the media) are subject to specific police practices – it seems as if deprived urban areas were operated under a "different" legal order which in turn requires "different" police codes (Jobard, 2005). According to research on the topic, police work

---

[122]   Original quote: *"Il y a un quartier qui n'est plus tout à fait sous les lois de la République, qui est tenu par un caïd"*. *"Quartier"*, the French word for neighborhood, has become a euphemism for groups of housing projects in French *"banlieues,"* – itself a euphemism for those neighborhoods on the outskirts of French cities which are often characterized by high-rise public housing and large communities of poor residents with roots in North and West Africa. Thus, while the first acceptation of *"banlieue"* can be translated into "suburb" in English, the equivalent of *"la banlieue"* as described by the French media would be "the projects" in the United States, and "housing estates" or "council estates" in the UK. To quote but a few related terms used in politics, sociology, and the French media, *"banlieues"* are associated with *"zones urbaines sensibles"* (sensitive urban zones) and *"quartiers sensibles"* (sensitive neighborhoods).

has to deal with specific problems depending on the space where it takes place (Herbert, 2006; Yarwood, 2007; Eick, *this volume*). Neoliberal urbanization, which fostered social inequality, is often understood as responsible for the existence of troubled urban areas. They are spaces in crisis, characterized not only by their isolation from urban centers and by old, dilapidated housing blocks, but also by residents whose socio-economic status and ethnicity make them the target of numerous discriminations, and moreover seems to be a challenge for French "republicanism."

It seems as if urban space - with its economic, social, urban, and political specifics - were inherently violent and, as such, would call for specific strategies in policing as well as for a rethinking of existing procedures. Such pragmatism can provide a justification for certain policies, for example the choice of a strict law-and-order approach. Consequently, the construction of the *banlieue* in France as a spatial category is a determining element of police work; the punitive ideology of the penal state rests on the existence of such a category and is reinforced by its repetitive use. The power of those categories is not merely symbolic, it is performative, since the larger signifying structures that they are part of become the basis for action. Police work results neither solely from the everyday practices of police(wo)men nor from the bare implementation of political commands and instructions (from the respective responsible government). Police work cannot entirely be explained by dialectical relations between so-called "cop culture" and police institutions; it is also shaped by discursive categories. Specific words and phrases such as "depressed area" have become so pervasive that they now equip police officers with sets of interpretation for society itself.

In this study, I explore how spatial categories are created and used by the French police who work in so-called "troubled" areas. My aim is to show how spatial division and social categorization are linked within a discourse of conflict framing police work and security work spaces. In my analysis of how space is discursively produced, I will use the term "territory" in its French acceptation (see below). My research framework is grounded into two disciplines: French social geography (Aldhuy, 2006; Lévy and Lussault, 2000; Séchet and Veschambre, 2006) and German cultural geography (Gebhardt, Reuber, and Wolkersdorfer, 2003; Glazse and Mattissek, 2009).

In the first part of the paper I will explain the research design, concepts, and methods as well as significant elements of the social, political, and spatial context. In the two sections following, I will analyze the results of the research and begin with the discursive constitution of territoriality through conflict narratives, followed by the linkage between territoriality and violence. In the conclusion, I will discuss the results of the research.

Research: concepts, design, methods

POLICE TERRITORIALITY

Many English-speaking geographers have demonstrated how police practices can contribute to the production of space – more specifically, to the production of *urban* space (Fyfe, 1995; Herbert, 2003). Police work[123] includes observing and controlling space, as well as developing spatial strategies and putting them to work. Space is therefore one of many policing tools, so much so that one can talk about a "geography of policing" (Fyfe, 1991). Police work depends on territoriality for strategic and organizational issues related to the deploying of security forces, the setting of geographical limits of the police's areas of jurisdiction, and the location of police stations (Herbert 1996). Knowing and mastering social spaces are two prerequisites of police work; police work itself contributes in turn to the production of urban space. I suggest conceptualizing police work as a form of territorialization.

In the everyday language about security and police, the usual and prevailing French word for territory – *territoire* – has two main acceptations (Dieu, 2009); the first one refers to the division of the national territory into police jurisdictions. In

---

123   While police work covers numerous institutions (cf. Monjardet, 2002; Brodeur, 2003: 350-353; see Eick, *this volume*), this paper focuses on public order police units.

this case, the word *"territoire"* refers to more than the spatial equivalent of institutional action defined by the dealing with responsibilities and missions of employees in a given space. It also hints at exerting control over space, surveying and mastering it. The area of jurisdiction – the local space that the state puts "under the care" of police authorities – is, in a way, a synecdoche for the national territory itself. In its second acceptation, *"territoire"* refers to police work itself since police practices shape space. *"Territoire"* then calls forth notions of experience, of one's knowledge of a place and its inhabitants, and of one's ability of exercise authority over them. Such uses of the word "territory" in policing point to the fact that a "territory" is not an arbitrary space, but rather a space defined by one's sovereignty over it. It evokes the concepts of appropriation (peaceful or violent), law, legitimacy, and control – and, in some cases, resistance to and contestation of control.

The scientific discussion about the notion of territory is controversial, but its understanding is still essential to the study and practice of social geography in the French-speaking world. Most of the time, what is meant by *"territoire"* is the appropriation of space by a group or a person and its role in the construction of identities in connection with political, historical and economic processes (Di Méo, 1998). The term "territoriality" therefore challenges static conceptions of space and allows researchers to establish that there is no such thing as a "territory object" (*chose-territoire,* Aldhuy, 2008) – space is a *process* of constant re-appropriation and identification. Such notions allow for the conceptualization of power relations produced by space (Ripoll and Veschambre, 2006) and the physical and symbolic dimension of spatialized conflicts. I find the French-speaking definition of *territoire* useful insofar as it refers to the shaping and production of territory through diverse social practices. Police work is a social practice of territory production; police territory is more than a functional space, it is a shaped space and a specialized statement of power (see Fernandez and Scholl, *this volume*). What is of particular importance in this notion is the link to power relations, how groups with opposite interests might vie for dominion over an area. Territories are the basis for the establishment of an "us" that opposes a "them"; what is appropriated *by* a group is always appropriated *from* another group. On the other hand, the English-speaking definition mainly establishes territories as the spatiality of the modern state, i.e. a specific historical phenomena which is closely related to the notion of border (see Elden, 2010; Kuus and Agnew, 2008; Paasi, 2008; Painter, 2010). This acceptation of territory is relevant to this study in that it brings up the idea of a "space of state sovereignty" through which the population can be controlled.

"INSECURE" FRENCH SUBURBS

The French term *"banlieue"*, which is sometimes reductively translated into "suburb" or "poor suburb" in the international press, refers to several distinct phenomena. France's larger metropolitan areas are all composed of several towns gathered around a central city; each one of these peripheral towns is a suburb, whether well-off or poor. The term *"la banlieue"* generally refers to the groups of housing projects that were built in these peripheral towns and over the years have become depressed areas equated with a host of "social issues."[124] Social scientists have studied these spaces within the theoretical framework of urban planning and architecture (cf. Dufaux and Fourcaut, 2004), and given attention to the social and economic trends that have produced them. The *banlieues* are commonly understood as the result of industrialization combined with the creation of a cosmopolitan urban working class. The collapse of the French colonial empire and waves of postcolonial migration led to the development of an immigrant working underclass. *Banlieues* are featured in studies about deindustrialization (Duchêne and Morel-Journel, 2000; Beaud and Pialoux, 2003) and the demise of fixed collective identities (Bacqué and Sintomer, 2001). In the political realm,

---

124   The use of generic phrases such as "banlieue" (suburb) and "quartier sensible" (sensitive or troubled neighborhood) is controversial, since it contributes to lumping together strikingly different situations and thus to the creation of a stereotypical spatial category which breeds discrimination. These phrases fail to convey the complex way in which urban planning is tied to economic and social issues.

the emergence of *"quartiers sensibles"* (sensitive neighbor-hoods) as a discursive notion in texts, institutions and policies has led to the creation of a separate, identifiable category of public action (see Map 1),[125] and has reified debates over related social issues (Tissot, 2007). "Riots" and social unrest are particularly contentious themes among the researchers who attempt to interpret violence in the *banlieues* (Esterle-Hedibel, 2002; Mohammed and Mucchielli, 2006; Mouhanna, 2003; Schneider, 2008).

The trope of *"la banlieue"* has also given way to the solidifica-tion and dispersion of representations that have had a substantial impact not only in political and administrative institutions and among the general public, but also on residents themselves (Four-caut, 2000). The media have played a key role in the production and dissemination of such representations. The treatment of *"la banlieue"* as a full-fledged news category (cf. Sedel, 2009) reflects the intensity of the competition that exists among the groups vying for dominance over the discourse on suburbs, in particular about the origins of their problems and solutions to address them. Main-stream narratives characterize the *banlieue* as an insecure place and link the insecurity to urbanism characterized by large-scale housing, to employment and social crisis, and/or to the failure of immigrant integration. Where *banlieue* as place is a product of neoliberal politics, *banlieue* as a concept is a product of neolib-eral discourses. Apart from these hegemonic narratives, which can be found in dominant media as well as in the political sphere, counterhegemonic narratives have also emerged (Germes and Tijé-Dra, 2012). A broad range of social movements, mainly on the local level,[126] try to reframe the signification of *banlieue* in the public debate, preferring for example the more positive phrasing *"quartier populaire"*. This reframing considers the inhabitants of the *banlieue* as victims of economic and racial discrimination resulting from neoliberalism and surviving postcolonial everyday

---

125   Map 1 shows that area-based public policies in France focus on large housing estates rather than on single-family-housing neighborhoods, which are mostly not included in the *"Zone Urbaine Sensible"* of Clichy-Montfermeil (Département Seine-Saint-Denis).

126   Such counter-hegemonic discourses can be found in political rap texts as well as in formalized social movements such as the Forum Social des Quartiers Populaires (so-cial forum for "working-class neighborhood"). For this purpose, see: Tijé-Dra (2011).

racism. Another reframing rallies for a positive and proud identification with the stigmatized *banlieue* and emphasizes the
potential for autonomous development. The handling of the
phrases *"banlieue"* and even *"quartier sensible"* in social science
is controversial for many reasons; they are informal and normative categories of mainstream narratives and/or public policies.
Although the terms have deeply influenced the development of a
research field in the social sciences, they should not be taken for
granted as concepts, but on the contrary questioned or even challenged as powerful categories. Debates and campaigns among
social movements as well as in the social sciences are trying to
reconfigure the neoliberal language through the promotion of
other words and ways of speaking.

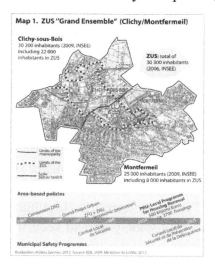

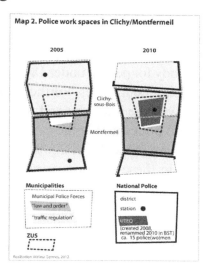

Today's hegemonic discourse, which emerged in the
1970s, closely links French suburbs to the notion of urban
crime (Germes et al., 2010). This explains to a large extent
why suburbs have been the targets of law-and-order measures
for decades. Those measures include "specific" and localized
law-enforcement efforts, as well as local safety measures (cf.
Dikeç, 2007b: 193-204; Bonelli, 2008). Not only are suburbs
unequivocally considered unsafe, they are also often portrayed
as counter-places whose ultimate symbolic role is to provide an
anti-exemplar for an ideal French society against which a "republican" identity can be asserted (Germes and Glaze, 2010).

SPACES OF POLICE WORK IN FRANCE

At the end of the first decade of the 21st century, security had become a central theme of political debate and an important dimension of public policies worldwide. This was and is the case in France as well. The "repressive turn" in the policing of the French *banlieue* goes back to the middle of the 1990s (Dikeç 2007a: 1201). In 2000, discourses of "insecurity" and repressive penal policies and control procedures, focusing particularly on deprived neighborhoods, were already present in the fields of police work, justice, and education (Bonelli and Sainati 2000). New laws about public order such as the *Loi sur la Sécurité Quotidienne* (2001), the *Loi "Perben" de Programmation pour la Justice* (2002), the *Loi d'Orientation Pour la Sécurité Intérieure I* (2003) and *II* (2009) enforced the police and judiciary response to minor offences (Tévanian 2003), for example, respectively: penalization of petty fraud; longer temporary custody for people under 18 and a ban on loitering in entryways of housing complexes. Furthermore, these penal laws transformed the way the judiciary and police function, increasing the power of the police and at the same time giving priority to statistic-led policing (Mucchielli 2008). While Nicolas Sarkozy's important role in these developments both as the right-wing Minister of the Interior (2007) and as the president of the French Republic (2007-2012) cannot be ignored, most researchers highlight the fact that these policies are part of a widely spread security ideology predating Sarkozy; the beginning of the "republicanist" repressive turn is generally dated back to the left-wing Minister of the Interior Chevènement (1997).

My aim is to study the discursive categories used by the police to designate space in the French suburbs and thus to produce territories of police work. This paper is based on empirical evidence gathered from a dozen semi-structured interviews with civil servants responsible for law enforcement at the local level, including members of the National Police (some who worked at police stations, others at the level of the central directorate for public security (*Direc-*

tion *Centrale de la Sécurité Publique*, DSCP),[127] and in the departmental directorates (*Directions Départementales de la Sécurité Publique, DDSP),* as well as commissioners of municipal police forces. The following table offers a short presentation of the main characteristics of national and municipal police in France.

Table 1: Comparison of two urban police institutions in France: National and Municipal Polices

	National Police	Municipal Police
Political Authority	Ministry of the Interior	Mayor of the municipality
Organization	Centralized national institution subdivided into 8 services ("Central Directions" for border police, intelligence services, military police, judiciary police, public security).	Local institution, organization depends on function.
Territory of competence	Depends on the directions. Public Security Police is spatially subdivided in 102 departmental directorates and further into 462 urban districts (as big as one or two municipalities).	The whole municipality (about 3,500 urban municipalities are divided into 36,000 municipalities in France).[1]
Fonctions	Depends on the directions. For the Public Security Police (DCSP): "assistance, prevention, public order."	Depends on the mayor's decision: Basically, traffic regulation and violation, application of municipal bylaws, public order. Restricted use of weapons.
Legal competence	Depends on the directions. The Public Security Police is responsible for major or minor offences (The Judiciary Police are responsible for major crimes).	Responsible for minor offences. Recorded major offenses and crimes have to be handed off to the National Police.
Worker Status and Recruitment	After national competitive examination, recruited as a public employee of the state. Possibility of transfers on a national level. (about 78,000 police workers in the *DCSP* in France).[2]	After local competitive examination, recruited as a local level as a public employee of the municipality (about 20,000 municipal police workers in France).[3]

1   Malochet, Virginie 2010. «Les polices municipales: points de repères.» In: Note rapide, Institut d'aménagement et d'urbanisme, 515 (September), at: http://www.iau-idf.fr/fileadmin/Etudes/etude_734/NR_515_web.pdf.
2   Ministry of the Interior 2009. *Les polices municipales: points de repère,* at. http://www.iau-idf.fr/fileadmin/Etudes/etude_734/NR_515_web.pdf.
3   Ibid.

---

127   The DCSP is the uniformed patrol and response arm of the French National Police.

In order to conduct the interviews, I selected towns which are located in the near periphery of Paris[128] and included at least one *"Zone Urbaine Sensible"*[129] (cf. Map 1). This delimitation of the research field indirectly constituted a preliminary definition of what was meant by *"quartier sensible"* in the study, but was also an important requirement for the pertinence of the interview material. It must be noted that the French urban police is under the control of two separate institutions (see Table 1). The National Police (*"Police Nationale"*) is a centralized institution which is closely related to the French Ministry of the Interior. The Municipal Police's prerogatives and methods depend on the Mayor, and so differ greatly from town to town. The Municipal and National Police's territories overlap (see Map 2). Map 2 shows one of my case studies: the municipalities of Clichy-Sous-Bois and Montfermeil, both in the *Département* Seine-Saint-Denis. The local geography of police districts and the territorialization of the dispositive changed heavily between 2005 and 2010 (cf. Map 2). In 2005, both Clichy and Montfermeil were part of two separate National Police districts. The *UTEQ* unit, created 2008, is responsible for the whole *ZUS,* a large-housing estate spread over both municipalities (see Map 1). National police districts were locally reorganized in 2010 in order to unite the two towns into a new National Police district. Whereas both towns have a Municipal Police station, significant differences in municipal policing between Clichy and Montfermeil have been noted. While the Clichy municipal police are mainly concerned with traffic regulation, the armed municipal police in Montfermeil are very engaged in surveillance, repression of offences, and demonstrative presence in public spaces, in conformity with the "blue in the street" axiom. Nonetheless, the Municipal Police in Montfermeil conducting patrols in

---

128   In order to respect the interviewees' anonymity, the municipalities and areas of ju-
         risdiction they worked in have not been disclosed. It has been necessary however to
         make one reference to one of the interviewee's specific situation.

129   "Sensitive urban zones" (ZUS) are urban areas whose social and economic circum-
         stances have made them high-priority targets for urban policy, as recognized by the
         law of November 14, 1996.

single-family neighborhoods, avoid entering the main large housing estate, and, by doing so, draw an unexpected and unconventional border within its "own" municipal territory.

The interviews started with the interviewees presenting and explaining the procedures performed in their own area of jurisdiction. Then they were asked specific questions about *banlieues* and *UTEQ* police units (*Unités Territoriales de Quartier*, see below). During the interviews, I did not ask my partners about their representation of space, but rather about the spatiality of police work. Space remained in the background of the interview. The collected statements were then used as the basis for a study of local police officers' discourse on social space. While this exploratory study cannot pretend to be an accurate picture of one unified discourse that would sustain police activity, it does identify a range of discourses that circulate within the police. An analysis of the interviews has shown that police members resort to conflict narratives strongly rooted in territorial identifications. By territorial identifications I mean the discursive process of delineating a place and identifying or not identifying subjects with it (*"it's my place and not his/her place"*) within the context of a conflict narrative.

DISCOURSE OF CONFLICT: A METHOD

The research method used in this paper is based on the post-structuralist approach to discourse analysis, as presented by Mattissek and Reuber (2004) as well as Glasze (2007), who reinterpret and formalize the Foucaldian approach to discourse. In this approach, meaning is constructed through the arrangement and combination of elements within sign-systems; a discourse is characterized by the regularity of statements, i.e. the regularity of the combination – or articulation – of elements. Meaning is never fixed because of the permanent and changing re-articulation of elements. Consequently, discourses are temporary, fragile, and fluid. However, when certain patterns of articulation and meaning dominate and "neutralize" other patterns and thus other meanings, a discourse becomes hegemonic. Hegemonic discourses temporarily decide over the legitimacy of a certain social order. This conception of discourses as the (powerful but fragile) articulation of elements allows the conceptualization of the constitution of collective identities. Identities are socially and discursively constructed through a delimitation and demarcation from a "constitutive outside". In other words, the "we" appears only with the constitution of an "other". Discourse analysis consists therefore of the collection of recurring words and phrases from corpuses made up of different individual statements to uncover an overarching discourse. In other words, it is not concerned with "what is said", with the actor's intention to mean something, his opinions or views about social spaces, but rather exposes the ways in which singular occurrences exemplify "ways of saying" and the structures of language. Thus, my focus is neither the representation nor the meaning of space but the spatial discourse, which is to say the various articulations of "space." Spatial structures which can be found in the language (in/out, here/there, beyond) constitute an important frame for meaning, and as such an interpretation level for the everyday work of the police. Notions, including spatial notions, are correlated and linked to each other with equivalences and oppositions. This method of discourse analysis allows one to identify and code speech patterns, spatial terms or spatializations, and the linguistic statement of conflict during interviews (cf. Glasze and Mattissek, 2009). This method, in the way it is developed by German-speaking cultural geography, is particularly suitable for the study of discursive demarcations of (in)security discourses, in so far as these discourse are built on oppositions between dangerous/endangered (Glasze, Pütz, and Schreiber, 2005).

In this paper, speech patterns are studied through an analysis of the use of proper and common nouns, personal pronouns, possessives, as well as ellipses and phrases that refer to people, groups, or institutions more or less explicitly; this forms the first step of the analysis, in which I studied the main characters in policing narratives. The second step of the analysis focused on the spatial dimension of statements through the systematic collection of common or proper nouns referring to places or spatial entities, as well as prepositions, adverbs, and verbs of location and direction. With this second step, the discursive relations (such as (non-)identification or (non-)belonging) linking space and subjects can be identified. The third step of the analysis was devoted to the statement of conflict. It was based on an analysis of syntactic forms denoting negation and semantic elements referring to opposition, power, obstacles, and circumvention. Finally, the territorializations in the police discourses were studied. The discourse of territoriality rests on an entanglement connecting individuals, spaces, and related situations of conflict. Significant quotes that reflected major trends in the interviews have been excerpted and will be studied in the following pages. In those quotes, words referring to *characters, spaces,* or *conflicts* will be visually signaled by the use of small capitals, bold type and underlining, respectively. My analysis will start with formal descriptions and move on to more interpretative comments.

Police work as discursive ordering

The first step was to identify the characters developed in the discourse. The collected statements present the typically loose structure that is characteristic of all natural conversations: the first-, second-, and third-person pronouns might not refer to the same signifier (the same word might in turn stand for the speaker, the police, one group or another, for example); agents are not systematically made explicit and can be merely implied (cf. quotes 4, 5).[130] Yet in the collected statements, three main, recurring agents have been identified. First, the speaker himself (here, a member of the national or local police), identifies with "the police." Interviewees used different pronouns to refer to the police: sometimes the third person (cf. 1, 6: "*signaler l'arrivée de la police;*" "*ils ont vu la police*"), sometimes "*on*" – the

---

130   The full quotes are reproduced below.

French indefinite third-person pronoun – (cf. 3, 5: *"on peut pas;"* *"On n'y va pas"*), at other times the first person plural or even the second person, when the speaker wished to include the interviewer and anyone listening to paint a more vivid picture of a scene (cf. 3: *"Quand vous rentrez"*). The police was then the subject of the discourse – a sparsely defined subject of an informal collective, which fits well with and reproduces the strong collective identity of police workers. The individual or group targeted by police activity is the second most frequent participant mentioned in most sentences. The police's "adversaries" are almost always referred to in the third person plural and in the masculine (cf. 5, 6: *"ils se sauvent;"* *"c'est chez eux"*; except for 3: *"on vous met"*). The vocabulary used (*"bande,"* *"caïd,"* *"leaders délinquents,"* *"individu guetteur"* [dont le rôle est de signaler]" in occurrences 2, 1, 6, and 7) identifies the character primarily with a group organized around leaders, and secondarily as a group that questions the rules and laws enforced by the police. *"Ils"* ("they") stands for an anonymous adversary. It evokes most commonly the narrative trope of the young man from the suburbs, a potential offender and a potential threat (cf. Hancock, 2008). Finally, one finds a more elusive and less recurring character: the "residents that wish for peace," pitted against to the minority of (petty) criminals who threaten them (see also Germes and Glasze, 2010; Rodenstedt, *this volume*). The three characters identified are thus placed in opposition each to the other along boundaries drawn by the aims of police work.

References to space are clearly organized in the statements, while hinting at a more complex geography. The most frequent place mentioned is the housing project, or the larger *banlieue* (cf. quotes 3, 2: *"là, cette cité-là"*; *"Quand vous allez dans les quartiers"*). Those spaces are described as closed (cf. 3, 1: *"vous tombez dans un cul-de-sac;"* *"qu'un seul accès"*), along with their dependencies (cf. 5: *"ils se sauvent dans les bois!"*) and the related hiding places (cf. 5: *"ils vont...dans les caves"*). They are narratively opposed to a vaguely defied "outside" corresponding to the surrounding area (cf. 6: "*les policiers, c'est en dehors de [la cité]*"). The verbs of movement used imply the existence of this place as the place people in the *banlieue* "come back" from or "run to" when they "are chased" (cf. respectively 3, 6). Not only does this antinomic coupling recall an existing dichotomy between two spaces, but it also evidences the fact that the spatial opposition constitutes a meaningful and efficient structure in policing discourses. The recurring outside/inside pair plays a decisive discursive role since it parallels and thus confirms the opposition that exists between the first two characters identified above.

The police, as participants, belong to the "outside," and, logically, their adversary belongs to the *banlieue* (cf. 6: "*Ils ont une logique de territoire, c'est chez eux, et puis les policiers, c'est en dehors de [la cité]*"). This clear-cut pairing of roles and territories with characters is based on a grid of discursive parallels and oppositions which is structured around two elements: the police and the suburbs. The complementary elements (the police's "adversaries" on the one hand, and what lies outside the suburbs on the other hand) are both only vaguely designated despite their structuring role in the speech patterns studied. This process evidences how spatial categories (here, the troubled suburb or housing project) can be used by the speakers to refer to social groups without having to name them; in other words, because of an implicit but meaningful categorization, references to space or place can be substituted for the description of a social group. The discursive ordering seems to be the first task of police work. The next section examines how a socio-spatial discourse sustains various phrases used in the statement of conflict.

Municipal police: from conflict to territoriality

The theme of conflict appears in the interviews through syntactic structures, lexical forms – in negative statements for the most part – and in semantic units, as well as through the above-mentioned pairings and oppositions. Conflict is always described as closely linked to the disputed territory;

in most cases, it revolves around circumventing or bypassing "other people's territory" or remaining there (in order to avoid a clash or a showdown). The following quotations are from municipal police forces.

1	Quand il n'y a **qu'un seul accès qui permet d'accéder au quartier**, il suffit de METTRE UN INDIVIDU GUETTEUR à l'entrée pour signaler **l'arrivée** de LA POLICE. (municipal police commissioner)	When there is **only one way to access the housing project**, PLACING A WATCHMAN at the entrance to make it known that THE POLICE are **coming** is enough.
2	Quand VOUS **allez dans les quartiers**, c'est bien d'y aller à pied, mais à pied VOUS faites une <u>interpellation</u>, VOUS en faites quoi DU TYPE. Et s'il y a UNE BANDE **juste à côté**, <u>hostile</u>, ILS vous <u>cassent la tête</u> des DEUX POLICIERS INTER-VENANT. (municipal police commissioner)	When YOU **go into the housing projects**, it is a good thing if YOU can walk there, but if YOU're walking and YOU have <u>to question</u> SOMEONE, what do YOU do with THE GUY. And if there's a GANG **right next to** YOU, and THEY're <u>hostile</u>, THEY will <u>beat up</u> THE TWO INTERVENING POLICEMEN.
3	Quand VOUS **rentrez**, VOUS tombez dans **un cul-de-sac**, comment VOUS faites si <u>ON VOUS met</u> une voiture <u>en travers</u> ? VOUS sortez pas, vous <u>abandonnez</u> VOTRE VOITURE et VOUS <u>courez</u>. [...] Et là, **cette cité-là**, c'est... ON <u>peut pas</u> **y mettre un pied** parce que... ON <u>peut même pas</u> **rentrer** avec LE VÉHICULE [...] C'est **chez EUX**... (municipal police commissioner)	When YOU **drive in** and YOU find YOURSELF in a **dead-end**, what can YOU do if SOMEONE <u>blocks the way</u> with a car? YOU don't get out, YOU leave YOUR CAR and YOU <u>run</u>. [...] That **specific housing project** is... NO ONE can **set foot in it** because... NO ONE can even GET IN with the vehicle. [...] It's THEIR **place**...

These words run the gamut of conflicts that may occur when the municipal police tries to enter one of the housing projects: the police are observed (which corresponds to a reversal of the roles, since the police become the object of their initial mission – to observe and control others) and they must deal with adversity (cf. 2: *"s'il y a une bande juste à côté, hostile"*). Narratives that describe how spaces are bypassed establish a limit to both spaces, and, as such, it sets a border between them (cf. 3: *"on peut pas y mettre un pied"*). These words refer to the housing projects' architecture and to their layout, which are systematically identified as obstacles to the presence of the police and the carrying-out of its surveillance mission (cf. Romieux, 2007; Landauer, 2009). The interviewees sometimes blame pedestrian paths because they lead to dead-ends and are not car-friendly. They also find fault with high passageways and roofs, which can be used as observation desks from which the adversary can watch the police or even launch attacks on them. According to the interviewees, avoiding clashes is a mutual task: police officers avoid going into housing projects just as much as "gangs" avoid the police when they are in the housing projects.

4	*ILS se sont <u>mis à</u> **courir** quand ILS ont vu LA POLICE.* (Commissioner of a municipal police)	*THEY <u>started</u> **running** when THEY saw THE POLICE.*
5	*A chaque fois, ILS <u>se</u> **sauvent** dans les bois ! ON **va** <u>pas</u> LES **chercher dans les bois**. Ou alors ILS **vont dans les parties communes, dans les caves**, etc. ON <u>n'**y va** pas</u> hein.* (Commissioner of a municipal police)	*Every time, THEY **<u>flee into</u> the woods!** WE <u>don't</u> **go looking for** THEM **in the woods**. Or THEY **go into common areas in buildings, like cellars**, etc. WE <u>don't</u> **go in there**, of course.*

It could seem paradoxical to interpret those passages as referring to conflicts since they describe the act of *avoiding* clashes (cf. 5: "*on n'y va pas;*" "*ils se sauvent*"), but to mention avoiding conflict is also to imply its potentiality. Conflict is circumvented in favor of a *status quo* on both sides. The border between the police's and its adversaries' territories seems to be decided by how events play out.

6	[Il s'agit] *DE <u>LEADERS</u> DÉLINQUANTS qui font un peu <u>régner</u> LEUR loi, et quand ILS voient des VÉHICULES DE POLICE, qui font tout pour <u>LES discréditer</u>, LES POLICIERS, qui font tout pour <u>LES</u> **chasser** du **territoire**. ILS ont une logique de **territoire**, c'est **chez** EUX, et puis LES POLICIERS, c'est **en dehors de [la cité]**.* (Commissioner of a municipal police)	*These men are the <u>LEADERS</u> OF GANGS and THEY <u>rule over their land</u>, so to speak, and, when THEY see POLICE CARS, THEY do everything THEY can to <u>discredit</u> THEM, to <u>discredit</u> POLICEMEN, and to **chase** THEM <u>out</u> of the **territory**. THEY reason in terms of **turf**: it's THEIR **home**; then again, POLICEMEN belong **outside of the housing projects**.*
7	*Il y a un **quartier** qui n'<u>est plus tout à fait sous les lois</u> de LA RÉPUBLIQUE, qui <u>est tenu par</u> un <u>CAÏD</u>.* (Commissioner of a municipal police)	*Here is a **neighborhood** which it seems <u>is not really</u> under the laws of THE FRENCH REPUBLIC anymore; it is now under <u>BOSS</u> rule...*

There is a process of spatial appropriation on both sides and both territorializations are mutually exclusive; they establish both groups' sovereignties over their own respective places. The matter of conflict leading to the constitution of territories is, according to the municipal police narrative, the law. Beside the legitimate law of the police, the law of the *"caïd"* (boss; cf. quote 7) emerges: the conflict is not structured by the narration of offences or crimes, but by the assertion of another and illegitimate law. Territory is a narrative tool in the conflict, since it allows the demonstration of spatial appropriation and the setting of limits. Thus, conflict narratives attest and materialize the existence of the "other", of an "adversary" (see Rodenstedt, *this volume*). The discourse analysis conducted leaves no doubt as to the fact that conflicts are not the result of preexisting territorial rivalries, but rather that the conflict's narrative leads to territorializations. Interestingly, such production of territory through discourse is essentially based on a pervasive conflict – to the point that non-confrontational situations[131] do not seem to play a role in territorialization.

This analysis must be considered within the particular context of the French Municipal Police, which is an additional police force under the authority of Mayor of (often small) municipalities. The direction of municipal police forces depends therefore on political relationships and demands from the most active groups of citizens, and is therefore embedded in small-scale urban politics. The establishing of an additional municipal police force is unsurprisingly based on the need to secure an "endangered" voting population from an "external" threat – in this case, the "other" people from the housing projects. Even when the municipal police concentrate on a strong law-and-order approach, they don't have the capacity, legal or concrete, to manage security problems with a large extent or complexity. Their aim is to prevent through scare tactics; all other cases must be referred to the National Police. The work of French Municipal Police is today therefore more about engendering a sense of security than about repressive intervention.

---

131   The interviews indeed mention the "peaceful inhabitants" of large housing estates. These inhabitants are not described as interacting with the police, but exclusively as a counterexample distinguished from the young male "adversaries". They are described as being women, old, or/and well-meaning people who fear the young criminals and seek police protection.

The unités territoriales de quartier (*UTEQ*): a discourse of violence

As mentioned above, in addition to Municipal Police, I also conducted interviews with the National Police. The description of police work in these interviews centered particularly on the recent implemented *Unités Territoriales de Quartier* (*UTEQ*). They are one of the many law enforcement initiatives which have been implemented in the *banlieue* for the last few decades. The implementation of law enforcement initiatives targeted at depressed areas seems to result in part from an old hegemonic insecurity discourse. As early as the 1990s, France's intelligence agency (*Renseignements Généraux*) created units whose task was to keep watch over troubled neighborhoods – their official aim was to deter and defuse "urban violence" (Bonelli, 2001; Dikeç, 2007b). The 1990s also saw the creation of plain-clothes units called the Anti-Crime Brigades (*Brigades Anti-Criminalité*) who were meant to intervene as fast as possible in cases of *flagrante delicto*. The brigades can reach any place in an area of jurisdiction or *département* quickly. They work mostly night shifts, focusing on *banlieues* and other "trouble spots." Between 1999 and 2002, community-police units were deployed primarily in *banlieues* in order to improve communication between the police and residents, as well as to prevent crime (Mouhanna, 2008). *Banlieues* are thus the object of specific policing initiatives that indicate a shift in the implementation of safety measures from a national and regional level to the local level. With the *Contrats Locaux de Sécurité* (*CLS*, "Local Safety Contracts" between the State and the Municipalities, identifying needs and strategies for safety, created in 1997) and the *Conseils Locaux de Sécurité et de Prévention de la Délinquance* (*CLSPD*, "Local safety and Petty Crime Prevention Councils" created 2002, councils of local public and private actors for the local fight against and prevention of crime),[132] small areas within the towns are defined as "trouble spots" or as endangered places needing security measures. The

---

132   *CLS* and *CLSPD* are both initiatives of the government, but locally implemented by the mayors, and established through partnerships with local actors. The mayor is the president of the *CLSPD*.

state, public administrations, and municipalities joined forces to determine which areas in a town could be identified as "trouble spots." This process comprised assessing the safety level of a zone, organizing meetings with representatives from all the relevant institutions (the National Police, the Municipal Police, and the judiciary, but also schools, hospitals, companies, etc.), and launching prevention initiatives under collective supervision. The goal was to develop "made-to-measure" procedures to prevent petty crime locally (Bonelli, 2008). The spatialized dimension of police initiatives is mostly based on the zoning enacted through the French urban policy called *"Politique de la Ville"*[133] (Dikeç, 2007b); policing is based on the policy's definition and division of the French territory into "sensitive areas" based on socio-economic criteria (such as employment, demographics, housing, or education – see Map 1).

In 2008, two other governmental measures were implemented in order to reach the goal of safer *banlieues*. The daily presence of a visible police force on foot (the *UTEQ*) in limited areas was complemented by new mobile police units within *départements*, whose goal it is to intervene promptly to maintain order (*CS, "Compagnies de Sécurisation"*). Those two units, both inaugurated in the Seine-Saint-Denis in 2008, have complementary roles, but they cover distinct areas and intervene in different cases. The first *UTEQ* were deployed in April 2008 to those areas identified from the *DDSP* as "the most sensitive," then they were phased in over time to intervene in further troubled French metropolitan areas.[134]

---

133   The principle of the *Politique de la Ville* is similar to the *CLS* and *CLSPD*: the principles and the agendas are defined from the government, but locally implemented by the municipalities, in the form of a contract between government and municipalities, but also *régions* and *départements* (broader districts), in combination with partnerships with local actors.

134   *UTEQ* are small units that hold jurisdiction over small areas within depressed neighborhoods, which makes them appear as yet another kind of *police de proximité* ("proximity police," an early French version of community police). Yet they were precisely meant as a departure from community policing, since their mission was to "to maintain respect for the authorities and for the law, where and when it must be maintained" (*"faire respecter l'autorité de l'Etat et le respect de la loi, là où il le faut et à l'heure où il le faut"* – quoted from M. Alliot-Marie, Ministre de l'Intérieur, 14 January 2008). In 2010, new units, the similar *"Brigades Spéciales de Terrain"* ("special field squad") succeeded the *UTEQ* in the same neighborhoods. In August 2012 they were replaced by similar new "Zones de Sécurité Prioritaires".

The third part of this paper does not aim at analyzing the validity or success of *UTEQ*, but to study how they are represented in the police discourse. *UTEQ* have a significance that goes beyond the spatialization of police work. The territory, as a space of sovereignty, is identified explicitly as the *UTEQ*' target, since they find their justification in the narratives of conflict described above. Yet the study of police officers' discourse on *UTEQ* proves that those units infringe upon the territorial limits identified in the second part of this study. The next section – the more interpretative part of this analysis – will focus on the interviewees' discourse on *UTEQ* to demonstrate to what extent those units infringe upon the territories of their adversaries and to examine how they handle and solve conflict.

VIOLENCE-PRONE AREAS

The *UTEQ* are first and foremost defined in relation to the area in which they can intervene, which corresponds to a very specific institutional territory within the larger areas of jurisdiction of other police units (cf. 8).

| 8 | Disons que l'UTEQ par exemple, on va parler de l'UTEQ de S., elle est **cantonnée** à un **secteur particulier**. Donc son **secteur** d'investigation c'est **la cité de F.** [...] Pourquoi ?... parce que c'est **une cité** particulièrement _criminogène_ de la circonscription et du département. (National police, local official). | Let's say that UTEQ – for example, let's pick the UTEQ of S., the UTEQ is **limited** to a **particular sector**. So **the area** in which it can investigate is **the F. housing project**. Why? ...because it's a particularly _violence-prone_ **housing project** in this area of jurisdiction and in the département. |

"Sectors" within urban areas are limited to a few blocks, high-rises or streets (see Map 2). They are treated as self-contained units, whose links with their surrounding areas are overlooked. Most of the time, they correspond to housing projects and *banlieues* already classified as a "Sensitive Urban Area" (*Zone Urbaine Sensible*) by the French "*Politique de la Ville*." However, interviewees declare crime rates as the main criterion that determines where those zones start and where they end. Thus, the *UTEQ* initiative rests on the assumption that some places foster crime. This assumption has been repeatedly questioned within the field of critical criminology;

studies have shown how, through a chain of oversimplifications, an individual responsible for criminal activity will be considered "criminal," which in turn will lead to the social group s/he belongs to being classified as such, until eventually the space identified with the group is considered "criminal" (Belina, 2006). The small-scale territorialization of police work is reflected by the progressive scale restriction of the geo-criminal units of analysis in policing practice – quarters, neighborhoods, blocks, streets (Weisburd et al., 2009) – and the fragmentation of police work into smaller and smaller spaces. Groups of individuals will be policed mainly because they are in a violence-prone area. The "sectors" where the *UTEQ* work construct, by definition, "the others'" territory. Consequently, the police are led to trespass the boundaries established by their own discourse on banlieues.

MASTERING AND REPRESENTING
The interviewees' descriptions of police work highlight how mastery is achieved over the others' territory.

9	*Les UTEQ ont même une formation encore plus poussée sur la connaissance de **leur quartier**. [...] **Ce sont des territoires limités** pour qu'ils puissent bien les connaître et qu'ils puissent être connus des HABITANTS **du quartier**. [...] Les UTEQ ont la même formation sur la sociologie, la topographie **des quartiers dans lesquels** ils interviennent.* (National police, departemental directorate)	*The UTEQ' training includes an even larger part on the specificities of **their assigned housing projects**. **Their areas** are small so they can know them well and so the RESIDENTS in **the housing projects** can become familiar with them. The UTEQ have the same level of training in the sociology and the topography of **the areas where they intervene**.*
10	*Donc concrètement on va avoir DIX FONCTIONNAIRES À PIED qui **patrouillent dans un secteur**.* (National police, local official)	*So, concretely, there are going to be TEN CIVIL SERVANTS **patrolling a sector on foot**.*
11	*Là, ILS ont une vocation <u>plus répressive</u> quand même. ON <u>**occupe le terrain**</u>. ON <u>pacifie</u>. Et ON prend contact avec LA POPULATION, ON rend service à LA POPULATION, ON <u>sécurise</u>, ON noue des contacts avec LA POPULATION.* (National police, local official)	*There, THEY are meant to be <u>more punitive</u>, I mean. WE are <u>**all over the place**</u>. WE <u>calm things down</u>. And WE make contact with THE LOCAL POPULATION, WE give THEM a hand, WE make the area <u>safer</u>, we establish relations with THE POPULATION.*

Controlling this territory includes several processes: the police must be trained in advance, they must be visible, and they must conduct intelligence activities. The police officers' discourse on the *UTEQ*' practices, constantly reaffirming an exceptional situation in the targeted sectors, is remarkable for its repetitive mention of the third character previously identified – the silent "population" which constitutes the majority (cf. 9, 10, and 14: "*tout le monde*"), belongs neither to the police nor to their adversaries, and yearns for peace. The residents are treated as potential informers, but they are also those who can witness the police's reestablishment of their rule over the territory. Patrolling on foot (cf. 10: "*patrouiller à pied*") and "being all over the place" (cf. 11: "*occuper le terrain*") stand in opposition with the strategies of conflict avoidance mentioned above; such an invasive re-appropriation of the dangerous place constitutes an attempt to extend the limits of the police's territory. Police work in the *banlieues* consists of "making" territory – the bodily presence of the police is therefore a form of appropriation. The police's discourses confirm that the *UTEQ* unit also has a symbolic function: it is meant to assert the power of the state where the state's sovereignty is threatened.

AMBIGUOUS VIOLENCE

The police officers' discourse on *UTEQ* bears a very specific relationship to violence.

12	Parce que voilà il y a beaucoup de <u>criminalité</u> et puis il fallait que LA POLICE... QUE LA POLICE d'abord fasse partie des..., <u>arrive à s'imposer</u> **dans le secteur** pour que LA POPULATION puisse <u>mieux vivre</u> tout simplement. (National police, local official)	Because you see, there is a high <u>crime rate</u> there, and then THE POLICE had to... THE POLICE had first to be part of... had to effectively <u>establish ITS authority</u> **in the sector**, IF THE POPULATION was to just <u>live better.</u>
13	Au départ ON a eu pas mal de soucis. Puisque le premier jour de la mise en place de l'UTEQ ON a eu DEUX FONCTIONNAIRES <u>blessés</u>. Mais depuis la situation s'est normalisée. (National police, local official)	In the beginning there was a lot WE had to deal with. Since the first day the UTEQ was established TWO OF OUR CIVIL SERVANTS were <u>wounded</u>. But since then, the situation has become normalized.
14	C'est-à-dire POUR NOUS, une **UTEQ** qui <u>PREND des cailloux</u>, ça veut dire qu'ELLE <u>dérange</u>. Parce qu'ELLE <u>prend des cailloux</u> d'un côté et TOUT LE MONDE est content qu'ELLE **soit là** de l'autre. (National police, central directorate)	I mean, FOR US, a **UTEQ** being pelted with stones is obviously a sign that IT <u>disrupts things</u>. Because IT is <u>being pelted with stones</u> on the one hand, and EVERYONE is happy IT's **there** on the other hand.

The second character identified in the previous part of the study, the police's adversary – here, the participant responsible for violent acts – pervades the conversation (s/he is implied in past participles and adjectives, cf. 13: "*blessés*," cf. 14: *prend des cailloux*"), but is never concretely identified. These acts of violence, by lacking an agent, become closely associated with their setting: the sector – the *UTEQ'* "territory" – as if the violence was built into these spaces. It is the presence of the police (cf. 14: "*soit là;*" cf. 12: "*s'imposer dans le secteur*") that seems to trigger those acts of violence. They are described as natural, even *necessary*, because they seem to perform a cathartic function. As such, violence underlies the existence of *UTEQ* – their work is about violence. Their ultimate goal is the reassessing of power relations through the breaking down of pre-existing violence in order to build a new symbolic order. Paradoxically, the discourse on *UTEQ* makes violence appear normal. The ambiguity that defines the relation between the state and violence crystallizes in the police officers' discourse and through the territories it shapes. As such discourse is structured on conflict, the notion of territory ends up contributing to the legitimization of clashes, and is seen as a preliminary condition to the restoration of the symbolic order within the *banlieues*.

Conclusion

The discourses articulated by the police about French "troubled neighborhoods" studied in this paper repeatedly resort to markedly territorialized narratives of conflict. The discourse establishes three characters, first by distinguishing between police and inhabitants, and then by distinguishing among the inhabitants between "adversaries" and "peaceful people". These characters are constituted by a grid of oppositions and equivalences. The discursive combination of characters and places is remarkable: the unnamed "adversaries" are identified only through their belonging to the banlieue, while the police subject belongs to an unnamed place. This grid of oppositions and equivalences is structured by a conflict narrative: characters (based on places) and conflicts occur simultaneously since they constitute each other. Narratives of escape, intrusion, and strategies of conflict (non-)avoidance shed light on how territories' limits are negotiated. The conflict draws on a mobile border between the police and their "adversaries," thereby defining the territorial sovereignty of both characters; only then are the territorializations constructed. The everyday work practice is the construction of police territories. In this study I highlighted the police discourse of the bodily practice of presence/absence in the banlieue. The second section of this paper showed how the suburbs are constructed as scenes of territorial disputes pitting the local Municipal Police against petty criminals. Nevertheless, as has been demonstrated in the third section, the French National Police's declarations on UTEQ units, that policing those areas means infringing on set boundaries. Trespassing amounts to a show of force in which violence, considered as a necessary evil in the police's reclaiming of troubled neighborhoods, has an ambiguous status. The two police – national and municipal – are different institutions with different functions and missions. They therefore draw on two different territorial narratives of conflict embedded in the same banlieue discourse.

The statements collected from interviews conducted with police officers about troubled neighborhoods largely reflect and adapt the dominant discourse on French depressed suburban areas. A collective "we"-identity is associated with France, the state as an abstraction, the state and public institutions, republican values, and security. This "we"-identity is at the same time opposed to a "they"-identity, associated with otherness, foreignness, disorder, and dangerousness (Germes and Glasze, 2010). In the study mentioned, we showed this discursive structure of the hegemonic French discourse about banlieue in a corpus of texts from the media; police discourses draw on the same discursive model. Police then identify with the collective "we"-identity – per definition of their missions and role. The re-articulation of the hegemonic French banlieue discourse by police depends on the (political) definition of police missions: discursive territorializations in the National Police differ from those of the Municipal Police. These naturalized territorializations in turn shape the interpretation of facts, give meaning to experiences, and consequently frame police work.

A range of questions arise about this specific manifestation of the hegemonic discourse. Is this re-articulation only a repetition and therefore a simple confirmation that police subjects identify with a hegemonic discourse? What are the relations between these police discourses and the French state? To what extent are my results specific and particular to the French case study, and to what extent do they refer to a broader context? (Wacquant, 2006)

This police discourse about the suburbs applies specifically to the context of the *Politique de la Ville*. Discourses construct particular areas as places housing a range of social, economic, racial, and security problems, which have to be solved with area-based policies. In this way, discourses form the conditional framework for the possibility, acceptance, and achievement of urban policies. The convergence between urban regeneration programs and police practices (which is obvious in the case study of Clichy-Montfermeil – see Maps 1 and 2; see also Bonelli, 2000) is part of a broader transformation through spatial sanitization. This housing program's goal is to create a new urban landscape with smaller, clean, and fenced-off buildings, as well as numerous public services for the new population. In accordance with the social mix principle of the *Politique de la Ville*, a substantial part of the renewed homes are intended for middle-class inhabitants, displacing the predominantly poor, migrant former population of large families. Such a production of "safe", "aesthetical" and "attractive" places in the area surrounding Paris attempts to re-value (the marketability of) space (see also Raco, 2003). In this narrow context, the re-articulation of a hegemonic discourse by agents of a key institution is part of a broader dispositive. A comparison of such police declarations with speeches of presidents of the French republic, prime ministers, and interior ministers would show numerous similar words and phrases (see also Germes and Glasze, 2010). It shows the importance of questioning the circulation and (re-)appropriation of discourses, particularly within the hierarchical police, and within the close political sphere (Rimbert, 2000). It is important to note that the whole spectrum of re-articulation possibilities by police(wo)men is not reflected in my small set of interviews, since I observed neither moderations nor divergences from the dominant discourse.

The empirical evidence gathered has to be linked to the French context: its urban history, its postcolonial geographies, and its social issues and law enforcement measures. The analysis of this evidence should attempt to interpret the identity construction which underlies the hegemonic discourse. Discourses on the *banlieues* by the police, as well as by numerous other subjects, take part in the discursive matrix of the constitution of a counter-place. The "badlands of the Republic" (Dikeç, 2007b) are said to be unsafe, constitute a threat to public order, and also jeopardize the values of mainstream society. The discursive constitution of *banlieues* as counter-places reaffirms and solidifies a dialectical opposition to the threatened "French Republic" or "Nation" (Germes and Glasze, 2010). What is meant by "French Republic", "French Nation", or "French State"? What has to be understood under the collective "we"-identity (constituted in antagonism to the banlieue), beyond the fact that the terms designating this collective identity vary slightly depending on the corpus of texts or interviews, beyond the fact that it is definitively not a *thing* or a *phenomena* that should be identified once for all – but nothing more than an empty category? The crucial question is to determine to what extent this collective identity has to be understood either as "France" or as "Republic", "Nation", "State". Without overlooking the particularities of the French context, my aim is to question the focus on "French collective identity". The first reason is that the analysis of such a collective identity does not allow the full explanation of the hegemony. The second reason is that it could essentialize the French case study and overlook the convergence with other cases.

One must then consider the French *banlieues* within the context of socio-spatial segregation in post-industrial cities, discrimination in postcolonial societies, shrinkage of the welfare state, and the shift to more law-and-order approaches in policing and penal institutions. The crisis of the *banlieues* can be explained by neoliberal trends; moreover, hegemonic discourses about banlieue and dominant explanations of a crisis inherent to some places can be interpreted as neoliberal discourses, in so far as they mistake the problem *in* a place for the problem *of* the place. The first false premise of a disconnected place – the banlieue – oversees the interdependence between places and relations of domination through space. The second false premise of endogenous causes (and therefore solutions) for the crisis oversees the interdependence in political and economic inequalities. The police discourses I analyzed have to be recontextualized in the context of the advanced marginality (Wacquant, 2006) and penal state (ibd.; also: Dikeç, 2007a).

The discursive construction of a conflict-prone territory does not appear as a constitutive element of police culture but as a conceptual framework that informs the police's mission of preventing and punishing crime, in a context where the increasing enforcement of the penal state is a response to advanced marginality. Are these police discourses the expression of a penal state? Although it could be possible to maintain that they are reflecting a pre-existing state, I argue rather that they aid in the construction of the (penal) state (parallel to many other discourses and practices) – (see Painter, 2006; Kuus and Agnew, 2008). Police officers identify with a loose collective "we"-identity by re-articulating a discourse about the banlieue and thus taking part in the constitution of a State – which can be qualified as a penal state in a neoliberal context.

Thanks to such spatial discourses, police work and police officers are embedded in neoliberal politics. Territorial conflict narratives provide the framework that structures police work as well as social spaces, and also shape police officers as individuals. How do territorialized discourses influence police officers' identity? How is the hegemonic discourse in so doing repeated or transformed? What then are the alternative spatial discourses available, and what spatial identifications do they rely upon?

References

Aldhuy, Julien 2006. "Modes de connaissances, intérêts de connaître et géographie sociale" In: Raymonde Séchet and Vincent Veschambre (eds.), *Penser et faire la géographie sociale*. Rennes: Presses universitaires de Rennes: 31–46.

Aldhuy, Julien 2008. "Au-delà du territoire, la territorialité?" *Géodoc,* 55: 35–42.

Bacqué, Marie-Hélène and Yves Sintomer 2001. "Affiliations et désaffiliations en banlieue". *Revue française de Sociologie,* 42 (2): 217–49.

Beaud, Serge and Michel Pialoux 2003. *Violences urbaines, violence sociale: Genèse des nouvelles classes dangereuses.* Paris: Hachette Littérature.

Belina, Bernd 2006. *Raum. Überwachung. Kontrolle.* Münster: Westfälisches Dampfboot.

Bonelli, Laurent 2001. "Renseignements généraux et violences urbaines." *Actes de la recherche en sciences sociales,* 136 (1): 95–103.

Bonelli, Laurent 2008. *La France a peur. Une histoire sociale de l'"insécurité.* Paris: La Découverte.

Bonelli, Laurent and Gilles Sainati (eds.) 2000. *La Machine à punir.* Paris: L'Esprit frappeur.

Bonelli, Laurent. 2000. "Des populations 'en danger' aux populations 'dangereuses.'" In: Laurent Bonelli and Gilles Sainati (eds.), *La Machine à punir*. Paris: L'Esprit frappeur: 17–52.

Brodeur, Jean-Paul 2003. *Les visages de la police. Pratiques et Perceptions.* Montréal: Les Presses de l'Université de Montréal.

Di Méo, Guy 1998. *Géographie sociale et territoires.* Paris: Nathan.

Dieu, François (ed.) 2009. *Les nouveaux territoires de la sécurité. Cahiers de la Sécurité.*

Dikeç, Mustafa 2007a. "Revolting Geographies: Urban Unrest in France." *Geography Compass,* 1 (5): 1190–206.

Dikeç, Mustafa 2007b. *Badlands of the Republic.* Oxford: Blackwell Publishing.

Duchêne, François and Christelle Morel-Journel 2000. "Cités ouvrières et banlieues: la filiation oubliée." *Géocarrefour,* 75 (2): 155–64.

Dufaux, Frédéric and Annie Fourcaut 2004. *Le monde des grands ensembles.* Paris: Créaphis.

Elden, Stuart 2010. "Thinking Territory Historically." *Geopolitics*, 15 (4): 757–61.

Esterle-Hedibel, Maryse 2002. "Jeunes des cités, police et désordres urbains." In: Laurent Mucchielli, and Philippe Robert (eds.), *Crime et sécurité.* Paris: Editions La Découverte: 376–85.

Fourcaut, Annie 2000. "Pour en finir avec la banlieue." *Géocarrefour*, 75 (2): 101–05.

Fyfe, Nicholas R. 1995. "Policing the City." *Urban Studies*, 32 (4-5): 759–78.

Fyfe, Nicholas R. 1991. "The Police, Space and Society: the geography of policing." *Progress in Human Geography*, 15 (3): 249–67.

Gebhardt, Hans, Paul Reuber, and Günter Wolkersdorfer. 2003. "Kulturgeographie – Leitlinien und Perspektiven." In: *Kulturgeographie.* Heidelberg: Spektrum: 1–27.

Germes, Mélina and Georg Glasze 2010. "Die *banlieues* als Gegenorte der *République.*" *Geographica Helvetica*, 65 (3): 217–28.

Germes, Mélina, Henning Schirmel, Adam Brailich, Georg Glasze, and Robert Pütz 2010. "Menaces pour l'ordre social?" *Annales de Géographie*, 675: 515–35.

Germes, Mélina, Andreas Tijé-Dra 2012. "Banlieue." In: Nadine Marquardt and Verena Schreiber (eds.), *Ortsregister.* Bielefeld: transkript, 32–38.

Glasze, Georg 2007. "Vorschläge zur Operationalisierung der Diskurstheorie von Laclau und Mouffe in einer Triangulation von lexikometrischen und interpretativen Methoden." *Forum Qualitative Sozialforschung,* 8 (2).

Glasze, Georg and Annika Mattissek 2009. *Handbuch Diskurs und Raum.* Bielefeld: transcript.

Glasze, Georg, Robert Pütz, and Verena Schreiber 2005. "(Un-) Sicherheitsdiskurse: Grenzziehungen in Gesellschaft und Stadt." *Berichte zur deutschen Landeskunde*, 79 (2/3): 329–40.

Herbert, Steve 1996. *Policing Space.* Minneapolis: University of Minnesota Press.

Herbert, Steve 2003. "Coercion, Territoriality, Legitimacy: The Police and the Modern State." In: *Handbook of Political Geography.* London: Sage: 169–81.

Herbert, Steve 2006. *Citizens, Cops, and Power.* Chicago: University of Chicago Press.

Jobard, Fabien 2005. "Le nouveau mandat policier: Faire la police dans les zones dites de 'non-droit.'" *Criminologie*, 38 (2): 103–21.

Kuus, Merje and John Agnew 2008. "Theorizing the State Geographically." In: *The SAGE Handbook of Political Geography.* London: Sage: 95–106.

Landauer, Paul 2009. *L'architecte, la ville et la sécurité*. Paris: Presses Universitaires de France.

Lévy, Jacques and Michel Lussault (eds.) 2000. *Logiques de l'espace, esprit des lieux. Géographies à Cerisy*. Paris: Belin.

Malochet, Virginie 2010. "Les polices municipales: points de repères", at http://tinyurl.com/abtjcqw [accessed 18 January 2013].

Mattissek, Annika and Paul Reuber 2004. „Die Diskursanalyse als Methode in der Geographie." *Geographische Zeitschrift*, 92 (4): 227–42.

Ministry of the Interior 2009. "Les polices municipales: points de repère", at http://tinyurl.com/alomrle [accessed 18 January 2013].

Mohammed, Marwan and Laurent Mucchielli 2006. "La police dans les quartiers populaires: un vrai problème!" *Mouvements*, 44 (2): 58–66.

Monjardet, Dominique 1996. *Ce que fait la police*. Paris: La Découverte.

Monjardet, Dominique 2002. "Les policiers." In: Laurent Mucchielli and Philippe Robert (eds.), *Crime et sécurité. L'état des savoirs*. Paris: Editions La Découverte: 265–74.

Mouhanna, Christian 2008. "Police: de la proximité au maintien de l'ordre généralisé?" In: Laurent Mucchielli (ed.), *La frénésie sécuritaire*. Paris: La Découverte: 77–87.

Mouhanna, Christian 2003. "Le policier face au public. Le cas des banlieues." In: Sebastian Roché (ed.), *En quête de sécurité*. Paris: Armand Colin: 241–53.

Mucchielli, Laurent (ed.) 2008. *La frénésie sécuritaire*. Paris: La Découverte.

Paasi, Anssi 2008. "Territory." In: John Agnew, Katharyne Mitchell, and Gerard Toal (eds.), *A companion to political geography*. Malden, MA: Blackwell: 109–23.

Painter, Joe 2006. "Prosaic geographies of stateness." *Political Geography*, 25 (7): 752–74.

Painter, Joe 2010. "Rethinking Territory." *Antipode*, 42 (5): 1090–118.

Raco, Mike 2003. "Remaking Place and Securitising Space." *Urban Studies*, 40 (9): 1869–87.

Rimbert, Pierre 2000. "Les managers de «l'insécurité». Production et circulation d'un discours sécuritaire." *SAINATI:* 161–201

Ripoll, Fabrice and Vincent Veschambre 2006. "L'appropriation de l'espace: une problématique centrale pour la géographie sociale." In: Ray Séchet and Vincent Veschambre (eds.), *Penser et faire la géographie sociale*. Rennes: Presses universitaires de Rennes: 295–304.

Romieux, Charles 2007. *Logement social et traitement de l'insécurité*. Paris: L'Harmattan.

Schneider, Cathy Lisa 2008. "Police Power and Race Riots in Paris." *Politics & Society,* 36 (1): 133–59.

Séchet, Raymonde, and Vincent Veschambre (eds.) 2006. *Penser et faire la géographie sociale*. Rennes: Presses universitaires de Rennes.

Sedel, Julie 2009. *Les médias & la banlieue*. Latresne: le Bord de l'eau.

Tévanian, Pierre. 2003. *Le ministère de la peur. Réflexions sur le nouvel ordre sécuritaire*. Paris: L'Esprit frappeur.

Tijé-Dra, Andreas 2011. *Eine andere banlieue? Vorschläge zur diskursanalytischen Untersuchung gegenhegemonialer Sprecherpositionen und Raumkonzeptionen*. Mainz: Geographisches Institut.

Tissot, Sylvie 2007. *L'Etat et les quartiers. Genèse d'une catégorie de l'action publique*. Paris: Seuil.

Wacquant, Loïc 2006. *Parias urbains. Ghetto, banlieues, Etat*. Paris: La Découverte.

Weisburd, David, Wim Bernasco, and Gerben Bruinsma 2009. *Putting Crime in its Place*. Dortrecht: Springer.

Yarwood, Richard 2007. "The Geographies of Policing." *Progress in Human Geography*, 31 (4): 447–65.

URBAN (IN)SECURITY – A SYNOPSIS AND FURTHER QUESTIONS

Kendra Briken and Volker Eick

Policing in neoliberal times increasingly relies on the co-existence and cooperation of heterogeneous stakeholders. Their collective effort stabilizes the respective capitalist economies. Policing is no longer, if it ever has been, an endeavor of the state alone (Kempa, 2011). As this anthology illustrated, the interests of state and non-state policing apparatuses – to some degree competing but in major parts overlapping – draw on different sets of powers and deploy control technologies ranging from unpaid patrol guards in the so-called disadvantaged neighborhoods to sophisticated IT equipment directed against protest movements. Far from believing in an overarching 'security architecture' or in a 'police extended family,' this edited volume, based on different theoretical and empirical approaches, allows an understanding of similarities and differences of a diverse landscape of policing and understandings of 'security.'

Grand pictures of policing and control have their merits insofar as they illustrate defining features of current societies and also help us to understand tendencies within the most advanced capitalist nation states better. In this perspective, the analyses of policing and crime fighting strategies proposed by scholars such as Garland (2001), Wacquant (2009) and Graham (2010) are significant. The chapters of this anthology mark the existence of divergences across space and place and are informed by empirically based analysis of urban policing within 'actually existing neoliberalism.' That said, this volume is inspired by an empirically informed analysis of urban policing under an 'actually existing neoliberalism.' Far from being eclectic, we believe that the surplus value of this volume stems from providing a broad array of case studies that are concerned in particular ways with urban (in)security. Each contribution highlights specific, path-dependent developments and the particularity of each case study allows more general assertions, as the following concluding remarks will underline.

Defeating dichotomies

It is widely agreed that there is no single definition of 'security,' but security should rather be understood as an "umbrella term" (Valverde, 2011: 5) embracing different forms of governance. What is more, the term security functions as an empty signifier utilized to hide many kinds of power relations. Security deploys the masks of fear, threat, crime, and/or incivilities. To criticize the latter, the Copenhagen School used the term "securitization" (Buzan et al., 1998), whereas the 'Anti-Security Manifesto,' which is based on a rather materialist critique, suggested instead to refer to "pacification" (Neocleous and Rigakos, 2011). These approaches, their different theoretical backing notwithstanding, share the attempt to overcome the binary construction that underlies the notion of (in)security. Pacification, understood as a mode of governing, is a bargaining *process* which can be observed empirically, and is composed of identifiable actors, detectable interests, unequally distributed power and traceable technologies. As the authors of this volume either implicitly or explicitly point out, such an understanding allows for questioning the so-called security projects by unveiling the underlying conflicts, power structures and interests instead of perceiving 'security' as part of the problem or even as an element of the solution.

Seen from such a perspective not only the production and consumption of 'security,' but also the urban is to be understood as an undetermined *process* with the ability to shift, at times, from a marketplace to a battleground and vice versa, thus making particular types of policing necessary. Not surprisingly, the presented empirical material refers to the problem of 'security' as an independent as well as a dependent variable. As the contributions to this volume show from a number of perspectives, many transformations such as the growth of the commercial security can be explained through a re-definition of 'security.' As, among others, Bob Jessop (2013: 19) reminds us, a finance-dominated accumulation regime refers to "a free market plus an authoritarian 'strong state'," and it is for this reason that security turns into a marketable good. In turn, incidents such as 9/11 or the Mumbai bombings in November 2008 may be used as arguments for diminishing transparency and democratic oversight as well as encouraging 'Othering' processes and even torture and targeted killings in the name of 'security' (Eick, 2012). In other words, the empty signifier is filled with presumed threats or with the permanent 'state of emergeny'. It no longer hides its post-democratic roots, namely

> the paradox that, in the name of democracy, emphasizes the consensual practice of effacing the forms of democratic action. Postdemocracy is the government practice and conceptual legitimization of a democracy after the demos, a democracy that has eliminated the appearance, miscount, and dispute of the people, and is thereby reducible to the sole interplay of state mechanisms and combinations of social energies and interests (Rancière, 1998: 101-102).

Within the context of the neoliberal state, this 'third way' leads to the neutralization of political antagonisms by inventing factual constraints. 'There is no alternative,' the famous TINA logic utilizes 'security' to manage its populace scrupulously and in authoritative manner. In the workfare regime – a decisive ingredient of the neoliberal state – TINA also enables governments to define the urban poor as a sign of decreasing 'security' with regard to the well-being of the *Gemeinschaft*. In such a way, the preaching of neighborhood-watch schemes evokes security provision as an 'empowerment' tool for the populace in a neocommunitarian sense. Here, the postulate of 'no rights without responsibilities' includes even the aspect of self-policing of the urban poor.

Such a reframing of security by state institutions, for-profit, and nonprofit organizations allows for new modes of staging security on different scales, while incorporating additional or reassembling existing stakeholders. Some scholars refer to 'nodes' of policing to analyze such reframing and practice. The theoretical concept of "nodal policing" (Johnston and Shearing, 2003) suggests that security providers are interconnected and sensitizes for unexpected constellations between them. It clarifies, that the "police are only one node in a network that works to govern security" (Shearing, 2005: 58), but rather fails to account for particular power relations stemming from the structure of capitalist society as such (Cox, 2013). In this respect, the network approach seems to be more critical. It conceptualizes security by being produced by various networks of actors from both the public and the private realm. By deploying the 'capital metaphor,' it shows how each actor of a security network is able to mobilize particular resources and technologies in order to maximize their position within the network (Dupont, 2004). Nevertheless, attempts to operationalize 'nodes' or 'networks' still remain unsatisfying. Quantitative data are difficult to collect and academics in the field of (anti-)security research as a rule hesitate to apply quantitative techniques (Dupont, 2006). In turn, qualitative data alone do not allow for a meaningful generalization, while attempts to analyze discourses as speech acts often fail to grasp the intersection between the state and the subject, thus ignoring social structures within capitalist societies (Ranasinghe, 2013).

We believe that the combination of existing data bases, a sociological sense for 'thick descriptions' and materialist ethnographic approaches have proven to be fruitful as, among others, Rigakos (2002, 2008) has clarified for the Canadian context. Further, as the contributions in this volume show, taking into account the *process* and the 'historical making' of specific constellations needs to be acknowledged for a critical (anti-)security research.

Scaling security

As *Margit Mayer* has displayed in the opening chapter of this volume, urban and social movements on each and every scale encounter specific social and power relations. The question when, where, and how such struggles occur, remains an empirical question. However, oppositional movements which strive to block or to roll back the contemporary neoliberal onslaught have begun to mobilize on different geographical scales in strategic, sometimes highly creative ways.

These multi-level and multi-scalar contestations in neoliberal times are developments of and responses to adjusted policing strategies. As this volume clarifies, the state police apparatuses, the commercial security sector, nonprofit organizations and associations inspired by either neighborhood-watch schemes or militias are phenomena on both the local and the global scale. The project of neoliberalism with its aggressive attempt to forge new scalar hierarchies, in which unrestricted capital mobility, unfettered market relations, intensified commodification and zero-sum competitions are announced and executed, permanently aims at its institutionalization. While the neoliberal project comprises the reorganization of the global, national, regional, and local scale, neighborhoods in particular are in need to respond to such challenges and thus are increasingly a site of neoliberal policy experiments. A telling case study for such rescaling is the chapter of *Andrew Wallace* on the 'creation of community,' a reordering project of the urban setting being adjusted to the 'demands' of the British neoliberal model. As several scholars have clarified from different perspectives (Pütter, 2006; Crawford, 2009), 'community policing' is one of the concepts *à la mode* at least in western democracies. The (self-)responsibilization of 'decent' citizens for respect and civility leads to what *Volker Eick* describes as "protective prosumerism" – namely, the consumption and production of policing by the very same stakeholders. Protective prosumerism, or prosumerist policing, addresses the idea of an 'activated' civil society and, more generally, the exploitation of human resources by way of deploying volunteers (sometimes involuntarily) into policing measures. Protective prosumerism is deployed not only by neighborhood-watch schemes but also by nonprofits delivering services to the local job centers and even by global sports associations. Based on the concept of the workfare state, the exploitation of human resources under the umbrella of 'doing something meaningful' for oneself and the community thus successfully dovetails the active production and consumption of 'security.'

Pacifying perspectives

By the late 19th and early 20th century, industrial workers became the greatest threat to the capitalist state. By establishing modern welfare regimes, particularly in continental Europe, the capitalist state aimed at pacifying parts of the working class by granting selected social rights (Eick, 2011) and, in so doing, also laid the foundation for the establishment of mass-consumption patterns. It is beyond the scope of this conclusion to further detail the development of modern industrial labor conflicts but, importantly, the intimidation of the working class continued, and the early 20th century provided the breeding ground for commercial security companies as strike breakers (Nelken, 1926; Shalloo, 1933; Bock, 1976). From the 1960s onwards, grassroots initiatives and social movements emerged (Castells, 1973). In turn, the intimidation and pacification of the working class started to reach beyond the production sphere (i.e. the factory), now encompassing the reproduction sphere and, in particular, the urban realm.

The respective policing of a dissenting populace, as in the case of the alterglobalization movement analyzed by *Luis Fernandez* and *Christian Scholl,* combines the criminalization of protest with the centralization and militarization of police forces enforcing 'counter-insurgency' strategies. Fast policy transfer became one particular characteristic of capitalist learning and practice (Brenner et al., 2010), including the transfer of policing strategies. The 'Othering' of protesters opposed to the 'brave' neoliberal citizen applies to the global protest 'elites' and to those suffering from unemployment, poverty and hunger due to the austerity measures at the behest of the international financial institutions as in the case of Lithuania, analyzed by *Arunas Juska* and *Charles Woolfson.* While the activists of the alterglobalization movement might be able to leave the protest site, the only 'exit' option for the violently pacified Lithuanians seems to be emigration. Lithuania (and its neighboring states) became the one laboratory of the European Union for experimentation with austerity measures and with policing strategies against emerging dissent. The economic reconfiguration in post-communist economies has been a 'smash and grab' process of a new 'kleptocracy' backed from the very beginning by 'policing by threat,' as Juska and Woolfson clarify. In Portugal, Greece and Spain as only recently the so-called financial crisis led to violent clashes between the police and the populace (Birke and Henninger, 2012; Roth, 2012). Just as in Lithuania, however, the strategy of 'accumulation by dispossession' (Harvey, 2003) results in growing numbers of emigrating citizens. While the multi-level and multi-scalar contestations under an 'actually existing neoliberalism' are obvious, successful counter-strategies by urban and social movements, trade unions and dissenting populace, as Mayer highlights, are still to be developed.

This is of high importance not the least because 'traditional' modes of pacification and overt violence by the police are combined not only with 'counter-insurgency' measures but also with so-called 'preventive' instruments that encourage active participation of the populace. From such a perspective, one can read "protective prosumerism," the model developed by *Volker Eick* in this volume, and *Andrew Wallace*'s community-generating "brother's keeper" as a participatory policing technique speaking to the conception offered by the 'Anti-Security Manifesto' (Neocleous and Rigakos, 2011). Participatory policing then would equate 'self'-pacification and, in turn, comes across as a reversed version of 'Othering.' While, as *Ann Rodenstedt* clarifies in her Swedish case study, 'Othering' processes are used to distance one group from another, the variegated forms of 'community'-generating policing strategies create moments of 'Gathering.' Thus, self-pacification allows for visualizing an in-group and stigmatizing the 'Other', sometimes even working or living in the same neighborhood as for example sex workers or homeless people, while addressing the individual as a potential co-manager of policing strategies.

As *Alison Wakefield* and *Peter Gahan* with his colleagues highlight in their workplace studies, pacification duties also offer time and space for cooperation (among employees) and for processes of cooptation. As their empirical material illustrates, security guards, just like their state police counterparts, are not immune against attempts by citizens to coopt them for individual purposes even though such services are not part of their contracts (Eick, 2004; Bareis, 2007: 177-179; Briken, 2011). Work places and urban environs always provide opportunity structures for collective resistance and action as described by *Mayer* for urban movements, and therefore, pacification may be contested. Retracing the history of walls as "territorilizing agents," *Samantha Ponting* and *George Rigakos* clarify that 'traditional' separating control technologies are still of high importance for the capitalist project. separating control technologies such as walls are still of high importance for the capitalist project. Walls are a technique of pacification, enabling those in control to count, to observe, to enclose, and to surveil excluded and/or dangerous classes; in the most extreme cases, walls even equate life and death decisions. Separating space, thus defining an inside and an outside, is also the topic of *Andreas Lohner*. A collection of his photographs taken from the Corcoran Project reveals how deeply rooted the concept of walls is in our everyday lives as a 'normal' concept .

Accounting actors

Looking behind the obscure curtain of 'security' and its dazzling and deafening discourses enables an understanding of its provision as waged labor and employment conditions. In their respective chapters, *Peter Gahan, Bill Harley* and *Graham Sewell, Anibel Ferus-Comelo* as well as *Volker Eick* and *Alison Wakefield* argue that state and non-state policing is above all a form of work. In turn, security understood as a product is not at all as 'fluid' as scholars such as Zedner (2003) try to convince us. The daily life of security workers instead is 'hard,' their tasks are boring and at the same time wide-ranging, the 'product' to be delivered is clearly defined, although becoming invisible once it is provided successfully, and entails the duty to represent the respective customers. The contributions in this volume clarify that the characteristics of commercial security provision have a global validity – from Australia to the UK, from Germany to India, demands and duties, stresses and strains for the workforce resemble each other and do not differ that much. Beyond the poor working conditions, there is another remarkable similarity: In all discussed countries, only a small minority of market leaders is able to skim off substantial profit. Their ability to offer complete 'premium security' packages and their capacity to tender a wide range of services, as *Eick* and *Wakefield* show for Germany and the UK, even enabled their integration into the 'architecture' of the state apparatus.

Beneath the 'big players,' small- and medium-sized self-appointed security experts are on duty. As *Anibel Ferus-Comelo* points out in the Indian case, paid protection and safeguarding for the few means shock and awe for the many; the cooperation of commercial security guards with burglars being just one example. In turn, the global players try hard to convince the public that only small-scale security providers are the proverbial 'bad apple' and demand intensified regulation of the market. By the same token though, just as other global companies like Nike or Apple hire subcontractors, the commercial security industry is known for subcontracting. However, reliable market data on subcontracting are hardly available and therefore, consistent and systematic analyses are lacking (Briken, 2011).

Contracts and non-contractual agreements between commercial security providers and the state further complicate the provision of urban (in)security. In its attempt to police the neoliberal economy, the state may appear as a competitor, a contractor or a partner, and the role chosen by both the state and the commercial security industry depends on the context (White, 2011). As *Alison Wakefield* stresses, the British state is still the primary source for providing legitimacy to the commercial security sector. In the UK, commercial security providers actively ask for direct control by state institutions through statutory regulation. At first sight, this might solve the problems outlined by *Anibel Ferus-Comelo* in the Indian case. She reveals how the uncontrolled and uncontrollable emergence of the so-called security providers in Goa in fact increases consumers' insecurity instead of calming their fears. Therefore, regulation might stabilize the relationship between the state and the industry to the benefit of all customers. But as *Wakefield* points out, the need for regulation demands further regulation and constant fine-tuning, because regulation needs regulatory agencies, personnel to be qualified and additional institutions. It therefore further triggers a demand for supplementary regulations, qualifications and competences to be regulated. What is predictable therefore is that sooner or later new needs for control and regulation will emerge.

Collective cross-examination

In times of 'glocalized' neoliberalization, the most important goal of today's urban policy is to mobilize city space as an arena of market-oriented economic growth. Roll-out neoliberalism has established some flanking mechanisms and modes of crisis displacement such as local economic development policies and community-based programs to elevate social exclusion. It has introduced new forms of coordination and inter-organizational networking among previously distinct spheres of local state intervention, so that ultimately, social, political and even ecological criteria have become intertwined and at the same time redefined in an attempt to promote economic competitiveness. Social infrastructures, political culture and ecological foundations of the city are being transformed into an economic asset. Already with the deregulation and the dismantling of the welfare state in the 1980s, distributive policies were increasingly replaced by measures of reinforcing urban competitiveness; as a consequence, sociospatial polarization intensified, whereas wealth and economic opportunities became more unevenly distributed. It is against such a background that critical studies on 'urban (in)security' or 'pacification,' as suggested in the Anti-Security Manifesto, should focus their approaches theoretically as well as empirically also on socioeconomic conditions. As this volume underlines, there a wide range of critical interventions concerned with state and non-state policing phenomena emerging since the advent of neoliberalism already exists. What is needed is a more systematic, interdisciplinary and comparative approach, comparing global as well as local pacification projects, their different scales and scopes. Further, a commitment to the globally and locally oppressed should be an additional precondition to allow for a meaningful use of the term 'critical' research on policing.

References

Bareis, Ellen 2007. *Verkaufsschlager. Urbane Shoppingmalls – Orte des Alltags*. Münster: Westfälisches Dampfboot.

Birke, Peter and Max Henninger (eds.) 2012. *Krisen Proteste*. Berlin: Assoziation A.

Bock, Gisela 1976. *Die 'andere' Arbeiterbewegung in den USA von 1905-1922*. München: Trikont.

Brenner, Neil, Jamie Peck, and Nik Theodore 2010. "After neoliberalization?" *Globalizations*, 7 (3): 327–345.

Briken, Kendra 2011. *Produktion von 'Sicherheit'? Arbeit im Bewachungsgewerbe*. Düsseldorf: Hans Böckler Stiftung.

Buzan, Barry, Ole Wæver, and Jaap De Wilde 1998. *Security: A New Framework for Analysis*. Boulder, CO: Lynne Rienner.

Castells, Manuel 1973. *Luttes urbaines et pouvoir politique*. Paris: Librairie de François Maspero.

Cox, Kevin R. 2013. "Territory, Scale and Why Capitalism Matters." *Territory, Politics, Governance*, 1 (1): 46–61.

Crawford, Adam (eds.) 2009. *Crime Prevention Policies in Comparative Perspective*. Cullompton: Willan.

Dupont, Benoît 2004. "Security in the age of networks." *Policing and Society* 14 (1): 76–91.

Dupont, Benoît 2006. "Delivering security through networks: Surveying the relational landscape of security managers in an urban setting." *Crime, Law and Social Change*, 45 (3): 165–184.

Eick, Volker 2004. "Jenseits des Rechtsstaats. Kommerzielle Sicherheitsdienste schaffen sich eigenes Recht." *Grundrechte-Report 2004*. Frankfurt/M.: Fischer: 148–151.

Eick, Volker 2011. "'Welfare Queens' und 'altrömische Verhältnisse': Paradigmen der Stigmatisierung Erwerbsloser in den USA und Deutschland." *Soziale Arbeit*, 60 (10-11): 384–390.

Eick, Volker 2012. "'Kill Decision.' Mit Drohnen von der Air Force zur Chair Force." *Infobrief der Rechtsanwältinnen und Rechtsanwälte für Demokratie und Menschenrechte*, 33 (107): 28–35.

Garland, David 2001. *The Culture of Control*. Chicago: University of Chicago Press.

Graham, Stephen 2010. *Cities Under Siege. The New Military Urbanism*. London: Verso.

Harvey, David 2003. *The New Imperialism*. Oxford: Oxford University Press.

Jessop, Bob 2013. "Revisiting the Regulation Approach." *Capital & Class*, 37 (1): 5–24.

Johnston, Lee and Clifford D. Shearing 2003. *Governing Security: Explorations in policing and justice*. London: Routledge.

Kempa, Michael 2011. "Public Policing, Private Security, Pacifying Populations." In: Mark Neocleous and George S. Rigakos (eds.), *Anti-Security*. Ottawa: Red Quill Books: 85–105.

Nelken, Sigmund 1926. *Das Bewachungsgewerbe*. Berlin: Verband der Wach- und Schließgesellschaften.

Neocleous, Mark and George S. Rigakos (eds.) 2011. *Anti-Security*. Ottawa: Red Quill Books.

Pütter, Norbert 2006. *Polizei und kommunale Kriminalprävention*. Frankfurt/M.: Verlag für Polizeiwissenschaft.

Rancière, Jacques 1998. *Disagreement*. Minneapolis: University of Minnesota Press.

Ranasinghe, Prashan 2013. "Discourse, practice and the production of the polysemy of security." *Theoretical Criminology*, 17 (1): 89–107.

Rigakos, George S. 2002. *The New Parapolice: Risk Markets and Commodified Social Control*. Toronto: University of Toronto Press.

Rigakos, George S. 2008. *Nightclub: Bouncers, Risk and the Spectacle of Consumption*. Montreal and Kingston: McGill-Queen's University Press.

Roth, Karl Heinz 2012. *Griechenland – was tun?* Hamburg: VSA.

Shalloo, Jeremiah P. 1933. *Private Police*. Philadelphia: The American Academy of political and Social Science.

Shearing, Clifford 2005. "Nodal Security." *Police Quarterly*, 8 (1): 57–63.

Valverde, Mariana 2011. "Questions of security: A framework for research." *Theoretical Criminology*, 15 (1): 3–22.

Wacquant, Loïc 2009. *Punishing the Poor*. London: Duke University Press.

White, Adam 2011. "The new political economy of private security." *Theoretical Criminology*, 16 (1): 85–101.

Zedner, Lucia 2003. "Too much security?" *International Journal of the Sociology of Law*, 31 (3): 155–184.

EDITORS AND AUTHORS

Kendra Briken is a research assistant at the University of Bremen, CRC 597 "Transformations of the State," Project: "Transformation of the State as Employer: Public Employees' Role Perception and their Interest Representation in International Comparison" (kendra. briken@sfb597.uni-bremen.de). She has recently published articles in the journals *Kritische Justiz* (4/2011) and *Social Justice* (38/2011) and a monograph on private security work, *Produktion von 'Sicherheit'? Arbeit im Bewachungsgewerbe* (Hans-Böckler-Stiftung, 2011).

Volker Eick is a political scientist in the Faculty of Social Sciences, Humboldt Universität zu Berlin, Germany (eickv@zedat.fu-berlin.de). His research has been published in R. Lippert and K. Walby (eds.), *Policing Cities* (Routledge, 2013), L. Huey and L. Fernandez (eds.), *Rethinking Policing and Justice* (Routledge, 2011); K. Haggerty and C. Bennett (eds.), *Security Games* (Routledge, 2011); H. Leitner, J. Peck, and E. Sheppard (eds.): *Contesting Neoliberalism* (Guilford, 2007).

Luis A. Fernandez is the author and editor of several books, including *Policing Dissent* (Ruttgers, 2008) and *Shutting Down the Streets* (NYU Press, 2011). He is currently the Director of the Program of Sustainable Communities at Northern Arizona University (Luis.Fernandez@nau. edu). He is also an associate professor in Criminology and Criminal Justice in the same university.

Anibel Ferus-Comelo is a Mumbai-born independent scholar based in Goa, India (anibelfc@gmail.com). Her doctoral research in economic geography (London) explored globalization and labor strategies in the global electronics industry with a comparative focus on Silicon Valley (US) and Bangalore (India). She has worked extensively with unions and community-based workers' centers supporting the rights of low-wage workers, and continues to illuminate corporate geography and labor standards in different industries. Her publications include a co-edited book *Globlisation, Knowledge and Labour* (Routledge, 2010), policy reports, and articles in peer-reviewed journals and books.

Peter Gahan is professor of management at The University of Melbourne (pgahan@unimelb.edu.au). He has published widely on labor market regulation, unions, workplace innovation and high performance work systems. He is currently chief investigator on a research projects examining the evolution of business regulation, and its consequences for worker protection; the impact of legal reforms on collective bargaining; and the management of security work, from which this paper is derived.

Mélina Germes is a researcher in political geography and urban studies at the Centre Marc Bloch (CNRS/ Humboldt-University, Berlin; germes@cmb. hu-berlin.de). She has recently published two papers, "Neue Kulturgeographie - Débats et perspectives au sein de la nouvelle géographie culturelle germanophone" (*Cybergeo: European Journal of Geography*, 556, 2011, with Georg Glasze and Florian Weber) and "Die *banlieues* als Gegenorte der République. Eine Diskursanalyse neuer Sicherheitspolitiken in den Vorstädten Frankreichs" (*Geographica Helvetica*, (3) 65, 2010: 217-228, with Georg Glasze).

Bill Harley is professor of HRM and Organisational Studies at the University of Melbourne, Australia (bharley@unimelb.edu.au). Bill's research focuses on the labour process and in particular on employee experiences of management practices. His work has been published in leading international journals including *Work Employment and Society*, *British Journal of Industrial Relations* and *Journal of Management Studies*.

Arunas Juska is an associate professor of sociology at East Carolina University, USA (juskaa@ecu.edu). He specializes and writes extensively on the Baltic region, with especial focus on rural development as well as policing in Lithuania. His research in collaboration with Dr. Charles Woolfson is published in Crime, Law and Social Change (2012) and in K. Goodall, W. Munro and M. Malloch (eds.), *Building Justice in Post-Transition Europe* (Routledge, 2012). His articles have also appeared in *Policing and Society* (2009) and *Police Practice and Research* (2006)."

Andreas Lohner is a visual artist (www.andreaslohner. com) with a particular interest in 'security,' space and power. The works from his Corcoran series focus on the shaping of space as a form of societal action. He currently lives and works in Hamburg, Germany.

Margit Mayer teaches comparative and North American politics at the Freie Universität Berlin, Germany (mayer@zedat.fu-berlin.de). Her research focuses on urban and social politics and social movements. She has published on various aspects of contemporary urban politics, urban theory, (welfare) state restructuring and social movements. She co-edited *Urban Movements in a Globalising World* (Routledge 2000), *Cities for People not for Profit* (Routledge 2011), *Neoliberal Urbanism and Its Contestations* (Palgrave MacMillan 2011).

Samantha Ponting received a Master's degree in Political Economy in 2012 from Carleton University in Ottawa, Canada. Her current research explores walls, racism, and geographies of labour under capitalism, particularly in Palestine, North Africa, Central America, and gated communities in the West.

George S. Rigakos is Professor of the Political Economy of Policing and Chair of the Department of Law and Legal Studies at Carleton University. (george_ rigakos@carleton.ca). Most recently he has published *Anti-Security* (Red Quill Books, 2011, together with

Mark Neocleous), *Nightclub: Bouncers, Risk and the Spectacle of Consumption* (McGill-Queen's University Press, 2008), and edited (together with John L. McMullan, Joshua Johnson, and Gulden Ozcan) *A General Police System: Political Economy and Security in the Age of Enlightenment* (Red Quill Books, 2009). He is also head of the Editorial Collective for *Red Quill Books*.

Ann Rodenstedt is a PhD candidate in human geography at the Institute for Housing and Urban Research, Uppsala University (ann.rodenstedt@ibf.uu.se). At present, Ann is writing her thesis about how residents of the upper-middle class in Malmö, Sweden, create secure and controlled home territories and how their discourses of fear become manifested materially as well as socially in the neighborhood.

Chris Scholl (c.scholl@uva.nl) is an Amsterdam-based activist researcher currently teaching Social Movements and Gender Studies at the Political Science Department of the University of Amsterdam. His research interests revolve around globalization, social movements, and social control. He received his Ph.D. from the same university and is co-author of *Shutting Down the Streets* (NYU Press, 2011) and author of the forthcoming book *Two Sides of a Barricade. (Dis)order and Summit Protest in Europe* (SUNY Press, 2012).

Graham Sewell is professor of organization studies and human resource management in the Department of Management and Marketing, University of Melbourne, Australia. He has published extensively on workplace surveillance and his work has appeared in journals such as the *Administrative Science Quarterly*, the *Academy of Management Review*, *Sociology*, and *Organization Studies*. He is also a senior editor of *Organization Studies*. Graham has held visiting positions at the University of California's Berkeley and Santa Cruz campuses, and from 2004 to 2005 he was the

Ministerio de Educación y Ciensias de España visiting professor at the Universitat Pompeu Fabra, Barcelona. His latest book, *Technology and Organization: Essays in Honour of Joan Woodward* (with Nelson Phillips and Dorothy Griffiths), was published by Emerald in 2010.

Alison Wakefield is a criminologist specialising in security and risk management, based at the Institute of Criminal Justice Studies, University of Portsmouth, UK. Among her publications, she has authored *Selling Security: The Private Policing of Public Space* (Willan Publishing, 2003), which was shortlisted for the British Society of Criminology Book Prize 2003; and she is editor of *The Sage Dictionary of Policing* with Jenny Fleming (Sage, 2009) and *Ethical and Social Perspectives on Situational Crime Prevention* with Andrew von Hirsch and David Garland (Hart Publishing, 2000). Alison also works closely with the private security sector in the UK, serving as a director and fellow of the Security Institute, the UK's leading member association for security professionals, and as academic adviser to the Chartered Security Professionals Registration Authority, a new oversight body for senior UK security professionals.

Andrew Wallace is Senior Lecturer at the School of Social and Political Sciences, University of Lincoln (awallace@lincoln.ac.uk). His interests include urban relegation and renewal, citizen empowerment and community building. He published a monograph in 2010 with Ashgate entitled *Remaking Community? New Labour and the Governance of Poor Neighbourhoods*. He is currently researching community planning in London and the aftermath of the 2011 London riots.

Charles Woolfson is professor of labor studies at REMESO, Institute for Research on Migration, Ethnicity and Society, Linköping University in Sweden (charles.woolfson@liu.se). During 2000-2009 he lived in Lithuania, including for three years from 2004-2007 as a Marie Curie Chair.

Lightning Source UK Ltd.
Milton Keynes UK
UKOW06f1502200214

226833UK00006B/14/P